Sport and Play

IN AMERICAN LIFE

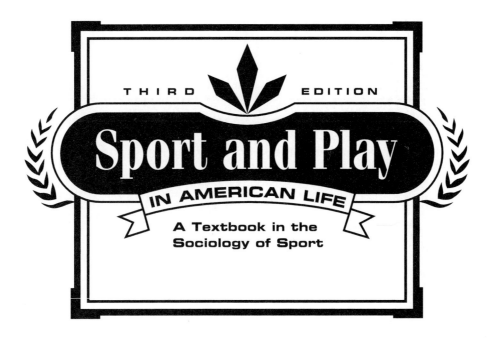

THIRD EDITION

Sport and Play

IN AMERICAN LIFE

A Textbook in the Sociology of Sport

Stephen K. Figler

California State University, Sacramento

Gail Whitaker

San Francisco State University

Brown & Benchmark
PUBLISHERS

Madison   Dubuque, IA   Guilford, CT   Chicago   Toronto   London
Caracas   Mexico City   Buenos Aires   Madrid   Bogota   Sydney

Book Team

Executive Editor *Ed Bartell*
Editor *Scott Spoolman*
Production Editor *Kristine Queck*
Art Editor *Tina Flanagan*
Photo Editor *Rose Deluhery*
Permissions Coordinator *Vicki Krug*
Visuals/Design Developmental Specialist *Janice M. Roerig-Blong*
Production Manager *Beth Kundert*
Visuals/Design Freelance Specialist *Mary L. Christianson*
Marketing Manager *Pamela S. Cooper*

A Division of Wm. C. Brown Communications, Inc.

Executive Vice President/General Manager *Thomas E. Doran*
Vice President/Editor in Chief *Edgar J. Laube*
Vice President/Production *Vickie Putman*
National Sales Manager *Bob McLaughlin*

 Wm. C. Brown Communications, Inc.

President and Chief Executive Officer *G. Franklin Lewis*
Senior Vice President, Operations *James H. Higby*
Corporate Senior Vice President and President of Manufacturing *Roger Meyer*
Corporate Senior Vice President and Chief Financial Officer *Robert Chesterman*

Cover design by Sailer and Cook Creative Services

Cover image © Marvin E. Newman/The Image Bank

Copyedited by Jeff Putnam

A Times Mirror Company

Library of Congress Catalog Card Number: 94-71514

ISBN 0-697-15242-1

Printed in the United States of America by Wm. C. Brown Communications, Inc.,
2460 Kerper Boulevard, Dubuque, IA 52001

10 9 8 7 6 5 4 3 2

To Howard, who shows the way, and to Jill, who gives form, substance, color, and joy to my life.

Stephen Figler

To my family, for their love and support—especially to Jan and Korbie, who fill my life with happiness.

Gail Whitaker

Contents

Preface

Sport has a splendid and potentially approachable ideal, perhaps even more attainable than the ideal states of most other societal institutions. (Could we imagine, for example, equitability in politics or fairness throughout the business world?) Play, however, is joyful, and so, potentially, should sport be. We claim to "play" sports, and many watch athletic events for pleasure and diversion. Sport also potentially, and sometimes actually, provides pleasures of association, a path for mastery and self-expression, honor for achievement, and the sense of community. Sport further has the potential to foster education, release tension, provide employment, and even to yield riches.

Yet sport and athletics seem to be submerged in an embarrassment of ethical failings and scandals, economic excesses and inequities, legal issues, overzealousness, drug use, criminal behavior, player and fan violence, and exploitation ranging from youth sports through professional ranks and the Olympics. At this writing the attack on Olympic figure skater Nancy Kerrigan has leapt from the sports pages to become front page and prime time news, momentarily displacing Title IX inequities in women's school sports and the Black Coaches Association's near boycott of NCAA basketball games as the prime topic of sports news. As you read this, other problems in sport will be occupying public concern. This is as certain as the daily reporting of scores and standings and the unending pre-game flack designed to whip up and satisfy interest in whatever the next "big game" is.

Still, with all of these problems, there remains an enchantment about play and sport, something encouraging in a world that looks bleak for the "X-Generation," you folks taking this class in the sociology of sport. We feel joy in the joy we see in athletic striving and performance. Perhaps we even get to experience some of that joy in our own performance, whether our skills are meagre or great or somewhere between, whether our sweat pours onto a "venue" surrounded by paying spectators or on a playground surrounded by people who couldn't care less about what we are doing out there. We may not shine as brightly as the stars, but we have earned our own twinkle when we get to play and to compete. In a way we are luckier than the stars, because our own play and sport may have a sense of purity, done for the doing rather than for some tangible reward. Plus, we get to enjoy the stars' performances on TV or in person, if we can afford it.

Clearly, however, in American society we can't escape sport, even if we wanted to. Sport assaults us at every turn, although for millions of Americans, it is like being hit with a warm breeze in January. We revel in play and sport. We anticipate it, enjoy it, and reflect on it. Unfortunately, in this last decade of the 20th century, we seem to be headed in the other direction in overdrive, a yawning gap between the ideal of sport and its manifestation in the real world. Too bad that so much of sport has turned serious and sour. That is the space within which this text dwells, the vast and seemingly growing difference between the ideal of play and sport and its colder, harder, more painful reality. This is why near the end of each chapter we present "social engineering," attempts to bring closer together the drifting apart of the ideal and the real in play and sport.

Sociology of sport strives to cut through such myths, folk beliefs, and misconceptions as character development in sport, athletes as role models, and widespread social mobility through sport. If we fail to learn about such things, we are liable to perpetuate the myths and misconceptions, fail to help solve the problems, or simply not use the full potential that sport ideally offers.

Sociology of sport is not a prescriptive "how to" discipline. You will not learn how to play a flexing zone defense, prevent or repair an ankle injury, or "motivate" an athlete to superlative performance. These, along with such concerns as playing rules and eligibility guidelines, are the *text* of sport. Sociology of sport, instead, considers the *context* of sport. Context focuses on the meaning of what happens in sport, where sport fits—or does not fit—into society and why. What sport does *to* and *for* players, coaches, parents of athletes, owners or managers of teams, officials, writers, spectators, etc., is the essence of sociology of sport, as is the place of sport within societal institutions.

Although sociology of sport is not a "how to" discipline, it can still be practical and useful. Comprehending the place of sport in society in general and coming to understand more specifically such things as varying value structures and purposes of sport at different levels, the perspectives of men and women or blacks and whites, political uses of sport, aggression and violence among players and spectators, and how cheating becomes endemic, can help the sport practitioner forestall or surmount problems. Seeing *that* problems exist is a necessary first step to solutions, which is the specific way that sociology of sport is a "practical" discipline, while not being a "how to" branch of knowledge.

Some students using this text will be new to the discipline of sociology, while many more will have, at best, only a passing acquaintance with social theory, methodology, and statistics. For these reasons, graphs, tables, and quantitative analysis are kept to a minimum. Research conclusions are offered, but are used sparingly compared to some other texts in the field. It is left to those students who are curious and capable of interpreting statistical information to plumb the numerous references provided at the end of each chapter.

While the book is divided into separate topical areas, the disciplines and concerns are not completely distinct. Section One orients the students to underlying definitional and theoretical concerns. These chapters consider how and why society—American society in particular—works and how and why it does not work. Section Two provides a developmental look at sport in American life, beginning with youth sport, extending to school and professional sports, and finishing with the new and growing concern for sport in later years. Section Three focuses on five particular issues through which sport touches our lives: aggression and violence, political "intrusion" into sport, racism, sexism, and the creation and purpose of heroes.

Bridges exist between the various areas of concern, and we must often cross back and forth before we can understand the territory on either side. We have attempted to provide various perspectives of sport and play. The text includes some psychology, anthropology, economics, pedagogy, and a healthy dose of history, as well as significant amounts of sociology, its home discipline.

We wish to acknowledge the help of Scott Spoolman and Steve Lehman, who were instrumental in the development of this third edition, as well as John C. Pooley, East Stroudsburg University, PA; Jody Brylinsky, Western Michigan University; Diane Chamberlain, Brigham Young University; and James D. LaPoint, University of Kansas, for their insightful review comments.

SECTION I

The Sociological Orientation

$\mathbf{W}$e live in a complex, dynamic social world with a rich diversity of inhabitants, interrelationships, personal and collective values and goals, resources, lifestyles, and modes of interaction. At first glance it may seem an impossible task to sort out with any certainty or predictability the patterns of human behavior that structure and give meaning to our lives. How can we come to understand the underlying principles of social order, much less consider possible changes in that order that might make it better for us? Especially, how can we approach the study of such a large and encompassing endeavor as sport, with all of its perplexing dimensions and applications, and make it understandable within the larger sociocultural picture?

The key to such an approach is sociology, the science concerned with the structure of human organization and the systems of human relationships. Sociology offers us the conceptual and procedural tools we need to unlock the mysteries of collective human behavior and to discover what is and is not true about our social world. Most important for us, it can enable us to separate fact from fiction within the institution of sport, our chief concern.

In the first chapter of this text, we will identify some key developments in the history of American sport that are of broad sociological interest. We will then establish some basic understandings shared by sociologists about the study of sociological phenomena. Using sport-related examples, we will define some key terms, identify the various levels of social interaction, and introduce the process by which sociologists investigate questions of sociological relevance such as those we will explore within the context of sport.

Do individual members of society share the same values and aspirations, or are we constantly and necessarily at odds with each other? What is the relationship between the individual and the larger group? Is equilibrium a desirable or even a possible social condition? Is conflict good, bad, necessary, avoidable? Finally, how do such initial assumptions about the social order itself influence how we view sport, how we identify the variables that affect sport-related issues, the methods we use to examine them, and the conclusions we draw about them? In Chapter 2, we will discuss two distinct views, or theories, of society and especially of sport. We will see how these two theories interpret sport-related issues, lead us to alternative conclusions, and suggest different future directions for sport.

"Sport builds character"—or so it is widely believed. Is this true? If so, what kind of character does it build, and how? In Chapter 3, we will explore socialization, the process by which we learn to do what is expected of us. We will discuss how this process guides us toward certain behavior patterns and away from others. We will see how individuals are socialized into, out of, and through the institution of sport, and evaluate the belief that sport fosters positive behavioral patterns. In the process, we will examine and compare competitive values in American society and American sport, and we'll consider alternative forms of sport competition.

How much room for individual difference does the social system allow? How far can we deviate from the path of law, rule, or custom without incurring the wrath of our fellow citizens? What kinds of deviance do we see in sport, and how can we judge its seriousness with regard to the larger social order? In Chapter 4, we will examine the concept of deviance and the range of factors that bear on the deviance of various participants in the world of organized sport.

CHAPTER 1

Background and Overview

Puritans we are not. American culture is fettered no longer by the strict and restrictive moral code of the early colonial settlers. No longer is attending church—or a funeral—the highest form of entertainment on a Sunday afternoon. Indeed, play and sport have come to dominate and vastly influence the lives of contemporary Americans in ways unimagined by even the most farsighted Puritans. But how have our attitudes and behaviors changed so drastically in only three and a half centuries? To begin to understand, it will help to look quickly at America's evolution through three economic stages: colonization, industrialization, and extensive mass consumption (Stone 1972). In each period, play and sport have taken on different characteristics and have touched different groups of people. In this quick look, we can begin to see how activities once thought to be wasteful and even sinful not only have gained acceptance and grown into a multibillion-dollar industry, but have become one of America's central institutions.

The Development of Play and Sport in North America[1]

In the colonial era, when life was less certain, when energies were directed toward surviving the winter and surviving attacks by Native Americans and the British, gaining a foothold on the land was a primary motivation in life.

---

[1]The focus of this text is play and sport in the United States and (to some extent) Canada, together properly called North America in order to distinguish the area from Central and South America. In the interest of readability, however, we will refer to the North American region simply as America.

Anything not productive to this end was considered frivolous. Recreation, though considered a basic human need, was to be satisfied only in constructive and socially productive ways (Lee 1964). The straitlaced seriousness of a heavy Puritan influence and the Protestant work ethic in early bloom left little time for unproductive activities such as play and games, although subsequent generations tended to embrace play more readily (Struna 1977).

Certainly, very young children, particularly those too young or too small to be of real help in daily chores, were allowed the freedom to play. Once youngsters reached the size and age when they were capable of contributing to the family's survival, even in the most meager way, they were set to tedious and time-consuming chores that often rendered playtime a mere wish. A very real devil and his perdition lay in wait for those, old and young, who strayed.

In the Southern colonies, playtime was considered more of a legitimate portion of the day or week and an acceptable outlet for energies (Spears and Swanson 1978). This difference in the perception of play between the Southern colonies and those on the middle and northern seaboard may have resulted from the more tolerant religious influence in the South.

At least as important as religion in making play a legitimate part of Southern life were economics and climate. The economy of the North came to focus on manufacturing, while the South was predominantly agrarian. Many of the play and game forms so acceptable and commonplace in the South were functional because of the lifestyle, work, and survival skills they involved. Thus, much "play" time was spent in hunting, fishing, and riding horses. In addition, certainly a great deal more of life was spent outdoors in the Southern colonies than in the North because of the milder climate (Bennett 1977).

Even in the North, however, the colonists' lives were not devoid of play. This is attested to by the proverb, originating in the 17th century, that "All work and no play makes Jack a dull boy" (Howell 1955). Play existed despite the moral breast-beating against its frivolity. Tag, wrestling matches, climbing, hoop rolling, and other contests among youngsters, and horse racing, marksmanship, and card games among adults were common. Sometimes work and play were combined, as in barn raising, corn husking, and quilting bees. The modern counterparts to these activities are the agricultural and homemaking contests at county fairs that make a game of activities that are essentially work.

In general, however, play in colonial America was restricted to the few hours of leisure that might be found in a long, hard week of work. Particularly, once a person reached the "age of responsibility," indulging in play carried with it varying feelings of guilt, carefully nurtured by the moralists of the time.

Industrialization, the Leisure Class, and Sports

With the 19th century came industrialization and the great growth of urban centers, but in the early, darker years of industrialization, work for the masses was little less time- and energy-consuming than it had been for the colonists. This factor, along with a lingering religious influence keeping righteous and God-fearing citizens from profaning the Sabbath, left little time for the working-class person to play.

Play and "sporting" endeavors, however, blossomed among the upper-class industrialists, the group that Veblen in 1899 caustically called the "leisure class" (1967). Sociologist Gregory Stone (1972) suggests that conspicuous participation in play and sport were obvious means for those in the leisure class to maintain their distinction from the common masses. American leisure class sportspeople were "conspicuously unserious" about their play, similar to the approach taken by British upper-class sportspeople. The amateur code of conduct, still expressed clearly in modern times in the Olympics, also fostered distinction between the leisure class and the working class. Members of the leisure class could afford the time and money to remain "purely" amateur athletes. Members of the working class could not.

Veblen (1967:271–72) considered sports among the working class "an occasional diversion rather than a serious feature of life." In contrast, he characterized the leisure class as having an "addiction to athletic sports, not only in the way of direct participation, but also in the way of sentiment and moral support."

Those who became wealthy and thus new members of the leisure class often marked their new status by taking up sports. This, along with a tendency for lower classes to emulate upper classes, suggests why the late 19th and early 20th centuries saw a broadening of sports participation in America.

Play and Sport in Modern American Life

The primary focus of this text is not on the past, but on modern American life, the period that Stone (1972) calls "high mass consumption." Broad and strict religious sanctions against play have been relegated primarily to history. Our current technology has transformed America from a production-oriented economy to a consumer-oriented one. Both factors have allowed play and sport to fill vast amounts of leisure time in the lives of Americans.

This text will call on you to be an observer of America. As de Tocqueville did in his classical analysis of American life a century and a half ago, try to observe American society as an outsider. Gain some perspective, and you may view American life and its nuances more clearly than you have as a participant immersed in its flow, its effects, and its consequences.

From this vantage point as participant-observer, one of the first things you may notice is that modern American culture seems preoccupied with play, games, and sport. The economy is permeated with advertising using the medium of sport and its personalities. The athletic image is used to sell automobiles, cologne, coffee makers, and underwear, not to mention the expected standbys of beer, breakfast cereals, and candy. The mass media (newspapers, magazines, radio, television, and movies) display or report athletic contests, examine their sociological, psychological, and humanistic content, and even offer parodies of sport in the guise of real sport.

De Tocqueville, observing in the mid-19th century, concluded that a most striking aspect of America was "the general equality of conditions" of its citizens (1946:3). This observation holds true in the latter 20th century, probably more so than it did during de Tocqueville's time, particularly if we understand that his observations of "citizens" did not include the Southern slaves and Native Americans, who were neither citizens nor "equal" to those of European descent who dominated American culture.

Like many other observers of cultures and social organization, de Tocqueville gave play and games short shrift. This may have been because he and other observers (Veblen being an exception) felt play forms to be unimportant in a "serious" analysis of American life. Nevertheless, the equality noted by de Tocqueville has been a major contributor to the widespread influence of play forms in American life. As a modern observer during a period when play forms are more apparent, you may infer that in order to better understand American society and culture, it would be beneficial to focus on, to seek to understand, and to interpret America's preoccupation with play and sport.

A more recent visitor to America, Welsh poet John Davies, with fresh eyes and insight, caught the essential spectacle of professional sport while observing an indoor soccer match (Davies 1985):

a night out at the Tacoma Dome

                    well here's a howdy-do
        at a soccer match
                where the unshy daughter
        of a power saw and a laser
                                performed open-skull surgery
                    rending the starspangled banner
        while the crowd stood still
                                though pierced from ear to ear
                    relying on the flag
                        hands clamped over hearts
                            protectively
            and the flag survived

over-amplified then
an orchestra of muscles:
THUS SPAKE ZARATHUSTRA
drifting of hallelujah smoke
with lightning spikes
and the voice of God
declaiming Laydees an Jentlemen
but just
the Tacoma Stars came
flicking a football like a nervous thought
at the Cleveland Force and
I hope to god
said Gill
they're going
to restore our faith in human
failure
which they did

Source: Davies, J. 1985. *The Visitor's Book*. MidGlamorgan, Wales: Poetry Wales Press.

We ask that as Veblen and Davies have done, you also strive to see how sport and American culture reflect each other.

Our text will follow this plan: first providing the reader-observer with some basic tools to aid observation and understanding, then delving into the broad areas of life touched by play and sport. For the remainder of this introductory chapter, we will first consider the similarities and differences among play, games, sport, and athletics, then orient ourselves toward sociology as a method of observing and interpreting the patterns of American life.

Play, Games, Sport, and Athletics in Perspective

Since we will be using these terms throughout the text, it is important that we understand the similarities and differences among play, games, sport, and athletics. A number of writers attempt to define these terms by looking to their etymology, in which the Latin, Greek, or French roots are used to clarify definition. This is done particularly with *sport*. This tactic is often more confusing than helpful, however, because the forms of words and their meanings, both denotation and connotation, change over time and geopolitical context. Thus, while the French *desport* may originally have meant "to divert oneself" in the French cultural context, it does not necessarily follow that its derivative, *sport*, carries the same meaning in late-20th-century America, or late-20th-century France for that matter. Therefore, in defining key words, we will avoid their etymology and focus instead on present context.

Johan Huizinga in *Homo Ludens* describes the characteristics of play as follows (1955:13):

> . . . a free activity standing quite consciously outside "ordinary" life as being "not serious," but at the same time absorbing the player intensely and utterly. It is an activity connected with no material interest, and no profit can be gained by it. It proceeds within its own proper boundaries of time and space according to fixed rules and in an orderly manner. It promotes the formation of social groupings which tend to surround themselves with secrecy and to stress their difference from the common world by disguise or other means.

Caillois (1961:9–10) analyzed Huizinga's conception of the characteristics of play and restated them as follows:

1. Free involvement—play is voluntary.
2. Separated from "non-play" by spatial and temporal limits (lines, ropes, nets, innings, holes, maximum or minimum points).
3. Uncertainty of outcome—especially where competition is an element of the play activity, efforts are often made to insure that both or all sides begin evenly and that the process is "fair." Thus, play is not play if it is not fair play.
4. Unproductive—no material gain comes from playful activity.
5. Rules govern the procedures.
6. Make-believe—play stands apart from "real life."

More recently, Garvey (1977:4–5) attributed to play these characteristics:

1. Play is pleasurable, enjoyable. Even when not actually accompanied by signs of mirth, it is still positively valued by the player.
2. Play has no extrinsic goals. Its motivations are instrinsic [sic] and serve no other objectives. In fact, it is more an enjoyment of means than an effort devoted to some particular end. In utilitarian terms, it is inherently unproductive.
3. Play is spontaneous and voluntary. It is not obligatory but is freely chosen by the player.
4. Play involves some active engagement on the part of the player.
5. Play has certain systematic relations to what is not play.

While many more scholars have attempted to analyze play[2] and its components, one characteristic seems to appear often: its separateness from "reality." Huizinga, Caillois, and Garvey all seem to agree on this thought. For example, to illustrate Garvey's last characteristic listed above, attacking behavior during play is accepted as mock attack (unreal or nonliteral) rather than as literal attack with its consequent dangers. Play ceases when the attack or the danger becomes real.

---

[2]The interesting topic of *why* humans play is tangential to our present concern with *how* we play. Sage (1979) discusses briefly but thoroughly theories of why people play.

In contrast, theologian Michael Novak in *The Joy of Sports* (1976:40) insists that "Play is reality. Work is diversion and escape." Play, according to Novak, is real because it concerns living and life in the present tense. Work, on the other hand, is unreal because it is motivated by and directed toward something past, such as paying bills and debts, or future-oriented, toward goals such as saving, security, and improvement.

Reality exists only in the present tense. We can only "be" now. Our "becoming" is oriented toward a future nonreality, something that we hope to become but are not yet. Play and sport, for Novak, are pure "now-ness." All that matters is what is going on now, within the confines of the activity. Indeed, one of the difficult tasks of coaches is to keep players' minds on and in the game or match at hand. When we leave the mental state of "play," we return to activities that attempt to cover for our past debts or plan for our as-yet-unrealized future.

> The serious ones say that sports are escape. It seems far more true to the eye, the ear, the heart, and the mind that history is an escape. Work is an escape. Causes are an escape. Historical movements are an escape. All these escapes must be attempted; I take part in as many as I can. But the heart of human reality is courage, honesty, freedom, community, excellence: the heart is sports (Novak 1976:42).

Novak's perspective is refreshing and introduces a possible resolution to Huizinga's unsatisfactory view of play as unreal. However, Novak's view is not wholly satisfactory either, since he fails to distinguish between play and sport. We can readily imagine sports in the future used as a means for improving one's life, as a tool of politics, and for other worldly purposes ulterior to play. We might suggest that sport is rather like a chameleon—it takes on the hue of its environment.

How do play and sport, games and athletics resemble each other? How do they differ? In common parlance these terms may be used interchangeably or in the same context. Our purpose in defining them more closely is not an attempt to change their common usage, but rather to allow the readers of this text to see the shadings of difference among these terms so that our communication may be more precise and shared. These four terms, or categories, should not be conceived as distinct, but rather as positions on a continuum of physical activity possessing the aura, if not the reality, of leisure (see Fig. 1.1).

Edwards (1973) points out that although some aspects of these activities are different in gradation only, other categories have particular aspects that absolutely distinguish one form of activity from the others. For example, each category or position on the continuum is characterized more or less by *fun*.

FIGURE 1.1   *Continuum of Physical Leisure Activity.*

That is, while we may have fun in all categories, in play, fun is a necessary component. It is not a necessary component for the other three categories. To explain this more fully,

1. In play, fun is essential; play ceases when fun ceases (i.e., when the activity becomes drudgery or work).
2. In games, fun is usually present, although compulsion or obligation to finish the game may keep participants involved even after their pleasure ceases.
3. In sport, fun is hoped for and expected, but is not a necessary ingredient of the activity.
4. In athletics, fun is completely irrelevant and may be unlikely, considering the pressures involved.

Rather than being present to a lesser or greater extent in all categories, certain characteristics exist in some categories but are totally absent in others. Competition, for example, is a necessary component of games, sport, and athletics since each points to a particular outcome or culmination of the activity. Play, on the other hand, is noncompetitive in its purest state, since play has no set beginning or end and has only the state of enjoyment, rather than a victory of some sort, as its goal.

Keeping in mind that we are conceiving the four forms of activity as areas on a continuum rather than as mutually exclusive categories, what are the attributes most characteristic of each area and what are the particular characteristics that distinguish given categories from the others?

Play

Freedom.   Play tends to be free. Participants enter and exit of their own volition. To the extent that play is ordered or controlled by some external authority figure such as an elementary school teacher ("Playtime!") or one's mother ("Go out and play in the yard"), the activity may be less "playful," unless the player wants to play anyway. In other words, it is difficult truly to play if you do not want to play.

Limits.   Play tends not to be limited in time and space. One can, if not may, play anywhere at any time. A ballpark with foul lines designating "out of play" is unnecessary. Play can occur in a field, at home, at school, in a business office (more or less surreptitiously), or on the surface of the moon. Play may become less playful or less free when someone says, "Time to stop playing!" but such edicts do not necessarily and immediately put an end to the play activity; fear of punishment might, however, put a severe crimp in the joyfulness of the play.

Rules and Authority. In play there are few rules. Such rules as exist are flexible and often change at a player's whim. As long as the new rule is agreed on, play continues. Disagreement and conflict bring an end to the playfulness of play.

Play has no imposed authority figure. Authority resides within the players during play. A well-meaning adult who tries to interject or impose his or her own conception of "the rules" simply interferes with the play in progress.

Outcome. Play is devoid of competition since competition implies a degree of gain or loss that is difficult to pursue given the freedom of time, space, rules, entry, and exit inherent in play.

Motivation. The primary motivation of play is pleasure. If the activity is not fun, it is not play. In the absence of fun, any activity becomes work.

Investment. Finally, play is characterized by an absence of investment. True play requires no money, planning, training, or ego-investment. While play may occur in their presence, it is quite possible, if not more probable, for play to occur in their absence.

Games

Freedom. While games also tend to be free, there is less complete freedom in games than in play because games usually have a specific beginning and a specific end. Therefore, when one enters a game, one is implicitly obligated as a player to participate until the end (although there is less obligation to oneself in a game such as solitaire).

Limits. Games tend to be confined within specific limits of space (i.e., boundaries) and time (either temporal limits or completion of designated activities such as capturing other players or holes or innings played).

Rules and Authority. Games tend to be played by rules that may be changed on agreement. However, this is less likely to occur than in pure play because games are pointed toward a specific outcome that may be obscured or subverted by mid-game rule changes.

Outcome.   When a game is begun, it is understood that there will be a winner and a loser, and that some degree of competition will be required to determine the winner. This is the key distinction between games and play. While in pure play there are no winners or losers, in a game all entrants share the assumption that each is trying to win, whether or not the game actually culminates in a definitive outcome.

Investment.   Since games imply winners and losers, there may be a degree of emotion or ego investment involved, although such investment tends to be small compared to that found in sports and athletics. In other words, games are primarily recreational, with relaxation, exercise, human interaction, and enjoyment providing the primary motivations.

Games, like play, need not be physical, while sport and athletics require physical exertion. For purposes of comparison with sport and athletics, however, we will consider primarily play and games of the physical type.

Sports

The difference in character between games and sports is dramatically greater than the difference between play and games (thus the greater distance between the two in Fig. 1.1), with sports tending to take on more of the character of work and relinquishing some of the appearance of play and games.[3]

Structure.   Sports imply a structure of teams and leagues. There are more restrictive controls over entry into and exit from sports participation than there are in the prior two categories.

Authority.   Sports tend to have a hierarchical authority pattern within given competing groups. Coaches exist to guide and/or dictate to players. At least one level of external authority (Little League Baseball, the AAU, state high school sports associations) also exists to dictate regulations, schedules, and conduct. While rules in games may or may not be codified (i.e., written), these rules may be altered or transgressed by agreement among players of a particular game. This is not so in sports; rule changes in a sport must be channeled through an authority that governs the sport.

Investment.   Sports are significantly more competitive than games, and it follows that there is significantly more investment of time, energy, money, and ego in sports. This greater degree of investment, and a concern for won-lost records in addition to the outcome of the contest at hand, is a key distinguishing feature of sports, as Edwards (1973), among others, points out.

---

[3]Jaeggi (1967) has found some empirical support for this contention in Europe.

Quite often, the investment aspect of sports equals or outweighs their recreational aspect. The recreational Sunday golfer, tennis player, or runner who has significant ego investment (and often monetary investment in equipment) may be clothing his or her "game" in the raiments of sports. On the other hand, many weekend participants legitimize their sports involvement by joining sports clubs or tournaments with achievement as their express goal. Problems can occur when some recreationally inclined players engage in contests with more ego-invested opponents, or when the motivation changes in mid-contest. What began as "just a game" sometimes becomes something more.

This scenario illustrating possible crossed lines of communication among participants might be a problem among middle-class adults or possibly in intramural sports. In situations such as inner-city basketball contests, the games are seldom "just games" because of the long-range goals of many of the players and often because of the scarcity of playing space and the need to work or play hard in order to keep playing.

Athletics

Sports and athletics are often thought of as synonymous and tend to be used interchangeably (Edwards 1973). A distinction, however, is not only useful but necessary in a world seemingly exploding with sportive activities of all kinds and degrees.

In simple terms, we may conceive of athletics as "sports in spades." Athletics outsports sport. If sports are highly structured, the category of athletics is virtually rigid. If sports limit access and exit, athletics is absolutely restrictive. This is particularly apparent in the rigid guidelines governing participation in college and Olympic athletics.

Although sports have their modest forms of authority hierarchy, systems of athletics place athletes on the lowest status level of an extensive authority structure with the smallest voice in procedures, despite the fact that athletes are the essence of athletics. Athletes and social critics such as Hoch (1972), Scott (1971), and Edwards (1969) have publicly bemoaned the pawn-like status of players.

Regarding goals and motivations, athletics also outdistances sport. Sports require some investment, while athletics is big business. Sports are competitive, while in athletics, "winning is the only thing." It would be nice but totally irrelevant in athletics if the athletes were having fun.

The distinction between sports and athletics, in Keating's words (1964:28), is based on a difference in "attitude, preparation, and purpose of the participants." Sports are basically pleasurable diversions characterized by moderate effort, while participation in athletics is characterized by intense dedication and sacrifice. The term *sports,* as used in this text, will refer to the category of activities that is more conducive to fun than athletics and is, at least by degree, less serious and consuming than athletics. *Sport* (in the singular form) will be considered a generic term for sports, athletics, and even some competitive physical games.

What Is Sociology and What Is Its Focus?

Given this brief overview of the concepts to be explored in this text, we are ready to introduce the process we will be using to make our exploration meaningful. Essentially, we are embarking on an analysis of American society through play and sport. What then does the discipline of sociology involve? What are its concerns?

Sociology has been defined as the study of systems of social action and of their interrelationships (Inkeles 1964). Sociology is the science concerned with the structure of human organization and the systems of human relationships. As a science, it tests the assumptions that we make about our social environment.

Implicit in our definition of sociology is the belief that there is order in human relationships. That is, sociologists believe that when two or more human beings interact, something more than chaos is occurring, although at times the order in this interaction may not be apparent. If human interaction is random and unpredictable, there is no reason to study it. Social scientists, however, believe not only that there is order in human interaction, but that it can be predicted and possibly controlled if enough is known.

Sociology of Sport as a Subdiscipline

There is little that cannot be studied from a sociological perspective, that is, from the point of view of the relationships among living beings and their social organization. Nothing in this world exists in a void. Every occurrence has impact on or implications for persons and groups around it.

Sociology is divided into subdisciplines based on other institutions or disciplines. Thus, while most of us know sociology as a general science of its own, there is also the sociology of law, of deviance, of small groups, of medicine, of art, of the aging, and of cities (i.e., urban sociology), to mention only a few. There is even a sociology of sociology that investigates the role relationships, statuses, normative and deviant behaviors, attitudes, and trends within the field of sociology.

Sociology of sport is a relatively new subdiscipline. Its inception as a field of study may have been formally marked by the publication of an article in 1965 by Gerald Kenyon and John Loy called "Toward a Sociology of Sport." In this article, the authors defined sociology of sport as "the study of the regularity and departure from it of behavior in the sports context." Since the Kenyon and Loy article, there has been rapid acceptance of sociology of sport as a subdiscipline, at least within the field of teacher training, if not yet completely in the parent discipline of sociology. Its rapid acceptance as a key course within the physical education curriculum, and a recent proliferation of journals focusing on the field, may be taken as signs that the emergence of this subdiscipline was timely, if not overdue.

The Domains of Sociology

Sociology is concerned with four domains of human life: (1) social systems, (2) institutions, (3) small groups, and (4) the individual social act. These four domains will be discussed in order of the most encompassing to the least, the general to the specific.

Social Systems. A social system has been described as "two or more individuals who have developed a set of mutual obligations and expectations as part of an ongoing and complex relationship" (Larson 1973:245). Social systems may be as small as two interacting persons. Somewhat more broadly, Allison (1979) has described a game as a social system, since a game consists of statuses and roles, expectations, interactions, and goals—those elements that constitute a social system.

The term "social system," however, generally refers to a larger, more complex system of interrelationships such as a nation, a tribe, the systems of intercollegiate athletics, a particular league or conference, or a team in which all interacting members have obligations to the group and expectations of it. We will consider the social system to be the setting—complete with regulations, obligations, and expectations—within which the smaller domains function. Our social system, unless otherwise stated, will be North American society.

Institutions. The subsystems contained in the social system are called institutions (Inkeles 1964). The four general categories of institutions are the family, the polity (including the judiciary and subsystems that make and enforce laws), economic institutions, and a large category called expressive-integrative institutions. This last category includes religion, education, and sport, among others, all of which function to transmit societal values. The family and the expressive-integrative institutions are often more specifically called socializing institutions.

Socializing institutions exist specifically, but not necessarily exclusively, to transmit values, attitudes, mores, and normative behaviors. Sport is included as a socializing institution because it involves the transmission of significant amounts of value, attitude, and normative behavior, in addition to leisure and skill-learning. In Chapters 2 and 3 we will address in detail the socializing and other functions of sport at the institutional level.

The Small Group. As we focus more closely on the smaller parts of social organization, they become progressively less abstract. The group is an aggregate of people with a common goal or reason for being together. An aggregate of people without a common goal is a crowd, even if at one time the members of the crowd had shared a common goal. Presumably, we have all experienced being in a crowd that thought itself a functioning group. An aggregate of people becomes more crowd-like and less group-like when the goals of its individuals do not support the group goal. A basketball team with five individual stars functions more as a crowd, that is, less as a cohesive team, than one in which the players perform mutually supportive roles.

Groups characteristically contain various roles and statuses. These seem to emerge, not necessarily by plan, but as a natural concomitant of group process. A *role* is an expected behavior, including its rights and obligations. An actor or actress plays a role according to the way the person portrayed would be expected to behave (that is, not "out of character"). *Status* is a position encompassing certain attributes that distinguish people in a group. Status represents a place or a position in relationship to others, while role refers to the behavior defining the differences among statuses.

Child and parent, student and teacher, prisoner and jailor, client and lawyer, lawyer and judge, athlete and coach, and athlete and referee all represent different statuses between pairs of individuals. Particular role behaviors are expected and, in some cases, demanded; penalties can be imposed for deviations. Even where penalties are not assessed, problems within groups or institutions may ensue when status or role inconsistencies occur. Such inconsistencies lead to crossed lines of communication or violated expectations, which may result in a breakdown in group function. Parents, for example, expect to tell or show the child how to behave, not vice versa; players expect the coach to tell, show, or advise them how to play, not vice versa. If these status and role relationships are violated, and expectations are not met, group function and social interaction can break down.

An individual may play as many roles, and thus have as many statuses, as groups he or she is in. At times, a single status may have numerous roles, possibly leading to role conflict. The roles of "woman" and of "athlete," as we shall discuss in Chapter 12, are potentially conflicting.

The player who, after college graduation, becomes an assistant coach of the team on which he or she played may have difficulty shifting role relationships in accordance with the shift in status from player to coach. It is not unusual to hear the complaint that "he (or she) is not the same person" after a change in status from player to coach, or even the relatively minor status change to team captain. While the problem may come in part from lack of acquired skill in the new role on the part of the new coach or captain, much of the problem is likely to stem from the old teammate-buddies who harbor false expectations that the promoted person will attempt to retain the old role relationship and relate to them in "the same old way." The status is, in fact, different, with new responsibilities, making it virtually impossible for the newly promoted person to relate in the old way while still doing the job entailed by the new status.

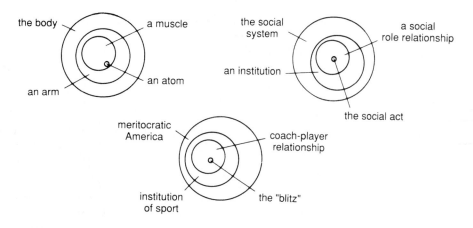

FIGURE 1.2 *Relationships Among the Domains of Sociology.*

The Individual Social Act. The fourth domain of sociology is the individual and his or her social act. This is the life thread running through each of the three other domains. In sociology, the individual is studied in relationship to these other domains.

Figure 1.2 represents how the individual social act relates to the group, to the institution, and to the social system. Using a biological point of reference (following Inkeles 1964), consider the relationships among an atom, a muscle that many atoms might constitute, the arm that this muscle helps to move, and the body of which the arm is a part. From the sociologist's perspective, the equivalent relationships are an individual's specific social act, the role relationship that acting person has in his or her relevant group, the effect of that group on the relevant institution, and the effect of that institution on the functioning social system. Since football seems pervasive in much of American life, let us look for illustration to the fairly common "social act" of a linebacker blitzing (rushing through the offensive line) in order to knock down the opposing quarterback. This one social act has two goals: (1) to break up the play in progress, and (2) to intimidate the quarterback in the hope that this will interfere with subsequent plays.

The act of hitting the quarterback fits into the role relationship or group domain because the coach of the team either ordered a player to commit this action or sanctioned it, since the intent is to further the group goal of victory in the game. Victory-seeking behavior is congruent with the institution of sport, which is predicated on athletic competition, a process of determining differences in performance and ability (i.e., winners and losers). The institution of sport, in turn, is congruent with the American social system, which has as its raison d'etre the philosophy that one's place within the social system

"STANLEY CAN'T PLAY THE PIANO UNTIL HE'S FINISHED HIS FOOTBALL LESSON."

Reprinted by permission: Tribune Media Services.

should be determined by one's ability and achievement. Thus, individual social acts have importance in that they are either congruent or incongruent with the group, the institution, and the social system.

Context and the Social Act

In order to illustrate the importance of context (i.e., social setting) and perspective in sociological analysis, another single act will be presented along with its place within the domains of sociology. We have used the example from football of a linebacker knocking down a quarterback for his personal and his team's gain. Compare this act to that of a street mugger. The mugger knocks down a person who has something that the mugger and the mugger's gang (if he or she is a "social" mugger) want. This individual act of mugging serves the needs of the gang/group as well as being within the scope and expected behavior of the criminal element of society, which represents a social system of its own. There is nothing inconsistent or abhorrent from the perspective of the mugger, particularly when one realizes that many criminals believe the victims ask for their victimization. Many muggers and other criminals often justify their acts with the belief that the streets are their territory, particularly at certain times of the night, and that the victims should "know better" than to present themselves as targets.

Law-abiding citizens may feel righteous in believing one act to be socially acceptable because the quarterback volunteers to play football, while the other act is wrong because the person who is mugged because he works late and is out on the street at night has only volunteered to work late, not to interact with the mugger. However, the judgment comes from one's point of view. Even within sport, the rightness or wrongness of given acts of aggression are increasingly coming under question as attitudes and points of view change (see Chapter 9).

The Sociological Process

The sociologist's work tends to focus on issues—that is, questions of social relevance that involve more than one point of view. Issues can be stated in the form of questions, such as "Should athletes be allowed to take drugs?" or "Should college athletes get preferential treatment?" A systematic approach to social issues includes four kinds of activity: (1) pure description, (2) evaluative commentary, (3) social critique, and (4) social engineering.

Pure Description.   In order to analyze a social issue effectively, the sociologist must first describe the existing situation and clarify concepts that are important to understanding the issue. For example, in order to tackle the issue of whether athletes should be allowed to take drugs, the sociologist must first establish which athletes (Olympic? professional? collegiate? high school?) are being addressed, which drugs (anabolic steroids? amphetamines? diuretics? marijuana?) are in question, and the current situation regarding drug use in athletics (How much is legal? How much is allowed by Olympic/league/conference rules? How widespread is it? What effects does it have?). The pure description phase of a sociologist's analysis helps to prevent misunderstandings about the nature of the issue or the concepts related to it.

Evaluative Commentary.   After clarifying the issue itself, the sociologist must next identify the major positions taken on the issue, and then examine and evaluate the evidence supporting each position. For example, a range of positions on the issue of drug use may be sorted, from (*a*) no nonessential drugs should be taken by any athlete, to (*b*) only legal drugs should be allowed, to (*c*) professional athletes only should be allowed to take any drugs they wish, to (*d*) there should be no restrictions on drug use by any athletes. The sociologist then evaluates the various positions by examining the results of scientific studies relating to the issue, and by weighing the arguments offered by athletes, coaches, members of the medical profession, league officials, and others representing each position. Through this process, the strengths and weaknesses of each position are clarified, and the most defensible positions should emerge.

Social Critique. The purpose of social critique is to identify those conditions in various institutions within the social system that bear on the issue in question. Drug use by athletes within the institution of sport cannot be understood fully without some appreciation for the pressure put on athletes and coaches by an achievement-oriented society with a capitalistic interest in outcome, a religiously based work ethic, an educational system that is all too willing to overlook illegal activities as long as they maximize athletic performance, an entertainment industry with a major focus on sport, media attention that can warp the self-image of young athletes and stunt their emotional growth, a medical profession that promises a pill for every ill, and a government with a vested interest in using superiority in sport as evidence of political superiority. Social critique sheds light on the issue by putting it in perspective with regard to the overall societal picture.

Social Engineering. Ultimately, the goal of sociology is to improve society, that is, to make whatever changes are needed in order to create a better social order. Once the sociological process has identified some desirable changes, the next logical step is to institute those changes. Social engineering is everyone's task, however, not just the sociologist's. If, for example, sociological inquiry reveals that the best solution to drug use by athletes includes building effective drug education programs into the training of young athletes, then it is the responsibility of everyone connected with youth sports to put such education programs into place. Social engineering, then, links the political process with the academic process. It is responsible citizenship in action, informed by well-controlled, systematic sociological investigation.

The four-step sociological process described above is a sound approach to the analysis of any social issue. In this text, we will suggest how this analytical framework can be applied to each of the issues addressed.

Summary

Over the course of American history, play and sport have continued to figure prominently in the activities of various groups. In the modern era, sport has become firmly and pervasively embedded in our culture. Analyses of play, games, sport, and athletics point to increases from one to the next in structure, intensity, and external control, with athletics characterized as "sports in spades." To study such phenomena, sociologists operate within the increasingly specific domains of social systems, institutions, small groups, and the individual social act. The sociologist's systematic approach progresses from pure description to evaluative commentary to social critique, with the ultimate goal of illuminating directions for social engineering.

References

Allison, M. T. 1979. "The Game: A Participant Observation Study." *Journal of Sport Behavior* 2(2):93–102.

Bennett, B. 1977. "Sport in the South up to 1865." *Quest* 27(Winter):4–18.

Caillois, R. 1961. *Man, Play and Games.* Glencoe, IL: Free Press.

Davies, J. 1985. *The Visitor's Book.* MidGlamorgan, Wales: Poetry Wales Press.

Edwards, H. 1969. *Revolt of the Black Athlete.* New York: Free Press.

Edwards, H. 1973. *Sociology of Sport.* Homewood, IL: Dorsey Press.

Garvey, C. 1977. *Play: The Developing Child.* Cambridge, MA: Harvard University Press.

Hoch, P. 1972. *Rip Off the Big Game.* Garden City, NY: Doubleday.

Howell, J. 1955. "Proverbs, 12 (1659)." In *Familiar Quotations* (13th ed.), edited by J. Bartlett. Boston: Little, Brown.

Huizinga, J. 1960. *Homo Ludens.* Boston: Beacon Press.

Inkeles, A. 1964. *What Is Sociology?* Englewood Cliffs, NJ: Prentice-Hall.

Jaeggi, U. 1967. "Sport und Gesselschaft." *Sociology International* 5(1):57–80.

Keating, J. 1964. "Sportsmanship as a Moral Category." *Ethics* 85(1):25–35.

Kenyon, G. S., and J. W. Loy, Jr. 1965. "Toward a Sociology of Sport." *Journal of Health, Physical Education, and Recreation* 36:24–25.

Larson, C. J. 1973. *Major Themes in Sociological Theory.* New York: David McKay.

Lee, R. 1964. *Religion and Leisure in America.* New York: Abingdon Press.

Novak, M. 1976. *The Joy of Sports.* New York: Basic Books.

Sage, G. H. 1979. "Sport and the Social Sciences." *The Annals of the American Academy of Political and Social Science* 445:1–14.

Scott, J. 1971. *The Athletic Revolution.* New York: Free Press.

Spears, B., and R. A. Swanson. 1978. *History of Sport and Physical Activity in the United States.* Dubuque, IA: W. C. Brown.

Stone, G. P. 1972. *Games, Sport & Power.* New Brunswick, NJ: TransAction Books.

Struna, N. L. 1977. "Sport and Societal Values: Massachusetts Bay." *Quest* 27 (Winter):38–46.

de Tocqueville, A. 1946. *Democracy in America.* New York: Oxford Press.

Veblen, T. 1967. *The Theory of the Leisure Class.* New York: Viking Press (reproduction of original text published in 1899).

CHAPTER 2

Perspectives on Society and Sport

Probably all of us could give a passable description of an elephant—unless, of course, we had been without sight from birth and had never seen an elephant or had an elephant described to us. Now picture several blind men attempting to discuss what an elephant looks like. They decide to approach an elephant to determine what it is like. One touches a leg and says an elephant is like a sturdy tree. Another touches its flank and describes the elephant as being like a broad wall. A third touches the end of its tail and says an elephant is like a large brush. Another touches its ear and describes the elephant as being like a soft, warm blanket. Yet another touches its trunk and jumps back in alarm, crying out that the elephant is like a snake.

Which one is right about what the elephant is like? Of course, they all are right. And they all are wrong. What they "see" and describe depends on their perspective—where they are relative to the elephant and what their experience has been.

Our description of the social system in which we live, its effects on us, and our place within it, depend on our point of view—our perspective—which to a large extent is based on and limited by our experiences and our willingness to consider other points of view. To varying degrees we are all blind about the world. A central purpose of sociology and this text is to expand our perspective to give us insight into, if not necessarily fostering agreement with, other points of view.

Sport is our elephant. Because sport has become so ubiquitous in American culture, fed to us daily in large doses through the print and electronic media as news or as a commodity, it is easy to grow blind to sport, even if we have played or coached. It is sport as a commodity, as more than fun and games or mere diversion, that interests us sociologically. This is where social issues lie, where battle lines are drawn, where the dominance of one group over another leads some to challenge the status quo out of fear of being co-opted or coerced into accepting their subservience (Boggs 1981; McKay 1986).

However, we should not overlook the play element in American society, and especially the relative legitimacy and power of those who advocate and support each in times of limited resources. An example of such difference in perspective occurs in nearly every town and city in the country concerning battles over land use. Should our recreational land and resources be used for the open and unstructured use of the populace to play and exercise as they see fit, or should we build more ballfields, racetracks, and gymnasiums to accommodate formal, structured competition? The former serves personal needs, while the latter feeds people into and through the system of sport that in many ways reiterates the nation's competitive structure. Is play as "legitimate" a use of public land and money as sport?

Since many of us seldom consider sport beyond its entertainment role, we may not see the place of sport in the social system and the effects that play, as a free-form activity, and sport, as an institution, have on individuals and groups. Looking beyond the entertainment role of sport in American society, let us consider first the tools we can use to examine the social system and its workings. Then we can see how sport as an institution fits within that system.

The Nature of Theories

Theories are tools that serve as abstract explanations of beliefs about reality; they are attempts to describe and interpret bits of the world. The existence of more than one theory about a phenomenon ("bit of the world") or set of phenomena is evidence of disagreement about the "truth" or explanatory validity of any of those theories. For example, as we shall see in Chapter 9, several theories compete in attempting to explain where aggressive behavior comes from and what is the social-psychological result of acting aggressively. (Is aggression "gotten rid of," or is it "learned" and thus more likely to be repeated?) Ultimately, one of the competing theories may prove to be more supportable than others, although this is more likely to occur in the natural sciences in which the subjects being studied (rocks, cells, etc.) do not have volition or the ability to interpret and react as humans do to what is being said or concluded about them.

Theories about society are shaped by people's past experiences, current needs, and future hopes. At given points in history one perspective may be more popular or reflective of current events than others, rather than one being "true" and the others "false." For example, theories about the propriety of competitive sports or even simply time devoted to play within the school day have varied depending on the era and place (Chapter 6). A second example is the benefits of unstructured play compared to organized sports, especially for youth (Chapter 5). A third considers the concept of femininity and the effects of sports participation on gender socialization (Chapter 12). In each example, "truth", i.e., what is generally thought to be true at a given point in time based on then-current knowledge, bias, and interpretation, changes with time and social conditions.

Opposing Views of Social Reality: Theoretical Perspectives

Our point about competing views of "truth" can be seen through a "macro" theory, that is, one that tries to describe how humans organize ourselves and behave *en masse*. In the 17th century, English political philosopher Thomas Hobbes, struck by the essentially self-serving nature of humans, posed the question of how social order is possible. In his book *Leviathan,* first published in 1651, Hobbes pondered how it is that we are able to pattern our behavior in cooperation with other humans and create and maintain our social organizations. Known as the Hobbesian Question, this "problem of order" can be considered the starting point of all sociological theory (Turner 1978). Comparative theoretical perspectives on phenomena such as socialization and social inequality may be viewed as alternative responses to the Hobbesian Question.

Let us first look at comparative views of socialization. Each of us has a conception of right and wrong, appropriate and inappropriate behavior, "good" attitudes and "bad" attitudes. Our beliefs about right and wrong are largely the product of our particular socialization. The term *process of socialization,* which we will consider in greater detail in Chapter 3, refers to the ways in which we learn and internalize specific attitudes, values, and mores as proper. Seldom are we aware that we are being socialized since these views tend to be inculcated unconsciously. Rather, we tend to accept them as correct, as if there is no other real truth. ("Clearly, education is a good thing. How could those Amish discourage their daughters from getting an education! That is wrong-headed behavior.") These internalized beliefs, and the behaviors that follow, tend to be congruent with our view of the social system. If our behaviors differ from the social norm, especially if we break rules or laws, we will be labelled aberrant, deviant, or socially and perhaps even legally "abnormal."

Comparison: The Process of Socialization

The process of socialization is found in the relationship between the individual and the social system in which he or she lives (Parsons 1964). However, there are two ways of looking at this process. Advocates of one view see socialization as preparation of the young or new members of the social system for responsible adult roles within the existing, fixed society. From this perspective the social system develops and maintains *conformity,* helping individuals to "get along" and "make their place" in society. Opposing this view of socialization is the belief that the social system *coerces* individuals to accept the system's values and normative behaviors (if not necessarily its social hierarchy) at the expense of their own self-interest. The social system, from this second perspective, is an adversary to individuals rather than a foundation.

The difference in perspectives stems from how one responds to the Hobbesian Question. Does the social system exist to serve its individual members, or is it their place to serve and support the system, even to unhappy personal consequences? Of course, the individual and society are in many ways mutually dependent, but the question of priority remains. If the needs of the individual and the needs of the system conflict, which should be served? An example of such conflict can be seen in our system of justice based on our constitution's Bill of Rights. The Bill of Rights favors the individual, sometimes resulting in criminals being set free at the expense of communal safety. Other societies take a radically different perspective, seeing public safety as more important than individual rights. The Hobbesian Question is appropriate to ask not only regarding individuals in relation to the social system, but also for the individual in relation to institutions, such as sport, which are integral parts of the system.[1]

Functionalism

As a theory of social order, *functionalism* emphasizes the institutional mechanisms that help society to operate. The underlying assumption on which functionalism rests is that societal mechanisms—specifically, institutions—endure because they are useful to and consistent with the needs of the existing society. According to Parsons (1964:218), a structure or institution "either 'contributes' to the maintenance (or development) of the system or it is 'dysfunctional' in that it detracts from the integration, effectiveness, etc., of the system." Further, Merton (1951:51) suggests that functional structures (those that contribute to the system) elicit "adaptation or adjustment" to a given social system, while those that are dysfunctional lessen adaptation or adjustment.

The essence of functionalism is that each part of the system serves primarily the maintenance and continuity of that system. Each part helps the system sustain its equilibrium, keeping it not only operating but thriving. The social system is a well-coordinated and reasonably efficient machine with its

---

[1]Other theories may be used to analyze the relationship between individuals and society (e.g., social exchange, symbolic interaction, etc.). However, we will leave a broader comparison of theories to texts specifically focusing on social theory. Our discussions will be limited to a comparison of functionalism and conflict-coercion theories because they represent diametrically opposed perspectives and can best serve the purpose of opening our minds to different ways of interpreting institutions, attitudes, motives, and behaviors that we might not otherwise question.

main purpose being its own survival and growth. The primary socializing institutions of family, religion,[2] and schools function in congruence with the social system. In this century, sport has also grown into a pervasive socializing institution.

While the less-structured and -rewarded activities that we might categorize under play and games may also encourage mainstream attitudes and values, they do so informally, apart from institutionally derived processes (rewards and punishments). "Playing fair," for example, has a different meaning during recess than it may have for interscholastic athletes. On the playground, playing fair carries the sense of everybody having a fair chance and being treated equally. On interscholastic teams, fairness is more likely to mean taking advantage of others without breaking rules, and star athletes are often given more latitude by the institution's representatives—coaches, teachers, and even administrators.[3]

According to functionalism, the social system resists change that threatens its stability, although this tendency toward equilibrium is relative rather than absolute (Black 1961). Moderate change and even deviation are permitted so long as they do not throw the system off kilter. The system may welcome new forms and discard old ones that no longer serve adequately or efficiently. When variations prove harmonious, they will be adopted, just as the motor car was adopted despite its adverse effect on the horse-and-buggy industry. A given institution (or industry) will be sacrificed if the system is better served by a competing new form.

Within sport, might not the amateur athlete be an anachronism (except among the very young and the very old), no longer serving a purpose? If so, this category is destined to vanish, like the horse and buggy.[4] The Association for Intercollegiate Athletics for Women (AIAW) met its demise when the more entrenched and powerful National Collegiate Athletic Association (NCAA) expropriated the AIAW's governance of women's collegiate athletics. When a structure no longer serves a function, the social system discards it. This is the law of the jungle on a societal level.

---

[2]Most religions socialize individuals toward the values, attitudes, and behaviors of the encompassing social system. In America and Canada, such small but established religious sects as the Amish and Hutterites deviate to varying extents in integrating their followers to the mainstream culture. Some of these sects are tolerated, while others are persecuted because of their deviations from mainstream culture.

[3]In theory everyone is equal, but like the pigs in George Orwell's *Animal Farm,* some animals are more equal than others.

[4]The Olympics now allows professionals to compete and permits those athletes who have yet to declare their professional status to be paid through escrow accounts; the NCAA now allows professionals in one sport to compete collegiately in other sports.

The Social Functions of Sport

Numerous sociologists (including Allardt 1970; Wohl 1970; Luschen 1970; Gruneau 1975; and Sage 1979) describe sport in functional terms, that is, as supporting the social order. Stevenson and Nixon (1972) detail five functions by which sport helps the social system operate smoothly and efficiently:

1. Socioemotional function
2. Socialization
3. Social integration
4. Political function
5. Social mobility

Let's look at each function separately.

Socioemotional Function

Stevenson and Nixon divide the socioemotional function into three categories: (1) management of tension and conflict, (2) feeling of community, and (3) reassurance of ritual.

Conflict and Tension Management.   While sport may help to release psychological tension, how well sport serves this cathartic function may depend on the type and level of activity. *Exercise* and *games* appear more likely to release tension than *sports* and *athletics.* In sport and athletics investment of time, money, and ego are more likely to undermine relaxation and enjoyment, especially if the result is defeat. The topic of catharsis (venting of tension) is considered at length in Chapter 9.

Camaraderie and Community.   Feelings of friendship and belonging within a group may be fostered through play and sport. Camaraderie, i.e., fellowship, is available to fans as well as to athletes. Stevenson and Nixon note, however, that such feelings of affinity are not necessarily reciprocated. Athletes and coaches are traded, fired, or simply leave "their fans" for greener pastures. Similarly, fan support of a team tends to fluctuate with its success, and owners of teams may move to more lucrative locales despite loyal fan support. The sense of community derived from sportive activity also operates at the lesser competitive levels such as youth leagues, high school sports, and even adult league sports like softball and bowling. How well this socioemotional function operates depends on many intervening factors.

Reassurance of Ritual.   Sports seasons and the championships that punctuate them pass regularly through our lives, eagerly awaited by some and tolerated by others. Given the media saturation of major sports, few people in

America could not be aware of the World Series or the Super Bowl. Students, alumni, and many faculty avidly anticipate autumn and the fortunes of their school's football team. Basketball and ice hockey help the long winter months pass. Come spring, sportswriters wax poetic about the return of the robins and the clean, sharp crack of hickory on horsehide (even though neither is used any longer to make bats and balls).

Preseason training camps, the regular seasons, and the championships are anticipated events in the lives of millions of Americans. We have come to rely on sports for a measure of our psychic stability. We see sports events as rituals, "allaying anxieties and uncertainties" (Stevenson and Nixon 1972:123). A key historical event illustrates this, although many other examples can be found. On Friday, November 22, 1963, President John F. Kennedy was assassinated, plunging the nation into shock and mourning. At the time we were engaged in a Cold War with the Soviet Union and had recently confronted Cuba over the placement of nuclear missiles, while what would become the Viet Nam War loomed. The question arose widely as to whether Americans should be playing and watching football while we mourned our slain president. High school and college games across the nation were canceled or postponed, but the National Football League played that Sunday during the officially declared "national day of mourning." The ritual of Sunday professional football was preserved because a shaken nation needed the sense of stability, the psychic reassurance, that it provided.

In 1968 the murder of Martin Luther King, Jr., which caused widespread rioting, resulted in the cancellation of only one major league baseball game. On October 17, 1989, a devastating earthquake struck the San Francisco Bay area, aborting the third game of the World Series between the Oakland A's and the San Francisco Giants. The World Series was delayed ten days for cleaning up rubble and repairing buildings, bridges, and freeways, then it was continued, largely on the grounds that America needed the reassurance of this annual sports ritual.[5]

These events provide at least anecdotal support for sport serving a function of psychic reassurance for our society. How stabilizing sport actually is in times of crisis remains open to question. While the ritualistic benefits of sport may exist, we should not overlook financial reasons, such as lucrative television and advertising contracts, as the basis for their continuation during crises.

Socialization Function of Sport

If we assume that boys learn productive and socially approved attitudes and values through sports competition, several questions should arise. If this is true for boys, is it also true for girls? Are such behaviors as competitiveness

---

[5]The authors of this text, one in San Francisco and the other in Sacramento 90 miles to the east, both experienced the quake.

and assertiveness societally counterproductive for girls? Are "playful attitudes," such as participation for fun rather than achievement, anathema to the work ethic of formal, structured sport and athletics? In other words, would widespread adoption of the former hinder inculcation of the latter?

Do specific values (e.g., teamwork, drive to achieve, respect for authority) arise naturally in sport, or must they be taught? Are these values inherent in sport, or must they be taught? How and where are they being taught? What of negative socialization? Are dependency and cheating as easily learned through sport as independence and honesty? Such questions will be addressed in Chapter 3.

The process and outcomes of socialization are central to this course. The socialization process is central to our concerns and deserves extensive consideration.

Integrative Function

People who associate themselves with sports teams, whether as active participants or fans, gain an identity with those teams (Petryszak 1978; Albonico 1967; as well as Stevenson and Nixon). When the element of rivalry is added, a feeling is engendered of "us" (the in-group) against "them" (the enemy or out-group). Many high schools and colleges thrive on keen rivalries: Nebraska versus Oklahoma, Harvard versus Yale, Texas versus Texas A & M, Army versus Navy, and Stanford versus Cal-Berkeley among the most enduring. In baseball, the Dodgers and Giants transported their long rivalry from New York to California, both moving to the West coast in 1958 to maintain their lucrative adversarial (us versus them) relationship and galvanizing an existing rivalry between Los Angeles and San Francisco.

When we encounter fans of "our team," there is an immediate, if tenuous bond. We have something to talk about, to cheer or commiserate over, a point of communal aspiration. This is central to Coser's (1956) perception that conflict is functional for individuals and for the social system, because the "safe conflict" of sport rivalry helps to coalesce groups.

Symbolic integration with the group appears through the display of team colors and decals, insignia-bearing clothing, and banners and blankets, all stating allegiance to "our team." Such displays of group integration presume values congruent with sport and the social system. Is patriotism ever greater than during wars and the Olympics?

Integration should be symbiotic (mutually beneficial), as well as symmetrical (mutual allegiance). As the sportive form moves closer to economic enterprise ("sport," and certainly "athletics" in our lexicon), it seems that the mutuality of this integration is lost. Players' integration with a team can be taken from them through release or being sold or traded. Since fans' sense of integration with a team is a matter of personal choice rather than career, it cannot be taken away, even if the fan moves or the team is moved.

Political and Social Mobility Functions

The political and social mobility functions of sport are extensively discussed in Chapters 10 and 11, respectively. Despite the frequently voiced lament about the "intrusion" of politics into sport, we must realize that it is irrelevant whether or not politics *should* intrude into sport. Since the height of ancient Greek civilization and its Olympics, politics and sport have been inseparable. It is more fruitful to consider the *means by which* politics and sport connect.

Sport is clearly an avenue for social mobility for some. Those who have gained economic success and social status through sport are highly visible. Among the questions we will address in Chapter 11, focusing on social mobility through sport, are how and the extent to which this function works, especially for minority groups, which may devote effort and hopes disproportionately to sport.

The Function of Inequality

Contrary to the position of Stevenson and Nixon, Gruneau (1975:142) suggests that the maintenance of "institutionalized inequality" is the primary social function of sport. Gruneau bases his belief on several linked "functional assumptions," among them:

1. Achievement and recognition through competitive processes such as sport serve to integrate people into American society.
2. Sport fosters and makes explicit social stratification. Money and status, which are rewards for success in sports and athletics, make achievement desirable, thus attracting competent people.
3. Sport provides an avenue for achievement and upward social mobility. Besides immediate tangible rewards, jobs and associations may yield more permanent status, if not even greater wealth.

A single concrete example of Gruneau's tableau of inequality through sport would be the youngster who first learns in youth sports to compete and to become a "team player." He or she learns also that rewards come that are not gained by those who don't compete or who compete and fail, rewards ranging from ice cream cones to special treatment to college scholarships to a lucrative athletic career with the potential of paying the very successful more in one year than their professors and physicians may earn in a lifetime. Thus, the function of sport is to make explicit the incentive for competing that lies at the basis of the American social system.

Note that we have been discussing the social functions specifically of *sport*, because formal sport has become an American institution comparable to schools and religion, including hierarchies, shared norms, and systems of reward. While *play* has considerable social and psychic importance and effect, play cannot be said to serve a broadly societal function.

Inequality from Functionalist and Conflict Perspectives

The development, organization, and ongoing process of human society can be explained by two opposing theories: *functionalism* and *conflict-coercion theory*. There are other points of view that we might use to analyze the relationship between individuals and society (e.g., social exchange theory, symbolic interactionism, etc.). However, we will leave a broader comparison of theories to texts specifically focusing on social theory. Our theoretical discussion will be limited to a comparison of functionalism and conflict-coercion theory because they represent diametrically opposed points of view and so can best serve the purpose of opening our minds to different ways of interpreting institutions, attitudes, motives, and behaviors that we might not otherwise question.

Since social systems are not "thinking" beings, maintenance of inequality cannot be "purposeful" (Gruneau 1975; Page 1969). Rather, inequality is the product of hierarchical social systems and serves the "needs" of those who occupy positions of power and who, to some extent, control the system. (For the moment we are couching our comments in the conflict perspective.)

Inequality, from this viewpoint, is the motivating mechanism of the functionalist view of social order. Inequality is not only a fact of life in a hierarchically arranged society, it is the core of such a society. Societies having more than one status level—upper, middle, and lower classes, and perhaps even finer gradations—are referred to as *stratified*. In highly stratified societies, such as the England from which the American colonists escaped, there is little movement between the levels. In highly stratified societies, one's achievements or contributions would not change one's social status because such status or rank tends to be inherited, rather than a reward for achievement. Thus, inequality is fixed.

In a less-stratified society, one's accomplishments, if deemed societally or publicly valuable (e.g., athletic stardom), may lead to a measure of upward mobility, although the highest echelon is still likely to remain closed if one has not been born to it.[6] Even in a moderately stratified society, mobility is likely to be partly a matter of ascribed characteristics, that is, based on who the achiever is rather than what the achiever has done (Parsons and Shils 1951). High salaries awarded for achievement aside, the upper echelons of power (status) reside with management, and, in sport as well as in business and government, African Americans and other minorities have tended to be excluded from management positions. (see Chapter 11). Similarly, high achievement in women's athletics has not resulted in status equivalent to the status resulting from high achievement in men's athletics. (see Chapter 12).

---

[6]"High society" is less a function of money than of breeding, which includes not only family status, but "proper" (i.e., elite) schooling and friends (Aldrich 1988).

Consistency and Stasis Within the Social System

The functionalist view of social order does not imply that a society, or even a particular institution within that society, is a completely congruent value structure. Value systems have their own "preferred, permitted, and proscribed modes," with variations to the central value theme built into the system (Kluckhohn 1958:319). Intentional deviation from rules (e.g., cheating) is not a preferred mode of achievement, yet it may be permitted or overlooked if it serves a "greater good" (e.g., group success or even the individual success of the striver who is exhibiting otherwise laudable behavior). Rules may accommodate "cheating." Fighting in ice hockey is tacitly encouraged by the meagre penalty of a few minutes off the ice compared to game banishment in basketball. Cheating moves toward the proscribed end of the range of deviant behavior when it threatens the structure of the system.

Every society has a complete array of possible value orientations, from the dominant ones to the variant or deviant ones. There may be inconsistencies or anomalies within the functionalist view of society, such as with Pooley's (1972) study of ethnic soccer clubs in Milwaukee, in which he concluded that sport may serve to inhibit rather than to foster integration into American culture. In general, however, consistency, congruity, and stability are integral to society from the functionalist perspective.

How the System Perpetuates Itself.   A steady state is implied from the functionalist view: institutions exist, power is invested in particular people or offices, and values are lauded because they work, all of which lead toward stasis rather than change. While institutions within a social system are modified, vary in importance, and may even be replaced (Hagen 1962), from the functionalist perspective, equilibrium is the natural condition of society, despite periodic evolutionary change. This may be observed both in the 20th century growth of sport and in the relative decrease in the importance of religion in the lives of Americans. Sport, in other words, has appropriated some of the role of religion. Thus, while particular social institutions may wax and wane, the process of socialization remains steady.

Using functionalism as an explanation of social order, agencies or institutions (such as family, school, religion, and sport) are the *means* that help to fulfill societally determined *needs* in order to foster the *end* or goal of that society, the ultimate goal being a society's own continued existence and growth. The same goal of self-perpetuation can be attributed to each institution or agency serving the social system. The International Olympic Committee (IOC), for example, is not likely to recommend its own demise or even to suggest anything that might threaten its position of authority. The IOC functions to provide and ensure fair athletic competition in the Olympics, but it also functions to ensure the continued existence of the Olympics as well as itself. The growth of professionalism in international athletics imperiled the supremacy of the IOC's dominance over international competition. This led to a "functional" decision to let professionals participate in the Olympics and even allow payments to athletes defined by Olympic rules as amateurs. While this rule change deviated significantly from the longstanding "amateur ideal" of the Olympics, it deflected a serious threat to the power and control of the IOC and, therefore, was a functional, system-maintaining decision.

When we speak of a "system" perpetuating itself, we mean an actual structure of governance and tangible reward (school, politics, formal athletics). Play has no formal structure, no territory to be jealously guarded, and no reward scheme to be coveted. In the absence of vested interests, it is surprising that unstructured play has any legitimacy in a goal-oriented society such as America. The values of play—pure fun, freedom to enter or exit at one's whim—are anathema to formally structured and goal-driven activities. The socialization taking place in play is *not* the socialization of sport and athletics.

The functionalist perspective is the view of social order taken, tacitly or explicitly, by many scientists, politicians, businesspeople, teachers, coaches, and athletes, possibly because it supports and justifies the system in which people employed in these areas are more or less thriving. The unequal distribution of rewards advertises that they have "done well" through the system. As we shall see, however, a very different perspective may be taken by those for whom the system is not working and for whom the system is failing to provide access to position, prestige, power, and wealth.

Social Darwinism

Charles Darwin's theory of biological evolution said that individuals (and species) that demonstrate the strongest survival traits will prosper at the expense of those who are weaker. "Survival of the fittest" has been extended to social conditions, yielding "Social Darwinism" (Hofstadter 1955). According to the Social Darwinist perspective, those who have fought to the top, gaining power, status, and wealth, are the most highly evolved and adapted. Those at the lower socioeconomic levels are believed to be there because they do not have either the inherited ability or the fortitude to gain access to the rewards of their social system.

Intelligence as an inherited trait is a key factor that purportedly determines who is "the fittest" (Blum 1978), but physical soundness is also one of the bases of Social Darwinism. Competitiveness of all kinds is presumed to weed out the weak and less competent and to provide the system with the most productive and highly evolved individuals in positions of power and wealth. From this perspective, the high esteem afforded top athletes is consistent with the theory.

Social Darwinism is a variation of the functionalist perspective, interpreting success as directly related to functionality, or competence. Inequality is viewed as natural because not everyone is capable of performing at a level that reaps societal rewards. Social Darwinism tends to designate *whole groups* of people as more or less highly evolved, more or less functional, and therefore more or less deserving of society's bounty. Specifically, the theory fosters the belief in the natural superiority of certain races of humans (primarily those from Northern Europe) and the comparative inferiority of other races. Its popularity as a descriptor and predictor of human behavior and social order rose in the late 19th century and fell in the middle to late 20th century. As with any theory, one can only guess about its future.

Discrimination against subgroups is an alternative explanation for their low socioeconomic status. Nevertheless, Social Darwinism has impacted organized sport to the extent that it must be acknowledged. In Chapter 11, we will see how it has been especially consequential for the black athlete.

Conflict-Coercion Theory

The prior section expounds on the view that the social system and its institutions are beneficent and worthy of support. An alternative perspective views the social system as oppressive, coercive, and in dire need of radical change. From the conflict-coercion perspective, social order and organization change, if at all, at an *evolutionary* pace not rapid enough for those who are oppressed. *Revolution* is required to overcome oppression. A system of continual change was expounded in the *dialectic* of Friedrich Engels and Karl Marx early in the 19th century. The dialectic is primarily an economic model to explain inequality and social order, which also describes the mechanism for this continual change (Fig. 2.1).[7]

The dialectic assumes that for every belief (*thesis*) there is a contrary belief (*antithesis*). These beliefs are competing forms of social order in continual conflict over which will prevail. Since they represent opposing and incompatible social systems, conflict between thesis and antithesis is inherent. From conflict a *synthesis* will emerge. Once established and empowered, however, this synthesis becomes the new established doctrine (thesis) and carries with it its own contradictions (antithesis). This introduces a new round of conflict, which generates a new synthesis, ad infinitum.

While the dialectic is an underpinning of communism, it more widely explains conflict between ideas or groups vying for primacy in any system. Oppressors and oppressed, owners and producers, management and labor all vie for dominance. The specific form that conflict takes is necessarily revolution, since those in power are loath to relinquish their position of dominance.

As McKay (1986) suggests, the core of the issue is *hegemony,* the domination by a power-elite (most often white and male, and to the point of this

---

[7]Although the dialectic is primarily a model explaining changes in the means and relationships of economic production, Marx and Engels believed that economics was responsible for the form of all other institutions in a society as well as its normative values. (See Fisher, *The Essential Marx,* 1970.)

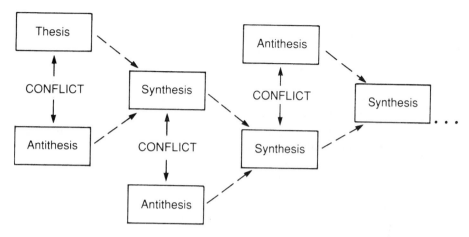

FIGURE 2.1 *The Dialectic Mechanism of Social Change. (See Fischer, The Essential Marx, 1970.)*

text, nonathlete sports management) over the unempowered masses (nonwhite, female, worker/athletes).[8] From the conflict perspective it matters not how much money professional, college, or even Olympic athletes earn if they remain otherwise discommoded, enslaved, or taken advantage of as African Americans, as women, or as athletes in general. This domination occurs whenever and wherever sport is packaged and sold as a commodity. This ranges from the professional level to the Olympics, as far down the sports hierarchy as youth league sports.

Conflict (revolution) occurs between the classes in a stratified society because those who hold high status seek to maintain their advantage (which they see as deserved, either through achievement or the ascription of "birthright"). Meanwhile, those relegated to lower status levels seek to usurp power, prestige, and wealth on the grounds that they have been cheated out of those scarce resources by a system that keeps the lower classes downtrodden. The *coercion* part of conflict-coercion theory can be seen in the laws and rules, social and economic pressures, and the propaganda put forth by the established socializing institutions of school, religion, and sport. The oppressed lower classes are coerced into remaining loyal to the system despite the barriers that this system places in the way of their gaining a share of the society's rewards. According to Marxism, the only hope of the oppressed is revolution, replacing the system with a "fairer" system of their own.

Conflict-coercion theory can be directly applied to sport. Gruneau (1975, 1983) proposes that the nature, functions, and internal structure of

---

[8]Critiques of society (and the institution of sport) have come from several different conflict perspectives, including Marxists, neo-Marxists, and post-Marxists. For the purposes of this text we will ignore the distinctions among these philosophic positions.

organized sports and athletics systems are determined through their relation-ships to the ruling class and to the social system's economic structures con-trolled by the ruling class, defined as those who have power over an organiza-tion's form and function, and thus who dominate the unempowered "workers." This description applies to the relationship between a coach and his or her athletes[9] or between ruling organizations such as the NCAA, IOC, or the ownership of professional leagues and their athletes.

Formal sports organizations are controlled by capitalistic interests for their own wealth and aggrandizement, rather than for the benefit of players or fans (an assertion that might even apply to highly structured youth sports such as Lit-tle League baseball; see Chapter 5). The oppressive coercive relationship mani-fested in sport includes, according to Gruneau (1975:136–37), the following:

1. Sport is wedded to material gain and must be seen in this light (not sim-ply as recreation and entertainment.)
2. Sport is intimately associated with differences in wealth and power.
3. Competitive sport reflects bourgeois (i.e., middle class, upwardly mo-bile) ideology; as a meritocratic, mobility-oriented institution, it fosters a false consciousness and false hopes for the lower class.
4. Sport, particularly the professional variety, alienates athlete-workers from each other, pitting them against each other (e.g., many athletes vying for few positions), thus undermining social revolution.
5. "Competitive sport" cannot exist in a classless society because competi-tive sport is not, by its nature, egalitarian (i.e., distinguishing between re-warded winners and nonrewarded losers.)

Sport as an Opiate

Karl Marx declared that "religion is the opiate of the masses." Philosopher Paul Hoch (1972) feels that in the latter part of the 20th century sport has become the opiate of the masses. An opiate is a narcotic that dulls the senses and pro-vides a false sense of well-being. Marx called religion an opiate because it de-flected the concern of the masses from their poor and oppressed condition, focusing their attention instead on the presumably greater rewards of the af-terlife (e.g., "The meek shall inherit the earth," *Psalms,* 37:11). Religion, seen through Marxism, serves those in power, since it undermines the lower classes' potential for revolution.

Sport, according to Hoch, has emerged as the new opiate of the masses in part because it has replaced religion as a broad socializing institution. The

---

[9]A particular coach may or may not use an autocratic style, but rarely does a coach *not* have the freedom to establish dominion over his or her team if the coach desires this kind of system.

opiate-like quality of sport occurs through its illusory world that diverts the physical and psychic energies of the masses. In the psychic domain it provides either satisfaction through association with a winning team or the fellowship of commiseration with a losing team. Fostering dreams of upward mobility, sport allows a very few participants to gain enough success to rise through several socioeconomic levels, while planting false hope in the minds of the masses. So long as they believe that they can profit and rise through the social system, the masses are not likely to seek destruction of that system.

Organized, high-level sport is believed to redirect the economic, political, and social frustration of individuals into the "safe" channel (safe for the system and those in power) of sport, whether that channel is active participation in the arena or passively expressed in front of the television or in the stands (Petryszak 1978). From the radical Marxist perspective (Gruneau 1975), sport, by distinguishing winners and losers, is a faulty system since social inequality is wrong whether it comes from birthright (ascription) or from relative merit (achievement). Any institution that fosters inequality is seen as defective.

Lenk's view of sport is less starkly critical while still retaining the conflict-coercion perspective (1977:175):

> The social criticism of sport is not directed against every demand for achievement but only against the ideology of the achieving society which subordinates all other requirements to the raising of production and achievement which is oriented to the assurance and creation of privileges of a class-conditioned kind. . . .

Whether or not sport acts as an opiate, it is seen by those who hold the conflict-coercion perspective as misdirecting energies that could be spent more productively in rectifying a faulty social order. Functionalists see sport as an emotional "outlet" and a means for mobility; conflict-coercionists see sport as at best a diversion and at worst another of the ruling class's instruments for oppression of the lower classes, only marginally more palatable than sweatshops.

Perhaps the value of the Marxist perspective is less in providing a model for insurrection than in presenting us with a different " 'way of seeing' power, domination, exploitation, and liberation" (McKay 1986:266). The perceived coercion of the worker-athletes is no small part of this theoretical perspective on sport. Players are viewed as servants to the ruling-class owners/managers, who seek to keep their workers at odds with each other and thus less likely, in the pain of their oppressed state, to turn on the owners/managers. (High school or college coaches and athletic directors may also be counted among owner/managers because they exercise virtually total control over athletes.) Such oppression causes a bubbling ferment beneath the calm surface of the established social order. Authoritarian decision making, in which the worker-athletes have no voice yet must obey, serves as a focal point of conflict within sport organizations (Oglesby 1974; Eitzen 1986).

The Theories of Social Order in Contrast

Our intent in outlining the functionalist and conflict-coercion theories is not to present either of them as necessarily "the way things are." Instead, these diametrically opposed views serve as alternative perspectives for interpreting social order (including that of sport), the roles that institutions play, the effects of those institutions on individuals, and, of course, the ways in which individuals might assess their own system.

Why should we limit our theoretical analysis to just these two perspectives? C. P. Snow used the dichotomizing device, and his rationale (1963:15–16) shall stand for ours:

> I have thought a long time about going in for further refinements [of the "two cultures"]: but in the end I have decided against. I was searching for something a little more than a dashing metaphor, a good deal less than a cultural map: and for those purposes the two cultures is about right, and subtilising any more would bring more disadvantages than it's worth.

Functionalism and conflict-coercion theory do not exhaust the "cultural map," but they do show us how someone can observe a phenomenon—sport or a process within sport—and come to conclusions very different from those of another viewer holding a different perspective. Is organized youth sport beneficial or harmful to kids? (Two people viewing the same game might arrive at opposite opinions.) Does the system of intercollegiate athletics exploit participants, or does it provide a viable avenue for mobility? Does participation in sport teach antisocial or prosocial behavior? What is the effect on society (or individuals) of allowing females to participate in the same activities as males, whether it be big business, the front lines of war, or athletic contests?

Functionalism is a relatively static model that focuses on the equilibrium or stability of a social system, operating on the premise that the vehicle of society is chugging along quite well, thank you. Change in the system is recognized but is perceived as periodic rather than constant—brief transitional periods between long "steady states"—with minor adjustments designed to make the system ever more efficient. In contrast, the conflict-coercion theory is a dynamic model emphasizing frequent, if not constant change, while recognizing moments of stasis during which the pressure toward renewed upheaval is rebuilding. From this view, the system is faulty and needs an overhaul or even a whole new engine. Differences between the two theories arise in large part from the focus of the former on social *structures* and the latter on social *processes* (Hagen 1962). Let's bring these abstractions to the more tangible level of perceptions and behaviors of individuals.

Some people view the world and their social system as agreeable, supportive, and stable. Although change occurs, it is evolutionary and does not shake the basic structure of society, nor should it. People holding this perspective tend to be those who are gaining the system's rewards—status, income—to a level that they find acceptable. Even greater status and earnings may be achieved if one is willing to work harder. Thus, inequality is acceptable since it provides incentive for those who desire to better themselves. Participation in the system at whatever level is consensual, that is, not forced on one, nor is one prevented from participating by institutional barriers. Individuals enter an un-written, seldom spoken contract with their social system and the agencies serving it, which says, in essence: "If I strive to do well (work hard), the system will do well by me." According to this view, the institution of sport is integral to society, providing both socialization and a means for upward socioeconomic mobility for those who invest what it takes to achieve it.

In contrast, those who see conflict and coercion as most descriptive of social reality consider their social system and institutions as unbalanced, un-fair, and ripe for "improvement." They see inequality as society's failure to support all of its members: no person (or race or gender) is more valuable than another; therefore, all deserve support by the society. People are coerced to participate in a society that does not treat them fairly, while their desire for bringing about social change is blunted through system-fostered opiates such as religion and sport.

Revolution is necessary to bring about change since those holding power and privilege will not voluntarily relinquish their advantage (Lenski 1966). The institution of sport, a tool of oppression and false hope, needs to be democra-tized, humanized, and liberated (McKay 1986). Sport could serve as a counter-balance, a "personalized reaction" to an increasingly commodified and imper-sonal world (Allison 1987).

Seeing sport exclusively from either extreme perspective fails to take into account its complexity. However, discussing sport in terms of these ex-tremes provides useful conceptual frameworks from which we can interpret social order and the role of sport within that order (Gruneau 1975; Lenk 1977). For those who hold the functionalist view, the script of society is writ-ten; the agents merely act it out. For those who hold the Marxist view of recti-fying the system, the script is to be determined by the actors (agents). Their plot is dialectic change and their theme is materialism, the drama to be played out on an economic stage.

TABLE 2.1 *Comparison of Two Views of Social Order*

Theory	Societal Mechanism	View of Inequality	Outcome
Functionalist	socialization	provides incentive	thrive by "fitting in"
Conflict-coercion/ Marxist	dialectic	improper and changeable	revolt to gain equity

NOTE: "Play" does not fit into this comparison because the concept of inequality is anathema to play.

Social Unrest in Sport

An example of coercion and conflict leading to revolution and perhaps ulti-mately to radical change in the structure of a sport occurred in men's profes-sional tennis in 1989 when the Association of Tennis Professionals (organized by and for players) split from the ruling Men's Tennis Council (entrepreneurial tournament organizers) to establish their own tour (Comte 1989). This sort of restructuring of the system is more likely to succeed in professional men's ten-nis than in a team sport since team sports require a more extensive manage-ment hierarchy with power domains to protect, and because teams are owned by wealthy nonplayers who "own" the players. These players are the primary means of production of the athletic commodity that owners peddle to the public. Tennis players, in contrast, are independent contractors, and so their livelihood is less dependent on a management structure.

Another example of unrest within a sport social system occurred in inter-collegiate athletics, although this was not a matter of individual worker-athletes rising up *en masse* to protest, but of individual schools banding to-gether to challenge what they perceived as oppression on the part of the NCAA organization that governed them. Schools fielding top-level collegiate football programs may not appear to be an "oppressed" group. Indeed, it is dif-ficult to work up much sympathy for schools that wield multimillion-dollar budgets. Yet athletic program administrators at more than 60 "big-time foot-ball" institutions felt oppressed within the NCAA structure because their inter-ests were ignored by the majority of the NCAA membership. These schools formed the College Football Association in 1984, threatening defection and the possible collapse of the NCAA. This threat of revolt did not result in the demise of the NCAA or even the kind of radical restructuring of the organiza-tion that some defectors wanted, but it was enough counterpressure to force the NCAA to provide these institutions with more decision-making power.

Amateur athletes may have the least control over their own athletic des-tinies, yet they are the least likely to foment conflict because they are not a co-hesive group. Individual players are likely (and correctly) to fear that they have too little status to make their views heard and even less power to force change. Instead, they are coerced into complying with whatever those in power (coaches, administrations) want and demand of them because athletes know that they are replaceable parts in an athletic machine. Only after achiev-ing fame and wealth do they have any sort of a pedestal from which to speak out, at which point they are less likely to rail against a system that has treated them well. Perhaps something that militates even more against their voicing complaints (or even realizing that complaints are called for) is the primary mo-tivation engendered in them throughout their sport experience, which is to achieve and be rewarded *individually*. While some athletes may be team-mates, every other athlete is the opposition, since team membership is a status won through intragroup competition.

Ingram and Loy (1973) point out that, particularly in amateur sport, athletes are completely outside the authority hierarchy and are simply the raw material for the systemic goal of prestige and wealth to be accumulated by those who operate the system. To illustrate, NCAA rules forbid college basketball players to reap any concurrent rewards for their efforts beyond the basic scholarship, while their coaches may earn hundreds of thousands of dollars from athletic equipment manufacturers. An athlete who resists falling into line risks not only censure (and perhaps loss of eligibility as dictated by the NCAA) but the ire of his or her coach.

You as Conformist or Change Agent

Picture yourself as a teacher/coach beginning your career in a social system: a school. (Many, perhaps most, careers in which an individual enters an existing hierarchical structure could serve as an example.) You are fresh from college, loaded with ideas to improve "the system." However, those who have been thriving in that system are likely to resist your grand ideas for change and improvement. They also may feel threatened, since your call for change implies criticism of what they have felt to be good, or at least workable (i.e., functional).

If tolerant, the established power structure might say: "Wait until you've been around for a while. You'll see that your newfangled ideas won't work." Underlying this position is the sense held by those who are invested in the system that their system has evolved, stood the test of time and does not require change. A less tolerant response to the neophyte change agent might be: "Don't make waves. Conform or be gone."

The question that every new teacher/coach entering an existing system must address is, "Do I mold myself to the existing system that hired me, or do I try to improve it?" The problem is compounded when system agents at the school that hired you did so in part because of your education or experience, the very things likely to give you ideas for improvement; yet, the agents you work with (and under) may be threatened by and resistant to change. Does the teacher/coach serve the system or his or her own conscience? Does the system work well enough, or is it so flawed that it needs to be changed? Is social engineering part of your work role, or should you leave that to others and just teach or coach or . . . ? Is it your "place" to "fit in" or to change things, to conserve or to alter? These questions refer to structure-shaking change, not simply new ideas to improve or streamline a system's ongoing process.

Not long ago, one such issue of social engineering centered on the question of coeducational physical education classes. Let's say a newly hired teacher, the ink on his or her degree still wet, feels that coed physical education is the right learning experience and the wave of the future. This neophyte teacher might wonder why he or she is meeting with opposition, perhaps considerable resistance. While the neophyte might look on this item of social engineering as merely a bit of streamlining or improvement, those already invested in the system, the "old-timers," could perceive a threat. Certainly any change is an implicit criticism of the way they have been doing things. What does the neophyte teacher do: conform to the old ways or make waves? If you feel strongly enough that you are right about this issue, that the "establishment" is wrong, and that people are being coerced into doing things "the old way," what do you do: go along with the status quo or try to overturn the entrenched power structure to "make things right?"

Your answers will likely come from the life experiences that you bring to a situation, which include but are not limited to your formal education. The questions should be consciously asked and the decisions consciously made. Perhaps this issue is not big or broad enough to lead you to seek structure-shaking change. The structure may be flexible enough on this issue or those in power wise enough to avoid a confrontation by yielding or compromising in order to preserve the structure. There may be other issues, however, on which the lines of conflict are clearly drawn and compromise is not an alternative.

Summary

Pervasive social structures, such as the several systems of formal sport and athletics thriving in America, exist because they serve societal functions. Among these are socioemotional functions, socialization of neophytes, integration of individuals into groups, political functions, fostering of social mobility, and reiteration of inequality, which serves as an incentive toward personal advancement.

The condition of formal sport, more so than informal or casual play or games, presents a contest between individuals or teams vying for a prize/ outcome that only one can attain. The process of striving, from a societal perspective, supposedly imbues culturally lauded values, attitudes, and behaviors, e.g., teamwork, dedication or commitment, confidence, and competitiveness, as means toward the desired end of victory and its resulting rewards (society's incentives: "the carrot"). A narrow reward structure, however, may lead to violations of other culturally lauded values, such as fairness, honesty, respect, etc., especially if there is no "carrot" associated with them. Thus, if "character" is a rubric for the body of traits that a society encourages in its members, then we might question the adage that "sport builds character." This is a question we will broach directly in the following chapter.

How well each of these functions work and how appropriate each function is remains a matter of perspective. Are people helped or hindered by the social functions that sport serve, or do these functions instead serve mainly to support those already in power? Can people improve their lives through sport, or does it merely serve as an opiate keeping them from improving their lives in other ways?

How individuals answer these questions may depend on their experiences and indoctrination. Despite the absence of value-neutral "right" or "wrong" answers, the informed, intelligent person must ask, because only through such inquiry can we hope to understand what is happening and try to bring sport closer to its potential for doing well. Functionalism and conflict theory are two diametrically opposed theories that can act as a framework through which we can assess what is occurring in and through sportive activity throughout its full spectrum from play to formally organized, fully competitive athletics.

References

Albonico, R. 1967. "Modern University Sports as a Contribution to Social Integration." *International Review of Sport Sociology* 2:155-64.

Aldrich, N. W., Jr. 1988. *Old Money: The Mythology of America's Upper Class.* New York: A. Knopf.

Allardt, E. 1970. "Basic Approaches in Comparative Sociological Research and the Study of Sport." Pp. 14-30 in *Cross-Cultural Analysis of Sport and Games,* edited by G. Luschen. Champaign, IL: Stipes.

Allison, M. T. 1987. "Kaleidoscope and Prism: The Study of Social Change in Play, Sport, and Leisure." *Sociology of Sport Journal* 4:144.

Black, M. 1961. *The Social Theories of Talcott Parsons.* Englewood Cliffs, NJ: Prentice-Hall.

Blum, J. 1978. *Pseudoscience and Mental Abilities.* New York: Monthly Review Press.

Boggs, C. 1981. "Politics of the Knowledge Industry." *New Political Science* 5/6:89-97.

Comte, E. 1989. "ATP Sets $38-Mil Calendar." *Sports, Inc.* Jan. 23:3.

Coser, L. 1956. *The Functions of Social Conflict.* New York: Free Press.

Eitzen, D. S. 1986. "Athletics and Higher Education: A Conflict Perspective." Pp. 227-37 in *Sport and Social Theory,* edited by C. R. Rees and A. W. Miracle. Champaign, IL: Human Kinetics.

Fischer, E. 1970. *The Essential Marx.* New York: Herder and Herder.

Gruneau, R. S. 1975. "Sport, Social Differentiation, and Social Inequality." Pp. 117-84 in *Sport and Social Order,* edited by D. Ball and J. Loy. Reading, MA: Addison-Wesley.

Gruneau, R. S. 1983. *Class, Sports, and Social Development.* Amherst, MA: University of Massachusetts Press.

Hagen, E. E. 1962. *On the Theory of Social Change.* Homewood, IL: Dorsey Press.

Hoch, P. 1972. *Rip Off the Big Game.* New York: Anchor Books.

Hofstadter, R. 1955. *Social Darwinism in American Thought.* Boston: Beacon Press.

Ingram, A., and J. Loy. 1973. "The Social System of Sport: A Humanistic Perspective." *Quest* 19:3–23.

Kluckhohn, F. R. 1958. "Variations in the Basic Values of Family Systems." *Social Casework* 39:63–72.

Lenk, H. 1977. *Team Dynamics.* Champaign, IL: Stipes.

Lenski, G. 1966. *Power and Privilege: A Theory of Social Stratification.* New York: McGraw-Hill.

Luschen, G. 1970. "Cooperation, Association, and Contest." *Journal of Conflict Resolution* 14(1):21–34.

McKay, J. 1986. "Marxism as a Way of Seeing: Beyond the Limits of Current 'Critical' Approaches to Sport." *Sociology of Sport Journal* 3:261–72.

Merton, R. K. 1951. *Social Theory and Social Structure.* Glencoe, IL: Free Press.

Oglesby, C. 1974. "Social Conflict Theory and Sport Organization Systems." *Quest* 22:63–73.

Page, C. H. 1969. *Class and American Sociology.* New York: Schocken.

Parsons, T. 1964. *Essays in Sociological Theory.* New York: Free Press.

Parsons, T., and E. A. Shils. 1951. *Towards a General Theory of Action.* Cambridge, MA: Harvard University Press.

Petryszak, N. 1978. "Spectator Sport as an Aspect of Popular Culture." *Journal of Sport Behavior* 1:14–27.

Pooley, J. C. 1972. "Ethnic Soccer Clubs in Milwaukee, a Study in Assimilation." Pp. 328–45 in *Sport in the Sociocultural Process,* edited by M. M. Hart. Dubuque, IA: W. C. Brown.

Sage, G. H. 1979. "Sport and the Social Sciences." *The Annals of the American Academy of Political and Social Sciences* 445:1–14.

Snow, C. P. 1963. *The Two Cultures: and a Second Look* (Mentor ed.) New York: Cambridge University Press.

Stevenson, C. L., and J. E. Nixon. 1972. "A Conceptual Scheme of the Social Functions of Sport." *Sportwissenschaft* 2:119–32.

Turner, J. H. 1978. *The Structure of Sociological Theory* (revised ed.) Homewood, IL: Dorsey Press.

Wohl, A. 1970. "Competitive Sport and Its Social Functions." *International Review of Sport Sociology* 5:117–25.

CHAPTER 3

Socialization Through Sport:
Competition, Values,
and Morality

*Winning! Oh, you really can't say enough good things about it. There is noth-
ing quite like it. Win hands down, win going away, win by a landslide, win
by accident, win by a nose, win without deserving it. Winning is the tops. Winning is the name of the game. Winning is what it's all about. Winning is the
be-all and the end-all, and don't let anybody tell you otherwise. All the world
loves a winner. Show me a good loser, said Leo Durocher, and I'll show you a
loser. Name one thing that losing has to recommend it. You can't. Losing is tedious. Losing is exhausting. Losing is uninteresting. Losing is depressing. Los-
ing is boring. Losing is debilitating. Losing is compromising. Losing is shame-
ful. Losing is humiliating. Losing is infuriating. Losing is disappointing.
Losing is incomprehensible. Losing makes for headaches, muscle tension, skin
eruptions, ulcers, indigestion, and for mental disorders of every kind. Losing is
bad for confidence, pride, business, peace of mind, family harmony, love, sexual potency, concentration, and much much more. Losing is bad for people of
all ages, races, and religions; it is as bad for infants as for the elderly, for
women as for men. Losing makes people cry, howl, scream, hide, lie, smolder,
envy, hate, and quit. Losing is probably the single biggest cause of suicide in
the world, and of murder. Losing makes the benign malicious, the generous
stingy, the brave fearful, and the healthy ill, and the kindly bitter. Losing is
universally despised, as well it should be. The sooner we get rid of losing the
happier everyone will be. (Roth 1973: 287–88)*

Winning is valued in American society as is a "winning attitude"
(i.e., competitiveness), perhaps independent of the actual achievement of victory. Winning is the central value in American society, even more consequential than honesty or "fair play," since only victory is tangibly rewarded by our

formal structures (institutions). Those behaviors and attitudes that are rewarded we can assume to be those the social system wants to be socialized into its members.

For many of us, the sentiments expressed by a sportswriter in Philip Roth's *The Great American Novel* (presented at the beginning of the chapter) fairly well represent our feelings about winning and losing, success and failure. For others, it may be overstated. We like to win and try to win when we play, but winning is not so great nor losing so demeaning as Roth's sportswriter suggests.

There is an obvious lack of logic in Roth's final sentence. At least as far as traditional modes of economic and sportive competition in the modern world go, we could not "get rid of losing" without also getting rid of winning. Winners are often defined by their dominance over losers. Winning and losing are the results of the process we know as competition. In this chapter we will consider the socialization of people into the American value system. We will discuss competition as a dominant force in American life, its manifestation in sports, and various value-oriented responses to competition within American society. We will also consider the place of competition and sport within the framework of American morality. By chapter's end, we hope that you will have an understanding of the cultural, moral, and philosophical foundations of competition in America. If we laud competition for ourselves and for our children and students, we should understand its place in our society, its benefits and consequences.

Does sport build character? If so, is it the type of character we would like it to build? These are the issues addressed here. In the *pure description* phase of our analysis we will focus on the process that sociologists call socialization. We will also describe the related concepts of competition and the values attached to it. Our *evaluative commentary* will focus on the effectiveness of sport as an agency of socialization, including the nature of the values sport fosters. *Social critique* will be apparent in comparisons drawn between the values promoted within sport and those of the larger socioeconomic environment. Finally, *social engineering* is, as always, up to us all; however, we will suggest some alternatives to the current competitive focus of sport.

The Process of Socialization

Socialization can be defined simply as the process by which we learn to do what is expected of us. Every role we play (e.g., daughter/son, brother/sister, student, employee, athlete) with respect to every activity we pursue (e.g., household chores, studying, doing our jobs, playing sports) must be learned.

Socialization occurs when we learn and adopt the "right" (as defined by our society or subculture) behaviors, attitudes, and values. We do this by watching others be rewarded or punished. We become socialized to "fit in" to our society, to be similar rather than different. We may experience some conflict during our socialization if a subgroup to which we belong carries a set of attitudes and values incongruent with those of mainstream society. An example of such conflict can be seen in some teenagers who are torn between modes of dress and hair style adopted by peer subgroups to which they are attracted, especially if this calls for a radical change. Two considerably less benign examples of socialization conflict in adolescence concern gang violence and drug use. When mainstream and subculture attitudes, values, and behaviors conflict, choices favoring the subculture can be explained by the subgroup's greater immediacy to the individual than the society's. Peers are powerful agents of socialization, often more powerful than the social system's designated agents—parents, teachers, coaches, and heroes.

Each of us probably holds different values, attitudes, and opinions on a variety of topics. *Values* are abstract general standards, each focusing on a general belief that something or some behavior is good or bad. An *attitude* represents a predisposition to act, think, and feel in a certain way based on a given value. *Opinions* focus on given situations and are specific judgments regarding a particular attitude (Broom and Selznick 1968).

Since opinions focus on given situations, they may appear to be contrary to a generally held value. For example, one may value racial equality, yet hold the opinion that school busing to achieve racial equality is wrong. One may value competition and have a predisposition to act competitively, yet believe that holding the Olympics in Beijing, China, is wrong because of that government's oppressive tactics against free speech, that organized competition for seven-year-olds is wrong, or that women competing in athletics is wrong. Since each of these opinions represents a specific and different application of competitiveness, they are not necessarily inconsistent.

A *cultural value* has been defined as "a widely held belief or sentiment that some activities, relationships, feelings, or goals are important to the community's identity or well-being" (Broom and Selznick 1968:54). America is too broad and has too great a diversity of people to say that all Americans believe in a particular set of values. We can say, however, that achievement and success are at least as highly valued in America as they have been in any other culture (Calhoun 1981; Kluckhohn and Strodtbeck 1961; Williams 1970; Loy 1978). And, as Sage (1980:114) has so concisely pointed out, "The primary social process by which success in America is to be achieved is through competition."

A Model of Socialization

Robert Hess (1971) has developed a model that explains, through seven specific elements, the process of socialization (Fig. 3.1). Each element serves a necessary function to effect socialization and to integrate individuals into the social system's matrix of normative behavior.

Agencies.   The first element in Hess's model is the *institution* itself, the social *agency*. Institutions include the family, schools, religion, the polity, the military, and sport, each containing infrastructures. "Family", for example, can include the nuclear family (parents and children) or the extended family (grandparents, aunts and uncles, etc.). Schools are grouped into elementary school, secondary school, and collegiate or postsecondary levels. Sport is subdivided into the distinct agencies of youth, high school, collegiate, and professional levels, as well as Olympic and adult recreational sports.

Agents.   *Agents* represent the second element in Hess's model. They foster the maintenance of each of the socializing agencies. Social agents include parents and grandparents, teachers and school administrators, the clergy, elected officials, officers of the military, police and judges, and coaches and referees within sport. Much socialization comes from peers, that is, those on the same status level, such as playmates, classmates, and teammates, who have already established themselves within the agency.

Neophytes.   Those who are new to a group are the primary objects of the socialization process. This includes infants and immigrants, youngsters undergoing confirmation or some other religious rite of passage, school freshmen or transfer students, military inductees, and rookies in athletics.

Normative attitudes and values.   These are transmitted to the neophytes. In the American social system these tend to include competitiveness, achievement orientation, respect for if not deference to authority, respect for property rights, and conformity, among other things.

Processes.   Normative attitudes and values are transmitted by and through such processes as role modeling and reward and punishment. Grading in schools, for example, provides reinforcement of interpersonal competitiveness and achievement. Traffic tickets punish disrespect for the law. Repetition of the Pledge of Allegiance in schools and the national anthem at athletic events presumably helps to ingrain patriotism. Role modeling as a process of cultural transmission is apparent in father mowing the lawn while mother cooks in the kitchen, and in famous athletes peddling a product on television.
   Extrinsic rewards such as blue ribbons, olive wreaths, trophies, hugs and kisses, ice cream, a job, or cash are often provided to symbolize and reward victory. These extrinsic rewards vary in importance according to the level of competition (consider for example the playground "Olympics" versus the international Olympics) and within given levels of competition according to the individual psyche and physical needs. In sports and athletics, it is sometimes assumed that pure amateurs (i.e., those to whom no tangible rewards accrue) compete for the *intrinsic* rewards of participation and victory, while professionals compete for money, fame, and whatever else of

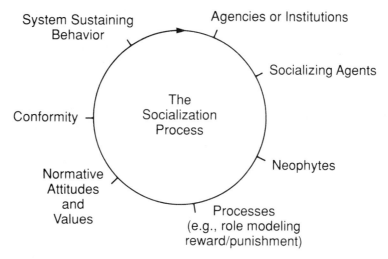

FIGURE 3.1   *The Process of Socialization. (Adapted from Hess, 1971.)*

value victory brings them. We know, however, that many professionals compete because they love the process of competition, with the engagement in the competitive activity being its own reward. Likewise, many amateur athletes, so-called simply because they are not paid directly and openly for performing, actually participate for tangible and intangible prizes such as scholarships, trophies, and public recognition, as well as lucrative endorsement contracts.

Conformity.   "Fitting in" is the direct outcome of these processes, adopting culturally condoned behaviors ranging from standing for the national anthem, to keeping the lawn neat or the kitchen tidy, to striving for high grades, a high batting average, or career success. As mentioned previously, various subcultures (e.g., racial, ethnic, socioeconomic) may instill values and condone behavior differing from those promoted by other groups. Nevertheless, conformity by some definition is the goal of socialization in subcultures as well as the larger social system.

System-sustaining behavior.   This is the culminating element in this model of socialization, providing continuity within the social system. Here, neophytes, who have internalized the culturally condoned attitudes and values and translated these into societally consistent behaviors, now become peer agents helping to socialize the next wave of neophytes.

We all can recall times when we have been neophytes in a new social setting, whether it was a new school, a town, job, or team. We probably were unsure of how to behave or, particularly when we were young and our sense

Calvin and Hobbes
by Bill Watterson

of self was forming, what values to hold as proper. The process that we used to learn the "right" behaviors—including modes of dress and grooming, styles of speech and walking, and goals to be desired and strived for—was first to observe those around us who were already well entrenched in our new social system. We were then likely to emulate those who seemed to garner the rewards of high status. As freshmen or rookies, we looked to the established students or players to mold our own developing behaviors and, to some extent, our values. This is the socialization process at work.

While this process operates the same for females as for males, females are less effectively socialized into sport participation because there is less opportunity and reward for females in sports (discussed at length in Chapter 12). We may even say that females are socialized *not* to be athletes when and where such rewards do not reach the level afforded males (Lichtenstein 1987).

Playing time is primarily a function of a player's talent. Those with outstanding ability may transgress normative behavior patterns more often than less-talented individuals. It is certainly not unheard of, however, for an agent (e.g., team coach or office manager) to hold back someone with great talent if he or she fails to comply with normative behaviors. A deviant group member, no matter how talented, poses a potential threat to efficient group functioning and its goal of team victory. Any social system has its own survival as a primary goal. Anyone representing a threat to its smooth functioning is open to punishment, reprisal, and eventual banishment.

Resocialization After Sport
To be socialized into a particular role means learning that adopting that role is good and rewarding. As we must be socialized *into* our various roles, we may also need to be socialized *out of* them when we can no longer practice these roles. To be socialized out of a role, i.e., to be *resocialized*, means learning

that *not* doing it is acceptable and carries its own rewards. The social and psychological adjustments necessary during resocialization from a role can be more difficult and painful than the process of socialization into that role. The "empty nest" syndrome is evidence of the sometimes traumatic experience of parents whose children have grown up and moved away, leaving them no one to nurture. Similarly, retirement from a lifelong career can be extremely hard if the retiree has nowhere else to put the time and energy which had been devoted to work.

Formally organized and hierarchical sport domains such as youth leagues, high school and collegiate programs, the Olympics, and professional leagues provide the participant with a role or persona that is recognized as "athlete." Often, this athletic identity is a central part of the participant's self-concept and a major source of self-esteem. Even many club and recreational players carry this "athlete persona." For such people, the shift to less competitive status or out of sport altogether is likely to require a major socialization adjustment with regard to expectations, goals, and behaviors. Resocialization out of sport is likely to be especially stressful when (*a*) the athlete's level or intensity of involvement in the sport was high; (*b*) retirement from the sport is involuntary and/or precipitous; (*c*) retirement from the sport entails downward mobility in the form of less income and/or lower status (e.g., celebrity); (*d*) the athlete has no activity with which to replace his or her sport involvement; (*e*) the athlete's self-concept is largely centered on his or her athletic accomplishments, necessitating a major "ego adjustment" on retirement; or (*f*) the athlete goes through the process of retirement without the benefit of counseling or other mechanisms for easing the transition (Rosenberg 1984; Blinde and Greendorfer 1985; Werthner and Orlick 1986). Although these conditions are most acute for professional and other elite athletes, they are not uncommon among collegiate, high school, and serious recreational athletes.

Specifically, the process of resocialization might include such concerns as recasting of aggressive drive to make it functional in the nonsport world, learning to restructure blocks of time that had been controlled by coaches, "weaning" from the subservient coach/athlete role pattern, and finding direction and purpose in a world that defines success more broadly than victories and championships. Often the athlete has to go through the experience of resocialization with little help or advice due to the relative scarcity of athletic counselors or other agents of resocialization.

Competition and the American Value System

Defining competition is not an easy task, despite its being a word, a concept, and a behavior common to us all. The etymology of competition, "to seek together" (Lawther 1972), is inadequate to explain its many manifestations in the modern world. We must add that participants are seeking an objective in opposition to each other, so that all seekers cannot attain it (Berkowitz 1962).

Sherif (1976:19) allows for competition to exist within a single person, as long as measurement of performance is against a socially shared standard. For example, measuring yourself against the best marathon time in your state is competing. Measuring yourself against your own best time, according to Sherif, is not competing. While attempting to improve on one's previous best is laudable, Sherif reserves the term *intrapsychic comparison* for activities lacking a standard for social comparison.

The definition of competition can be simplified without violating the precepts noted above. For our purposes, we shall define competition as *the pursuit of a scarce prize.* A prize is "scarce" when it is valued and sought by more than one competitor. The greater the number of competitors, the more desirable it is. The more difficult it is to obtain, the scarcer it is.

Pursuit is the *process* of competition, while the prize is its *product.* Competition does not exist in the absence of either element. One may compete emphasizing either the process (i.e., participation for its own sake) or the product (i.e., "winning at all costs"). One cannot compete, however, in the absence of either component.

We will use this definition of competition throughout the text as a measure of the character and level of competition under consideration. We might predict that the character of competition occurring between Sunday tennis players or intramural basketball teams, since little more than ego is at stake, emphasizes the pursuit component of competition—the process over the product. Here, the act of participation is more important than winning, in contrast to, say, Wimbledon or the NBA championship.

How "competitive" a person or team acts often depends on their degree of satisfaction with anything less than first place. Philip Roth's sportswriter, quoted at the opening of this chapter, cared far more for the product—the outcome of competition—than for the process of attaining that outcome. Many Americans would agree with this philosophy, whether or not we are really comfortable with it. In business, for example, the product is characterized in terms of "the bottom line" (i.e., net profit). How the victory or profit was achieved is secondary to attaining it, which reflects a cultural emphasis on product over process.

The Place of Cooperation within Competition

Cooperation is a corollary process to competition rather than being contradictory to it. Cooperation is necessary to much sports competition. The most obvious examples of intergroup cooperation include agreements as to playing schedules and rules. More subtle intergroup cooperation may occur in the myriad ways in which teams obtain and exchange players or, for example, when teams agree not to entice another team's coach. Such intergroup "cooperation" can reach the level of illegality if it serves to restrict the marketplace of talent (to be discussed further in Chapter 7).

Intragroup—within team—cooperation is, of course, essential to sport. At its epitome, all players on a team yield their own personal needs and goals for the benefit of the team and its superordinate goal: victory. While each player competes within the team for playing time or stardom, many cooperate by taking a lesser role. However, within sport, cooperation is not an end in itself. Rather, it is a means to more effective competition. One is not rewarded for perfecting cooperation; rewards go to winners, who are likely to have exhibited a cooperative strategy.

Zero-Sum Competition

A common form of competition is characterized as "zero-sum," although nothing in our definition (or Berkowitz's or Sherif's, for that matter) restricts competition to this form. Zero-sum competition between two individuals or two teams in a given event will result in a winner (+1) and a loser (–1), totaling zero. If the contest ends in a tie, that outcome also totals zero, as if the contest had not been played.

While "zero-sum" may well describe the outcomes of isolated competitive events, it is less descriptive of the larger picture of organized sports and athletics, particularly in terms of the distribution of rewards. In professional athletics, for example, the winners rarely take all of the rewards and leave none for the losers. In major league baseball, playoff money is shared by teams according to their final ranking, although the lion's share, of course, goes to the winners. In college athletics, money earned by a school for television and tournament or bowl appearances is shared with other schools in the conference.

In many athletic events such as gymnastics, wrestling, swimming, track meets, and ball game tournaments, there is one overall winner and more than one loser. These forms of competition are likely to result in a *negative-sum* outcome. If there are ten competitors, whether in a single race or in a league, there will be one winner and nine losers. Thus, only a small portion of the participants can achieve the success defined by winning the top prize.

"Am I a loser—a 'minus'—if I don't win?" Expectation states determine the extent to which finishing lower than first place is deemed to be failure. A team or individual that believed itself to be near the bottom of the group in ability might count itself successful with a third place finish. That success would still likely have to be qualified and explained for others, since American culture is so oriented toward unqualified success, particularly in sport.

Economic Competition in America

The competitiveness of the American economic system supposedly reflects the competitiveness of our character. Economic competition is the foundation of capitalism. The open market is supposed to produce the best product at the cheapest price, reaping the greatest reward for those who are the most competitively efficient. Once America left the realm of the cottage industry, however, open economic competition lasted but a few decades. The result of such open laissez-faire competition was the rise of wealth and power concentrated in the hands of a few "robber barons" (Carnegie, Stanford, Rockefeller, DuPont, and Mellon, among others). The effect that these top competitors had on the open marketplace of capitalism was the destruction of their competition.

In the 1880s the American economy had become so dominated by a few industrial giants that antimonopoly and antitrust legislation, in particular the Sherman Antitrust Act, was enacted in 1890 to ensure that a single company could no longer control a particular market. In other words, to foster competition the federal government had to rein in the best competitors, who, in a fairly short period of time, had destroyed competition in their particular marketplaces. Although the American economic system is certainly more competitive than socialist state economies, such as those in Sweden or Cuba, it contains elements of economic socialism; consider its myriad regulations of industry, parity prices for farmers, the welfare system, social security, a federally subsidized transportation industry, and the Fair Trade laws. Yet, the myth of a free and open American economy dies hard. America is still often viewed as a competitive system that requires constant reinforcement through schools and sports (Curry and Jiobu 1984; Riesman and Denney 1951; Thompson 1959). Support also exists for competition as a cultural value and a means toward child training (Grove and Dodder 1979).

There is some belief that competition is overemphasized as an American cultural value (Devereaux 1976; Orlick and Botterill 1975; Guttmann 1988; Martens 1976; and Leonard 1974). Sadler (1973) says that mindless allegiance to competition as a value leads to competitive excess. Ellis (1976) criticizes its pyramidal form in which an increasing number of people are eliminated from participation at successively higher levels, a pattern that is particularly noxious at the preadolescent level. Some critics decry the destructiveness of competitive propaganda in the Olympics (Curry and Jiobu 1984; Filho 1978; and Howald 1978), while others suggest that outcome-oriented competition in schools is destructive (Davidson 1955; Bailey 1977; McEwin 1981; and Guttmann 1988). These wide-ranging conclusions show that competition is not the unquestioned value that we might think it to be (McCormack and Chalip 1988).

Alfie Kohn (1990, 1992) goes furthest in criticizing competition as a cultural value. Kohn believes that competition brings out our darker side, which, contrary to the belief of some, is not the essence of human nature. He projects that the "Hobbesian Question" (which we raised in Chapter 1) leads one to wonder how naturally selfish homo sapiens can live communally. Kohn says, instead, that we naturally want to cooperate rather than to compete, but modern culture, and particularly American society, foster destructive competitiveness. Kohn advocates a restructuring of our institutions—family, school, sport, and business—so that success is not achieved at the expense of others. Success, he says, can come from cooperation *as the goal,* rather than simply cooperation as a tactic within competition. He would eliminate grading and ranking in schools and business and would eliminate athletic competition as counterproductive to the welfare of individuals and our society.

Feminist writers have been especially critical of the assumption that competition is an important emphasis in American life (Lugones and Spelman 1987). The world of economic competition has long been dominated by men; women in our culture have been socialized to place much stronger value on cooperation and compassion. Even those women who are competitive athletes often are uncomfortable with the notions of direct confrontation, physical aggressiveness, and conquest that so often are associated with athletic success. Many choose instead to focus on achieving personal excellence in ways that do not entail a cost to others (Lichtenstein 1987).

Sport As an Agency of Socialization

We have been focusing on competition as an American cultural value, particularly as manifested in sport. Geertz (1972) shows in his analysis of Balinese cock fighting that sport provides a medium through which we can observe an array of values, status mechanisms, and other aspects of a culture. Lipsky (1978:351) also describes the social drama of sport as encouraging spectators and participants to accept the cultural values supported in sport:

> The sports aesthetic can be seen as facilitating the internalization of the 'proper' attitudes toward mobility, success, and competition. In this way, sports is the symbolic expression of the values of the larger political and social milieu.

Like family, religion, and school, sport serves as an agency of cultural transmission, helping to socialize participants to values that tend to be congruent with the culture. The cultural values inherent in sport participation and the value of sport to society and to personal development are well recognized. However, this may be based on folk belief rather than on evidence. School athletic programs have been linked with such social values and psychological benefits as health, happiness, emotional maturity, morality, cooperativeness, competitiveness, teamwork, compliance with rules and authority, sportsmanship, fair play, democracy, achievement, and social competence (Educational Policies Commission 1954). Social attributes attached to sport participation reflect the perceptions of theoreticians, administrators, and observers of the social process in sport (Harragan 1977; Berlage 1982). These values and benefits coalesce into what Edwards calls the "dominant American sports creed" (1973).

Does Sport Build Character?

The folk belief that "sport builds character" (Rafferty 1971; Ford and Underwood 1974) implies that sport *causes* character traits (assumed to be good traits) to develop in participants, particularly youngsters. Seldom addressed is the question of whether sport actually "builds" or causes good character traits to develop or whether those people already possessing these traits become selected into the sports sphere. Schafer (1976) found that interscholastic athletes tended to be less delinquent than nonathletes, but he questioned whether conformity to rules was actually taught in sport or whether a selection process was responsible for athletes' lower delinquency rate. Nonconforming youngsters might have chosen not to participate in sports (self-selection), or they might have been rejected by adult controllers of these sports as undesirable.

Further clouding the role of sport as an agency of character development are findings that indicate that the type of character promoted in sport and exhibited by athletes is not always positive by societal standards. Bredemeier and Shields (1986a) found that moral reasoning in sport is more egocentric than in daily life, and further (1986b) that college athletes exhibit patterns of moral reasoning significantly less mature than those of college nonathletes. Beller (1990) suggests that college athletes need a moral reasoning intervention program. Heyman (1986) found that athletes often have difficulty giving adequate attention to nonathletic priorities, suffer from high levels of stress and burnout, and struggle to control expressions of aggressiveness that are encouraged within sport but disallowed in other areas of their lives. Although we cannot assume that sport causes such problematic findings (any more than we can assume that sport causes the development of positive characteristics), this kind of evidence certainly does not speak well for the validity of the "dominant American sports creed."

Morality in American Sport: Criticisms

The close link between sport and religion that appears to exist in American culture has caused at least one cleric to bemoan the "sterility of religion" and the "idolatry of sports" (Michener 1976:385). While many athletes profess religious convictions, either privately or publicly through evangelical organizations such as the Christian groups Athletes in Action and Sports Ambassadors, athletes rarely take a public stance on moral and ethical problems in sport such as greed, drugs, violence, and cheating (Deford 1976).

Greed seems rampant in sports among both owners and athletes. At least from the conflict-coercion perspective, greed can be viewed as an inherent failing of the capitalist competitive system. In contrast, the functionalist perspective considers the open-ended opportunity to make money as an incentive toward self-improvement and thus the betterment of the social system. Greed from the capitalist perspective is simply charging what the market will bear; the value of a product or service (whether it be a widget or an athlete's talent and fan-drawing power) is determined by what purchasers are willing to pay (i.e., owners "buying" players and fans purchasing the resulting entertainment, or sporting goods manufacturers "buying" athlete endorsements and the public buying the resulting product). Begun in 1972 Nike, the athletic shoe and sports apparel company, was a $2 billion company by 1990, with income exceeding the combined tickets sold and TV revenues of the NBA, NFL, and Major League Baseball (Katz 1993). Michael Jordan makes $20 million a year from his Nike endorsements alone. Tennis player Jim Courier makes $26 million over four years from Nike, while the company pays its Indonesian factory workers the equivalent of $1.35 a day (Katz 1993).[1]

Drugs, Violence, and Cheating as Competitive Tactics.　Performance-enhancing drugs are publicly condemned because they undermine the essence of human competition and because drugs often have detrimental immediate or long-term side effects. Yet drug usage is rampant in many sports. Whether they're steroids to increase strength and bulk, diuretics and emetics to quickly reduce weight, or amphetamines and barbiturates to control emotional states, drugs seem to have become an integral if not pervasive part of athletics. Violent tactics and cheating are often viewed as ethical problems, but also as essential to the contests in which they occur if they are instrumental in attaining victory.

Values in sport are measurable, and the ultimate measure is victory. This is similar to the business world, in which "the bottom line" provides the ultimate measure of worth, supported by what we might call "The Virtue of Single-Mindedness," in which attaining the prize (victory, dollars) supercedes all process values (honesty, fair play, health, etc.). In essence this ethic says, "Forget *how* we win, so long *as* we win." Strategic violence and cheating are condoned as a means to the sole acceptable outcome: victory. (If sufficient tickets and beer are sold, this may temporarily substitute for victory).

Periodic scandals in collegiate athletics suggest that cheating in pursuit of victory is rampant. In 1988 six of the eight members of the Southwestern Conference were penalized by the NCAA for major recruiting and academic rules infractions in their football programs. (The 1993 movie, *The Program*, directed by David S. Ward, characterized the combination of drug usage, violence, and cheating that is rampant in collegiate football.) Specific during-contest violations of rules may pale in comparison, yet they indicate how rules designed to proscribe behavior are strategically broken to foster a competitive edge. Holding and other forms of illegal interference are taught as useful tactics in contact sports such as football, water polo, and basketball. Young

---

[1]At that wage, it would take an Indonesian worker in a Nike factory a third of a year to earn enough money to buy one pair of $155 Air Jordans.

catchers in baseball and softball are taught to "pull" pitches into the strike zone to fool umpires. A strategic faked injury has long been a part of games structured by time, to the point where rules have been adjusted to control this form of cheating. Examples of strategic cheating proliferate in other sports as well. Rules do not control cheating; they merely present an additional challenge until new strategies are devised to circumvent the newer rules.[2] As these behaviors become increasingly acceptable in the single-minded pursuit of victory, we might ask whether the definition of transgression has shifted from the act of cheating to the result of getting caught at it. (See the discussion of *anomie* in Chapter 4).

"The Temptation of Roland Agni"

This chapter opened with a quote from a sportswriter in Philip Roth's *The Great American Novel* extolling victory and vilifying defeat. Roland Agni, another character from the same novel, is the only star on a hopelessly inept professional baseball team. Roland is faced with a moral choice: whether or not to cheat to ensure his own future in baseball as well as a measure of success for his team. Specifically, Roland must decide whether to feed his teammates Wheaties containing an "extra ingredient" guaranteed to make them win. Roland's dilemma is whether to cheat in order to win or to remain moral and continue to lose. His response to the "mad scientist" offering him the choice is interesting:

ROLAND: "But—but, if I feed the boys these Wheaties—is that what you want me to do?"

MAD SCIENTIST: "Exactly! Every morning, just a little sprinkle!"

R: "And we win?"

MS: "Yes! You win!"

R: "But—that's like throwin' a game."

MS: "Like what?"

R: "Like throwin' it. I mean, we'd be winning when we're supposed to be losin'—and that's wrong. That's illegal!"

MS: "Throwing a game, Roland, is losing when you're supposed to be winning. Winning instead of losing is what you're supposed to do!"

R: "But not by eatin' Wheaties!"

MS: "Precisely by eating Wheaties! That's the whole idea of Wheaties!"

---

[2]Cheating may be defined in a variety of ways and is distinguished from actions that completely destroy the goal structure of the contest. Here, we informally define cheating as *actions beyond the rules, but within the structure of the game, which the perpetrator has a reasonable chance of getting away with* (Avedon 1971). Viewed in this light, cheating resembles strategy.

R: "But that's real Wheaties! And they don't make you do it anyway!"

MS: "Then how can they be 'real' Wheaties, if they don't do
what they're supposed to do?"

R: "That's what makes them 'real'!"

MS: "No, that's what makes them unreal. Their Wheaties say
they're supposed to make you win—and they don't. My
Wheaties say they're supposed to make you win—and they
do! How can that be wrong, Roland, or illegal? That is keeping your promises! That is being true to your word! I am
going to make the most hopeless baseball team in history
into a team of red-blooded American boys! And you call that
'throwing a game'? I am talking about winning, Roland, winning—what made this country what it is today! Who in his
right mind can be against that?"

The mad scientist asks, rhetorically, why it is acceptable for corporations
(such as General Mills, manufacturer of Wheaties) to be less than honest in advertising their products but not okay for athletes to lie and cheat. He concludes that there is no difference: athletes should not be held to a standard of
purity greater than that which exists in business. However, the *ideally* stated
ethic against cheating is very different from the *reality* of athletics. Through
his characters Roth is saying that moral ideals in athletics are convenient but
burdensome fictions. They falsely justify the exalted position we give to athletics and athletic stars. Business has no such ethic or image to uphold, so ironically business could be considered more honest than athletics. Advertising and
selling have long been guided by the tenet of caveat emptor, "Let the buyer
beware." Thus, lying, deviousness, and cheating are institutionalized and accepted in business.

In sport, cheating is formally discouraged through rules. In reality, though,
cheating is commonly accepted as a viable strategic weapon, with rules functioning not as barriers to cheating, but as obstacles to be circumvented on the
path to victory. Contrary to the ideals often espoused in American sport, honesty and adherence to codes of conduct are not absolute values. Instead, honesty and morality are contingent on the outcome: only if one can be assured that
honesty does not jeopardize winning should one risk moral behavior.

Contingent Values.   A belief in contingent values, according to Kohlberg
(Duska 1975; Kurtines and Greif 1974), is the highest level of conscience and
moral choice. Rather than cheating or stealing being absolutely good or evil,
they are good or evil depending on conditions and consequences. Cheating may
be condoned, for example, if the other team is doing it also. Cheating or strategic violence may be more acceptable (or less reprehensible) if the stakes are
high enough. Transgression may be recast as acceptable, with the real crime relegated to getting caught, unforgivable only if it costs the team the game.

A concrete example of contingent morality appears regularly in sport. Acceptance of money beyond expenses by amateur athletes had long been forbidden. Yet this was so common in international athletics that amateurism was redefined to make taking money acceptable. In many Olympic sports now, professionals compete, although not for the level of money they normally command.

Jerry Tarkanian (former basketball coach at the University of Nevada–Las Vegas), who has been cited for NCAA violations while coaching at two different universities, distinguishes between "serious violations of rules" and "acts of decency" (Smith 1978). Tarkanian, in his own defense, suggested that much of what he did for his athletes, such as providing them with transportation, spending money, and gifts, while technically infractions of NCAA rules, fell into the category of "common decency to a fellow human" (Smith 1978:5). Tarkanian added that these acts of kindness were not significantly different from the benefits many professors provide for their students.

There is a difference, however, that relates to the consequences of these acts. A physics professor may provide unlimited funds to support a top student's work with little danger of creating a category of "tramp physics jock." If one coach, on the other hand, could exercise his or her "humanity" at will, so could other coaches. College athletics, unlike physics, are publicly competitive, garnering publicity and the potential for millions of dollars for the institution. For better or worse, these conditions do not exist in physics or any other academic discipline. Neither is there an ethical distinction between amateur and professional physicist. Therefore, subsidization of physics "jocks" is not an issue, but payment to amateur athletes is a moral issue so long as a distinction between amateur and professional exists.

Whether product-focused competition, through which attaining "number one" status far outshines any other value, is morally right or wrong must be answered individually. Its consequences for individuals and for society are open to speculation. Some see a bleak future with continued rampant competitiveness further eroding other values and human relations. Others see competition as integral to the American social fabric. The issue is certainly not as clear as Roth's sportswriter suggests. Nor may the consequences of rampant product-focused competition be as dire as social critics would have us believe.

Comparative Value Positions in Sport

Despite a prevailing pressure toward political conservatism and authoritarian control in sports and athletics, value positions periodically ebb and flow within the institution. Kew (1978) categorizes these value orientations in sport as the Lombardian Ethic, the Counterculture Ethic, and the Radical Ethic.

The Lombardian Ethic: or, "The Virtue of Single-Mindedness."   The Lombardian Ethic dominates American sport, lauding competitiveness above all other values. Because it is the reason for competing, winning is the ultimate

FIGURE 3.2   *The "Lombardian Ethic" of victory as the sole worthwhile outcome of sports is attributed to Vince Lombardi. Whether or not he actually believed in and lived this ethic is uncertain. In his name, however, the ethic has attracted a widespread following in sports, business, and politics. (Photo courtesy of the Green Bay Packers.)*

value and goal, exemplified in the famous dictum attributed to Vince Lombardi, coach of the Green Bay Packers in their glory years, that "Winning isn't everything; it's the only thing." Accordingly, values other than competitive domination are irrelevant to survival in a cold, hard, hostile, dog-eat-dog world.

Although Lombardi probably believed that various other social values, such as obedience and loyalty, are conducive to winning, these were by-products and paled in importance to victory. This "Virtue of Single-Mindedness" is exemplified by success and its rewards, which come to those who persevere on the straight and very narrow path to victory. All other values pale next to victory: honesty is a luxury, served only when and if dominance is assured. Loyalty is characterized as devotion to the group (i.e., team) goal of success rather than to individuals—aging warriors no longer able to "cut it" on the field of battle will be released to make room for someone who can get the job done. Participation for its own sake diminishes as the tangible rewards of victory increase. As Sherif states (1979:4), "The focus is so narrow that all other values are subordinated to a moment of truth . . . the prize of such overwhelming value that nothing else counts."

The Counterculture Ethic. The second value orientation identified by Kew, the Counterculture Ethic, lauds competition, but primarily as a process, with significantly less emphasis on the outcome of victory or defeat. Competing (that is, participating) is conceived as more important than winning. Winning is irrelevant except as a reflection of the quality of effort. Grantland Rice's famous quote, it matters "not that you won or lost, but how you played the game," provides a motto for the Counterculture value orientation.[3] Personal feelings and meanings drawn from the competition are of primary importance. Direct, head-to-head competition is less valuable than striving for personal improvement and approaching perfection of form (thus deviating somewhat from our definition of competition). This is an existential approach, which favors present-time orientation rather than comparisons with past performance or future striving. Adult recreational sport potentially comes closest to the Counterculture Ethic, as might such events as the Special Olympics and the Senior Games.

The Counterculture Ethic is similar to a conflict-coercion view of sport, rejecting many aspects of modern American society such as hierarchical relationships (i.e., unequal status resulting from differential achievement), external institutional controls, and competitiveness. A key belief of the counterculture is that sports achievement supports repressive and coercive methods of social control. Those imbued with the dominant sport ethic, on the other hand, accept these facets of social order as supporting an essentially beneficent society, which provides systemic rewards such as status, education, money, and jobs, if only the participants "play the game" well enough to succeed. Although success in a competitive system is, by definition, at the expense of other competitors (who have not "played" well enough to succeed), there is a presumption that other avenues exist through which success can be achieved.

---

[3]The "counterculture" as a social movement had, perhaps, its zenith in the late 1960s and early 1970s; the term, however, remains descriptive of a value orientation that runs contrary to the generally dominant product-oriented competitiveness of American society.

In reality, very few people will be found entrenched in either camp. We are more likely to see society in general and the institution of sport as more or less worthwhile and beneficial, rather than as absolutely beneficial or detrimental. Spady (1976:218) takes the middle ground, describing social life as "a highly complex struggle between the individual and the collectivity which demands compromises from both."

The Radical Ethic. The Radical Ethic suggests that playing well and winning are complementary and mutually supportive conditions. Both the means (playing) and the end (winning) are important in competition, but in contrast to the Lombardian Ethic, the means is preeminent. Winning deviously (i.e., by cheating) undermines its value to self and to society. This position is not radical in the sociopolitical sense, nor does it appear to be a radically new thought. Instead, the Radical Ethic in sport is the value orientation from which sports and athletics originated, in which playful, participation-oriented principles were paramount, rather than the more modern corporate form (Frey and Eitzen 1991). To return to this value orientation, after decades of the Lombardian Ethic in sport, would be radical, indeed.

Functionalist and Conflict Views on Sport and Socialization

The functionalist and the conflict theorist have distinctly different interpretations of the role of sport as an agency of socialization. For the functionalist, the institution of sport serves the needs of the athlete by providing an arena for the development of competence, health and fitness, achievement and success, etc. It provides role models in the form of athletic heroes and heroines, and it positively reinforces hard work and good performance with trophies, status, public recognition, and other extrinsic rewards. Further, it both reflects and instills the values of the broader culture, and it encourages the athlete to develop the skills and attitudes associated with success in sport and life in general.

The conflict theorist, however, sees the institution of sport as serving primarily the needs and purposes of the ruling class, oppressing and exploiting the athlete in the process. It promotes inequality, pitting individuals against each other for a few prizes that can only be won at another's expense. The conflict theorist sees sport perpetuating the cruel and empty myth that significant extrinsic gains are obtainable by all who desire and are willing to work for them. In reality (from the conflict perspective), sport makes conspicuous the few who do achieve success, holding them up as examples of the riches that can be won and misleading the masses into believing that such riches and status are truly within reach. Meanwhile, sport is packaged and sold to the unwitting public as entertainment, which dulls their consciousness and feeds the coffers of the already rich and powerful.

Alternative Views of Sport Competition

Philip Slater, in *The Pursuit of Loneliness* (1970), offers a parable describing the hold that competition has on American culture. He describes how those who believe in the benefits, the sanctity, and the purity of cooperation might remove the "invidious elements" from a competitive form, such as a foot race. The partisans for cooperative strategies, as organizers of the race, begin by removing the prize (extrinsic motivation), but finding that the racers and the spectators are still preoccupied with who will win, they attempt to alter or remove other elements of the event, such as identification of runners, timing devices, and even the track. In order to discourage comparison of performances, they forbid the runners to run parallel to each other or in a straight line. Of course, in their zeal to remove "invidious competition" from the race, they no longer have a race; rather, they have created a dance.

Those who criticize the overbearing and harmful effects of competition (aside from Kohn, mentioned above) do not go as far as Slater's parable. They do not want to abolish competition completely. Instead, they seek to alter those elements they perceive to be destructive.

> In any competitive structure, there are only two possible outcomes: a tie or inequity. So "winning" is present as a value in any competition, as is losing. But what is won and what is lost are issues to be discussed, considered, evaluated, and decided upon (Sherif 1979:16).

Redefining Rewards

In American culture there are many alternatives to our normative focus on winning contests and deriving tangible rewards (trophies, money, etc.). Altherr (1978), describing hunting in competitive terms, suggests that the product or "prize" of hunting has been redefined by hunter-naturalists who seek not heads or skins but contact with the animals, a photograph of the live animal serving as a tangible symbol of the "kill." Cheyenne warriors in battle exhibited possibly the epitome of competitive sportsmanship, conservation, and respect for the foe by counting victory merely in touching opponents rather than in killing them (Blanchard 1976). (Unfortunately for the Cheyenne, the white man "played" by his own rules.)

Altering Standards

Walsh (1975), Austin and Brown (1978), and Simon (1985) believe that the standards of comparison that underlie competition might be changed. Walsh suggests that the definition of success be liberalized to include perfection of form rather than simple comparison of scores. In game competition as we know it, victory is awarded to the participant who accumulates more points

(and, depending on the sport, sets and games) than the opponent. This overlooks poor performance since such factors as luck, the decisions of game officials, and an even poorer performance by one's opponent often enter significantly into the outcome. Instead, why not count only clearly winning plays—aces, passing shots, etc., in tennis, for example (Gallwey 1976)—to determine the winner of the contest?

Handicapping is a preset standard of comparison that allows for more than one winner. If a gambler bets on a losing team to beat the point spread, e.g., the team loses by two points when the expected margin is three, the gambler wins, yet the team that performed better than expected is still considered a loser. Why not reward the team on the short end of the final score with a win, or perhaps a half-win, if it does better than the "experts" expected? (This might give some legitimate purpose to oddsmakers, for better or worse.) The minor league Continental Basketball Association, in fact, awards ranking points not only for the winners of games, but also for quarters won.

The Iconoclast of Coaches: Winning By Losing

To this point we have considered competition as a dominant American value and have looked briefly into differing views of value systems. Now we will look at a man who, as head coach of a college football team, deviated significantly from the dominant and pervasive value system in coaching.

Stewart Ferguson was a star pass receiver and defensive terror at Dakota Wesleyan University in the 1920's despite being only 5′8″ and 160 pounds. He coached successfully at the high school level for several years, then at his alma mater, bringing Dakota Wesleyan its first undefeated football team. He also took a previously poor Wesleyan basketball team to the National AAU tournament five times despite never having played basketball competitively.

Ferguson was subject to the same occupational attitudes and pressures as other coaches. In his unpublished autobiography (1947) Ferguson relates that bending and breaking rules was the norm in coaching, particularly at the collegiate level, and that he conformed to this norm in order to win.

In 1935 Ferguson was hired at Arkansas A & M to attempt to turn a long-inept football program into a winner. He decided that he wanted to do it right this time, with true students instead of tramp athletes (who often moved from school to school changing their names) and without scholarships awarded specifically for football ability.[4] But his team, the Boll Weevils, continued to lose, and Ferguson was fired from his coaching position. He remained at A & M as a professor and watched the local boosters club take control of the athletic program in a blatant attempt to produce a winning team, which also failed, while draining the school's resources.

To this point, Ferguson's story could describe the careers of countless coaches, but here the story begins to take a unique turn. The university administration was on the verge of dropping football but decided to try one last time to attain a semblance of success. In 1939, Ferguson was offered a contract, which, at his insistence, did not depend on his winning a single game. He promised only that the team would not cost the university any money and might even bring in some revenue. His plan was to play most of the games away from home, traveling from one end of the country to the other. The team's expenses would be covered by gate guarantees from the schools they visited. Ferguson promised opponents that he would provide a wave of pregame publicity and that the hype, along with the fans' natural curiosity about a team from so far away, would bring a large enough crowd that both teams would make money.

This scheme set the stage for what transpired. The first of two unusual steps toward making the Boll Weevils a unique team was that Ferguson let his players run the team. When he first told them that they would have complete control, he also said that he wanted them to play for fun; they should treat football as a game and let him worry about the business side of football. His players interpreted "playing for fun" literally. They begin to play for laughs, making up plays as they went along for the entertainment of the fans and themselves. Some people interpreted this as the Boll Weevils trying to lose games. They weren't—they simply didn't care about winning.

Many players from the previous year's Weevils team quit. However, others were attracted by the opportunity to travel and an atmosphere that was free of the oppressiveness that they had come to expect from coaches.

---

[4]During this era scholarships expressly for athletic ability were controversial, a common occurrence but considered ethically questionable (Savage 1929).

The Weevils were capable of moving the ball forward, although they displayed bizarre antics when they were in danger of scoring, such as a play featuring nineteen laterals that brought the ball from the brink of the enemy goal back to their own. Whichever Weevil had the ball at that point would look for an opposing lineman and toss it to him for a touchdown. Their London Bridge defense in which everyone, including the Weevils' substitutes on the sideline, all fell down on cue, caused more than one surprised opponent to fumble. When they wanted to score, a particularly agile Weevil halfback was available who ran on his hands with the ball tucked between his feet. They substituted players on a bicycle and carried tired teammates off the field on a stretcher.

The Boll Weevils played to large, usually appreciative crowds who were seldom put off by the lack of "competition" because they were so well entertained. Ferguson's team gained a national reputation as the "Marx Brothers of Football" (Crichton 1940) with their fame and antics growing with each game throughout the 1939 to 1941 seasons.

Ferguson's Purpose.   Whether you find Ferguson's form of football to be refreshing and entertaining or a perversion of a great American game is irrelevant to our immediate concern. More pertinent is what Ferguson was trying to accomplish, how it was received at the time, and what degree of success he attained in delivering his three-fold message.

First, he believed that college football should be primarily an educational experience. To this end, he expanded the schedule to 13 games each year with only 2 at home to give his Arkansas-born and -bred young men a chance to see the nation. They spent considerable time away from campus but visited classes at other schools; they also conducted field work in their majors. Second, Ferguson questioned the prevailing ethic that winning was the only way to have fun. He believed that football was a game rather than a symbolic life-and-death struggle, so it should entertain players as well as spectators. His third message, most pertinent to this chapter, was ridiculing the win-at-all-cost syndrome that dominated college athletics. The Lombardian Ethic guided college athletics long before Vince Lombardi. Ferguson believed that values such as education, honesty, personal growth and health, and sportsmanship had become subservient to victory and were given credence only when they did not jeopardize the preeminent goal of victory.

Any lasting effect that Ferguson's satire might have had was buried by World War II. Shortly after the 1941 college football season ended, the Japanese attacked Pearl Harbor and college athletics were severely curtailed until the war ended. If given more of a chance to incubate and grow, perhaps Ferguson's satire of college athletics and the Lombardian Ethic might have had some lasting effect. On the other hand, with Ferguson as the lone critic inside the game, his message might still have withered and died. The NCAA would be unlikely to tolerate such behavior today, leaving Stewart Ferguson as the only person to try to ridicule and change from within the value system that guides big-time college athletics.

Boll Weevils-inspired cartoon of Oct. 15, 1940. (Used with permission of Wide World Photo.)

This leaves us with several questions. Does putting other values above winning mean that an individual or a team is violating the ethic of sport? Is sport primarily—or perhaps exclusively—about winning, or is the essence of sport found in the playing, with winning merely a reflection of the skill exhibited? Spiro and Sherif (1975) support a system of self-directed (i.e., player-directed) learning and control in sport since such a system is more conducive to retention of learning. While coaches may verbally support the educational values of athletics, few teams are structured to reinforce these values.

Competition in the Future: Two Views

What may we expect in the 21st century? What new trends will take hold and which current trends might recede in popularity? The increase in leisure time that once seemed a virtual certainty has been eroded by the growth in two-income families. In the late 1970s about 33 percent of families depended on two incomes. This is predicted to rise to an estimated 75 percent by the year 2000 (Wendel 1989). Joel Arthur Baker (author of *Discovering the Future: The Business of Paradigms*) says, "There's a growing noncompetitiveness in how we use our leisure time. I was on the Minnesota Outward Bound program for several years and many people told me that was a helluva lot more fun than beating somebody down at the club" (Wendel 1989:51). Jennings (1979:418), in a futuristic look at leisure and sport, addresses this point:

> "Free time" implies a period during which an individual is in charge of his or her own destiny. In deciding how to use their free time, people have the opportunity to practice the skills of future-thinking: examining alternatives, comparing costs and benefits, rating the probability of undesired or unexpected consequences, and considering how best to balance risk against reward.

These futurists seem to suggest a resurgence in the cultural respect afforded play and a concomitant reduction in the primal place given to structured, product-focused competitiveness. If this is to occur, however, there will need to be a concomitant raising or redefinition of the rewards ("prizes") that our social system applies to each type of leisure pursuit. Only with valued rewards might we come to be socialized (or resocialized) into play as we are into sport. By valued rewards we do not necessarily mean tangible rewards, such as money or trophies. General approval for play-like pursuits, especially if accompanied by high status, can lead to greater acceptance of play as compared to competitive quests.

It is these two approaches to competition—emphasis on participation (pursuit) or on the outcome of winning (the prize) that provides the framework to view sport as it might appear in the future.

Technosport.   Two decades ago William O. Johnson (1974) observed the two-pronged nature of competition and hypothesized two paths for American sport in the future: Technosport and Ecosport. Technosport would thrive in a future increasingly reliant or fascinated with technological innovation. Computers and advances in video reproduction are being designed to enhance both player performance and fan participation, particularly in highly organized and product-oriented sport.

Johnson illustrates Technosport with "Democracy Football," which allows fans watching on television to participate in the play selection through a computer linked from their television sets to the team's coach. Subscribers have their team's playbook and roster. The plays selected by the majority of fans are calculated instantaneously and relayed to the sideline, whereupon the coach "calls" the democratically chosen play. The other team's fans counter with a defensive play. Democracy Football would truly be "of, for, and by the people."

Edwards (1976) suggests, on the other hand, the possible collapse of highly technological sport. He considers highly organized sport to be an archaic institution because technology has eroded its underlying values.

Changes wrought by the technology of drugs (steroids, human growth hormone, blood doping, etc.), training techniques that program athletes' physical and psychic states and so dehumanize them, and genetic engineering may undermine the human essence of sport, the confrontation between two human beings (or teams), both pursuing the same scarce goal.

Ecosport.   In contrast to Technosport, Ecosport involves activities that are less staged and more natural. Johnson (1974) illustrates Ecosport through the "Never Never Game," in which teams come together to play a game that they have never played before and probably will never play again. The parameters of the game, such as field size and shape, type of ball or object, and goals, are determined by chance. All possible game permutations would appear in "The Never Never Game Book," each one selected by rolling dice. The laws of probability work against the same combination of game characteristics occurring twice with the same set of opponents. Without being able to anticipate the next game's characteristics, it is impossible to prepare specific strategies and to load one's team with giants as for basketball or behemoths as in football. The Never Never Game's lack of set structure rewards many different body types and abilities since the range of possibilities in the game will favor different body types and different skills at various times. Ecosport may be highly competitive, but its fluid structure discourages technological specialization.

Inner Games

The "inner game" approach to sport may influence the way Americans spend their leisure time. Traditionally, satisfaction from sports is based on defeating an opponent. The inner game dismisses ego involvement, which means suspending, if not eliminating, striving to win. In its place the "inner" approach to sport focuses on the quality of performance. Timothy Gallwey, author of The Inner Game of Tennis (1974) and Inner Tennis: Playing the Game (1976), describes a new way to score tennis matches that embodies this method. Rather than awarding the score on a given point to the person who kept the ball in play the longest, credit for a point is determined by the loser of the point. The loser decides whether the point was lost through his or her own fault, whether it was won by the opponent's good and unreturnable shot, or whether the point was evenly played and the termination occurred, perhaps, by luck. To gain credit for a point one must earn it through fine play, rather than as a result of luck or the opponent's poor play (such as a double fault). This "inner game" scoring system emphasizes quality of performance rather than mere outcome (Gallwey 1976).

The inner game approach to sports may ultimately provide a quantum leap, as George Leonard suggests (1974), in the skill and accomplishment levels of athletes. Focus on the functions of the mind, and particularly on specific functions of the brain, may add significantly to performance in golf (Wiren and Coop 1978). Leonard argues that it is the slow, tedious, analytic-inductive mode of teaching that has retarded rather than fostered progress in physical skill levels of Western world athletes. For support, he points to the "centered" or process-focused approach that allows Oriental-trained martial artists to break bricks, boards, and ice blocks with various parts of their anatomy, while the same tasks attempted by an "uncentered" or outcome-focused person would result in broken bones.

The New Games Alternative

There is yet another alternative to the syndrome of playing to win, failing, then failing to play. This alternative is New Games, developed by a San Francisco-based nonprofit organization with the goal of bringing play back into people's lives. One of its prime movers was Stewart Brand, who helped form the Point Foundation with his profits from the very successful *Whole Earth Catalogs*. The Point Foundation, in turn, formed the New Games Foundation after a highly successful and innovative New Games Tournament held in Northern California in 1974. The New Games Foundation subsequently grew to international scope; festivals and workshops have been held across the United States and in several other countries. The foundation has now been absorbed by the National YMCA, and several spin-off groups are continuing the New Games movement throughout the country and internationally, working with corporations and other organizations to bring alternative competitive forms to their recreation- and fitness-minded employees (Michaelis 1985 and 1988).

"New Games" is actually a misnomer as many of the activities are not new and many are pure play, not having the outcome attributes of games. The following excerpt by Bernie DeKoven (1977:1) explains the relationship between playing "new games" and old games:

> Look at the idea of newness, the phenomenon of the new game. When we're playing a new game, nobody's expert. We start off equal. We start off new.
>
> If the game isn't going well for us, well, look, it's a new game. We've never played it before, and maybe we should change it so we can have more fun. Who's to know? Who's to call us on it? After all, it's new.
>
> This is the event New Games is all about—discovering we have a right to decide how we want to play together. If a game is new, because we're new to it, we can look at the game, we can evaluate it, we can decide whether or not *it* is good. We're already good: we start playing from this premise. The only question is finding the right game, a game which we all feel good playing—good about ourselves, about each other, about the way we play together. We can do it because the game is new; because the game is new, because there is no official rule book or official anything, we become officials, we decide.

FIGURE 3.3   *"New Games" provide an alternative physical and emotional outlet to structured, restrictive, highly competitive sports activities. (Photo by Ron Bingham.)*

There is a competitive element in many New Games categorized as "soft war" games, such as those resembling tag. (Baseball and football are essentially games of tag.) Some of these games we might recall from childhood, such as Rock-Paper-Scissors, British Bull Dog, and Keep Away. Some are imports from other cultures, while still others, such as Brand's creation called "Slaughter," are developed by the players (Fluegelman 1976). New Games rules are fluid, changing to fit each situation. The point of New Games is that players should play to play, not to win, because the existence of winners as traditionally defined necessitates the existence of losers, and losers tend to quit playing.

Redefinition of winning and losing is crucial to the New Games concept. A conscious attempt is made to define every player as a winner by redefining winning as maximization of participation and pleasure, rather than as maximization of point totals or territory gained (Fluegelman 1976). In New Games tug-of-war contests, for example, some people pulling on the dominating side are likely to change in mid-tug to the weaker side, because the event is so enjoyable that participants want it prolonged. Few New Games are structured in a way that eliminates players. Most often a tagged or "out" player simply shifts to the other team rather than being banished to the sidelines, with the game continuing until exhaustion sets in or interest drifts.

New Games resemble pure play since the primary motivation for participation is the pleasure of doing it: one enters when one wants to have fun and quits when it is no longer fun, with no one else wielding the authority to prevent this. Yet, many other values associated with the traditional view of sporting competition, such as fair play, striving, and respect for others, are at least as valid in these unstructured New Games as they are in football, basketball, tennis, track, etc.

Redefining winners may appear futile, given the entrenchment of winning as a dominant goal in American culture. It would certainly be futile and foolish to suggest New Games as a replacement for traditional sport and athletics. New Games, however, are not represented as a replacement, but instead as an alternative to an existing sport and athletics structure. Traditional sport serves the culturally reinforced need to compete and to strive for special status and scarce prizes. Joy and tension release, however, do not necessarily result from sporting competition. New Games, on the other hand, provide a structure through which people can participate in competitive activities where emotional and physical release as well as joy are the primary objectives, to be experienced by every participant (what might be called a maximum-sum outcome).

American institutions socialize their members to consider competition as virtuous. American institutions incorporate some element of competitive reinforcement. By the nature of competition, most participants will lose, which often results in withdrawal of the defeated from the competitive fray. Since such traditionally defined competitive environments leave significant numbers of people discouraged, disenchanted, and unfulfilled, is it not wise to develop (perhaps even to market) some novel forms of competition designed to serve more participants in a more satisfying way? Why, after such attempts have been made, has the harsh, participant-eliminating form of competitiveness continued to dominate? (This is not as naive a question as it may seem. Neither nature nor nurture seem sufficient to explain the pervasiveness of the competitive ethic and its dominance over other values in American culture.) Are there still enough opportunities for traditional competition to satisfy Americans, or perhaps is it just as easy to avoid competition and still find satisfaction? These are questions that social commentators and social engineers need to consider.

Summary

Philip Roth's fictional sportswriter quoted at the chapter opening most closely reflects the dominant Lombardian Ethic on which American sport is based. The gap between our "sporting" ideals and its modern manifestation is filled, like an NFL uniform, with that singleminded Lombardian Ethic. Only in play and games, and *perhaps* at the early (youth) and late (elder) embodiments of sport, might we expect culturally lauded values encompassed by the word "sportsmanship" to be rewarded, particularly when such ideals threaten the pursuit of victory.

Alfie Kohn levelled strong criticism at competitive attitudes and behaviors, charging that they adversely affect human relations. Recall, also, that Coach Stewart Ferguson of the Boll Weevils found a way to make football a win-win situation by redefining success and scorning the importance of defeat. Of course, we could not have many people acting as Ferguson did—some would say one was too many—without completely altering sport to the point where it would be unrecognizable and would likely lose its prominent place in American society. (Kohn would say, "Good riddance.")

The question remains whether American society wants the ideals of sportsmanship fostered or whether the values and behaviors reinforced in more highly competitive activities are really what we want and thrive on. When and where victory-seeking and fair play come into conflict, which core value is passed from agents of socialization to neophytes? What values do we hold firmly, and which are contingent on whether they jeopardize our chances for the scarce prize of victory? Is our society moving toward more narrowly focused pursuit of victory, or are we broadening our goals to encompass playfulness? The following chapters address such questions.

References

Altherr, T. L. 1978. "The American Hunter-Naturalist and the Development of the Code of Sportsmanship." *Journal of Sports History* 5:7–22.

Austin, D. A., and M. Brown. 1978. "Social Development in Physical Education: A Practical Appraisal." *Journal of Physical Education and Recreation* 49(2): 81–83.

Avedon, E. 1971. "The Structural Elements of Games." Pp. 419–26 in *The Study of Games,* by E. Avedon and B. Sutton-Smith. New York: J. Wiley.

Bailey, C. I. 1977. "Inner Voices Limit Choices—Socialization in Play, Games, and Sport." *The Physical Educator* 34:183–87.

Beller, J. M. 1990. *A Moral Reasoning Intervention Program for Division I Athletes: Can Athletes Learn Not to Cheat?* Ph.D. Thesis, University of Idaho. Dissertation Abstracts International No. AAD91-07064.

Berkowitz, L. 1962. *Aggression: A Social Psychological Analysis.* New York: McGraw-Hill.

Berlage, G. I. 1982. "Are Children's Competitive Team Sports Socializing Agents for Corporate America?" Pp. 309–24 in *Studies in the Sociology of Sport,* edited by A. O. Dunleavy, A. W. Miracle, and C. R. Rees. Ft. Worth, TX: Texas Christian University Press.

Blanchard, K. 1976. "The Cultural Dimensions of Competition: An Ecological Analysis." *Proceedings of the NCPEAM* 79:68–75.

Blinde, E. M., and S. L. Greendorfer. 1985. "A Reconceptualization of the Process of Leaving the Role of Competitive Athlete." *International Review for the Sociology of Sport* 20 (1,2):87–93.

Bredemeier, B. J., and D. L. Shields. 1986a. "Game Reasoning and Interactional Morality." *Journal of Genetic Psychology* 147(2):257–75.

Bredemeier, B. J., and D. L. Shields. 1986b. "Moral Growth Among Athletes and Nonathletes: A Comparative Analysis." *Journal of Genetic Psychology* 147(1): 7–18.

Broom, L., and P. Selznick. 1968. *Sociology* (4th ed.) New York: Harper and Row.

Calhoun, D. 1981. *Sports, Culture and Personality.* West Point, NY: Leisure Press.

Crichton, K. 1940. "Football Is for Fun." *Collier's Magazine* December 23:21+.

Curry, T. J., and R. M. Jiobu. 1984. *Sports: A Social Perspective.* Englewood Cliffs, NJ: Prentice-Hall.

Davidson, H. A. 1955. "Competition: The Cradle of Anxiety." *Education* 76: 162–66.

Deford, F. 1976. "Religion in Sport." *Sports Illustrated* April 19 and 26, May 3 (three-part series).

DeKoven, B. 1977. "The Idea of Newness." *New Games Newsletter* Spring:1.

Devereaux, E. C. 1976. "Backyard versus Little League Baseball: The Impoverishment of Children's Games." Pp. 37–56 in *Social Problems in Athletics,* edited by D. Landers. Urbana, IL: University of Illinois Press.

Duska, R. 1975. *Moral Development: A Guide to Piaget and Kohlberg.* New York: Paulist Press.

Educational Policies Commission. 1954. *School Athletics: Problems and Policies.* Washington, DC: NEA.

Edwards, H. 1973. *Sociology of Sport.* Homewood, IL: Dorsey Press.

Edwards, H. 1976. "Change and Crisis in Modern Sport." *The Black Scholar* 8: 60–65.

Eitzen, D. S., and G. H. Sage. 1978. *Sociology of American Sport.* Dubuque, IA: Wm. C. Brown.

Ellis, M. J. 1976. "Coping With the Stresses of Intensive Competition." Paper presented to the International Congress of Physical Activities Sciences, Quebec, Canada.

Ferguson, S. A. 1947. *A Fool Is Born.* Unpublished autobiography.

Filho, A. P. deC. 1978. "The Important Thing Is No Longer to Take Part, but to Win. . . ." *Olympic Review* 127:295–96.

Fluegelman, A. (ed.). 1976. *The New Games Book.* San Francisco: Headlands Press.

Ford, G., and J. Underwood. 1974. "In Defense of the Competitive Urge." *Sports Illustrated* July 8:16–23.

Frey, J. H., and D. S. Eitzen. 1991. "Sport and Society." *Annual Review of Sociology* 17:503–22.

Gallwey, W. T. 1974. *The Inner Game of Tennis.* New York: Random House.

Gallwey, W. T. 1976. *Inner Tennis: Playing the Game.* New York: Random House.

Geertz, C. 1972. "Deep Play: Notes on the Balinese Cockfight." *Daedelus* Winter: 1–35.

Grove, S. J., and R. A. Dodder. 1979. "A Study of Functions of Sport: A Subsequent Test of Spreitzer and Snyder's Research." *Journal of Sports Behavior* 2(2): 83–92.

Guttmann, A. 1988. *A Whole New Ball Game.* Chapel Hill, NC: University of North Carolina Press.

Harragan, B. 1977. *Games Mother Never Taught You: Corporate Gamesmanship for Women.* New York: Rawson.

Hess, R. D. 1971. "The Acquisition of Feelings of Political Efficacy in Pre-Adults." Pp. 59-78 in *Social Psychology and Political Behavior: Problems and Prospects,* edited by G. Abcarian and J. W. Soole. Columbus, OH: C. E. Merrill.

Heyman, S. R. 1986. "Psychological Problem Patterns Found with Athletes." *Clinical Psychologist* 39(3):68-71.

Howald, H. 1978. "Medical and Pharmacological Means of Influencing Performance in Top Competitive Sports." *Olympic Review* 127:297-302.

Jennings, L. 1979. "Future Fun, Tomorrow's Sports and Games." *The Futurist* December:417-31.

Johnson, W. O. 1974. "From Here to 2000." *Sports Illustrated* December 23:73-83.

Katz, D. 1993. "Triumph of the Swoosh." *Sports Illustrated.* August 16:54-73.

Kew, F. C. 1978. "Values in Competitive Games." *Quest* 29:103-12.

Kluckhohn, F. R., and F. L. Strodtbeck. 1961. *Variations in Value Orientations.* Evanston, IL: Row and Peterson.

Kohn, A. 1990. *The Brighter Side of Human Nature: Altruism & Empathy in Everyday Life.* New York: Basic Books.

Kohn, A. 1992. *No Contest: The Case Against Competition.* New York: HM.

Kurtines, W. B., and E. B. Greif. 1974. "The Development of Moral Thought: Evaluation of Kohlberg's Approach." *Psychological Bulletin* 81(8).

Lawther, J. 1972. *Sport Psychology.* Englewood Cliffs, NJ: Prentice-Hall.

Leonard, G. B. 1974. *The Ultimate Athlete.* New York: Viking.

Lichtenstein, G. 1987. "Competition in Women's Athletics." Pp. 48-56 in *Competition: A Feminist Taboo?,* edited by V. Miner and H. E. Longino. New York: Feminist Press.

Lipsky, R. 1978. "Toward a Political Theory of American Sports Symbolism." *American Behavioral Scientist* 21(3):345-60.

Loy, J. W., Jr. 1978. "The Cultural System of Sport." *Quest* 29:73-102.

Lugones, M. C., and E. V. Spelman. 1987. "Competition, Compassion, and Community: Models for a Feminist Ethos." Pp. 234-47 in *Competition: A Feminist Taboo?,* edited by V. Miner and H. E. Longino. New York: Feminist Press.

Martens, R. 1976. "Kid Sports: A Den of Iniquity or A Land of Promise?" *Proceedings of the NCPEAM* 79:102-12.

McCormack, J. B., and L. Chalip. 1988. "Sport as Socialization: A Critique of Methodological Premises." *Social Science Journal* 25(1):83-92.

McEwin, C. K. 1981. "Interscholastic Sports and the Early Adolescent." *Journal of Early Adolescence* 1(2):123-33.

Michaelis, B. 1985. "Fantasy, Play, Creativity and Mental Health." Pp. 69-86 in *Recreation and Leisure: Issues in an Era of Change* (revised ed.), edited by T. L. Goodale and P. A. Witt. State College, PA: Venture Publishing.

Michaelis B. 1988. Personal interview. San Francisco, CA, October 10.

Michener, J. 1976. *Sports in America.* New York: Random House.

Orlick, T. D., and C. Botterill. 1975. *Every Kid Can Win.* Chicago: Nelson-Hall.

Rafferty, M. 1971. "Interscholastic Athletics: The Gathering Storm." Pp. 13–22 in *The Athletic Revolution,* edited by Jack Scott. New York: Free Press.

Riesman, D., and R. Denney. 1951. "Football in America: A Study of Cultural Diffusion." *American Quarterly* 3:309–19.

Roper, D. L., and K. Snow. 1976. "Correlational Studies of Academic Excellence and Big-Time Athletics." *International Review of Sports Sociology* 3(11):57–70.

Rosenberg, E. 1984. "Athletic Retirement as Social Death: Concepts and Perspectives." Pp. 245–58 in *Sport and the Sociological Imagination,* edited by N. Theberge and P. Donnelly. Ft. Worth, TX: Texas Christian University Press.

Roth, P. 1973. *The Great American Novel.* New York: Bantam.

Sadler, W. A., Jr. 1973. "Competition Out of Bounds: Sport in American Life." *Quest* 19:124–32.

Sage, G. H. 1980. "Sport and American Society: The Quest for Success." Pp. 112–22 in *Sport and American Society* (3rd ed.), edited by G. H. Sage. Reading, MA: Addison-Wesley.

Savage, H. J., 1929. *American College Athletics.* New York: The Carnegie Foundation for the Advancement of Teaching.

Schafer, W. E. 1976. "Sport and Youth Counterculture: Contrasting Socialization Themes." Pp. 183–200 in *Social Problems in Athletics,* edited by D. Landers. Urbana, IL: University of Illinois Press.

Sherif, C. W. 1976. "The Social Context of Competition." Pp. 18–36 in *Social Problems in Athletics,* edited by D. Landers. Urbana, IL: University of Illinois Press.

Sherif, C. W. 1979. "Competition-Cooperation in Sports and Academia." Unpublished paper presented to the faculty of Dickinson College, Carlisle, PA.

Simon, R. L. 1985. *Sports and Social Values.* Englewood Cliffs, NJ: Prentice-Hall.

Slater, P. 1970. *The Pursuit of Loneliness: American Culture at the Breaking Point.* Boston: Beacon Press.

Smith, S. 1978. "Tarkanian Denounces NCAA Before House Committee." *Chronicle of Higher Education* June 18:5.

Spady, W. G. 1976. "A Commentary on Sport and the New Left." Pp. 212–23 in *Social Problems in Athletics,* edited by D. Landers. Urbana, IL: University of Illinois Press.

Spiro, R. J., and C. W. Sherif. 1975. "Consistency and Relativity in Recall with Differing Ego-Involvement." *British Journal of Clinical and Social Psychology* 14(4): 351–61.

Thompson, M. K. 1959. "Motivation in School Learning." Pp. 450–70 in *Educational Psychology* (4th ed.), edited by C. Skinner. Englewood Cliffs, NJ: Prentice-Hall.

Walsh, J. 1975. "Developments in the Social Psychology of Competition." *Proceedings of the NCPEAM* 78:118–23.

Wendel, T. 1989. "Time: The Incessant Foe." *Sports, Inc.* January 2:49–51.

Werthner, P., and T. Orlick. 1986. "Retirement Experiences of Successful Olympic Athletes." *International Journal of Sport Psychology* 17:337–63.

Williams, R. M. 1970. *American Society: A Sociological Interpretation* (3rd ed.) New York: A. A. Knopf.

Wiren, G., and R. Coop. 1978. *The New Golf Mind.* New York: Simon and Schuster.

CHAPTER 4

Deviance in the World of Sport

An intercollegiate golfer falsifies her score card. A professional football player takes anabolic steroids with the consent of his coach. Parents subject their child to long, grueling hours of gymnastics practice. A college official alters an incoming athlete's high school transcript to make the athlete eligible. Drunken fans riot at a soccer stadium. Gamblers entice a basketball player to shave points. A baseball or fastpitch softball pitcher knocks down a batter who previously had homered.

Which of these acts is deviant?[1] Which should be condemned? Would extenuating circumstances make any difference in your judgment? What, if anything, should be the penalty for such acts? Might we secretly admire these acts and their perpetrators even while publicly denouncing them?

In the *pure description* phase of our analysis, we will discuss the concept of deviance both generally and within the context of sport. Our *evaluative commentary* will focus on the relative and situational characteristics of sport-related deviance, and on a comparison of functionalist and conflict views of deviance. *Social critique* will take the form of identification and discussion of a range of contributing and mitigating factors related to deviant behavior in sport. Finally, suggestions for *social engineering* are offered in our discussion of anomie and should arise as well from the reader's own reflections on the chapter as a whole.

---

[1]Since specific forms of deviance are discussed in other chapters, evidence of their existence and rate will not be provided in this chapter. Please refer to relevant chapters for specific evidence and references.

The Concept of Deviance

Like aggression (discussed in Chapter 9), *deviance* is a behavioral concept that defies simple definition. For example, is a "deviant" someone who is merely different? No; nonconformity is not necessarily deviance. On the other hand, if a behavior violates norm or rule, yet "everybody does it," is that behavior still deviant? Possibly.

At its most general, deviance is *straying from a path* (Matza 1969:10); this definition is a sufficient starting point for our discussion. The question of whether the "path" refers to rule and law, ethics, or normative behavior depends on one's point of view. However, don't let this mislead you into viewing deviance as something merely within a person's mind or as behavior that is important only if one wants to make it important. We must understand deviance because it can indicate serious problems within a society while at the same time serving important functions for that society.

Deviance as Situation-Specific Behavior: Spirit vs. Letter of the Law

Deviance is situation specific. Members of society are rarely always deviant or always conforming. Instead, they behave in ways considered deviant at particular times or under certain conditions. Killing a human being appears deviant, whether we look at it legally or ethically. Yet even killing is subject to the situation specific qualification before we can label it as deviant. Is killing deviant in war? In the electric chair? In self-defense? Opinions and even laws vary on each of these questions.

The behaviors we will be considering in the context of sport fortunately do not extend to the extreme of killing, yet they do include violations of law and rule, such as drug usage among athletes, violence, cheating in and around sport (including participants' illegal association with gamblers), and abuse and exploitation of athletes.[2]

The "path" that Matza refers to is constructed of the rules and values that a society espouses with congruent goals at the end of the path. Among the goals consistent with society's embraced values are the several behaviors that we encompass under "sportsmanship." There are shortcuts away from this path, however, and these shortcuts—rougher but quicker roads—also lead to desired goals. Among the more tangible goals that society also holds forth are victory, some victories bringing with them lucrative rewards. Play and games do not hold forth these lucrative rewards, so there is less general incentive to

---

[2]While playing infractions and fouling are rule-violating behavior, we do not consider fouling short of flagrant violence as deviant. We might be inclined to include boorish behavior of fans and greed of management as deviant, except that neither boorishness nor greed violate rule or law in America, and so are not defined as deviant, no matter how abhorrent we might find them. Gambling on sports by nonparticipants is legal in some jurisdictions and tacitly accepted elsewhere, so gambling also will not be considered as deviant for our discussion.

deviate from the path—take short cuts. People may cheat in games, but when they do, it is more for psychological reward than for tangible prizes flowing from the social system. In sport and athletics, however, the incentives to take shortcuts away from "the path" and toward the tangible prize may be great.

A case in point is the 1994 incident in which associates of ice skater Tonya Harding intentionally injured rival Nancy Kerrigan to foster Harding's access to an Olympic gold medal. Olympic fame and the millions of dollars reaped in its wake certainly provided incentive for such deviant behavior. Similarly, Gunther Parche admitted to knifing tennis star Monica Seles in 1993 to foster Steffe Graf's access to top world ranking. The difference in these two incidents is that Parche had no prior association with Graf, whom he simply adored in a deranged way, while the attack on Kerrigan was planned and carried out by associates of Harding.

We might further conceive of the path as having two lanes, one analogous to the "letter" of rule or law (i.e., a written code) and the other lane referring to the "spirit" or intent of rule or law. The metaphor is not perfect since play and games, as we defined them in Chapter 1, do not have immutable rules and certainly not formal laws from which deviation can be "caught" by societal agents who possess the power of penalty. Still, deviations from the play spirit may carry informal sanctions—perhaps with penalties similar to shunning in Amish society—as when others refuse to engage in further play with one who deviates from its spirit.

Concerning games, when all participants—or a majority, if the game process is democratic—agree to recast the rules to better fit their needs and desires, this is not deviance, since the spirit path of games is not being violated. Fair play is what the participants decide it should be, defining their own path so long as the spirit of fairness endures.

With sport and athletics, however, victory or defeat matters. Indeed, the outcome may be perceived as the very reason for engaging in that activity. While there may be some chagrin and accusation in sport and athletics over violations of their spirit[3], as when a loophole is found and exploited by one or more contestants, the real issue becomes legality rather than spirit. The spirit of sport and athletics is winning; the spirit of play and games is fairness in a context of fun. While we may argue that the spirit of sportsmanship *should* be imbued in sports and athletics, as it perhaps once was, this has become questionable in their modern manifestations.

Every sport has its examples of loopholes in the rules being found and exploited. Redshirting (originally allowed only for injured athletes) and tutoring by those who walk athletes through their courses are examples of exploited loopholes in college athletics. Blood doping[4] in track and cycling

---

[3]As seen in the code of the Little League, for example.

[4]Blood doping is the injection of blood into an athlete prior to competition to take advantage of the oxygen-carrying benefit of the additional red cells.

was a loophole in the drug regulations of those sports. The use of new materials or manufacturing processes, e.g., oversized tennis racquets, fiberglass vaulting poles, and high-compression golf balls, are examples of devising and marketing competitive advantages that deviate from the spirit of competition: fair play pitting individual against individual, each having fair access to the prize. The evidence that each of these cases represents a deviation from the spirit of competition can be seen in the alteration of rules to account for or limit these innovations. Examples can be found in any sport in which gaining an advantage toward victory is more highly valued than maintaining a level playing field.

Rather than being defined as deviant, however, the one who finds a loophole and exploits it in sport/athletics is more likely to be considered innovative and perhaps even be granted the accolade of "genius" (in the sports world's characteristic devaluation of that word). The difference here is of being dev*ious* rather than dev*iant.* The former is a strategy, the latter is an accusation. (See the discussion of outlaws and criminals later in this chapter.)

Labelling of Deviance.   Deviance is neither necessarily bad nor necessarily contrary to the way the majority of people act. Instead, an act is deviant because it is labeled that way, through laws and rules, by society. Anybody who breaks these laws and rules is labeled "deviant." Naturally, different societies have different laws and rules to define deviance. The concept of "free speech" provides an example. Speaking one's mind in the United States is a constitutionally guaranteed right. Those who would take the right of free speech from us are acting illegally and would be labeled as deviant and perhaps punished, or at least chastised. Speaking one's mind in Communist China or Iran is quite another matter. In such places, those who contradict governmentally sanctioned "truths" in speaking their minds are labeled as deviant and suffer the consequences, from censure to imprisonment, exile, or even death. (Recall the 1989 massacre of student protestors and others at Tiananmen Square in Beijing.)

Let's take this example of free speech and shift it to sport. Is a coach or athlete in the National Basketball Association allowed to speak his mind about the quality of officiating? No, because the subculture of the NBA has its own rules against speaking one's mind freely about the officiating of games. Those who criticize or complain are labeled as deviant by the rules and are punished. Criticizing authority is restricted by rules and penalties, i.e., labeled as deviant and punished, in many subsystems, despite the existence of a constitution governing the larger society that is supposed to protect that right. Rules and their enforcement are relative to time and place and what the particular agency of social control is willing to allow.

Rule and Law as Society's Definition of Deviance.   Rule and law are, theoretically, the evidence of agreement among members of a society—particularly a democratic one—about which behaviors are acceptable and which are deviant. Who and how many are actually labeled as deviant, however, is relative to the enforcement of rule and law. This tends to be inconsistent and is dependent on the mood, resources, and politics of enforcement agencies (Snyder 1985). As an example, white-collar crime tends not to be as harshly punished as crime committed by lower classes. What about adolescent delinquency? Is the lower rate of delinquency among high school athletes compared to nonathletes (evident in a wide array of research) a result of fewer infractions, or does it come from "reticence of rule enforcement agencies (schools, police) to label athletes as delinquent" (Snyder 1985:5)? In other words, it may be that high school athletes are allowed a measure of latitude to "stray from the path" similar to white-collar strayers. Why? Perhaps because both groups are so committed to culturally lauded achievement that their transgressions are forgivable.

Contrasting perceptions of deviance are rife throughout sport. One particular case in the society of intercollegiate athletics pits the NCAA against Jerry Tarkanian, former men's basketball coach at the University of Nevada, Las Vegas. This case advanced to the Supreme Court, suggesting that it has meaning beyond mere internecine warfare within college athletics (Lederman 1988). Tarkanian claims that the NCAA rules prohibiting him from providing food, clothing, and transportation to impoverished athletes unfairly label him as deviant, with Tarkanian seeing himself in the role of "Good Samaritan" rather than deviant. Thus, deviance is often in the eye of the beholder.

The treatment of youthful athletes by ambitious parents has often been questionable and ranged toward deviance in terms of the psychological welfare of the child. A recent example is the saga of professional tennis player Mary Pierce and her father, Jim, who, after years of psychologically abusive behavior toward his daughter, as well as her opponents, was banned from attending matches in 1993 (Jenkins 1993). In Jim Pierce's case, his deviant behavior was not questioned or apparently even investigated until it became a public embarrassment for the women's professional tennis tour.

How Does One Become Deviant?

Does involvement in a subculture in which others are or are perceived to be violating rule and law lead one also to deviate from the societally imposed path? If my opponent is fouling or my teammates expect me to foul, must I also foul? Take steroids? Restrict a child's life to little more than pursuit of athletic success because I believe that other parents are cracking the whip even harder?

Matza explains that "affinity yields permission instead of compulsion. Its consequence is liberty, or, if one prefers, license" (1969:112). In other words, as an athlete among steroid-using athletes, you are not *compelled* to take steroids along with the others, but your affinity with them makes it acceptable. This explanation does not suggest that taking steroids is legal, ethical, or harmless, only that the door to using them for performance enhancement is opened by others taking them. One must still be willing to walk through that door. The same process applies to parents and their sports prodigy children.

FIGURE 4.1 *Jerry Tarkanian, basketball coach at the University of Nevada, Las Vegas, enjoys the 1990 NCAA Championship with his team. (Wide World Photos, Inc.)*

According to Becker (1963) a person becomes deviant by passing through four stages: (1) being in a situation in which unethical or rule-violating behavior is an available option, (2) committing the initial violation, (3) continuing to violate, and (4) adopting a "career" pattern of deviance in which the person aligns himself or herself with others who are being similarly deviant and choosing to identify with that group rather than with rule followers.

Coaches who begin their careers with pure sporting intent and conforming ideals may develop contrary behaviors as they learn that "playing by the rules" jeopardizes their coaching careers (Snyder 1985). Coaching jobs depend on team records and team records often depend on factors over which a coach has little control, such as injuries and the unethical but competitively effective behaviors of other coaches. If the cheater is winning, can the ethically conforming coach expect to keep his or her job while losing? Is there a pull to cheat "just once" to capture a potential star athlete, perhaps making it easier to cheat "just once more," until a career pattern of cheating develops?

At this point the now-deviant coach may begin to see the rules and the rules enforcers as outsiders—"They don't understand what it takes to be a winner"—while rationalizing his or her own actions as justifiable "under the circumstances" (Sykes and Matza 1957). As long as team record is the primary criterion for coaching employment, coaches will be "motivated to use whatever legal and illegal means are available to control contest outcomes" (Snyder 1985:8). They will learn, through the rewards and punishments of the coaching occupational environment, to deviate from rules while devoting increased energy and ingenuity to keep from getting caught and suffering the consequences meted out by regulatory agencies.

The discussion in Chapter 12 about increased competitiveness in women's sports and the concomitant increase in rules violations is another example of the process of becoming deviant. In the absence of rewards and attention (not to mention opportunity) in women's sports prior to Title IX, there was less cheating and greater adherence to the traditional ideals of sport. As women's athletics and the rewards to be won in them grew, the number of formal rules spiraled upward along with the number of incidents of bending and breaking these rules. The result has been increased labeling of deviants (Farrell 1986). More rules means more opportunity for deviance; greater rewards means greater incentive for deviance.

We do not mean to imply that all or even most coaches and athletes choose the path of deviance. We only know how many have gotten caught, which is a relative few. Research is not likely ever to obtain reliable and valid data on how much of the iceberg this represents. Clearly, however, the rewards for competitive success and the punishments for failure are such in modern society as to provide considerable motivation toward deviant behavior.

TANK McNAMARA   by Jeff Millar & Bill Hinds

Deviance as a Relative Concept

Norms and rules change as a result of significant pressure from members of society or when the existing power structure and its social control agencies feel the need to change them, thus labeling some behaviors (and people) deviant and removing others from that stigma. Theoretically, all behaviors would be fair game for inclusion in or removal from the deviant label. However, this theoretical truth seems farfetched in some instances. While it might be within the realm of possibility that a shift in norms would cease to define point-shaving as deviant—changes in law now allow gambling on sports contests in some locales—such a change would be improbable since it would alter the nature of the event. It would no longer be a contest between two teams trying their best to win, thus threatening the structure of that social system. It would, instead, come to resemble professional wrestling and become showmanship in the guise of contest, rather than contest enhanced by showmanship. This is why legitimate sports agencies zealously guard their reputations and why members of the Chicago White Sox baseball team who threw the 1919 World Series—known as the Black Sox Scandal—were banned from professional baseball for life.

Yet, are there mitigating circumstances for such deviance? According to Asinof (1963) the Chicago players dealt with the gamblers because they were underpaid and treated badly by their owner, Charles Comiskey, and the players had no recourse through laws or the structure of Major League Baseball to rectify their situation. Clearly, they broke the rules and threatened the structural stability of baseball, although that structure could be considered blatantly unfair to the worker-athletes. Under such circumstances is deviance justifiable? Perhaps it was the Chicago players' specific choice of deviant actions (throwing games, thus violating the public's trust) that is so abhorrent rather than the simple fact that they were deviant.

We might be tempted to consider some deviant acts "understandable under the circumstances." We might be inclined, for example, to forgive a coach for altering an athlete's student transcript if the athlete's life would be at a dead end without college. Altering transcripts might also result from *role strain* that leads a coach to bend or break rules in order to improve the likelihood of earning a better record to keep his or her job. The coach may even justify these behaviors by claiming that the rules are unfair and needlessly restrictive, or that the enforcement agency is being unfairly selective in its prosecution (Tarkanian's claim). A similar rationale might be used by or for the athlete who takes steroids despite their harmful effects, illegality, and derogation of the essence of "sporting" competition.

Theoretical Perspectives on Deviance

The functionalist perspective and the conflict-coercion position hold distinctly different views of what constitutes deviance. These theories will help us gain a more complete view of deviance and should provide a foundation on which we can ground our own preferred conception of deviance. The final section of the chapter will distinguish between "criminals" and "outlaws" in terms of deviant behavior.

The Functionalist Perspective

Recall that functionalism focuses on social integration and solidarity within a society. The questions a functionalist asks are, "What consequences do individual acts have for society? Do they contribute to the ongoing welfare of the system (i.e., conforming behaviors, to be rewarded), or do they subvert the system (i.e., deviant behaviors, to be punished)?"

It should be noted that even functionalists see a certain amount of deviance as beneficial (i.e., functional) to the social system. One function that deviance serves is to define the boundaries of acceptable behavior. Since awareness of the boundaries of acceptable behavior is crucial to conformity, deviance is as functional to the social system and to its members as is conformity (Snyder 1985; Durkheim 1958; Parsons 1957).

Not all deviant behaviors are punished. A second function of deviance is to define areas of unacceptable behavior in such a way that individuals, and even groups, can "let off steam." This function is a cathartic one (not unlike "running amok" in some primitive societies) if the periods of tension release are confined in time, scope, and place. This sort of deviance is tolerated as long as it avoids serious harm to individuals or to the social system. Brawls among players at professional basketball games, coaches and fans berating referees and umpires (authority figures), and fans "rioting" after important contests serve this tension release function *within marginally acceptable bounds.* Only when the acceptable bounds are crossed is such

Reprinted with permission of the *San Francisco Examiner* (cartoon by Wiley).

deviant behavior seen as a problem and in need of curtailment, as with the escalation of fighting in ice hockey and vicious fan behavior at and around British soccer matches. Both soccer-governing agencies and the British government took the extreme sanctioning measure of temporarily banning British soccer teams from traveling abroad (Czuczka 1985).

Anomie Theory. Merton's (1938) theory of *anomie* extends the functionalist view of deviance by explaining when and why societies change, and, particularly, how they undergo moral deterioration.

Anomie is normlessness occurring when a society's standards of behavior break down; deviance is "a consequence of disjuncture between cultural goals and institutional access to goals" (Purdy 1985: 8). Members of a society will cease to share moral standards when they see the economic and status goals of their society as unattainable *as long as members remain within the society's ethics, rules, and laws.* The more people seek and obtain rewards through illegal means, the more others will see advantage in abandoning their commitment to conformity and will also seek "the easy way." Why play by the rules when the cheaters are prospering?

Anomie can explain much of the deviance observable in sport, as well as in business and politics. Because cheating and violence beget victory in sport, they also beget more cheating and violence. In sport or business one is not re-warded for playing by the rules; only winners get rewarded. If I believe my opponent is gaining advantage by deviating, I will be led to deviate unless I am willing to forego the rewards. This is the rationale used in ice hockey to justify violence, in collegiate athletics to justify breaching rules designed to control athlete recruitment and to keep them eligible, and the rationale used in a wide array of sports to justify taking performance-enhancing drugs (Moore 1988). The result is a society whose ethics are adrift.

> In competitive athletics, when the aim of victory is shorn of its institutional trappings and success in contests becomes construed as "winning the game" rather than "winning through circumscribed modes of activity" (i.e., fairness), a premium is implicitly set on the use of illegitimate but technically efficient means. The star of the opposing football team is surreptitiously slugged; the wrestler furtively incapacitates his opponent through ingenious but illicit techniques; university alumni covertly subsidize "students" whose talents are largely confined to the athletic field. The emphasis on the goal has so attenuated the satisfactions deriving from sheer participation in the competitive activity that these satisfactions are virtually confined to a successful outcome (Merton 1938: 675).

Made over 50 years ago, these observations describe conditions similar to today's. The seeds of anomie seem ever present in this arena of high stakes, quick fixes, rationalized shortcuts, and contingent morality.

The Linkage Between Goals and Means

We do not mean to suggest that all or even most of society's members will cheat in order to succeed. Merton (1938:676) sees five alternative ways in which people adapt or adjust to cultural goals and the institutionalized means for seeking them:

> I. **Conformists:** accept the goals, accept the means (Compete within the rules)
> II. **Innovators:** accept the goals, reject the means (Bend or break rules)
> III. **Ritualists:** reject the goals, accept the means (The "play" mind-set)
> IV. **Retreatists:** reject the goals, reject the means (Choose not to participate)
> V. **Rebels:** reject and substitute new goals and means (Redefine the activity)

The *goals* Merton refers to include simply a sense of achievement in play and games, or in more formal sport and athletics, money or other tangible prizes, status, and fame. The *means* include those culturally valued behaviors discussed in Chapter 3, such as perseverance, hard work, honesty, and abiding by ethics, rules, and laws.

Conformists adopt both the society's goals and the culturally accepted means of attaining those goals; this is the most common strategy adopted by individuals. As Merton points out, "Were this not so, the stability and continuity of the society could not be maintained" (1938: 677), and, indeed, it could not be called a society.

Innovators pursue the cultural goals and rewards, but because they are not well socialized, they reject culturally condoned means to obtaining goals and rewards. They may seek a quick and easy path to success and knowingly break rules to achieve success. ("Innovator" generally carries a positive connotation, but Merton used it in a pejorative sense to describe those whose behaviors negatively transform society.)

Ritualists reject the cultural goals, perhaps because they see these goals and rewards as beyond their reach, yet they adhere to society's standards of behavior. They continue to participate—in business, politics, sport, etc.—but they either accept the unlikelihood of winning or compete at a lower level. Ritualists may be involved in sport, but they participate as if it were play. To this extent, they are not well socialized to the society's conception of sport. They adhere to Grantland Rice's famous adage, it matters "not that you won or lost—but how you played the game." Ritualists are closest to the ideal of sport (Muscular Christianity discussed in Chapter 6), yet furthest from the reality of modern sport and society.

The *retreatist* rejects both a society's goals and the means for goal attainment. Since they are maladaptive to society, it shouldn't be surprising that retreatists are rare. Retreatists appear as society's dropouts. Retreatism as manifested in sport, however, does not carry the stigma of dereliction. Competitive sport does not inspire and attract everyone who is otherwise well adjusted. Yet those who don't care for competitiveness or its rewards may enjoy challenging physical activities such as recreational sports or New Games.

Rebels free themselves from standards of conduct and cultural values and attempts to "introduce a new social order" (Merton 1938: 678). Even an institution so culturally consistent as sport has had a few rebels break ranks. Billie Jean King (Chapter 12) and Harry Edwards (Chapters 10 and 11) are among the better known rebels within sport. Stewart Ferguson, that iconoclast among football coaches we met in Chapter 3, was a rebel since the purpose of his satire was to undermine what he considered to be a faulty status quo. Although he held no delusions about successfully creating a new social order in college football, he felt that the "society" of college football needed to see an alternative to its win-at-all-costs ethic.

We must remember that as deviance is situation specific, so the response also depends on the situation. A person might use one response in a given situation (e.g., conformity in school), a different response in athletics (e.g., ritualism), and yet another response in one's career (e.g., innovation). One may innovate (cheat) when competing, yet teach conformity (playing by the rules) to one's children in their athletic endeavors.

Innovators: The Primary Threat to a Society's Ideal Values.

When innovators attain scarce rewards more often than conformists, and as a result conformists are tempted to innovate, we have a state of anomie: disjunction between a society's goals and its means. Something must be done to realign them or the values of the society will change to find a new equilibrium with different, "emergent" values. In other words, if cheating, drug taking, and violence "work" as strategies to obtain desired goals, and there is not enough contrary pressure to bring behaviors back into line with a society's traditional values (its means), then those values atrophy as would unused muscle. Fairness, for example, may cease to be a cultural value, evolving instead into an icon, knelt to but not truly worshipped as much as the emergent deities of money, fame, and power. At this point cheating, drug taking, and violence become the new "shared values" and the society regains its equilibrium, for better or worse.

According to anomie theory, the primary concern of a stable, "functioning" society is with innovators (Merton 1938). Conformists are the source of a society's stability, while innovators undermine its foundation by calling into question its precepts of ethical conduct. Thus, *innovators are the kind of deviants that the society cannot ignore.* To the extent that innovators capture a disproportionate amount of society's rewards, the message to others is clear: it pays to violate rules and ethics. The society may claim to abhor cheating, drug taking, and violence, but if that conduct is rewarded, members of society will tend to adopt those behaviors.

This "end-justifies-the-means" doctrine—what we have earlier called the Lombardian Ethic—spreads through a culture and becomes a guiding principle for behavior when there is a "lack of cultural coordination" (Merton 1938: 681). This occurs when (1) winning and its rewards are excessively prized (i.e., product valued over process), and (2) the social organization itself prevents or limits access to goals through culturally condoned means—in other words, when playing fair ensures that you are going to lose. As members of the society come to believe, accurately or otherwise, that their best or only chance of winning is by deviating from rule and law, they cease to see this behavior as deviant and begin simply to weigh the profits against the possible penalties.

At the Seoul Olympic Games in 1988, Canadian sprinter Ben Johnson won the 100-meter dash in a showdown with Carl Lewis. He was later stripped of his gold medal and disqualified from Olympic competition when he was discovered to have taken steroids. One representative of the Canadian government stated that Johnson was doing what he had to do to win, given the pressure and rewards of modern sport (Cable News Network, September 27, 1988). This is perhaps the most infamous single example of the end-justifies-the-means doctrine used in sport. According to Merton, such deviance is a rational response to faults in societal order, in this case the disproportionate rewards garnered by Olympic winners compared to those who do not win the gold.

How to Reduce Deviance in Sport

The way to bring members of society back into alignment with its stated norms and thus reduce deviance is either to institute stronger social controls or to change the rules to legalize behaviors formerly defined as deviant. Here we can see how anomie theory is consistent with the functionalist perspective. It explains behaviors that deviate from a society's norms and leads to changes in perception of right and wrong.

Perhaps there is another way to reduce deviance in sport. Altering the environment that leads to deviance might negate the perceived need to resort to deviance. Would not reduction in stress also lead to reduction in drug and alcohol abuse? Might reduced drinking at games result in less fan violence? If coaches had more job security through tenure, would they be less likely to recruit illegally and undermine the academic side of their student-athletes' lives? These are changes in the sport environment worth consideration.

The Conflict Perspective of Deviance

Those who hold with the functionalist view of society (including its variant in anomie theory) define deviance as violation of rule and law. Functionalism perceives the rules and laws as paramount and those who break them as abnormal and deviant. In contrast, conflict theory holds that the source of problems and strains within a society derives from the rules and laws, not from the violators. Rules and laws serve as tools of the powerful and wealthy to maintain their exalted position and to keep the powerless and poor in their place. The process of socialization in which people learn to play "society's game" is seen here as simply a mechanism to preserve an oppressive, coercive status quo (Eitzen 1985).

According to conflict theory, when people who understand their plight and the unfairness of the system break laws, the lawbreakers are not wrong (deviant); rather, it is the laws and the lawmakers who are wrong (Hoch 1972). Breakers of unfair laws are simply trying to rectify the inequities built into those laws. Note that random lawbreaking is not condoned in conflict theory, only lawbreaking whose purpose is to make life more fair and equitable. Conflict theory distinguishes between *legal* deviance and *ethical* deviance. Legal deviance is simple lawbreaking; ethical deviance is doing what is wrong, whether or not it is illegal. Thus, unfair, coercive, and oppressive laws are wrong, and it is the law itself that is deviant (Eitzen 1985).

How is this conflict theory view of the social system's deviance manifested in sport? First and foremost, the humanity and the welfare of the athlete are sacrificed at the altar of victory and profit. Organized sport has lost the aura of play, becoming a commodity to which is attached great prestige and profit. A few athletes in several professional sports earn large salaries, while most earn relatively little over abbreviated careers, serving as virtual slaves to sports management. This is apparent (arguably) at the professional level, the primary difference at the lower levels of competition being an absence of salaries available to athletes for their toil. American Olympic athletes earn only expenses, college athletes earn only tuition and fees toward their education (which, itself, may be undermined by unscrupulous coaches and self-centered alumni), and high school athletes earn nothing but praise, all for the greater glory (and frequently the profit) of the organizations and those who run them. One might argue that this imbalance between toil and rewards applies even down to the organized youth league level where parental and coaching egos are served at the expense of the young athletes' needs.

Deviance as emanating from the power structure (Santomeier, Howard, Pilz, and Romance 1980) can also be seen in the underrepresentation of African Americans in management positions in collegiate and professional sport and the underrepresentation of women in management of even their own collegiate athletic programs (Birrell 1984) (discussed in Chapters 11 and 12, respectively). Further, management in ice hockey, football, and auto racing market the titillating violence of sport for profit and to the detriment of athletes and impressionable young spectators (Sugden 1981).

The threat of losing one's position or fear of letting one's team down leads athletes also to break playing rules to gain advantage (e.g., corking bats and scuffing baseballs) and to behave violently against fellow players, neither action being discouraged by management. Athletes who are unwilling to behave in this fashion because it compromises their own ethics or welfare are subject to punishment from management. A machine has no ethics, and conscience is deemed by management to be a flaw in the competitive mechanism, a defect likely to compromise group success and profits. Athletes are encouraged not to see their opponents as humans just like them, the better to narrow their focus on the singular goal of victory.

Too often in individual sports such as tennis, gymnastics, and swimming, children are molded into athletic machines and marketed by parents and coaches (perhaps not corporate, but still "management") whose sights are focused on prestige and profit. This may be less apparent (which is not to say absent) in American society, but becomes obvious when we look at the regimented training of young athletes in countries formerly within the Soviet sphere of influence (Morton 1963; Hoberman 1984; Seban 1976) and increasingly in Communist China (Seban 1976; Deford 1988; Reilly 1988; Swift 1988). A conflict perspective suggests that it makes little difference to the athlete whether the coercive pushing, prodding, and narrowing of their lives toward a singular athletic goal stems from government or from their own parents and coaches. The child athlete still is being controlled without full choice toward a goal of prestige and profit by someone who is relatively more powerful.

A child who refuses might be considered deviant by parent or coach and penalized by withdrawal of love or approval. The interscholastic or intercollegiate athlete who insists on obtaining the full measure of education or, worse, treating opponents humanely, is in danger of being viewed as deviant by the coach and may suffer loss of place on the team or even withdrawal of scholarship. The professional athlete who seeks to wrest control of his or her own future away from the dominant sport agency is considered deviant (e.g., Bill Walton, John Elway) and places his or her career in jeopardy. Of course, if the athlete is great enough, as in the case of Elway,[5] management may tolerate a little deviance, since they know in the long run there is a profit to be made from the "troublemaker."

The point, however, lies in how deviance is perceived. Management, the holders of power, label as deviant any straying from the rules that they themselves have defined, while those without power—players and occasionally fans—see management and its oppressive, unfair rules as deviant and in need of remedy.

A Naturalistic View of Deviance in Sport

Each of the perspectives discussed seems to explain something about deviance, although not everything. It is in part a matter of personal viewpoint as to which each of us might favor. Following Matza's lead (1969) we will take the position that deviance should not be forced into one or another paradigm. Human behavior is so complex that we may come to understand deviance better by viewing it more as a naturalistic phenomenon than as understandable only from a particular theoretical perspective. The naturalistic perspective suggests that deviance can be described by one or another theoretical box when the description fits, rather than trying to force all deviant behavior into one box. Matza believes that deviance should be viewed from the subject's position rather than from either a correctional (i.e., functionalist) or a romantic (i.e., conflict) perspective.

Drawing from the *West Side Studies* early in this century (1914:29–30), Matza illustrates the importance of viewing deviance from the perspective of those who would be labeled as deviant:

> The two chief sports of the Middle West Side [of New York City]—baseball and boxing—are perennial. The former, played as it always is, with utter carelessness and disregard of surroundings, is theoretically intolerable, but it flourishes despite constant complaints and interference. The diamond is marked out in the roadway, the bases indicated by paving bricks, sticks, or newspapers. Frequently guards are placed at each end of the block to warn of the approach of police. One minute a game is in full swing; the next, a scout cries "cheese it." Balls, bats, and gloves disappear . . . and when the "cop" appears . . . the boys will be innocently strolling down the streets. . . .When one sees the words "arrested for playing with a hard ball in a public street" written on a coldly impersonal record card in the children's court, one is apt to become indignant. But when you see the same hard ball being batted through a window or into a group of little children on the same public street, the matter assumes an entirely different aspect.

Baseball playing as deviance, then, is situationally specific. The community's view illustrated above is moralistic and not the view of the participants.

---

[5]Elway refused to play for the Baltimore Colts (currently the Indianapolis Colts), who had drafted him. His ability to also play professional baseball gave him leverage, and the Colts traded him to Denver, where he has considerably enhanced the balance sheets of the Broncos and the National Football League.

Did the players see themselves as deviant, even though they obviously knew that street baseball was illegal? Did they view the law as unnecessarily restrictive and unforgiving, and so itself deviant? Did the system, possessing the power to either modify the law or provide for the needs of the youngsters, do either, or did it ignore the youngsters, thus treating them as outsiders and making outlaws of them?

Criminals and Outlaws

> If you're honest, you sooner or later have to confront your values. Then you're forced to separate what is right from what is merely legal. This puts you metaphysically on the run. America is full of metaphysical outlaws. (Robbins 1980)

To follow through on Matza's suggestion for viewing deviance naturalistically, and to bring to bear on the issue of deviance those various parts of the theories we have been considering, we can view deviance in terms of the differences between criminals and outlaws. Outlaws and criminals are more similar to each other than either are to saints. However, the distinctions we can draw between criminals and outlaws can help us to better understand deviance. Although most dictionaries define one in terms of the other, our position is that both qualitative and perceptual differences can be drawn between criminals and outlaws, and that the perception of outlaws in a heroic or antiheroic light is shared by much of the public and by the outlaws themselves.

Criminals are "bad guys" who break rules and laws; outlaws are "good guys" who do the same thing. We feel bad when the criminal "gets away with a crime," while we may feel good when the outlaw "beats the system," often agreeing with the outlaw that the law, rather than the actor, is at fault. It is interesting to speculate whether women tend to share this distinction between outlaws and criminals. It is certainly more difficult to find examples from sport of women who have acted in ways that might place them in either category.

What is legal may be wrong ethically (i.e., in principle) but right practically or by convention (especially via subcultural mores). The athletic coach is potentially, perhaps even probably, an outlaw, since the coaching career in American society seems to encourage outlawry. Coaches break rules and yet we afford them hero status in spite of it, or maybe on a subconscious level (given our love for the outlaw type), because of it. To further clarify matters, let's focus primarily on one kind of sport deviant, the outlaw coach (although similar arguments might be made for athletes who take steroids or are violent in pursuit of their culturally exalted goals, or even for parents who dedicate their children's lives to athletic excellence).

The rules-violating athletic coach is often seen as an outlaw rather than a criminal because he or she ignores the possible consequences of breaking rule and law rather than consciously weighing those consequences (the latter being the criminal mindset). The behavior-restricting regulation is defined as bad, inappropriate, or unnecessary, and thus irrelevant to the outlaw coach, given what

TABLE 4.1 *Examples of "Outlaws" and "Criminals" in Sport*

Outlaws

Billie Joe Hobert (University of Washington quarterback, for accepting $50,000 while competing as an "amateur")

Michael Jordan (basketball All-Star, for gambling and associating with gamblers)

Rosie Ruiz (claiming first place among women at the Boston Marathon while running only a portion of the race)

Jerry Tarkanian (coach of the NCAA basketball champion University of Nevada, Las Vegas, for violating NCAA rules at two different schools)

Muhammad Ali (heavyweight boxing champion, for resisting the draft during the Vietnam War)

Criminals

Pete Rose (baseball All-Star, for tax evasion)

Mike Tyson (heavyweight boxing champion, for rape)

Vince Coleman (baseball All-Star, for tossing explosives into a crowd of fans and injuring a three-year-old girl)

Tonya Harding (US ice skating champion, for complicity in the conspiracy to injure competitor Nancy Kerrigan)

the world expects of coaches, which is to produce competitively satisfying entertainment. Victory is necessary; overwhelming, crushing victory is preferred.

Fans blithely overlook the highly successful coach's transgressions (even the not-yet-successful coach who is "giving his or her all" as well as his or her athletes' "all") in pursuit of the siren of success (Thomson 1977). The outlaw coach's transgressions are overlooked, as were the transgressions of Robin Hood, the James gang, and Bonnie and Clyde. As Sykes and Matza (1957:668) point out, "Robin Hood, and his latter day derivatives such as the tough detective seeking justice outside the law, still capture the popular imagination." It doesn't take much imagination to metamorphose that tough detective into the struggling, harassed coach or athlete.

Sport Promotes Outlaws

Who can be against some deviance in sport when the structure of American sport *promotes* deviance by encouraging violence, disrespect for rules, lack of concern for long-term health in favor of short-term achievement, greed, and dehumanizing behavior at the expense of fairness and sportsmanship (Eitzen 1981)? The public loves and envies outlaws (wishing they themselves had the nerve to buck the rules) because outlaws, by definition, are beyond, and thus fly free of, the law. Outlaw coaches ride the high ground beyond those picayune laws with which lesser persons would control them. How else to explain the worship of Woody Hayes, Adolph Rupp, John McGraw, Frank Kush, Billy Martin, Jerry Tarkanian, Bobby Knight, et al.?

Doonesbury

Occasionally, one of their own will offer public criticism when the deviance goes too far, as when Bill Walsh (football coach at Stanford) accused the University of Washington and its coach, Don James, of "running an 'outlaw' program." Walsh called the Huskies' football players "mercenaries" who live in "an athletic compound" and learn "none of the skills you are supposed to gain in college" (Graswich 1993:C1). The Washington football program was found in violation of enough NCAA rules to be banned from postseason bowls for two years. James quit his coaching position in the aftermath. Jerry Tarkanian, however, stands as the prototypical coach/outlaw who rose up and said to the NCAA, in effect, "Don't bother me 'cause I can't be bothered with you." Any outlaw worthy of the monicker would not deign to submit to the law or to the ciphers who attempt to impose it. He or she might say, if forced to recognize the forces of mediocre conformity, "You're only picking on me because you're jealous of my success."

Willingness to deviate should not be equated with predisposition to deviate (Matza 1969). Rather, willingness to deviate is a matter of emergent motives and amenability to violating rules when a person finds out that this is what "works" in providing access to highly desired goals and that not deviating probably means foregoing the goals. In other words, the outlaw cheats, or takes steroids, or acts violently on learning that it is necessary to do so. Thus, the outlaw deviates consciously and with intention, but without self-chastisement of his or her deviance: "I don't deviate because I like to deviate; I deviate to win."

Summary

Deviance is straying from the path of societally defined acceptable behavior. Deviance is situation specific, that is, one can be deviant in one aspect of life, for example in sport, while assiduously adhering to society's precepts everywhere else. Deviance can be assessed in straying either from the letter of law and rule or in violating their spirit.

Much of deviance as it appears in sport is a means for gaining goals deemed worth the risk of punishment. The decision to deviate is pragmatic. When deviance occurs frequently but is punished lightly, these acts become both practical and socially acceptable, resulting in anomie, in which a new set of normative values replaces the old. This is the end-product of "innovation" (as Merton uses the term). Whether a state of anomie—loss of standards, such as sportsmanship—has been reached in sport is a matter of personal judgment, although sportsmanship seems to be less a central part of the sport-athletic process than in the past. Behaving ethically may no longer seem feasible. Thus, traditional ethics and pragmatism are in conflict, with loss of the ability to distinguish what is "right" (equitable) from what "works" (yields success).

From the functionalist perspective, a modest amount of deviance serves society by helping to define the limits of acceptable behavior. In contrast, the conflict view considers rule breaking not to be deviant when and where the violations are of bad rules. In this case deviance is seen as bringing needed change to society. The naturalistic viewpoint may be the most useful, however, because right and wrong as reflected in rules and laws are relative to perspective. Here the crucial question is whether the actor is pursuing the American dream (as an "outlaw," if necessary) or is threatening the structure that holds forth that dream (a "criminal").

Before closing this chapter, we must clarify our position. Lest it seem as if we, the authors, are justifying, supporting, or excusing cheating in sport, steroid use, violence, or abuse of athletes, we wish to assert that we are disdainful of each and all of these behaviors. Our purpose is to explain behavior sociologically, and sociologically each of those behaviors is *understandable* from the several perspectives on deviance.

References

Asinof, E. 1963. *Eight Men Out.* New York: Holt, Rinehart and Winston.

Becker, H. S. 1963. *Outsiders: Studies in the Sociology of Deviance.* New York: Free Press.

Birrell, S. 1984. "Separation as an Issue in Women's Sport." *Arena Review* 8:21-29.

Czuczka, T. 1985. "Europeans Ban English Soccer Clubs." *The Sacramento Bee* (Associated Press) June 3.

Deford, F. 1988. "An Old Dragon Limbers Up." *Sports Illustrated* August 15:36-43.

Durkheim, E. 1958. *The Rules of Sociological Method* (trans. by S. A. Solvaay and G. H. Mueller). New York: Free Press.

Eitzen, D. S. 1981. "Sport and Deviance." Pp. 400-14 in *Handbook of Social Science of Sport,* edited by G. R. F. Luschen and G. H. Sage. Champaign, IL: Stipes.

Eitzen, D. S. 1984. "Conflict Theory and the Sociology of Sport." *Arena Review* 8:45-54.

Eitzen, D. S. 1985. "Conflict Theory and Deviance in Sport." Paper presented at the annual meeting of the North American Society for the Sociology of Sport, Boston, MA.

Farrell, C. S. 1986. "Big Jump in Money and Prestige Spurs Cheating in Women's Basketball, Coaches and Players Say." *The Chronicle of Higher Education* January 29:25.

Graswich, R. E. 1993. "UW Football Gets Blast From Walsh." *Sacramento Bee* May 25:C1.

Gross, E. 1978. "Organization Crime: A Theoretical Perspective." Pp. 55–85 in *Studies in Symbolic Interaction,* edited by N. Denzin. Greenwich, CT: Jai Press.

Hoberman, J. M. 1984. *Sport and Political Ideology.* Austin, TX: University of Texas Press.

Hoch, P. 1972. *Rip Off the Big Game.* Garden City, NY: Doubleday.

Jenkins, S. 1993. "Persona Non Grata." *Sports Illustrated* August 23:28–33.

Lederman, D. 1988. "Supreme Court Agrees to Review Case of Nevada Coach." *The Chronicle of Higher Education* March 2:A31.

Matza, D. 1969. *Becoming Deviant.* Englewood Cliffs, NJ: Prentice-Hall.

Merton, R. K. 1938. "Social Structure and Anomie." *American Sociological Review* 3:672–82.

Moore, K. 1988. "The Old Men and the Discus." *Sports Illustrated* July 25:56–69.

Morton, H. 1963. *Soviet Sport.* New York: Cromwell-Collier.

Parsons, T. 1957. *The Structure of Social Action.* New York: McGraw-Hill.

Purdy, D. A. 1985. "Functional Perspective of Deviance in Sport." Paper presented at the annual meeting of the North American Society for the Sociology of Sport, Boston, MA.

Reilly, R. 1988. "Here No One Is Spared." *Sports Illustrated* August 15:70–77.

Robbins, T. 1980. *Still Life with Woodpecker.* New York: Bantam.

Santomeier, J. P., W. G. Howard, W. L. Pilz, and T. J. Romance. 1980. "White Sock Crime: Organizational Deviance in Intercollegiate Athletics." *Journal of Sport and Social Issues* 4:26–32.

Seban, M. M. 1976. "Political Ideology and Sport in the People's Republic of China and the Soviet Union." Pp. 306–15 in *Sport in the Socio-Cultural Process* (2nd ed.), edited by M. Hart. Dubuque, IA: Wm. C. Brown.

Snyder, E. E. 1985. "Deviance in Sport: A Symbolic Interactionist Perspective." Paper presented at the annual meeting of the North American Society for the Sociology of Sport, Boston, MA.

Sugden, J. P. 1981. "The Sociological Perspective: The Political Economy of Violence in American Sport." *Arena Review* 5:57–62.

Swift, E. M. 1988. "Sleeker, Stronger." *Sports Illustrated* August 15:45–51.

Sykes, G. M. and D. Matza. 1957. "Techniques of Neutralization: A Theory of Delinquency." *American Sociological Review* 22:664–70.

Thomson, R. 1977. Sport and Deviance: A Subcultural Analysis. Unpublished Ph.D. dissertation, University of Alberta, Edmonton, Canada.

West Side Studies (I). 1914. New York: Russell Sage Foundation.

SECTION II

Sport Through the Years

This section treats sport as a developmental process. As with individual development, sport in society manifests growth and reaches a peak of intensity, followed by apparent decline. Underlying the section are questions about how we can make the best of it all, how we can bring contemporary sport at its various levels closer to the ideal.

Early in life, we Americans are introduced to sport and through it learn social skills, as well as sports skills . . . or we learn that if we shun sport or are shunned by it, that we are different, if not deficient. Chapter 5 addresses the organization and effects of both adult-organized sport and child-centered "disorganized" play. It considers what sport does *for* and what it does *to* young people as they grow into American society. Here appear the first intimations that, even for youngsters, sport is often more than play and, indeed, may be serious business.

Through the second and third levels of the three-tiered American system of schooling (elementary, secondary, college), sport continues its socialization function, expanding its purpose to include preprofessional skills training for individuals and economic, public relations, and group cohesion functions for communities and institutions. In doing so much sport may become the tail wagging its academic dog, creating ethical problems for institutions and educational goal attainment problems for student-athletes. A graduate of one midwestern university famous for its winning teams and notorious for a myriad of legal and ethical difficulties in its athletic program wrote to his school's coordinator of alumni affairs (sending a copy of the letter to the football coach). He complained that the school's graduates had difficulty finding employment outside of the state because "most major companies perceive the university as having forsaken education for football." The graduate recommended that the university do something to bring athletics in line with the institution's educational purpose. The football coach's callous and arrogant reply to the former student was, "You haven't lived long enough for me to consider your suggestions and proposals of much value."[1] Chapter 6 considers what is right and what is wrong in school-based athletics, suggesting some means for bringing campus athletics into line with their intended purposes.

What had been fun and games in childhood has grown to something yielding social status, fame, and perhaps the promise of education or career, finally metamorphosing into an industry in which economic profit or loss is the measure of its existence and the primary basis on which it functions. Chapter 7 focuses on the economics of sport, including media, legal, and judicial concerns about sport at the "big-time" intercollegiate and professional levels. Here sport is driven by the marketplace. It is the domain of sport in which ethics

---

[1]Wulf, S. 1989. "Good Riddance." *Sports Illustrated* June 26:15.

and even the subtleties of law often carry less weight than the corporate balance sheet. Here sport has "grown up" into a vigorous industry, despite the tender treatment sometimes afforded by sport in the courts.

As we age, our participation in and use of sport changes, perhaps back to what it had been early in our lives. Is the decline in sports participation with age a "natural" phenomenon, or is it due to people, agencies, and governments feeling that the elderly have less right to scarce sports resources, even though sports activity may help retard aging? Chapter 8 asks the general question: "If sport is good, why isn't it good for everyone?" In the process the chapter considers patterns of physical activity among the aging population and how and why these patterns might be changing.

CHAPTER 5

Kids' Play and Youth Sports

Is organized competitive sport good for young girls and boys? What benefits and what dangers does it entail? At what age, and under what conditions, do the benefits outweigh the dangers? How can we maximize the former and minimize the latter?

In this chapter, the *pure description* phase of our analysis will focus on aspects of the structure and cultural context of sport that bear on youths' experience. Our *evaluative commentary* will feature discussions of the pros and cons of organized youth sports. Our *social critique* will revolve around a comparison of children's and adults' needs and perspectives with regard to youth sports. Finally, ideas for *social engineering* will arise from a discussion of alternative models that have been proposed and/or established for youth sport programs.

Text, Context, and Transformation in Games

Childhood play and game forms develop for various reasons, some of which serve the child's needs and some of which serve the needs of society. These different sets of needs are not a problem, except where the needs of the child and the society come into conflict. In this chapter, we will look briefly first at consistency between forms of youthful play and the cultures that contain them. We will then focus on youth-oriented games and sport in American society and some conflicts among the needs of youth, the needs of social agents such as coaches and parents, and socialization into the adult world through organized youth sports.

Schwartzman (1978) identifies three aspects of games that help us to understand them in their social and cultural settings. These aspects of games are the *text* (rules and physical setting of the game), the *context* (social setting and meaning of the game), and *transformations* (changes in text or context).

In the childhood game of "jacks" the text involves reciting rhymes, bouncing the ball, and picking up as many jacks as one can. The context of jacks includes messages of friendship and association, as well as momentary status. Allowing a second bounce of the ball constitutes a transformation in text; competing with one's sister may transform the game's context by introducing the element of sibling rivalry. In baseball or softball, the text includes running, catching, hitting, and throwing, and sometimes guile, while the context includes team membership and achievement, as well as social status. The use of a batting tee for very young players is a transformation in the text of baseball, while the Little League World Series transforms its context to one of international pride and propaganda.

A Brazilian tribe of Indians, the Yanomamo, play a game many American youth play. Names for this game vary locally, but the essence of it is the trading of punches (Chagnon 1968). To American youth, it is a childhood game that supposedly indicates how tough a young person (usually male) is and how much pain he can endure and deliver. It usually passes out of the American male's repertoire fairly early in life, although in the athletic subculture, the game in various forms may last beyond adolescence. To the Yanomamo, however, it is a ritualized game forming an integral part of the system that determines adult male social status.

The text of the punching game is relatively simple. In Yanomamo society, the recipient of the blow raises one arm above his head and presents his pectoral muscle as a target. The hitter is restricted to the pectoral muscle, but may take a running start. This is followed by switching roles until one player cannot continue.[1] The text of the American punching game is similar, with local variations such as limiting the target to the deltoid muscle and/or limiting the run-up, sometimes to only the spread of a hand. The context of the game in American culture is youthful play, while in Yanomamo culture it is a serious game establishing adult social status. A transformation within the game may occur in American culture if the blows escalate to the point where it is no longer conceived of as "play" by the participants, but becomes a serious fight (Bateson 1971).

---

[1]The Yanomamo are heavy users of strong drugs that reduce the pain resulting from this game. The game is not recommended unless one is preparing to do fieldwork among the Yanomamo.

Why would a game similar in structure have different social meanings in two cultures? One reason might be found in the values of the culture. The Yanomamo live a highly aggressive life characterized by chronic warfare. Americans, although aggressive in another sense and having engaged in several wars, are essentially peaceful. In America, popular adult games and most youthful games take a different, less openly hostile form. While "hitting" is integral to football, it is simply one of a number of means to accomplish the primary game goals of amassing territory and points. In the Yanomamo punching game, hitting is the sole means of attaining the goal of inflicting pain. In both cultures, however, high status is associated with dominance. Within the contexts of both games are the messages of *machismo,* that is, being a tough man, able to "take it" and to "dish it out." However, the punching game in American youth culture establishes only momentary status between two individuals. Other attributes and accomplishments, such as athletic ability, humor, and attractiveness, establish more lasting recognition for American youth.

The concepts of text, context, and transformation are important because they help us to see the place of kids' play and organized youth sports in the lives of youngsters. In addition they help us identify how changes in one element can affect changes in others.

Organized Youth Sports

As youngsters grow and develop, the games that interest them change from a relatively low level of competition and loose structure into more organized and competitive activities. This greater level of organization and the control taken over by adults in order to achieve this organization are the main factors that distinguish youth sports from childhood play and games.

Distinguishing between child's play and organized sports, Webb (1969) sees the former emphasizing equality among participants with attention paid to the pleasure of playing, and with rules altered, created, or ignored by the players to ensure their own pleasure. In organized sports, success results from recognized differences in ability or performance levels as indicated by personal and team achievement records. Strict rules exist in order to ensure that these differences determined among competitors (wins, losses, and scoring championships) are valid. In child's play, however, the players often give an advantage to a weaker opponent (a head start or more players per side) in order to ensure equitable and enjoyable competition. These advantages or handicaps seldom appear in organized sports because they obscure the reasons for victory. Equitable competition is fostered in organized sports by age group, sex, weight and height restrictions in league play, and by performance tracks (such as novice, intermediate, and advanced) in organized individual sports such as gymnastics. Fairness is inherent, at least ideally, in both forms of youth activity. In kids' play, the fairness centers on equal access to participation and on equal enjoyment within the activity. In organized sports, fairness focuses on equal access to desired outcomes, particularly victory (Mantel and Vander Velden 1974).

The opportunities for youth to participate in organized sports have blossomed, literally becoming a billion-dollar industry. It is estimated that 25 million Americans between the ages of 6 and 16 compete in organized sports (Leonard 1988). Expansion continues for boys and new opportunities have opened for girls in the past decade.

Little League Baseball

Little League baseball began in 1939 as Carl Stotz's dream to provide an opportunity for boys to play real, full-blown baseball games with proper equipment, fields, uniforms, and umpires. By 1949, the original organization had spread from Williamsport, Pennsylvania, to over 300 leagues, although it existed in only 11 states. An article in the *Saturday Evening Post* in 1949 gave Little League national exposure and led quickly to its spread, not only across America, but throughout the industrialized, non-Communist world (Ralbovsky 1974).

In December of 1974, the United States Congress forced revision of the Little League charter to allow girls to participate. Furthermore, Congress mandated modification of the statement of the organization's purpose, replacing the goal of instilling manhood with that of developing citizenship and sportsmanship (Michener 1976).

Despite this change in the stated emphasis of Little League, competition, growth, and economic success remain the prime motivations of the movement, particularly in its executive offices. It is logical, then, to assume that the same motives permeate the Little League environment. Indeed, criticisms concerning overzealous parents and coaches have been voiced often and widely for at least three decades (Ralbovsky 1974; Brosnan 1963; Devereaux 1976; Horn 1977; Maggard 1978; Voigt 1974; Guttmann 1988; Hilgers 1988). These critics assert that being competitively successful is the primary motivation of Little League, with other social benefits and enjoyment of the players placing a distant second.

Organized Sports for Girls

Not until the 1960s did organized competitive sports for girls become widely promoted. In the 1970s increased participation for girls resulted from development programs sponsored by such organizations as the United States Olympic Development Committee and the Division for Girls' and Women's Sports of the American Association for Health, Physical Education, and Recreation (now called the American Alliance for Health, Physical Education, Recreation and Dance). Programs ranging from AAU age-group swimming to Lassie League and Bobby Sox softball became popular for girls (Felshin 1974). By 1980 more than a million American girls were playing soccer (Boutilier and SanGiovanni 1983), an indicator of the rapid growth in girls' youth sport.

FIGURE 5.1 *Organized youth league sports are available to youngsters barely past the toddler stage. When school sports begin, the schools and youth leagues often compete for the youngsters. Many school districts will not allow a youngster to play on a youth league team while he or she is on a school team.*

Problems in Youth Sport

In an exposé of youth league football, Underwood (1975:92) describes a "rat's nest of psychological horrors," such as parents and coaches falsifying birth certificates, starvation diets and reducing pills to make weight limitations, and various recruiting and playing-time violations all perpetrated by adults in an effort to circumvent rules they themselves designed to equalize competition among youngsters. Strong (1992) also found evidence that youth football coaches espouse other goals but in practice place winning above everything else.

Many of these transgressions appear also in Little League (Guttmann 1988). Where a rule exists, it seems someone will try to circumvent it in the name of competitive success, even when that success is at the preadolescent level. The question that we must address is whether this deviance from stated social and psychological ideals for youth sports is common or rare. Data to answer this question are minimal at present, but do not particularly support the view of Little League as a "den of iniquity" (Martens 1978).

Pros and Cons of Organized Youth Sports

Competition among youth need not be imposed by adult drives, but may emerge in youngsters spontaneously, particularly in a culture where competitiveness is a shared adult value that is constantly being modeled (Wallace 1970). While competitiveness may be a natural response of youth, the question remains whether it needs directed enhancement and elaboration by adults and, particularly, at what age youngsters will understand and accept it.

Hurlock (1971) identifies play activities preferred at various stages before adulthood and finds developmental patterns emerging. Infants (from birth to approximately 3 years) seem to prefer simple, repetitive, self-centered play. Childhood (from about 3 to 6 years) is characterized by more complex, imaginative, and other-oriented play involving testing of physical limits, particularly of their own bodies and the materials around them (e.g., mud, wood, or plastic). Children at this age have little concern for organized games.

Youths (from around 6 to 11 years) were found by Hurlock to prefer team games with a low level of organization and a moderate level of competitiveness. Identity with a group begins to gain importance at this stage of development. In the category that Hurlock refers to as adolescence (ages 12 to about 21), group play and identity is most important, competitiveness is a preferred play style, and rules are sought and adhered to. Organized athletics replaces loose group or "gang" play, although we do not know whether this reflects a spontaneous preference or results from imposition of adult-organized structure on this age group. The competitiveness that emerges around this age may be an outgrowth of the needs and desires of adolescents to associate in groups (Helanko 1964). The existence of multiple groups leads to comparison among them, and thus rivalry or competition develops (Sherif 1958).

These developmental stages become important when we measure them against the ages at which highly organized sports are provided for youth. Little League baseball begins at 8 years of age and ends at 12, but organized sports leagues and experiences exist for children younger than 8 years old in baseball, ice hockey, gymnastics, swimming, soccer, basketball, and other sports. The structures, rules, and competitiveness that characterize organized youth sports do not, according to Hurlock's work, fit the needs and desires of youngsters until about the age of 12. We might conclude, then, that organized sports for children under 12 serve adults' needs rather than kids', or at least serve adult perceptions of children's needs.

During the early growth period of organized youth sports, physical fitness, character development, sportsmanship and fair play, leadership, teamwork, and democratic living were generally stated as objectives and benefits of these activities (Berryman 1978). These statements of objectives and benefits still exist, but we are becoming increasingly aware that they cannot be achieved without attention to the developmental status of the young sport participant. Stein (1988) observes that, as children mature, the forms of competition appropriate to their developmental level progress from individual activities to parallel play (featuring low-level organization and cooperation) to lead-up activities to highly competitive group activities. Stein (1988:30) warns that "Children who are developmentally in individual or parallel play stages and thrust into highly competitive team or individual activities are truly at risk. These risks can be physical, psychological, emotional, and/or social." Thus, the objectives and benefits of youth sport programs may be achieved or they may be undermined, depending on how well we match the activity to the child's developmental level. A brief discussion of (1) physical, (2) psychological and emotional, and (3) social considerations follows.

Physical Considerations

The battle lines are well defined concerning the healthfulness of organized sports on young bodies. One side cites the established benefits of exercise in developing and maintaining physical fitness (Parker and Bar-Or 1991) and asserts that the physical training and stress imparted in youth sports develops strong bodies and a healthful attitude toward exercise and competition (Gilliam 1978; Corbin 1987; Gabbard and Crouse 1988). The other side claims that the importance of winning in youth sports and the physical stresses and strains endured to achieve victory are dangerous to growing young bodies and minds (Coe 1986).

Many critics point to damage in growing arm bones from throwing curve balls, knee and neck damage in football from practice drills that are patterned after college and professional drills, and overtraining in swimming. Supporters of youth sports reply that these practices are being controlled and are not so damaging as has been thought.

The documented evidence concerning physical damage to young athletes is not conclusive. Martens (1978) reports varying degrees of elbow damage in Little League pitchers, although he concludes that any risk is too much and that throwing curves should be eliminated until bone growth is completed. Francis et al. (1978) found former Little Leaguers had fewer elbow problems a decade later than nonplayers. They criticize the psychic pressures of Little League, but dismiss as myth the concern over long-term elbow damage. At least one group of medical specialists (Jackson et al. 1978) believes that in football the shearing effect on growing bones from such activities as blocking with the forearm and tackling the lower leg may be more damaging to youngsters than the twisting effect of throwing a curve in baseball.

Stanitski (1993) identifies two scenarios that tend to invite overuse injuries in young athletes. "One is when an inadequately conditioned athlete experiences high musculoskeletal demands. A second situation is when an extremely fit athlete overtrains" (1993:87). In a discussion of injuries including Little League elbow, Osgood Schlatter disease (an injury of the tibial tubercle, below the knee), Sever's disease (an injury of the heel and Achilles tendon), and stress fractures, Stanitski cites the following causative factors:

(1) *Equipment* (e.g., adult-sized balls, excessive racket string tension, hand paddles used for training in swimming, gymnastic dowel grips, inadequate footwear, and rigid or uneven floors, mats, and running surfaces).

(2) *Anatomy* (e.g., congenital or developmental anatomic variances, abnormal alignment, and incorrect mechanics of the foot and ankle).

(3) *Coordination* (i.e., attempting skills too advanced for one's genetic or developmental ability to control).

(4) *Training* (especially tissue overload from incorrect throwing, jumping, or running motions, excessive enthusiasm, or adult pressure).

A 1968 statement of guidelines for children's sports from AAHPER is more accepting of the chances for injury in children's sports than its earlier (1952) position. The existence of physical risks to youngsters is admitted in the 1968 position statement, but considered to be within an acceptable range. The more recent AAHPER statement places emphasis on the importance of proper training and age-size-ability grouping, good equipment, and the availability of a physician during games and practices (Rarick 1978). These ideas are reinforced in a 1979 AAHPERD publication, approved by the American Academy of Pediatricians, which presents the professional judgment of the National Association for Sport and Physical Education regarding competition for children (AAHPERD 1979).

Bailey (1978) and Gabbard and Crouse (1988) report research indicating that sports are not detrimental to developing hearts and bodies. However, Bailey (1978:104) adds the following warning:

> The body of a youngster is a wonderful machine with sophisticated built-in controls and instinctive limits defining sensors that in the absence of externally created pressures functions very effectively. It is the external pressure, particularly pressure exerted by ambitious adults . . . that should be a cause for concern.

New Zealand track coach Arthur Lydiard claims that the only situation in which a child should be allowed to run a distance longer than a sprint is cross-country, away from the pressure created by observers (Bailey 1978). If a stopwatch or any mode of comparison is used, however, an implicit observer exists along with a potential pressure on youngsters to live up to adult expectations of them.

The common denominator in most of these reports of the physiological effects of youth sports seems to be that the activities generally are fine for youngsters, but the extent to which kids are pushed, overtly or covertly by adults, may cause physical and emotional harm.

Psychological and Emotional Considerations

Childhood is a developmental process that involves more than just physical growth. Psychologically and emotionally, children's cognitive skills are maturing, their personalities are emerging, their values are being clarified, the priorities of their needs are shifting, and their self-concepts are becoming solidified (Fowler 1981; Cratty 1983). Participation in organized sport programs can be helpful to this developmental process, or it can be harmful. The cognitive complexity of sport can be a challenging and enjoyable source of learning for young minds, or it can be frustrating and defeating. Organized sport can offer youngsters opportunities to pursue activities that suit their own interests and personalities, or it can pressure them into activities that reflect what others want for them rather than what they want for themselves. The sport experience can provide children with numerous avenues for success, recognition, and a positive self-concept, or it can be a source of defeat, rejection, and a sense of personal failure. It can be fun and exciting, or it can be miserably stressful.

Pease and Anderson (1986) found evidence that children form lasting attitudes toward sport competition before the age of 10. It is important, then, that early sport experiences be emotionally positive ones. What does this entail? First, the sport experience should include careful, patient *instruction*. Children learn more slowly, in smaller amounts at a time, and more by imitation than adults do (Hardy 1986). The "coaching" of children in sport should be more a matter of teaching and demonstration than of refining skill or detailing strategy. Second, sport participation should be truly and entirely *voluntary*. Even young children display preferences for some activities over others (Fowler 1981). These patterns of individuality represent the emerging of unique personalities; they should be encouraged by a focus on variety and diversity in choices of activities (including the choice *not* to participate in organized sport). Third, the sport experience should include frequent *praise and encouragement* (Fowler 1981; Hilgers 1988). Children need the approval of adults, and they are highly sensitive to criticism (Fowler 1981; Cratty 1983). Adult pronouncements of success or failure, worthiness or unworthiness, are a major determinant of self-esteem in children's developing self-concepts. Positive reinforcement focused on children's efforts and the improvement of skills can make the sport experience a self-affirming one for every participant (Hilgers 1988).

Finally, the sport experience should put children under *no more stress than they can handle*. Numerous authors (Passer 1982; Smith and Smoll 1982; Cratty 1983; Roberts 1986; Bird and Cripe 1986; Hilgers 1988) have discussed the high levels of stress which are typically involved in youth sport competition, as well as the difficulty that many children have in coping with those levels of stress. Although competitive situations naturally produce suspense, performance anxiety, and the risk of failure and disappointment, such inherent stress need not have negative or debilitating consequences. Self-motivated athletes in a supportive environment do not necessarily exhibit excessive anxiety (Feltz, Lirgg, and Albrecht 1992). In fact, much of the stress of organized youth sport is imposed from without and is avoidable. Coaches and parents are two major sources of unnecessary stress and should be counseled on how to reduce their contribution to such stress (Lombardo 1982; Smith and Smoll 1982). Some authors (Smith and Smoll 1982; Bruns and Tutko 1986; Hardy 1986; Weiss 1991) also recommend that relaxation, meditation, and other stress-reduction techniques be taught to young athletes to help them cope with the pressures of youth sport.

Social Considerations

Contradictory research findings tend to undercut arguments for both the helpful and harmful social effects of participation in youth sports. On the positive side, it is argued that competitive youth sports provide a strong medium for socialization, although review of empirical findings provides little evidence that either positively or negatively valued behaviors and attitudes are learned through sport (Stevenson 1975; Leonard 1988). Studies do indicate, however, that, for both boys and girls, physical competence and athletic skill are positively correlated with children's status in their peer group (Gross and Johnson 1984; Evans and Roberts 1987).

Youth Sport: Reality versus Escape.   Among the very young, all who want to play usually are allowed to play, whether or not the activity is organized. In youth and adolescence there is increasing restrictiveness in organized sports, where the better players are selected and allowed to continue. In adult life only the best are allowed to participate at the highly organized level, although rather loosely organized sports are available through adult recreational programs.[2] Webb (1969:178) believes this increasing restrictiveness in organized youth sports fosters social adjustment to the realities of adult life, where not everyone can do what he or she wants. Webb believes that organized children's and adolescents' sports foster "committed and effective participation in [the adult social] system." Supporting evidence is found in children's increasing concern for success as they grow older and their decreasing concern over fairness (Mantel and Vander Velden 1974). Maintaining a concern for social values of play such as honor, tolerance of others, generosity, and courage as one grows older is, according to Webb (1969:178), "sophomoric and even moronic."

Whether or not you agree with Webb's strong statements, it is important to understand his reasoning. Webb is implying that the world of youth is idealistic and can afford to be. The adult world, however, is not so fair and

---

[2]Ironically, opportunities for moderate involvement in organized competitive sports are less available for adolescents than they are for adults since most adult leagues do not allow players under 18 years of age.

Reprinted with permission of Kathryn LeMieux.

equitable, and the problems encountered in youth sports help youngsters to adjust to the selective achievement orientation of the world, at least as it is perceived by Webb and many other adults.

The other side of the "sports as adjustment to adult reality" issue is no less persuasive and firm in its belief that youth sports should not only be inclusive of all but should also serve the playful needs of children in an environment removed from the pressures of impending adulthood. By progressively eliminating and discouraging youngsters from participation, this side argues, organized sports produce significant social and psychological harm (Orlick and Botterill 1975; Devereaux 1976; Underwood 1975; Bruns and Tutko 1986). One of the detriments of organized youth sports is its effect on malleable young egos. Roger Kahn (1971:90) writes eloquently of the effect of failure on men playing a boy's game. How much more painful might this passage be for a boy (or girl) with significantly less perspective, playing a youngster's game?

> Defeat, particularly dramatic defeat, confirms our worst image of ourselves. We are not effective, after all, not truly competent, not manly in crisis. We may dismiss a coach, but we cannot elude blame. We have failed. Everyone knows we have failed. We know it ourselves. We stand naked, before an unflattering mirror, hearing hard laughter, that includes our own.

The Mirror of Appraisal.   Self-evaluation in sport tends to be socially derived (Zajonc 1965; Smith and Smoll 1982; Horn 1985). Reflected appraisal may come from coaches, parents, or peers and is particularly important to the recipient when coming from these significant others (Chambers 1991; Brustad 1992; Weiss and Duncan 1992). Reflected appraisal may be subtle and unintentional (e.g., a smile or lack of one), but nevertheless has a great impact on the youngster's self-evaluation. Scanlan (1978) adds that youngsters are quite aware of the social evaluation potential in competitive situations. Given this awareness, and their own real or imagined inadequacy and doubts, many youngsters may prefer not to participate in sports, thus losing a major outlet for youthful energy, a source of friends, and group identity.

Morality Training.   Sportsmanship, fair play, equality, and democratic ideals fall within the category of moral-social benefits of sport. This morality-imbuing function of youth sports, however, is another area of concern having two opposing and strongly felt perspectives, with little hard evidence to support either side.

Chissom (1978) and Guttmann (1988) believe that organized youth sports programs are not providing a moral environment that will benefit either the youngsters or society. In support of this belief, Bredemeier et al. (1986) found that for both girls and boys, participation in contact sports was positively correlated with relatively immature moral reasoning. Chissom (1978) suggests that competitiveness and morality may be mutually exclusive, since competition by its nature establishes adversary relationships, rather than promoting good will, harmony, and trust. Along this line of reasoning, Webb (1969) believes that the simple, uncomplicated ethic of victory as a desirable state carries more weight than complicated and fuzzy concepts such as equality and sportsmanship.

Cheating even in such All-American events as the Soap Box Derby (Woodley 1974) supports this belief that in competition, ethics plays second fiddle to victory. The fact—or belief—that "everyone else cheats" seems to be sufficient justification for one's own cheating in the seemingly more important pursuit of success.

Far from condemning competition as undermining moral development, those who see morality training as an important social function of sport suggest that this can best be accomplished in the presence of intense competition. Kroll (1975) and Martens (1978) suggest that morality training would be meaningless and ineffectual in the absence of a strongly competitive environment. If ethics are to be nurtured (and they believe this should be the case), it must be done in an atmosphere where there is a real choice to be made, something valuable that is in jeopardy. In pure play and less competitive games and sports environments such as pickup contests, little is at stake, so it is relatively easy for youngsters to decide ethical issues in favor of sportsmanship, equality, and honesty. There is no real sacrifice, since victory and defeat carry little weight or lasting importance. However, for youngsters to make moral decisions favoring fairness (e.g., not cheating and allowing everyone to play) when a valued victory, rewards, and status are at stake is a highly desirable socialization outcome of youth sports and indicates a well-developed or developing morality.

This benefit could be nurtured by those in charge of youth sports. Chambers (1991) argues that sport experiences that include opportunities for negotiation and dialogue can enhance moral development. Some adults, however, foster behavior such as cheating and lying by modeling these behaviors or through explicit directives to youngsters (Guttmann 1988). Some critics of youth sports point to competition as the root of the problem when competition merely provides a pregnant medium for children's moral growth (Stein 1988). It is important to note, however, that while moral development is stated often as a social goal and benefit in youth league charters, seldom is there any means to pursue this goal or an evaluation of how well it is met.

Little League Syndrome

Despite an apparent general preference of Little League players for fun over achievement (although this certainly needs to be verified more widely), a malady may exist in players' attitudes and behaviors in and toward sports called Little League Syndrome (Figler 1981). To the extent that it occurs, Little League Syndrome may appear in three forms. One form, Wash-Out Symptom, is characterized by discouragement from continued participation and avoidance of situations that might lead to criticism from adults. Roberts (1978) describes a similar condition as "sports-learned helplessness."

Many youngsters leave organized sports simply because they fail to make the team. A substantial, if not overwhelming, body of research, however, supports the existence of Wash-Out Symptom as a problem by finding that many youngsters who leave competitive sports do so because of a belief that winning is overemphasized and enjoyment in playing is not emphasized enough (McPherson, Guppy, and McKay 1976; Devereaux 1976; Orlick 1973; Orlick and Botterill 1975; Klint and Weiss 1986).

The second malady, Burn-Out Symptom, also results in the youngster ceasing to participate, but in Burn-Out Symptom this may stem from too much participation, success, and pressure at too early an age. The causes might be physical, psychological, or a combination of elements (Rotella, Hanson, and Coop 1991). The phenomenon of highly successful youngsters leaving their sport at an early age has long been recognized in such physically demanding and time-consuming sports as swimming and gymnastics. This may also occur, however, in the less physically taxing but equally emotionally demanding organized youth sports.

The third form, Superstar Symptom, has an opposite effect to the prior two maladies, but it is also harmful. The characteristics of this malady are an overly competitive attitude, compulsive seeking of comparisons with and domination over others, and a compulsive seeking of approval and reassurance in many aspects of the young athlete's life. Need for achievement and approval are certainly not states to be avoided; in Little League Syndrome, however, they may become overly compelling and maladaptive, particularly for the preadolescent age group.

In recent years there has developed some discussion and theoretical analysis of Burn-Out Symptom (Smith 1986; Coakley 1992). On the whole, though, we still need significant testing to determine the extent that Little League Syndrome exists in all of its three forms. Criticism of Little League baseball and many other organized youth sports is sufficiently extensive that we should have some idea of what symptoms we are looking for and some framework to place them in, rather than simply making random criticisms. Analyzing behaviors of coaches and parents is certainly important. It is the effects on the attitudes and behaviors of youngsters, however, that is our real concern.

Kids' versus Adults' Needs in Youth Sports

It is estimated that as many as 80 percent of children drop out of competitive sport by the age of 12 (Roberts 1986). This is an appalling observation! Organized sports, populated by youth and run by adults, are in the potentially conflictive position of serving simultaneously the needs of two very different populations. Children want and need to express themselves, to behave spontaneously, and to test their physical and social abilities and limitations against other youth. Adults need to exercise control to better ensure the physical, psychological, and social development of youngsters. Children can tolerate far more chaos than can adults, while they care little if at all for the long-term benefits of sports participation. Because adults maintain control, however, organized youth sports tend to favor the needs of the adults rather than the youngsters.

Parents, Coaches, and Youth Sports

For children (both boys and girls), the most important reasons for participating in youth sports include improving skills and learning new ones, having fun, being challenged, and attaining physical fitness (Gill, Gross, and Huddleston 1983). Achieving competence and social approval are key goals (Roberts 1986). It appears to be crucial to the success of youth sport programs that adults avoid creating a conflict between these goals and their own objectives and expectations for youth sport.

A problem arises when some parents lose sight of other goals while becoming overly involved in satisfying their own needs for recognition (Lupo 1967; Waid 1979; McPherson 1982). In the process, they may create unhealthful anxiety (Dolan 1967; Bruns and Tutko 1986). The extent to which some adults will go to satisfy their needs for success through youth sports extends to illegal inducements and recruiting even at the junior high school and playground levels of competition (Lipsyte 1975; Guttmann 1988). Even supportive parents may develop conflicts between themselves over a child's athletic participation, and the resultant confusion can affect performance and even cause the child to drop out of participation (Rosenthal 1991).

While parental involvement—especially overinvolvement—certainly presents problems in Little League and other youth sports, a number of writers agree that coaches are the crucial element in whether youth sports are helpful or harmful to the players (Smoll, Smith, and Curtis 1978; Underwood 1975; Zarebsky and Moriarty 1978; Hilgers 1988). Smoll and Smith (1978), however, believe that most Little League coaches are maligned in their efforts and are better than their critics suggest. On the other hand, they suggest that coaches could do an even better job if they were trained to observe their own behaviors and if they had specific behavioral and social goals to aim for. In one study, coaches trained in these concerns tended to have players who displayed increased self-esteem over the course of a season, while coaches who did not have this training were associated with players whose self-esteem remained unchanged (Smoll and Smith 1978). More recent studies (Smith and Smoll 1990; Barnett, Smoll, and Smith 1992) reinforce this finding, indicating that children, especially those low in self-steem, respond most positively to supportive and encouraging coaches, and that training of coaches in desirable coach-athlete interactions has a positive effect on the self-esteem of young participants.

The Professional Model in Youth Sports

More study is certainly warranted concerning the perceptions, needs, and responses of youngsters to their sport experience. A clear impression projected by Little League and numerous other youth league activities, however, is one of a miniature model of big league professional sports. Both the structure of Little League baseball and its ambience is big league. The organization of Little League from the commissioner in Williamsport to local league officials to the "men in blue" follows faithfully the professional model of administrative and authoritative responsibility. The ladder of success in Little League parallels achievement in the big leagues, from pennants to playoffs to a nationally televised World Championship game, which, ironically, is more truly a *world* championship in Little League than in the big leagues. To round out the professional model, Little League also includes all-star games with gala pomp and circumstance.

The ambience could not be more professional, lacking only salaries, contractual hassles, and product endorsements. Contracts are, in fact, signed by players binding them to particular teams until their release is officially granted. (With the advent of free agency, professional athletes may have more freedom of choice than Little Leaguers.) Team names and uniforms in the professional image, along with many ritualistic trappings (such as playing of the national anthem and throwing out the first ball) add to the professional flavor. If bunting were allowed, the image of pint-sized professionals would be complete.

Ogilvie (1979) criticizes the professional model of youth league sports that stands in the way of a child-centered model. He suggests that a child-centered model, focusing on the intrinsic needs of youngsters to participate and to have fun, is more appropriate than a professional focus on achievement and success.

Brower (1979) suggests, however, that at some age the professional model in youth sports becomes at least somewhat more appropriate or acceptable. The key question here is at what point should we drop away the cloak of fun and games and make youth sports a learning experience for adult social reality? That is, at what point in youth sports does achievement and domination become more important than fun and fairness? The debate continues.

FIGURE 5.2 *Parental interference in youth sports has been severely criticized. Not surprisingly, however, it is the coach who has the greatest influence on the quality of experience youth obtain from sports. Training of youth coaches can increase the likelihood of a beneficial experience for the players. (Courtesy of Lynette Tanaka.)*

Alternative Models for Children's Sports

The focal point of the problems in youth sports is the issue of whether (or the extent to which) youth sports exist to serve the playful needs of children or to help assimilate them into a competitive society that operates with contingent morality. Should youth sports be a temporary sanctuary from adult pressures or should they be a forge on which youths are shaped and tempered for a world of adult competitiveness? Organized sport on the professional model is congruent with the "assimilation" side of this issue. Alternative models, however, serve the "playfulness" side of the issue. Often neglected by adults and thus made less legitimate in the eyes of youngsters, such alternatives are nevertheless authenticated by the call for reform in organized youth sport that has gained support in recent decades.

Transformations in Youth Sports

Little League and other organized youth sports began as responses to an atmosphere perceived not to be competitive enough for youngsters. Ironically, most of the suggestions for change in recent years have focused on reducing the extent or altering the form of competition in the lives of children. We will consider a few alternative approaches to youth sports.

The Youth Basketball Association.   The YBA is a league for preadolescent youth run through the YMCA and cosponsored by the NBA Players' Association, which requires each of its members to appear without pay at two YMCA clinics per year (McCartney 1976). During their clinics with YBA youngsters, the NBA players stress sportsmanship and skill development rather than competitive success. The rules, goals, and structure of the YBA de-emphasize competition and records of achievement.

Canadian Junior Ice Hockey.   Ice hockey is Canada's national game, probably even more so than baseball is America's national game. Junior hockey leagues, which exist as direct feeders to the professional game, are extensive in Canada. Because of the notoriety of Canada's junior hockey leagues for an aggressive (even hostile) and highly competitive level of play, Canadian sports officials, partly from parental pressure, have reassessed their goals and altered the objectives of youth hockey (Vaz 1974). Contrary to following the professional model from the time a youngster can skate and swing a hockey stick, as has been the case in most Canadian youth leagues, some leagues for younger players now forbid keeping score, much less maintaining standings and individual records (Tyler and Duthie 1979; Pooley 1979).

Youth Baseball.   Numerous suggestions for change have been directed at youth league baseball, with these changes primarily aimed at reducing the competitive pressure on youngsters (Gelfand and Hartmann 1978; Rarick 1978; Mayfield 1978; Smoll et al. 1978; Maggard 1978; Roberts 1978). Yablonsky and Brower (1979) suggest in particular that (1) the scorebook be eliminated, (2) players select coaches and umpire their own games, (3) every player on the roster bat in turn and share equal numbers of innings in the field, (4) more stringent restrictions be placed on innings pitched by a given player, and (5) an automatic base on balls be awarded for any breaking pitch. Kids will, of course, keep score in their heads, but the absence of an official record not only will allow them to de-emphasize the score, but will not afford parents and coaches a tangible means of comparing and manipulating youngsters.

Zarebsky and Moriarty (1978) see the crux of the problem less in the playing rules and more in the stated goals of Little League and how they are pursued. After an extensive six-year experimental study in Canadian Little League baseball, they suggest the following changes (note that some of these suggestions represent transformations of text while others focus on context):

1. Emphasize fun and socialization.
2. Conduct coaching clinics focused on social and psychological goals rather than on excellence.
3. Decrease emphasis on scoring and standings.
4. Eliminate scoring and standings from lower levels.
5. Eliminate all-star teams and championships at lower levels.
6. Increase local control.
7. Increase league competition and decrease tournament play.

8.   Distribute players based on age, size, skill level, and psychological needs while providing equal access to all interested players.
9.   Eliminate all disagreements with officials at lower levels of play.
10. Evaluate leagues on the basis of skill improvement and overall participation rather than on competitive success.

Normally, the most physically mature youngster in Little League becomes the pitcher. With the significant difference in maturation rate among youngsters close in age, the pitcher may dominate the game inordinately despite grouping by age.

If we were to find that pitching inordinately dominates Little League baseball games, pitching might be eliminated by use of one of the modern mechanical ball throwers. Not only could control be better assured for the direction of the pitches, but speed and trajectory could also be consistently maintained.[3] While throwing curves is considered a questionable practice for Little Leaguers, hitting curves is a skill that could be developed if a machine threw them. Speed of pitches could be tightly monitored and controlled, and leagues might be distinguished by the speed at which the machine is set rather than arbitrarily by age and size, neither of which is particularly relevant in noncontact sports.

Progression to more advanced leagues could be based more on performance than on age. For example, any player batting over .350 in the 40 MPH (speed of pitches) league would be required to move up to the 50 MPH league next year or at midseason. Any player under a certain standard would be required, or permitted, to move down a notch.

As girls' Bobby Sox softball develops widely, the same problem that exists in Little League could emerge. Fast-pitch softball is even more a pitcher-dominated game than is baseball. Thus, the pitching machine at the younger softball age groups could be considered as this sport grows in popularity.

We might expect, with a pitching machine, to see significantly more hitting, running, fielding, and throwing. A player could cover the pitcher's position as a fielder and players might rotate positions, playing at least one outfield, one infield, and one battery position each game. Those youngsters wanting to develop pitching skills could do so in practice or at home. There is no need to rush into pitching competition since control is the first thing that should be learned and a batter is irrelevant to developing control (an old auto tire works quite well as a target.)

In other team sports such as football, soccer, ice hockey, basketball, and field hockey, playing positions might also be rotated by regulation. This would ensure a more rounded sports experience for youngsters and would allow them wider experiences before becoming identified with and locked into a position.

Parallel or "House" Leagues.   Parallel leagues mean that for every highly competitive youth sports league, the adult sponsors would also be

---

[3]The twin wheel pitching machines are infinitely adjustable and much more controllable than the old sling action machines.

required to provide facilities and funds for youngsters who want simply to play the game in their own fashion without competitive pressure. Using baseball again as an example, every stadium provided for regular Little League activity would be accompanied by another field complete with backstop, bases, and mound for boys and girls whose interest is to "play" rather than to "work" at baseball. Coaches would be available, not to run practices or games, but to provide instructional clinics and to make sure that balls, bats, helmets, and catching gear were available. Since umpires and uniforms would be irrelevant, and balls could be used longer than in official games, the cost of the "parallel league" would be significantly less than the regular league.

No set schedule would be played; instead, games would be played at the youngsters' own discretion in pickup fashion and *by their own rules,* should they care to alter the regular rules. Not only would additional opportunity to play be provided, but also there would be an absence of competitive pressure, and the youngsters would be afforded the opportunity to experiment with their own playing techniques, imaginations, and ethics, aspects of growth sorely lacking in adult-run sports (Devereaux 1976).

A suggestion similar to parallel leagues has been made for Canadian junior hockey below the 14-year-old level (Pooley 1979). Windsor, Canada, already has a "house" league, in which standings are not kept, in addition to its competitive league (Tyler and Duthie 1979). Parallel or house leagues could also be adopted in many other sports. Pooley (1979) suggests that not only are kids' affective and developmental needs not met by highly organized and competitive sports, but their skill levels also suffer when emphasis in games is on outcome.

The reason that provisions should be mandated for such parallel opportunities for play is that the presence of a structured competitive league seems to make casual, pick-up type play somewhat less than legitimate. Adults should provide facilities and funds to make casual play legitimate in the eyes of those youngsters who cannot or will not join formal competition because of psychological aversion, slow development, lack of ability, or for those who simply do not care to play in adult-run, highly competitive leagues. (This might be attractive to delinquent youths or those who are bordering on delinquency and who may avoid structured and regulated play.)

A Bill of Rights for Young Athletes

In response to concerns such as those discussed in this chapter regarding youth sports, the Youth Sport Task Force of AAHPERD's National Association for Sport and Physical Education in 1977 drafted the following "Bill of Rights for Young Athletes":

1. Right to participate in sports.
2. Right to participate at a level commensurate with each child's maturity and ability.
3. Right to have qualified adult leadership.
4. Right to play as a child and not as an adult.

5. Right of children to share in the leadership and decision making of their sport participation.
6. Right to participate in safe and healthy environments.
7. Right to proper preparation for participation in sports.
8. Right to equal opportunity to strive for success.
9. Right to be treated with dignity.
10. Right to have fun in sports.

If sports are beneficial to youth, and if intense competition is not the only benefit to be derived from sports, then they should be available to all youth who are interested. Also, sports should be made more interesting and palatable to youths who have been turned off to or never have been interested in intense competition. These suggestions are not intended to be a panacea. They might, however, improve a highly questionable play and sports environment that currently exists for American youth. More attention needs to be paid to the various outcomes of youth competition. Greater effort could be directed toward attaining stated goals, and opportunities could be afforded for youth to experience different levels of play and competition.

Summary

The text of a game describes how the game is played; its context describes its significance within the culture. As children mature, both text and context undergo transformations, which may or may not be appropriate to the physical, psychological-emotional, and social status of the youngster. Organized youth sports have come under especially harsh criticism for the stress they have been known to impose on participants. Analysis of the literature reveals both advantages and disadvantages of organized competitive youth sports and suggests alternative transformations to maximize the benefits while minimizing the dangers.

References

American Alliance for Health, Physical Education, Recreation and Dance. 1979. *Guidelines for Children's Sport.* Reston, VA: AAHPERD.

American Association for Health, Physical Education, and Recreation Commission on Athletic Competition for Children of Elementary and Junior High School Age. 1952. *Desirable Athletic Competition for Children.* Washington, DC: AAHPER.

American Association for Health, Physical Education, and Recreation Commission on Desirable Athletic Competition for Children of Elementary School Age. 1968. Washington, DC: AAHPER.

Bailey, D. A. 1978. "Sport and the Child: Physiological Considerations." Pp. 103–12 in *Children in Sport: A Contemporary Anthology,* edited by R. A. Magill, M. J. Ash, and F. L. Smoll. Champaign, IL: Human Kinetics.

Barnett, N. P., F. L. Smoll, and R. E. Smith. 1992. "Effects of Enhancing Coach-Athlete Relationships on Youth Sport Attrition." *Sport Psychologist* 6:111-27.

Bateson, G. 1971. "The Message 'This Is Play.' " Pp. 261-66 in *Child's Play*, edited by R. E. Herron and B. Sutton-Smith. New York: John Wiley & Sons.

Berryman, J. W. 1978. "The Rise of Highly Organized Sports for Preadolescent Boys." Pp. 3-18 in *Children in Sport: A Contemporary Anthology*, edited by R. A. Magill, M. J. Ash, and F. L. Smoll. Champaign, IL: Human Kinetics.

Bill of Rights for Young Athletes. 1977. West Point, NY: Leisure Press.

Bird, A. M., and B. K. Cripe. 1986. *Psychology and Sport Behavior*. St. Louis: Times Mirror/Mosby.

Boutilier, M. A., and L. SanGiovanni. 1983. *The Sporting Woman*. Champaign, IL: Human Kinetics.

Bredemeier, B. J., D. L. Shields, M. R. Weiss, and B. A. B. Cooper. 1986. "The Relationship of Sport Involvement with Children's Moral Reasoning and Aggression Tendencies." *Journal of Sport Psychology* 8:304-18.

Brosnan, J. 1963. "Little Leaguers Have Big Problems—Their Parents." *Atlantic Monthly* 211(March):117-20.

Brower, J. J. 1979. "The Professionalization of Organized Youth Sports." *Annals of AAPSS* 445:39-46.

Bruns, B., and T. Tutko. 1986. "Dealing With the Emotions of Childhood Sports." Pp. 207-17 in *Fractured Focus: Sport as a Reflection of Society*, edited by R. E. Lapchick. Lexington, MA: D.C. Heath.

Brustad, R. J. 1992. "Integrating Socialization Influences into the Study of Children's Motivation in Sport." *Journal of Sport and Exercise Psychology* 14:59-77.

Chagnon, N. 1968. *Yanomamo: The Fierce People*. New York: Holt, Rinehart & Winston.

Chambers, S. T. 1991. "Factors Affecting Elementary School Students' Participation in Sports." *The Elementary School Journal* 91:413-19.

Chissom, B. S. 1978. "Moral Behavior of Children Participating in Competitive Athletics." Pp. 193-99 in *Children in Sport: A Contemporary Anthology*, edited by R. A. Magill, M. J. Ash, and F. L. Smoll. Champaign, IL: Human Kinetics.

Coakley, J. 1992. "Burnout Among Adolescent Athletes: A Personal Failure or Social Problem?" *Sociology of Sport Journal* 9:271-85.

Coe, P. 1986. "Endurance Training and the Growing Child." Pp. 32-43 in *The Growing Child in Competitive Sport*, edited by G. Gleeson. London: Hodder and Stoughton.

Corbin, C. B. 1987. "Youth Fitness, Exercise and Health: There Is Much to Be Done." *Research Quarterly for Exercise and Sport* 58:308-14.

Cratty, B. J. 1983. *Psychology in Contemporary Sport: Guidelines for Coaches and Athletes* (2nd ed.). Englewood Cliffs, NJ: Prentice-Hall.

Devereaux, E. C. 1976. "Backyard Versus Little League Baseball." Pp. 37-56 in *Social Problems in Athletics*, edited by D. Landers. Urbana: University of Illinois.

Dolan, J. P. 1967. "Parents of Athletes." Pp. 299-306 in *Motivations in Play, Games, and Sports*, edited by R. Slovenko and J. A. Knight. Springfield, IL: Charles C Thomas.

Evans, J., and G. C. Roberts. 1987. "Physical Competence and the Development of Children's Peer Relations." *Quest* 39:23-35.

Felshin, J. 1974. "The Social View." Pp. 177-279 in *The American Woman in Sport,* by E. W. Gerber et al. Reading, MA: Addison-Wesley.

Feltz, D. L., C. D. Lirgg, and R. R. Albrecht. 1992. "Psychological Implications of Competitive Running in Elite Young Distance Runners: A Longitudinal Analysis." *Sport Psychologist* 6:128-38.

Figler, S. 1981. *Sport and Play in American Life.* Philadelphia: Saunders.

Fowler, J. S. 1981. *Movement Education.* Philadelphia: Saunders.

Francis, R. et al. 1978. "Little League Elbow: A Decade Later." *The Physician and Sports Medicine* 6:88-94.

Gabbard, C. P., and S. Crouse. 1988. "Children and Exercise: Myths and Facts." *The Physical Educator* 45:39-43.

Gelfand, D. M., and D. P. Hartmann. 1978. "Some Detrimental Effects of Competitive Sports on Children's Behavior." Pp. 165-75 in *Children in Sport: A Contemporary Anthology,* edited by R. A. Magill, M. J. Ash, and F. L. Smoll. Champaign, IL: Human Kinetics.

Gill, D. L., J. B. Gross, and S. Huddleston. 1983. "Participation Motivation in Youth Sports." *International Journal of Sport Psychology* 14:1-14.

Gilliam, T. 1978. "Fitness Through Sports: Myth or Reality?" *Journal of Physical Education and Recreation* 49:41-42.

Gross, A. M., and T. C. Johnson. 1984. "Athletic Skill and Social Status in Children." *Journal of Social and Clinical Psychology* 2:89-96.

Guttmann, A. 1988. *A Whole New Ball Game: An Interpretation of American Sports.* Chapel Hill: University of North Carolina Press.

Hardy, L. 1986. "Psychological Stress and Children in Competition." Pp. 157-72 in *The Growing Child in Competitive Sport,* edited by G. Gleeson. London: Hodder and Stoughton.

Helanko, R. 1964. "The Birth Place of Sports." *Sosiologia* 2:58-62.

Hilgers, L. 1988. "Stress-Free Little League." *Sports Illustrated* August 22:90-91.

Horn, J. 1977. "Parent Egos Take the Fun Out of Little League." *Psychology Today* September:18.

Horn, T. S. 1985. "Coaches' Feedback and Changes in Children's Perceptions of Their Physical Competence." *Journal of Educational Psychology* 77:174-86.

Hurlock, E. B. 1971. "Experimental Investigations of Childhood Play." Pp. 51-70 in *Child's Play,* edited by R. E. Herron and B. Sutton-Smith. New York: J. Wiley & Sons.

Jackson, D. et al. 1978. "Injury Prediction in the Young Athlete." *American Journal of Sports Medicine* 6:6-14.

Kahn, R. 1971. *The Boys of Summer.* New York: Harper & Row.

Klint, K. A., and M. R. Weiss. 1986. "Dropping In and Dropping Out: Participation Motives of Current and Former Youth Gymnasts." *Canadian Journal of Applied Sport Sciences* 11:106-14.

Kroll, W. 1975. "The Psychology of Sportsmanship." Paper presented to the American Association for Health, Physical Education, and Recreation, Atlantic City, NJ.

Leonard, W. M. II. 1988. *A Sociological Perspective of Sport* (3rd ed.) New York: Macmillan.

Lipsyte, R. 1975. *Sportsworld.* New York: Quadrangle.

Lombardo, B. J. 1982. "The Behavior of Youth Sport Coaches: Crisis on the Bench." *Arena Review* 6:48-55.

Lupo, J. 1967. "Case Study of a Father of an Athlete." Pp. 325-28 in *Motivations in Play, Games, and Sports,* edited by R. Slovenko and J. A. Knight. Springfield, IL: Charles C Thomas.

Maggard, B. 1978. "Avoiding the Negative: Blue Jeans Baseball." *Journal of Physical Education and Recreation* 49:47.

Mantel, R. C., and L. Vander Velden. 1974. "Relationship Between the Professionalization of Attitudes Toward Play of Pre-adolescent Boys and Participation in Organized Sports." Pp. 172-78 in *Sport and American Society: Selected Readings,* edited by G. Sage. Reading, MA: Addison-Wesley.

Martens, R. 1978. "Kids' Sports: A Den of Iniquity or Land of Promise." Pp. 201-16 in *Children in Sport: A Contemporary Anthology,* edited by R. A. Magill, M. J. Ash, and F. L. Smoll. Champaign, IL: Human Kinetics.

Mayfield, L. 1978. "Introducing Youngsters to Organized Sports." *Journal of Physical Education and Recreation* 49:44-45.

McCartney, R. J. 1976. "Basketball Players Relax in the YBA; All the Stress Is on Fun." *Wall Street Journal* March 22:1,19.

McPherson, B. D. 1982. "The Child in Competitive Sport: Influence of the Social Milieu." Pp. 247-78 in *Children in Sport: A Contemporary Anthology,* edited by R. A. Magill, M. J. Ash, and F. L. Smoll. Champaign, IL: Human Kinetics.

McPherson, B. D., L. N. Guppy, and J. P. McKay. 1976. "Social Structure of the Game and Sport Milieu." Pp. 161-200 in *The Child in Sport and Physical Activity,* edited by J. G. Albinson and G. M. Andrew. Baltimore: University Park Press.

Michener, J. A. 1976. *Sports in America.* New York: Random House.

Ogilvie, B. 1979. "The Child Athlete: Psychological Implications of Participation in Sport." *Annals of AAPSS* 445:47-58.

Orlick, T. D. 1973. "Children's Sports: A Revolution Is Coming." *CAHPER Journal* 39:12-14.

Orlick, T., and C. Botterill. 1975. *Every Kid Can Win.* Chicago: Nelson-Hall.

Parker, D. F., and O. Bar-Or. 1991. "Juvenile Obesity: The Importance of Exercise and Getting Children to Do It." *The Physician and Sportsmedicine* 21:87-88, 91-92, 95-98, 104-06.

Passer, M. W. 1982. "Psychological Stress in Youth Sports." Pp. 153-77 in *Children in Sport: A Contemporary Anthology,* edited by R. A. Magill, M. J. Ash, and F. L. Smoll. Champaign, IL: Human Kinetics.

Pease, D. G., and D. F. Anderson. 1986. "Longitudinal Analysis of Children's Attitudes Toward Sport Team Involvement." *Journal of Sport Behavior* 9:3-10.

Pooley, J. C. 1979. "An Alternate Model to Reduce Competitiveness in Sports for Youth." *Review of Sport and Leisure* 4(2):65-88.

Ralbovsky, M. 1974. *Lords of the Locker Room.* New York: Wyden.

Rarick, G. L. 1978. "Competitive Sports in Childhood and Early Adolescence." Pp. 113-28 in *Children in Sport: A Contemporary Anthology,* edited by R. A. Magill, M. J. Ash, and G. L. Smoll. Champaign, IL: Human Kinetics.

Roberts, G. C. 1978. "Organized Sports for Children—Social Psychology of Sport Dimensions." *Proceedings: NCPEAM* 169-74.

Roberts, G. C. 1986. "The Growing Child and the Perception of Competitive Stress in Sport." Pp. 130-44 in *The Growing Child in Competitive Sport,* edited by G. Gleeson. London: Hodder and Stoughton.

Rosenthal, D. 1991. "The Impact of Family Conflict on the Junior Athlete." Pp. 138-42 in *Sport Psychology: Proceedings of the Maccabiah-Wingate International Congress,* edited by G. Tenenbaum and D. Eiger. Netanya, Wingate Institute: The Emmanuel Gill Publishing House.

Rotella, R. J., T. Hanson, and R. H. Coop. 1991. "Burnout in Youth Sports." *The Elementary School Journal* 91:421-28.

Scanlan, T. K. 1978. "Social Evaluation: A Key Developmental Element in the Competitive Process." Pp. 131-47 in *Children in Sport: A Contemporary Anthology,* edited by R. A. Magill, M. J. Ash, and F. L. Smoll. Champaign, IL: Human Kinetics.

Schwartzman, H. B. 1978. *Transformations: The Anthropology of Children's Play.* New York: Plenum.

Sherif, M. 1958. "Superordinate Goals in the Reduction of Intergroup Conflict." *American Journal of Sociology* 63(4):349-56.

Smith, R. E. 1986. "Toward a Cognitive-Affective Model of Athletic Burnout." *Journal of Sport Psychology* 8:36-50.

Smith, R. E., and F. L. Smoll. 1982. "Psychological Stress: A Conceptual Model and Some Intervention Strategies in Youth Sports." Pp. 178-95 in *Children in Sport: A Contemporary Anthology,* edited by R. A. Magill, M. J. Ash, and F. L. Smoll. Champaign, IL: Human Kinetics.

Smith, R. E., and F. L. Smoll. 1990. "Self-Esteem and Children's Reactions to Youth Sport Coaching Behaviors: A Field Study of Self-Enhancement Processes." *Developmental Psychology* 26:987-93.

Smoll, F. L., and R. E. Smith. 1978. *Psychological Perspectives in Youth Sports.* Washington, DC: Hemisphere Publishers.

Smoll, F. L., R. E. Smith, and W. Curtis. 1978. "Behavioral Guidelines for Youth Sports Coaches." *Journal of Physical Education and Recreation* 49:46-47.

Stanitski, C. L. 1993. "Combating Overuse Injuries: A Focus on Children and Adolescents." *The Physician and Sportsmedicine* 21:87-88, 91-92, 95-98, 104-06.

Stein, J. U. 1988. "Competition—A Developmental Process." *Journal of Physical Education, Recreation and Dance* March:30-32.

Stevenson, C. L. 1975. "Socialization Effects of Participation in Sports: A Critical Review of the Research." *Research Quarterly* 46:287-301.

Strong, J. M. 1992. "A Dysfunctional and Yet Winning Youth Football Team." *Journal of Sport Behavior* 15:319-26.

Tyler, J. K., and J. H. Duthie. 1979. "The Effect of Ice Hockey on Social Development." *Journal of Sport Behavior* 2(1):49-60.

Underwood, J. 1975. "Taking the Fun Out of Games." *Sports Illustrated* November 11:87–98.

Vaz, E. 1974. "What Price Victory?: Analysis of Minor League Players' Attitudes Toward Winning." *International Review of Sport Sociology* 9:33–55.

Voigt, D. 1974. *A Little League Journal.* Bowling Green, OH: Bowling Green University Popular Press.

Waid, R. 1979. "Child Abuse: Reader's Forum." *Runner's World* September:16.

Wallace, A. F. C. 1970. *Culture and Personality.* New York: Random House.

Webb, H. 1969. "Professionalization of Attitude Toward Play among Adolescents." Pp. 161–78 in *Aspects of Contemporary Sport Sociology,* edited by G. Kenyon. Chicago: The Athletic Institute.

Weiss, M. R. 1991. "Psychological Skill Development in Children and Adolescents." *Sport Psychologist* 5:335–54.

Weiss, M. R., and S. C. Duncan. 1992. "The Relationship Between Physical Competence and Peer Acceptance in the Context of Children's Sports Participation." *Journal of Sport and Exercise Psychology* 14:177–91.

Woodley, R. 1974. "How to Win the Soap Box Derby: In Which Craftsmanship Abets the Passion for Success to Produce a Tale of Moral Confusion." *Harper's Magazine* August:62–69.

Yablonsky, L., and J. J. Brower. 1979. *The Little League Game.* New York: Times Books.

Zajonc, R., 1965. "Social Facilitation." *Science* 149:269–74.

Zarebsky, J., and R. Moriarty. 1978. "SIR/CAR Studies Longitudinal Changes in Little League Baseball and Implications for Youth Sports." AAHPER Update December:13.

CHAPTER 6

Sport on the American Campus

School and sports. Academics and athletics. They seem naturally paired within American systems of education. Their relationships often seem like a marriage, sometimes tempestuous, but generally providing a union in which each partner seems to complement the other. This is particularly true in their espousal of cultural values, attitudes, and mores, such as competitiveness, achievement, perseverance, and respect for rules, authority, and group goals, whether the group is operationally defined as team, school, town, state, or nation.

In 1954 a national commission on education listed the following benefits that should accrue to people who participate in school sports (Educational Policies Commission 1954:1):

- emotional maturity
- social competence
- learning to win and lose
- obeying rules
- fair play
- discipline
- egalitarian values
- competitiveness

- health and happiness
- moral values
- building character
- sportsmanship
- teamwork
- democratic process
- meritocratic values
- cooperativeness

Nearly half a century later, we may not be so naive as to believe that all of these behavioral and attitudinal traits are actually learned in school sports. While much has happened in school sports to leave us cautious about the

FIGURE 6.1 *Athletics in schools and colleges has the potential to provide a student-centered learning experience that is a natural extension of the educational curriculum. (Photo by Yvonne M. Soy.)*

presumed social and socialization benefits of sports participation, beliefs still prevail that these benefits accrue to those who strive for athletic success.

Much of amateur sport in America, unlike other nations, is housed in systems of formal education. How consistent is sport with the purposes and functions of schools and schooling? While academics and athletics may march together, are they in step? Are they symbiotic and compatible in their values and elicited behaviors? Does sport serve the mission and goals of schools, or has it become the tail that wags the dog?

In the *pure description* phase of our analysis, we will examine the development of organized sport on the American campus and the history of related abuses that continue to cause concern. Our *evaluative commentary* will focus on the debate between those who maintain that student-athletes are getting a fair exchange for their talents and energy and those who argue that student-athletes are being unfairly exploited. We will evaluate these opposing views at both the high school and college levels, addressing as we go such areas of *social critique* as the purpose of education vis-à-vis the role of athletics programs, and power relationships involving coaches and athletes. Finally, we will suggest several areas of *social engineering* that show potential for reducing exploitation.

FIGURE 6.2 *The coach is a pivotal influence on whether athletes derive the intended educational benefits from school-based sports. (Photo by Faith Barbakoff.)*

It would be easy to accept the apparent symbiosis between sport and schooling since that is part of our lore. However, to understand the relationship we must address some concerns that make the marriage less than perfect. We should note that the compatibility of sport and schooling might vary at the several levels of education and competition.

The History of School-Based Sport: How Sports and Athletics Became Linked to Schools

Sports and athletics are now so intertwined with American schooling that it may seem as if it has always been so. During most of this nation's first century, however, the Puritan-spawned work ethic was instrumental in degrading physical play activity (Lewis 1966; Betts 1974). Linking of sport and American education did not begin until the Civil War era, although their affinity was such that the bond was quickly cemented. Because America's heritage is predominantly British, we must look to Great Britain for the origins of sport as an integral part of American education.

British Origins of School Sports

Early 19th-century British educators tolerated school sports rather than suffer student dissension. Thomas Arnold, headmaster at Rugby School from 1828 to 1842, however, permitted student self-government, which, as we might expect, led to increased play, games, and sports activities in the school setting. Students organized, financed, established rules for, and coached their own sports. These included rowing, cricket, football (soccer), and the ball-carrying version of soccer called rugby (Hackensmith 1966).

Thomas Hughes, a student at Rugby School, later chronicled the sporting life of English schoolboys in *Tom Brown's Schooldays,* published in 1857. The book would eventually play a monumental role in popularizing sport in American schools. The Clarendon Commission of the 1861 Parliament claimed that playing cricket and football generated social values such as team spirit and group loyalty.

By mid-century, headmasters had come to accept school sports if for no other reason than their value in fatiguing the boys and thus helping to reduce disciplinary problems. The dormitory or "house system" living arrangements at English schools also fostered athletic competition providing natural intramural rivalries (Hackensmith 1966).

Muscular Christianity

Muscular Christianity, a term describing the moral benefits to be gained from sports participation, was central to the development, growth, and legitimization of school sports. As historian John Lucas relates (1976:69–70),

> The Victorian age gave rise to a masculine concept of "a good sportsman" in the very largest sense of that phrase. It combined the widely accepted view of male physicality, honor, patriotism, religiosity, and a kind of Grecian discretionary balance. . . . The package [was] labelled "muscular christianity." Hughes defines a member of this fraternity as one "whose creed is to fear God, and walk 1000 miles in 1000 hours."[1]

Lucas (1976:66) adds, "The English must surely take the credit (or blame) for grafting onto play, values and outcomes of the highest order, and rapidly placing compulsory participation in school competitive games among its highest priorities."

Lucas suggests that the Muscular Christianity movement, particularly as it appeared through school sports, took hold because of societal forces created by the Industrial Revolution. The growing manufacturing society generated

---

[1]Lucas quotes Hughes from *Tom Brown at Oxford* (1861:126).

rising expectations, and many of the nonconformist religions that followed perceived sport as a "manly, moral, even mystical pastime" (Lucas 1976:66–67).

A prophetic warning note was sounded, however, by none other than Thomas Hughes, the trumpeter, if not the father, of Muscular Christianity in schools. Hughes warned, "These things 'athletic games' are made too much of nowadays, until the training and competition for them outrun all rational bounds." Hughes's warning was sounded over a century ago, in 1873 (Lucas 1976:72). Another early criticism of school sports was voiced by Sir Leslie Stephen, himself an accomplished athlete. Commenting on the character of college athletes, Stephen noted (1870), "Breathe a little more intellect into the masses of bone and muscle, and they could be really creditable persons."

The American Connection

Borrowing from the Muscular Christianity movement in Great Britain, a number of influential American clerics (including Henry Ward Beecher, Henry C. Wright, and Thomas Wentworth Higginson) preached a doctrine of physical health, vigor, and spiritual regeneration to combat the severe antiphysical Puritan ethic. Their ideas were adopted at Harvard, Yale, Princeton, and Amherst—institutions that influenced the curriculums and campus life of other schools.

The interest in sport on these campuses spread to schools in the West and South. If it was acceptable for college students, the nation's future leaders, to play games and sports, why not others? Was it not sport that helped to develop societally and morally laudable attitudes, values, and behaviors? According to Lewis (1966:42),

> Although the Muscular Christianity phase of social reform directly affected only a small segment of the population, its total impact must be measured in terms of the end results—the establishment of a new American institution.

The Growth of American School Sports and Athletics

Early Development of Sports in High Schools

Organized sports in high schools were modeled on collegiate athletic programs, particularly in their student-generated and student-directed beginnings. Later they were taken over by faculty and then influenced by boosters when their popularity grew. According to Spears and Swanson (1978), organized school-based high school sports programs flourished early in cities and later spread to rural schools.

At the turn of the century girls also participated in sports, especially basketball, although girls' sports programs tended to be intramural rather than interscholastic. An early proponent of sports for girls, Senda Berenson, expressed disdain for hypercompetitiveness as early as 1901: "The greatest element of evil in the spirit of athletics in this country is the idea that one must win at any cost—that defeat is an unspeakable disgrace" (Spears and Swanson 1978:188). Berenson was describing the Lombardian Ethic half a century before Vince Lombardi expressed it. Despite Victorian notions of feminine frailty, it gradually became understood that physical activity was healthy for females (Gerber et al. 1974).

High school girls' programs benefited from the increasing popularity of sport for both males and females through the "Roaring Twenties," but emphasized participation (process) rather than winning (product). (Chapter 12 discusses this topic further.)

The Beginning of Collegiate Athletics: Regatta

American intercollegiate athletics was born in 1852 with a series of rowing contests between Harvard and Yale. Rowing, or regatta, was originally organized, funded, and conducted by students. As its popularity grew, aided by much newspaper attention, university administrators took control of the sport. They exploited the public interest in regatta by hiring professional coaches who recast the formerly student-focused teams into athletic programs that served the public relations and financial needs of the institution (Lewis 1967).

As an extracurricular activity for the benefit of students and an economic enterprise for institutional aggrandizement, regatta quickly grew beyond the ability of school administrators to control it. Its popularity was promoted further by the construction of railroad spurs to take spectators from cities out to lakes and rivers suitable for rowing.

Many questionable and abusive competitive practices developed that later appeared in collegiate football, such as hiring tramp athletes. Within 25 years, regatta germinated, grew, and withered as a major sport on American college campuses (Lewis 1967). Regatta provides a prototype of the symbiotic link between amateur athletics and economic interests within and beyond the collegiate institution.

The Development of Football as the Major Exploitable Sport

Football became popular first in elite colleges, then spread to the broader American society (Green 1986). As its popularity grew, it became increasingly difficult for those who held to the sportsmanship ideals of Muscular Christianity to keep football in moderate perspective.

Football was established in the collegiate consciousness by the 1880s. Football's value to institutions of higher learning was predicated not simply on having a team to coalesce students and alumni but on victory. Early on, "Coaches . . . were hired to win rather than develop all-around, healthy young men" (Green 1986:205). By 1885 the Harvard faculty had had enough of the derogation of Muscular Christian ideals and the increasing levels of violence in pursuit of victory, banning football on their campus (Menke 1977). Interest in football was so widespread, however, that the sport returned the very

FIGURE 6.3 *Knute Rockne is best known as head football coach at Notre Dame. He was not only instrumental in bringing Notre Dame to prominence, but, with Gus Dorais, innovated the first effective passing strategy in football. (Courtesy of the University of Notre Dame.)*

next year, and Harvard resumed its position as the nation's dominant college team. While football had become firmly established in college life, the means and goals of the sport were widely and publicly debated (e.g., Roosa 1894; Hart 1890; Bowen 1908; Eliot 1908; Cooper 1914; Foster 1915).

Baseball as well as regatta were supplanted by football during this era as the major collegiate sport. Both continued as intercollegiate sports, as well as track and field and the new sport of basketball. However, during the decades surrounding the turn of the century, football was king on college campuses.

The Origin of Self-Governance in Collegiate Athletics
The year 1905 was a low point in an era of football brutality, culminating in the purportedly purposeful mauling of Swarthmore's great lineman Bob

The Center of the Line
Maxwell   Markle   James J. Lippincott

FIGURE 6.4 *Bob "Tiny" Maxwell, who anchored the Swarthmore line, was the object of the Penn team's efforts in their 1905 game. A picture of Maxwell emerging from the game bloody and battered inspired President Roosevelt to consider banning football. (Courtesy of Swarthmore College.)*

Maxwell by the University of Pennsylvania team. Momentum tactics such as the Flying Wedge and the moving defensive line (with defenders taking a running start at the stationary offensive line) had been wreaking havoc on players for nearly a decade. When leather helmets and other protective equipment were introduced to prevent injuries, it wasn't long before they were used as offensive weapons.

President Theodore Roosevelt, imbued with belief in the benefits of Muscular Christianity, felt that college football had grown beyond the ability of college administrators to control it. He was about to sign a bill abolishing the playing of football at colleges (not unlike the laws that make bullfighting and cockfighting illegal) when the presidents of several universities met with him, promising to establish their own intercollegiate organization to oversee sports, especially football. The result in 1906 was formation of the Intercollegiate Athletic Association (IAA), with 39 members serving as the first national governing body of college athletics. The IAA was created by college administrators expressly to control the vicious and brutal tactics then rampant in college football.

In 1910 this organization became the National Collegiate Athletic Association (NCAA), expanding its mission to cover all unethical conduct in collegiate athletics. A social control agency, though, is only as effective as the sanctions it is empowered to levy. Since the NCAA agency lacked the power to punish transgressors, compliance to regulations for the first four decades of the association's existence was more a matter of conscience (socialization) than social control. It was not until 1952 that the NCAA voted itself the power to punish violations of its rules.

Veblen: An Early Critic of Intercollegiate Athletics

Thorstein Veblen in 1918 published a diatribe on American universities called *The Higher Learning in America,* in which he railed against the presence of athletic programs on college campuses and the power they held. He called athletic events "side shows," the purposes of which were to provide "a certain, highly appreciated, loud tone ('college spirit') to the student body; and so it is felt to benefit the corporation of learning by drawing public attention" (Veblen 1965:119). Scholarships given athletes he called "threadbare subterfuges" for professionalism (1965:124).

Veblen felt that athletics, along with other forms of extracurricular "traffic" such as fraternal and social organizations, marching bands, and drama societies, might have their place in counterbalancing and making more tolerable the drudgery of academic pursuit. However, the drawbacks of the profit focus of football far outweighed this small benefit. Veblen's criticism of athletics represented an anachronistic 19th-century argument in a rapidly commercializing 20th-century world.

The Savage Report

By the mid-1920s the problems of ethical abuses and commercialization of college athletics had become epidemic, leading the Carnegie Foundation for the Advancement of Teaching to commission an investigation. The research was conducted by Howard Savage, who in 1929 published an extensive report, called simply *American College Athletics.*[2] Savage found college athletic programs failing to teach the social benefits that were touted as a reward for participation (1929:294):

> Such moral qualities as courage, initiative, and the group of characteristics included in the term "sportsmanship" are probably not inculcated by athletics at all. If through inheritance a young man or woman possesses them in whatever degree, athletic contests and games may effectually exercise them and through use strengthen them. The most that can be justifiably claimed is that athletics tend to develop in participants certain moral qualities that are already present.

---

[2]Savage studied 112 colleges and 18 high schools, interviewing school presidents, alumni, faculty, and athletes.

Savage (1929:297) cautioned, however, that even if some positive values such as courage and initiative might carry over from sport to life situations, so also may less salutary behaviors and values, such as "dishonesty, deceit, chicanery and other undesirable qualities," be reinforced in sport.

Hiring ringers—professional "tramp" athletes who went from school to school changing their names to sell their services—was only one of a long list of charges leveled at college football in the decades around the turn of the century. The list also includes extravagant expenditures, dishonesty, brutality, gambling, professionalism, demoralization of academic work, bad influence on high school athletics, employment of the "wrong kind of men as coaches," recruiting and subsidizing, and the "general corruption of youth" (Savage 1929:25).

Coaches and administrators denied these accusations, pointing to the

> bodily vigor and mental alertness of athletes, their manly character, their loyalty, and the qualities of leadership that their own [i.e., the coaches'] participation in athletics had engendered. [They] scoffed at the notion that any college athlete could be recruited or paid (Savage 1929:25).

Note that recruitment and subsidization of athletes were considered abhorrent, and well into the century's third decade these practices were vigorously denied by coaches and administrators. Yet Savage reported finding over 70 percent of the colleges he studied offering some form of athletics-related subsidy. Today, of course, athletic grants are permissible for both sexes, while virtually every college that fields athletic teams recruits players.

Prior to the 1970s, women's intercollegiate sport escaped most of the criticism faced by men's athletics, primarily because public interest in women's programs and institutionalized pressures to win were virtually nonexistent. Women's intercollegiate competition has existed since the 19th century. Until recently, however, women's programs were run by and for women and in accordance with a participatory, educational philosophy. They neither provided income from gate receipts nor prepared athletes for professional sport careers and so were free of the stresses that lead to corruption. Thus, criticisms such as those in the Savage Report were leveled only at men's intercollegiate athletics.

The Pattern of Deviance Continues

Recall from Chapter 4 that anomie—a sign of critical weakness in a social system—occurs when a significant number of system members accept the society's primary goal (winning) while rejecting the means (laws, rules, mores) that the society claims as standards of behavior (Merton 1938). Societal breakdown will increase if the society persists in rewarding only those who achieve goals, irrespective of the means used to attain them.

During the 25 years between 1952 and 1977, the NCAA brought charges of rulebreaking 993 times and found guilt in 548 of those cases (NCAA Enforcement Program, Part 2 1978). Between 1980 and 1988, the NCAA found 92 of its member institutions guilty of violating the association's rules, including 49 of 106 Division I schools (Lederman 1989). If we can conceive of Division I athletics as a small town and the NCAA as sheriff and judge (agents of social control), this is tantamount to 46 percent of the citizenry being tossed in jail over a 10-year period. This ignores the crimes of violence, drugs, theft, gambling, etc., that have occurred that NCAA regulations do not address. Perhaps it is clearer now why we distinguished between criminals and outlaws.

Why, with this long history of abuses and rules violations, hasn't the "social system" of intercollegiate athletics either crumbled under the weight of widespread transgression or altered its rules (means) so that fewer members of the system are defined as deviant (i.e., accommodated to modern "reality" rather than adhering to archaic standards)? Perhaps the answer lies in the lucrative fiction of high ethical standards. If college athletics were admittedly professional with only tangential interest in education while competing for Dear Old Siwash, the system would relinquish its mystique of being something other than professional entertainment. No longer would college athletics be the best of its own category. If college athletes were paid and academic eligibility rules were done away with, then the system of college athletics would openly become no more than the "minor leagues" for the NFL, the NBA, pro tennis, etc. Loss of its distinct amateur character (whether or not that character is fictitious), would endanger the luster of intercollegiate athletics and perhaps its audience. This speculation may explain why agencies charged with the welfare of the college athletics social system[3] continue in their struggle to maintain standards that have been grossly violated for decades.

The Issue: Exploitation or Exchange in School Athletics

> As an eighth grader at Marcus Garvey Elementary School in Chicago, Rashard Griffith should be enjoying a relatively simple life. Instead, he and his mother have spent the last eight weeks screening phone calls and dodging an expanding contingent of recruiters and reporters.
>
> Griffith's problem is also his gift: he is a talented 6-foot-10-inch basketball player who, at the age of 14, has been the object of an intense recruiting battle among Chicago high school coaches.[4]
>
> Elaine Griffith considered changing her number after one caller asked for "Joe." When she said that no one named Joe lived in her home, the caller asked, "Well, is there anyone in the house who's 6'10"?" (Rhoden 1989:C1)

Student-athletes receive fair exchange for their efforts and time when they develop the learning skills, knowledge, and career direction that other students attend college for and tend to obtain. They are exploited if they fail to gain an education while competing for and representing their school. Of course, some athletes may experience self-exploitation if they fail from laziness or disinterest to obtain the education that is made available (Figler and

---

[3]Along with the NCAA, governance is in the hands of the National Association of Intercollegiate Athletics (NAIA) and the National Junior College Athletic Association (NJCAA).

[4]In Chicago students are allowed to attend the high school of their choice.

Figler 1991). Because of the long and sordid history of school athletics, we must always consider the extent to which those associated with intercollegiate athletic programs foster or abet the exploitation of athletes.

Is a school-based athletic program "successful" when it produces winning teams despite failing to fulfill its educational promise to the student-athletes who comprise those teams? This question suggests another more philosophical question: Do school athletics programs exist for their own perpetuation, glorification, and profit or for the athletes' development and upward social mobility? From the functionalist perspective, school sports foster group solidarity, identity, and affirmation of group goals, outcomes that serve the collectivity. Schafer (1973:186) contends that "scholastic and intercollegiate athletics are likely to socialize the athlete . . . toward the technocracy, the established society, and the corporate state." For individuals who work within the system, shared values—perseverance, achievement-orientation, teamwork—may be fostered and affirmed. The rewards offered by the system for compliance—recognition, social status, the possibility of upward social mobility—are available in exchange for athletic striving. From this functionalist perspective, held by coaches, administrators, and many athletes, school sports are consistent with the purposes of the educational system, including upward mobility.

The conflict-coercion perspective sees school sports as exploiting athletes, generating a fruitless experience and empty sports consciousness that robs attention and energy from real social problems such as institutional oppression, while those who control school sport profit from it (Hoch 1972). School-based athletics is seen as coercing individuals into accepting a system that exploits them. Agents of the system—coaches, administrators, boosters, and anybody who profits from the system—foster this coercion by using athletes' desire to play as a tool for manipulating them toward behavior that favors victory and profit for the school, often at the expense of education and graduation. In the following two sections, we will discuss first high school sports, then intercollegiate athletics to determine whether and how athletes are receiving fair exchange or are being exploited.

High School Sports: Exchange or Exploitation?

The National Association for Sport and Physical Education (NASPE) in 1993 formulated a position statement on exploitation of high school athletes, defining exploitation as "any activities, actions, or outcomes that detract from an athlete's opportunity to participate in safe and healthful practices and contests" (NASPE 1993:I). Included among a list of exploitative conditions are the following:

- Recruiting athletes or influencing them to transfer to another school for the purpose of athletic competition.
- Use of drugs to enhance athletic performance.

- Retaining or "redshirting" athletes to gain maturity for an additional year of eligibility.
- Interstate televising of all-star contests and playoffs.
- Requiring or permitting injured athletes to participate in practices or contests.
- Uncontrolled dependence on corporate sponsorship for the support of interscholastic programs.
- Falsifying academic records to gain or retain eligibility.
- Conducting practices and games beyond the limitations prescribed by the controlling organization.
- Soliciting funds or products by athletes to defray the costs of participation in interscholastic athletics.
- Requirements or restrictions on the out-of-season experiences of athletes.

Laws, rules, and position statements such as this are means of social control formulated when socialization is deemed inadequate to protect the welfare of individuals or of institutions. There appears, then, to be a problem—or several problems—in ensuring that high school athletes receive fair exchange for their efforts.

Having Fun in High School Sports

Although the NASPE position statement does not address it, one "benefit" that we might consider as appropriate for adolescents engaged in sports is to have fun. When weighing fun against "serious" goal pursuit in virtually any organized physical activity patterned after and played with sportive rules, participants are likely to find seriousness carrying considerably more weight than fun, even if participants just want to have fun. In Czikszentmihalyi's (1975) classic study, he found high school basketball players less into the "flow" of their sport and more anxious about it than were rock-climbers, chess players, and those involved in musical composing.

Part of the seriousness of organized sport at the secondary level may be attributed to the purported academic, social, and physical benefits to participants. Considerable research over several decades has been devoted to testing these benefits.

Academic Benefits

During the 1970s and into the 1980s, many high school jurisdictions dropped minimal athlete eligibility requirements in the belief that such requirements removed the incentive for undermotivated or disadvantaged youth from attending high school. Sport was the carrot that would bring them back into the educational system. Another argument that led to dropping eligibility requirements was that sports participation in the school setting was considered a right rather than a privilege. By 1983 fewer than 100 school districts among 16,000 (less than 1 percent) across the United States held high school athletes to minimal academic performance standards (Lapchick 1987–88). In time, however, it became clear that an inordinate number of youth were concentrating mainly, if not solely, on sports while giving little effort to their schooling. By 1987 only five states (Maine, Maryland, Minnesota, New York, and Vermont) had not enacted some new minimal academic standards for high school athletes (Lapchick 1987–88). It would seem that academic leaders no longer are willing to accept the "dumb jock" stereotype and now—or, once again—are requiring more academic performance from high school athletes rather than accepting less.

The relationship between playing interscholastic sports and academic achievement in high school has received considerable attention over the years, with research indicating that athletes seem to get at least slightly better grades than nonathletes (Stevenson 1975; Hanks and Ekland 1976; Schafer and Armer 1968; Phillips and Schafer 1971; and Luther and Alvin 1977). Focusing on female high school athletes, Hickey (1992) found significantly higher grade-point-average than for female nonathletes.

Generally, there is little overlap between the skills and knowledge transmitted through the academic curriculum and those developed in extracurricular sport, although participation in athletics is believed to enhance work habits. However, high school athletes may compare favorably to nonathletes on grades for several reasons that have little to do with personal characteristics. Schafer and Armer (1968) suggest that one or more of the following factors may lead to an elevation in grades of high school athletes:

(1)   special assistance received by athletes
(2)   eligibility requirements for sports participation mandating that athletes maintain minimal academic standards
(3)   a preselection factor eliminating nonambitious students from the athlete pool
(4)   special status and privilege afforded to athletes

More cynical observers suggest that the grades received by athletes are deceptively inflated by such unscrupulous practices as athletes taking easy courses that keep them eligible but don't satisfy graduation requirements, teachers (either voluntarily or under pressure) assigning higher grades to athletes than they have earned, and the altering of athletes' grades before they appear on report cards (Dietz 1989).

Aspirations and Goals

Male high school athletes seem to benefit from having higher expectations or aspirations to attend college than nonathletes (Rehberg and Schafer 1968; Schafer and Armer 1968; Spreitzer and Pugh 1973; Luther and Alvin 1977; and Picou 1978). Hartzell and Picou (1978) report the same tendency toward higher aspirations among female athletes as compared to female nonathletes. Aspirations to

TABLE 6.1 *Participation in Sports at Three Levels**

Percentages relate to high school participants

	High School	College	Major Professional
Football	910,407	66,750 (7.3%)	1,260 (0.1%)
Basketball (Male)	521,023	23,750 (4.6%)	324 (0.1%)
Baseball	430,401	42,000 (9.8%)	700 (0.2%)
Tennis (Male & Female)	275,096	13,750 (5.0%)	@500 (0.2%)
Golf (Male & Female)	167,398	9,950 (6.0%)	@350 (0.2%)

*Data are 1992–93 figures obtained from the National Federation of High School Associations, the National Collegiate Athletic Association, the National Association for Intercollegiate Athletics, and the National Junior College Athletic Association (which does not include California Community Colleges). College participation figures are approximate as NAIA provided number of teams and average squad sizes.

attend college, however, may be a function of desire to remain in competitive athletics more than a reflection of an interest in a college education or the ability to thrive academically (Rehberg and Schafer 1968; Picou 1978).

What of the aspirations of high school athletes to become professional athletes? Is it better for student-athletes to strive toward an extremely remote chance of success (such as a professional athletic career) or toward a less seductive but more attainable type of success (such as in business, medicine or science, teaching, or social services)? "In high schools, kids pursue the dream, not aware that the chance of becoming a lawyer or doctor is much greater than that of becoming a National Basketball Association player," says Richard Lapchick, of the Institute for Sports in Society (Alfano 1989).

One seldom achieves without aspirations, but the distance between one's aspirations and the likelihood (or unlikelihood) of attaining those goals becomes problematic if and when the aspirants have no intermediate goals on which to fall back. This appears to be a problem particularly for black high school athletes who, according to one study (Lee 1983), aspire to become professional athletes at more than twice the rate of whites (47 percent to 22 percent). Perhaps even more telling was that 14 percent of the *nonstarter* black high school athletes surveyed aspired to become professional athletes. For athletes of any race who pursue and achieve an education, failure to achieve a professional athletic career should not leave them devoid of other acceptable options.

Socialization

Schooling teaches students to accept social norms, while the schooling process clarifies those norms for specific situations and circumstances (Dreeben 1968). This does not mean, however, that a norm learned in one setting necessarily transfers or generalizes to other settings. For example, competitiveness, which we presume is taught through sport and which is fostered relentlessly in American schools through the grading system, may not generalize to the individual's life beyond school. While the American economic system is primarily competitive, many Americans earn a wage or salary performing cooperatively within an organization.

The competitive environment of the playing field presents a set of circumstances very different from that of the classroom, despite their both appearing within the school setting. Although in both sports and classrooms individual excellence is assessed, failure can be shared collectively within a team but must be shouldered individually in the classroom. Success and failure, however, are more public in sport than in the classroom, which adds stress in the sport setting (Dreeben 1968). Nevertheless, even the relatively private failure in the classroom can be crushing if it reinforces one's self-perception as an intellectual outsider ("dumb jock"), frequently prompting athletes to retreat from academic competition, convincing themselves and each other that it is not important.

Still, athletics in the school setting can provide similar socialization to that occurring in the classroom. Striving or achievement-orientation is supported in both settings. Respect for authority also is fostered in each setting, although that becomes problematic to the extent that the socializing agent or role model—teacher or coach—condones or exhibits cheating behavior. Playing by the rules is tacitly encouraged in both athletics and academics, although this may be reinforced in terms of learning to use rules to one's greatest advantage, even to the point of bending or breaking the rules. Perhaps, at best, high school sport provides the opportunity to learn appropriate attitudes and values.

It is an article of faith that sports keep young people off the streets and acceptably occupied. High school athletics are presumed also to socialize participants away from deviant or delinquent behavior. Research in this area generally supports this belief (Schafer 1969; Buhrmann 1977; Landers and Landers 1978; Segrave and Chu 1978; Segrave and Hastad 1982).

Social Status

Male high school athletes often enjoy elevated social status in school and their community. In a classic study conducted during the late 1950s, James Coleman (1961) found among selected Midwestern high schools that athletic prowess is the most important factor relating to high social status among adolescents. About 15 years later, Eitzen (1976) again found athletes afforded high status in high schools. More recently, Thirer and Wright (1985) corroborated the same finding among male adolescents, indicating an even stronger pull of athletics as a source of male popularity in high school relative to other sources of status. (See Table 6.2.) The high status afforded athletes tended to decline as age increased, with higher family socioeconomic status, and in larger schools (Eitzen 1976; Thirer and Wright 1985).

TABLE 6.2 *Ranking of Criteria Males Use to Rate Popularity of Males* *

	Mean Rankings		
Criteria for Status	Thirer/Wright (1985)	Eitzen (1976)	Coleman (1961)
Be an athlete	2.20	2.20	2.20
Be in the leading crowd	2.21	2.15	2.60
Be a leader in activities	3.01	2.77	2.90
Make high grades, honor roll	3.38	3.66	3.50
Come from right family	4.05	3.93	4.50

Scale = 1–5; lower scores yield higher ranking

*Data from Thirer and Wright 1985:167.

Thirer and Wright (1985) and Feltz (1979) also considered the place of athletics in social status among female high school students.[5] In both studies athletics ranked low in the female status hierarchy, placing fifth of six options in the Thirer/Wright report and fifth of seven options in Feltz's study. In fact, Feltz reports that clothes were more important than athletics as status criteria to female adolescents.

While we can conclude that athletic participation seems to yield high social status among adolescents, this is not consistently true across the spectrum of American high schools. If there is a constant over the three decades from Coleman's study to the work of Thirer and Wright, it is the increase in the importance of being "in the leading crowd" to adolescents (Thirer and Wright 1985), although it is likely that each group may have defined "leading crowd" differently. More recent research (Chandler and Goldberg 1990) found high school boys in upstate New York identifying both outstanding athlete and outstanding student as desired roles, while girls identified with outstanding student and member of a leading peer group.

Certainly some questions remain concerning the "exchange" benefits of high school athletics, and such benefits—or liabilities—will vary from one situation to the next. However, research leads us toward a general conclusion that by the criteria of academic record, socialization, and social status, high school athletes tend not to be exploited.

---

[5]Coleman's and Eitzen's studies did not consider female athletics. In the 1950s, when Coleman gathered his data, there was little opportunity for athletic involvement among females. During Eitzen's study, athletic opportunities were increasing for girls, although the Title IX mandate to provide sports for girls had not taken full effect.

Intercollegiate Athletics: Exchange or Exploitation?

Scandals and efforts at reform in collegiate athletics over the prior two decades suggest that the question of exploitation or exchange for college athletes is less clear than it has been for high school athletes. The Knight Commission, the NCAA's own President's Commission, and the Amateur Athletic Foundation of Los Angeles were formed to address numerous problems within intercollegiate athletics, not the least of which is the academic progress and achievement of athletes.

Academic Progress

Until 1991 studies of the academic performance of college athletes tended to focus on single institutions. It was difficult to generalize these findings to a nationwide scale as the definitions of variables, such as graduation rate, differed between schools, even ranging widely within a particular institution. The graduation rate for football players at the University of Nebraska, for example, was calculated as 47.9 percent, 59.6 percent, 68.6 percent, 70.3 percent, *or 92 percent*, depending on which criterion was used (Eitzen 1987–88).[6]

Several studies over the years have indicated that athletes' academic performance does not suffer from their participation in intercollegiate athletics (Stecklein and Dameron 1965; Hanks and Ekland 1976; Braddock 1981; Jacobs 1983; Henschen and Fry 1984; Wulf 1985; Schurr, Wittig, Ruble, and Henriksen 1993). This contrasts with other studies concluding that college athletes do not fare as well academically as nonathletes (Goldaper 1974; Harrison 1976; Purdy, Eitzen, and Hufnagel 1985; Messner and Grossier 1982; Sutherland 1983; Vance 1983; Shapiro 1984; Adler and Adler 1985). Purdy, Eitzen, and Hufnagel (1985) measured several academic performance variables of athletes at Colorado State University through the 1970s. They found that

1. Athletes tended to have lower GPAs than the general student population.
2. Athletes in non-team sports tended to have higher grades and were more likely to graduate than those in team sports.
3. Scholarship athletes tended to achieve at a lower level than those not on athletic grants.
4. Athletes were admitted under special circumstances more frequently than nonathletes, and those admitted under these circumstances performed the poorest academically.

---

[6]The graduation figure depended on whether focus was on incoming freshmen given five years to graduate, only considered seniors who used full eligibility, included ultimate graduates from Nebraska or any other school attended later, or relied on "data" published in the University of Nebraska football recruiting brochure (the 92 percent graduation rate).

5. Revenue-producing sports harbored the greatest number of "problem" students.
6. Black athletes performed poorly throughout the range of indicators of educational achievement.

Shapiro (1984) found that while 80 percent of athletes entering MSU in 1953 graduated (compared to 45 percent of the general student body), only 61 percent of athletes entering in 1973 graduated (compared to 62 percent for the general student body). Thus, while the graduation rate of MSU students in general improved markedly over the years, the graduation rate of athletes fell sharply.

Female College Athletes.   Female college athletes have generally achieved at a higher level more consistently than male athletes (Mayo 1982; Jacobs 1983; Kiger and Lorentzen 1986; Birrell 1987–88). However, Blinde's (1989) meta-analysis indicated that the more women's athletics emulated the male Division I model, the more likely female athletes were to feel exploited, in sacrificing schoolwork, encouragement to take lighter course loads and unrealistic time requirements. Female athletes also felt exploited in patriarchal power relations and manipulation of their values by male coaches. Henschen and Fry (1984) also found that greater success in women's gymnastics at the University of Utah coincided with decreased academic performance. Yet, Meyer (1990) noted that female athletes at Michigan State University reported less academic conflict than female nonathletes with expectations for academic success in college increasing over time.

Black College Athletes.   Black male college athletes tend to fare poorly in college compared to white male athletes, black or white female athletes, and nonathletes (Spivey and Jones 1975; Edwards 1983; Naison and Mangum 1983; Eitzen and Purdy 1986; Kiger and Lorentzen 1986; *NCAA News* 1989c). Eitzen and Purdy (1986) attribute this to poorer preparation for college among blacks compared to whites and to coaches recruiting blacks with little attention to their academic background. One study suggests that in situations where education is not strongly reinforced, black athletes may lose whatever sense of ability to achieve they might have had over the course of their college years (Adler and Adler 1985). Of course, this could also be true of athletes of all races.

New Standards for Assessing Academic Performance

The absence of a standard means for comparison of graduation rates, along with a growing concern that college athletes were having their education undermined, led Senator Bill Bradley (Dem—New Jersey) and Representative Tom McMillen (Dem—Maryland), both of whom were All-America and NBA basketball players, to sponsor the Student-Athletes Right To Know Act. This

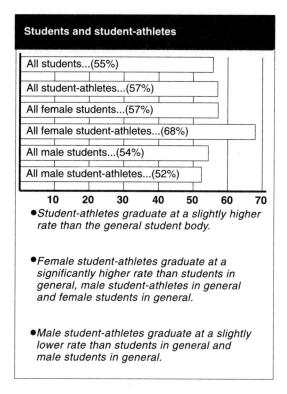

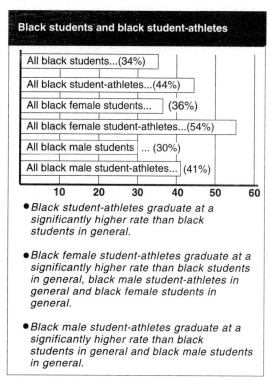

FIGURE 6.5   *1993 Composite NCAA Graduation Rates (From* NCAA News, *June 30, 1993, National Collegiate Athletic Association, Overland Park, KS.)*

legislation called for the federal government to oversee, gather, and disseminate graduate rates at universities, with NCAA Division I campuses targeted. To forestall such governmental intervention, the NCAA agreed to publish its own findings on graduation rates using standardized measures.

The results indicate that athletes in general tend to graduate at a rate comparable to nonathletes. Among the subgroup differences, female athletes tend to graduate at a higher rate, while among the black collegiate population, athletes graduate at a higher rate than nonathletes. (See Fig. 6.5)

NCAA Propositions 48 and 42: Setting Freshman Academic Standards

The NCAA has attempted to address the issue of academically underprepared athletes through its own legislation. What has become known in the popular media as "Proposition 48" was devised to limit eligibility for athletic competition during the freshman year in Division I or II schools to those who have met minimal standardized entrance test scores (a combined score of 700 on the SAT math-verbal or 15 on the ACT) or earned a minimum "C" average in 11 college prep high school courses. The standards have since been raised to include 13 core high school courses, in which a minimum grade point average of 2.50 is earned, and a 17 minimum score on the ACT college entrance test. Those who do not meet these requirements—"nonqualifiers"—are prohibited from competing during their freshman year; those who meet one of the requirements—"partial qualifiers"—may not compete but are eligible for financial aid.

Proposition 42, which would have denied participation in freshman-year sports to partial qualifiers was met with great dismay by the Black Coaches Association. Members felt that it weighed unfairly on black athletes and may even have been racist in its intent by reducing the number of black collegiate athletes. In protest John Thompson, basketball coach at Georgetown University, left the court during one of his team's games. The result of this controversy was repeal of Proposition 42 and introduction of a sliding scale—a below-minimum score on either GPA or standardized test scores may be balanced with higher than minimum on the other. This was intended to maintain the NCAA reforms demanding higher academic performance while paying attention to the cultural bias in standardized tests such as the SAT and ACT.

The purposes of such legislation are to give underprepared freshmen time away from the pressures of competition to improve their academic skills and to discourage those who are only interested in sports and have little interest in a college education. These rules impact more heavily on blacks than on whites, with 91.4 percent of those affected in the 1988–89 school year being black, according to an Associated Press survey of all Division I schools (Blum 1989).

The new standards, however, which allow six years to graduate, yielded a six percent higher graduation rates of athletes, with Proposition 48 "likely most responsible" for the increase ("Graduation Rates Jump by Six Percent" 1993). Broken down by subgroups, Table 6.3 shows the percentage increases in graduation rates following the application of Proposition 48, along with proportional changes. The data indicate that black and Hispanic athletes had by far the greatest proportional increases in graduation rates (26 percent and 21 percent, respectively).

Critics of Proposition 48 cast doubt on the raised graduation rates because the new standards eliminate or reduce the number of ill-prepared student-athletes. This purportedly diminishes the opportunity for higher education among those who most need it. However, junior college academic and athletic programs remain available to those ill prepared for four-year schools. This would seem to be the more appropriate route, either as a stepping stone to four-year schools or as an end-point for such student-athletes. The belief that ill-prepared student-athletes would benefit from exposure to those in four-year schools who have fully met entrance requirements overlooks the negative psychological effects of struggling students encountering daily those who are thriving.

TABLE 6.3 *Proportional Growth in Graduation Rates Following Proposition 48**

All Athletes	51 to 57%	(12% proportional increase)
Male Athletes	47 to 52%	(11%)
Female Athletes	61 to 68%	(11%)
Black Athletes	35 to 44%	(26%)
Hispanic Athletes	42 to 51%	(21%)
White Athletes	58 to 62%	(7%)
Football	45 to 51%	(13%)
Baseball	46 to 48%	(4%)
Men's Basketball	38 to 44%	(16%)
Women's Basketball	57 to 62%	(9%)

*Data from Kingston 1993:4.

Academic Performance of Athletes Compared by College and Conference

Recall that the federal legislation motivating the NCAA to gather and disseminate graduation rate data was couched as a "consumer" mandate so that athletes and their parents could more wisely select a school based on its recent history of graduating athletes. The premise here is that schools and conferences having a poor graduation record for athletes—and more specifically by sport, race, and gender—should be avoided.

The following data illustrate how widely the academic success of athletes can vary among schools and conferences. Figure 6.6 compares the graduation rates achieved by male athletes[7] in four conferences over a four-year period ("Graduation Rates of Scholarship Athletes in NCAA Division I" 1993:A36). The Big East clearly does quite well graduating its male athletes (67 percent, virtually identical to all full-time students), while the Big West appears to be particularly unrewarding to blacks, with only 15.7 percent of black male athletes graduating. The Big Ten is notable for scholarship athletes graduating at a higher rate than all full-time students (59.3 percent to 52.7 percent) and for black male athletes graduating nearly 10 percent more often than the average for all black male students.

Comparing individual schools can be even more revealing. The four schools shown in Table 6.4 were selected from the *1993 NCAA Division-I*

[7]This particular conference-focused report considered only male athletes.

Big East
Football Conference

8 members, 6 responded

All full-time student	67.7 %
All scholarship athletes	63.7
White male students	68.1
White male athletes	67.5
Black male students	42.5
Black male athletes	43.0

Big Ten Conference

11 members, 9 responded

All full-time students	52.7 %
All scholarship athletes	59.3
White male students	62.6
White male athletes	60.6
Black male students	33.7
Black male athletes	43.2

Southeastern
Conference

12 members, all responded

All full-time students	52.6 %
All scholarship athletes	45.7
White male students	50.9
White male athletes	51.7
Black male students	33.1
Black male athletes	26.4

Big West Conference

10 members, 9 responded

All full-time students	46.3 %
All scholarship athletes	38.3
White male students	47.3
White male athletes	35.3
Black male students	20.7
Black male athletes	15.7

FIGURE 6.6   *Comparison of Four NCAA Division I Conferences on Graduation Rate of Male Athletes (From* Chronicle of Higher Education, *July 22, 1992, page A36. Chronicle of Higher Education, Washington, DC.)*

Graduation-Rate Report to illustrate variety in region, athletic achievement level, and academic quality. California State University–Sacramento recently joined Division I as a scholarship granting athletic program after decades as a nonscholarship, Division II school. Ohio State and Florida State are among the athletic elite nationally. Stanford University is among the best academic institutions and has also won several recent national championships in baseball and women's basketball.

Note in Table 6.4 the wide range in graduation rates of athletes who have used up their eligibility. At Stanford more than 9 in 10 athletes (92 percent) who had exhausted their eligibility graduated, while at CSU–Sacramento the likelihood of graduation seems closer to even (58 percent). Even more stark are the comparative graduation figures for the various sports. Note, also, the low academic achievement at CSU–Sacramento (28 percent of football players in the 1986 cohort graduated; no black players graduated) ranging up to 77 percent (and 64 percent of black players) graduating from Stanford. Further, 73 percent of Stanford baseball players graduated, while at CSU–Sacramento no baseball players graduated. At Stanford, 92 percent of its top-rated women's basketball team graduated (and 100 percent of its black players), while only 13 percent of CSU–Sacramento's women's basketball team graduated. The figures for Ohio State and Florida State range between these extremes.

TABLE 6.4 *Comparison of Athlete Academic Performance at Four Universities**

	CSU–Sacramento	Ohio St.	Florida St.	Stanford
Avg-yrs to Graduate: All Ss	5.0 yrs	4.9 yrs	4.7 yrs	4.3 yrs
S-As	5.0 yrs	5.0 yrs	5.0 yrs	4.6 yrs
Graduation % —Exhausted Eligibility	58%	88%	75%	92%
Frosh Cohort Grad %: All Ss	37%	52%	52%	92%
S-As	34%	62%	45%	84%
M/W S-As	31/36%	59/70%	42/49%	82/90%
(# of Ss): HS GPA/SAT: FB	(102):2.62/881	(80):2.68/820	(97):2.63/822	(90):3.53/1069
BB	(49):2.68/800	(24):3.00/875	(36):2.86/845	(16):3.65/1181
M-BKB	(11):2.38/913	(12):2.57/—	(14):2.42/796	(14):3.86/1059
W-BKB	(14):2.59/763	(13):3.62/—	(15):3.45/—	(10):3.64/1043
Most Freq. Major: 83/84	Bus./Mgmt.	Education	Bus./Mgmt.	SocSci/Hist
84/85	Bus./Mgmt.	Bus./Mgmt.	Bus./Mgmt.	SocSci/Hist
85/86	Bus./Mgmt.	Education	SocSci/Hist	SocSci/Hist
86/87	Bus./Mgmt.	Education	SocSci/Hist	SocSci/Hist
Grad % by Sport (Black S-A)				
FB	28% (0%)	52% (30%)	41% (33%)	77% (64%)
BB	0% (0%)	64% (100%)	29% (—)	73% (—)
M-BKB	20% (20%)	23% (29%)	30% (43%)	69% (75%)
W-BKB	13% (0%)	57% (50%)	50% (50%)	92% (100%)

*Composite data over four years; from the *1993 NCAA Division I Graduation-Rate Report.*

Clearly, Stanford attracts (and only admits) the cream of the college-bound athletes, and perhaps it is unfair to use Stanford as a standard. However, CSU–Sacramento also compares unfavorably with Ohio State and Florida State. This is not to point a finger of blame, as other institutions likely have similar problems graduating athletes. The issue is whether athletes at particular schools are likely to have a fair chance at "exchanging" their athletic efforts for a viable education. If the coaches or counselors are not fostering their athletes' education, or if they are admitting students who are so poorly prepared that they are doomed to failure, these athletes are being exploited.

The American Institutes for Research (AIR) in 1988 found among 4,083 college athletes, that 95.2 percent of Division I football and basketball players expected at the time of enrollment to earn a college degree, as did 92.8 percent of athletes in other sports. Also at time of enrollment, 23 percent of football and basketball players aspired to become professional athletes, an understandable goal for adolescents. However, when 21 percent of the seniors still hold this aspiration, while few actually have a chance at a professional playing career, it is apparent that reality assessment and career preparation are not being fostered among these athletes. Athletes may have less-developed and more unrealistic attitudes towards their careers than other students (McKinney 1991). A primary purpose of higher education is to prepare students for a realistic future. To the extent that this is not occurring, is this not evidence of exploitation?

Other findings in the AIR study indicate:

- Football and basketball players had significantly lower Scholastic Aptitude Test (SAT) scores than extracurricular students (883 to 990 average composite scores).
- Football and basketball players had significantly lower SAT scores than other athletes (883 to 919).
- Both groups of athletes have GPAs that are significantly lower than those of other extracurricular students.
- Football and basketball players in more successful athletic programs compared to those in less successful programs:
  –had significantly lower GPAs
  –were more likely to have found courses too difficult
  –were more likely to have received incompletes
  –were more likely to have been on probation
- Athletes have more learning resources available to them (e.g., athlete counselors and support programs), but were less likely to consider academics their top priority.

While the AIR report hesitates to call their findings suggestive of exploitation, Robert Rossi, a principal researcher for AIR, states (1989:13)

"Student-athletes do indeed perceive it is more difficult for them to be students first and to take advantage of the personal development and growth activities at college because of their participation in intercollegiate athletics."

Other Concerns of College Student-Athletes

Steroid Use by College Athletes

Another potential area for exploitation—whether self-imposed or encouraged by coaches—is the use of performance-enhancing drugs, most notably, anabolic steroids. Since banning and testing for steroid use, the NCAA (1993) found male athletes decreasing their use of the drug, while use by female athletes has increased. Table 6.5 details this disturbing trend.

Role Conflict for the Student-Athlete

Conflict or strain between the twin roles of athlete and student is another potential problem for college athletes (Coakley 1982). Role conflict occurs when we find ourselves regularly in situations in which behavior or attitudes expected in one role clash with those of another role. The AIR study (1988)

TABLE 6.5 *Reported Anabolic Steroid Use by NCAA Athletes**

Men's Sports	1985	1989	1993
Baseball	3.5%	2.2%	0.7%
Basketball	3.6	1.6	2.6
Football	8.4	9.7	5.0
Tennis	3.6	2.2	0.0
Track/Field	4.7	4.1	0.0
Women's Sports			
Basketball	0.0	0.8	1.5
Softball	0.0	0.0	1.7
Swimming	0.7	1.0	0.6
Tennis	0.0	0.0	2.7
Track/Field	0.0	1.2	2.7

*Data from *NCAA Sports Sciences,* Winter 1993:1.

indicated that 55 percent of football and basketball players and 38 percent of athletes in other sports felt that it was difficult to be regarded as a serious student by professors (compared to only 13.5 percent of students in other extracurricular activities). Both groups of athletes felt it difficult to achieve the grades they were capable of earning, and found it harder to keep up with coursework than did other extracurricular students. These findings suggest that there is conflict between the roles of student and athlete, at least at the NCAA Division I level.

But an individual's being in two conflictual roles does not necessarily mean that he or she will suffer. Following the adage that, "If you want to get a job done, ask a busy person," greater energy and production may result from the combined roles rather than the requirements of one role undermining the other. While time is a constant, this synergistic (sum greater than its parts) model suggests that efficient use of time is critical and that serious commitment can enhance one's use of time (Marks 1977; Lance 1987).

The "Jock" Identity. Identity with the student role and emotional commitment to it has been a problem since the inception of the "dumb jock" image, which emanates from any of the following:

- low intellectual ability compared to other students.
- poor academic preparation relative to school standards.
- jealousy on the part of nonathletes.
- feelings of inferiority among athletes.

Our discussion of Muscular Christianity revealed that the "dumb jock" image existed as early as the mid-1800s. Recently it was quantified in a study of prejudice toward university athletes (Engstrom and Sedlacek 1991). Whatever its source, the "dumb jock" identity can cause considerable role strain, particularly if one feels obliged or forced to associate only with athletes. This has been a particular problem at schools with athletic compounds, or "Jock Dorms," which will be phased out by 1996, according to recent NCAA regulations. In the climate of big-time sports, athletes are publicly lauded for one role (athlete) and privately derided for the other (student). The scandals in college athletics over the past couple of decades have not helped to alleviate whatever role conflict or strain exists for student-athletes (Sack and Thiel 1985).

"Jock" Crime.   Delinquent and illegal acts by collegiate athletes have also caused alarm in recent years (Kirshenbaum 1989; Telander and Sullivan 1989; Reilly 1989; Associated Press 1989; Gup 1989) at such highly ranked institutions as the Universities of Oklahoma, Colorado, Washington, and Arizona. Football and basketball players dominate the list of athletes implicated in crimes ranging from public drunkenness and disturbing the peace to drug abuse, battery, rape, and attempted murder. An atmosphere of permissiveness on the campuses of big-time athletic powers tends to communicate to athletes the message that the only behavior monitored and expected of them is performance in the athletic arena; everything else, including studying and obeying the law, is optional. Unwillingness of universities to control lawlessness among their athletes deepens the conflict between role expectations of the student-athlete.

The Reform Movement in College Athletics

Intercollegiate athletics have been rife with problems and scandals for a century. Given the potential for money and fame to be made (or lost), can we expect exemplary behavior from those who have so much at stake? Reform has already begun, though, with publication of graduation rates a major step. However, given the century-long history of ignoring the welfare of student-athletes and misalignment between the purported aims and the reality of college athletics, diligence is required by those who would bring about reform. In terms of social engineering, there are several changes that can improve the environment and outcomes of college athletics.

Academic Support Programs for Athletes.   Academic assistance programs designed for athletes have existed at some campuses for over a decade. They may include monitoring of academic progress, tutoring, monitored and sometimes mandated study sessions, course scheduling, career and personal counseling, remedial classes, and test assessment. These programs are designed not only to improve skills, habits, and self-perception of athletes, but also to help them become more invested in their student role (Figler and Griffith 1982; Gurney, Robinson, and Fygetakis 1983; Snyder 1985; Figler 1987–88).

The effects of these programs have varied widely from positive results (Weber, Sherman, and Tegano 1987; Fletcher and Mand 1988) to negative (Ewing 1975; Naison and Mangum 1983; Monaghan 1986). A problem inherent in institutions providing special counselling to athletes is that institutional needs—e.g., to keep athletes eligible for competition—will hold sway over the athletes' needs for getting a good education and graduating, that is, exploitation over exchange. Exchange is more likely to occur through these support programs when they are housed in student services centers rather than reporting to and funded by the athletic department (Figler 1987–88).

Faculty Oversight. The faculty or academic senate on each campus should assess the academic performance of athletes at their institution on a regular basis (Weistart 1987; Figler 1987; Knapp and Raney 1987; Frey 1987–88). For reasons as yet unclear, faculty tend to be loath to adopt this task until a crisis hits their campus (Lederman 1987).

Presidents Re-Taking Command of Athletics. Ultimate control is in the hands of each school's president or chancellor, who makes all policy decisions on his or her campus. Problems within athletics began when presidents abdicated their role, handing decisions to athletic directors and sometimes to booster organizations. Campus presidents, along with their faculty, need to determine the athletics agenda on their own campuses instead of leaving that to athletics personnel and boosters (Padilla 1989). Presidents could retake command by simple fiat, although for a while some would have to withstand the displeasure of coaches, athletic administrators, and boosters.

Athletic Accreditation and Tenure for Coaches. If campus accreditation were tied to a "clean" athletic program, particularly one that graduates a representative proportion of athletes (including major sport athletes, black athletes, etc.), then CEOs would more likely govern their own athletic programs instead of farming that task out to those who represent athletic interests more than academic interests.

> *"If the basketball team has a 3.000 grade-point average and graduates everyone, and the coach goes 10-17, there would be a tremendous amount of heat on me to fire him. Anyone who says that's not true is a liar."* (Rudy Davalos, Athletics Director, University of New Mexico, quoted in the *NCAA News*, December 22, 1993, p. 4)

Coaches realize that their jobs depend primarily, if not exclusively, on producing winning teams; it is understandable (though not excusable) that winning is their highest priority. With the security provided by tenure, coaches could more easily broaden their goals, sacrificing victories for the health, growth, and education of their athletes when necessary. A recent study of presidents of NCAA Division I schools, along with 107 athletic directors and head football coaches, showed them favoring the use of graduation rates in evaluating coaches, although not counting more than 40 percent (Waggoner, Ammon, and Veltri 1993).

State Legislation. "The Texas Senate, fed up with the state's history of NCAA recruiting violations, adopted a bill March 6 [1989] that would make it a felony to bribe high school athletes to attend a particular college or university" (*NCAA News* 1989a:5). Twenty-seven states had legislation pending in 1989 designed to control abuses in athletics, an encouraging trend for those who see college athletics as repairable. Among these were 15 bills addressing anabolic steroids, 9 dealing with athlete agents, 4 concerning athletic scholarships, and 2 treating academic issues (*NCAA News* 1989b).

Agency Penalties. When an institution's athletic program is found to have violated association rules, that program is penalized by loss of rights to participate in postseason bowls and tournaments, restricted television exposure, and reduced scholarships. Investigations often take years, so those who suffer most directly—the athletes—often were not on the teams when the violations occurred. Coaches who were the perpetrators may escape direct penalties, often by moving to another institution, although recent NCAA rules attempt to penalize coaches instead of institutions.

Summary

In the legend of Faust, a man sells his soul to the devil in exchange for immediate knowledge and power. College athletes may not quite be selling their souls, but in their concentration on the immediate rewards of athletics, they endanger their future. Carrying the literary metaphor further, agents of the collegiate institution, including but not exclusively coaches, seem to be playing the part of the devil when they encourage young athletes to devote themselves to the present at the expense of their future.[8]

Viewing the relationship among college athletes, coaches, individual schools, and the structure of intercollegiate athletics (including its eligibility rules) from the functionalist perspective, we can see regulations as necessary in order to avoid chaos (i.e., dysfunction) and to maintain the system's direction and prosperity. From this functionalist perspective, rules are beneficial both to colleges and to *bona fide* student-athletes. Historically, at least, these rules and the structures of college athletics governance (NCAA, NAIA, NJCAA) were established to protect the health of athletes and their right to be involved in fair competition.

---

[8]The temptations of success in college athletics have become astronomical. Jackie Sherrill, former football coach at Texas A&M who was dismissed in part because of NCAA violations, was given $684,000 on termination of his contract, and also had his $300,000 home paid off by the university (Associated Press 1989).

From the conflict-coercion perspective, however, we see rules established by coaches for their teams and the regulations set by governing agencies severely abridging athletes' rights to participate and their access to fair exchange for their time and toil. One example of this perception may be seen in Proposition 48's limiting access of poorly prepared students from participating in collegiate athletics during the freshman year.

Competition within teams for scarce places on the roster and scarcer starting positions serves as the coercive mechanism by which coaches, as institutional agents, maintain virtually absolute control over players. Again, speaking from the conflict-coercion perspective, such control leads to oppression and exploitation when group goals (team victory) conflict with individual goals (academic success or individual achievement). The youth and relative inexperience of college athletes, as well as their vulnerability to institutional coercion, discourage them from joining together to alter exploitative practices and policies.

While high school athletics might be made more "healthful" or worthwhile than it is, few will question that high school athletes benefit from their involvement in sports. In contrast, the issue of exploitation—the extent to which it occurs, what it entails, who is being exploited—has plagued college athletics for over a century in wave after wave of scandals. It remains to be seen whether the current surge of reforms will lead to a system that provides all subgroups of student-athletes with more consistent exchange for their blood, toil, tears, and sweat on behalf of Dear Old Fill-in-the-Blank University.

References

1993 NCAA Division I Graduation-Rate Report. Overland Park, KS: NCAA.

Adler, P., and P. A. Adler. 1985. "From Idealism to Pragmatic Detachment: The Academic Performance of College Athletes." *Sociology of Education* 58:241–50.

Alfano, P. 1989. "Visions of the Pros Can Come Early." *New York Times* March 9:B9.

American Institutes for Research. 1988. *Report No. 1: Summary Results from the 1987–88 National Study of Intercollegiate Athletes.* Palo Alto, CA: Center for the Study of Athletics.

Associated Press. 1989. "Arizona Suspends Hutson, 2 Others." *The Sacramento Bee* April 5:D5.

Betts, J. R. 1974. *America's Sporting Heritage: 1850–1950.* Reading, MA: Addison-Wesley.

Birrell, S. 1987–88. "The Woman Athlete's College Experience: Knowns and Unknowns." *Journal of Sport and Social Issues* 11(1 & 2):82–96.

Blinde, E. 1989. "Unequal Exchange and Exploitation in College Sport: The Case of the Female Athlete." *Arena Review.* 13(2):110–23.

Blum, R. 1989. "Blacks Bear Brunt of Prop. 48." *The Sacramento Bee* (Associated Press). March 29:D1, D3.

Bowen, W. P. 1908. "The Evolution of Athletic Evils." *Western Journal of Education* 1:353-58.

Braddock, J. 1981. "Race, Athletics and Educational Attainment: Dispelling the Myths." *Youth and Society* 12:335-50.

Buhrmann, H. 1977. "Athletics and Deviance: An Examination of the Relationship Between Athletic Participation and Deviant Behavior in High School Girls." *Review of Sport and Leisure* 2:17-34.

Chandler, T. J. L., and A. D. Goldberg. 1990. "The Academic All-American as Vaunted Adolescent Role-Identity." *Sociology of Sport Journal.* 7(3):287-93.

Coakley, J. J. 1982. *Sport in Society: Issues and Controversies,* 2nd edition. St. Louis: C. V. Mosby.

Coleman, J. 1961. *The Adolescent Society.* New York: Free Press.

Cooper, C. S. 1914. "Domination of Athletics." *Education* 35:129-39.

Czikszentmihalyi, M. 1975. *Beyond Boredom and Anxiety.* San Francisco: Jossey-Bass.

Dietz, D. 1989. "How State High Schools Bend Pass-to-Play Law for Athletes." *San Francisco Chronicle,* June 5.

Dreeben, R. 1968. *On What Is Learned In School.* Reading, MA: Addison-Wesley.

Edwards, H. 1983. "Educating Black Athletes." *Atlantic Monthly* August:31-38.

Eitzen, D. S. 1976. "Athletics in the Status System of Male Adolescents: A Replication of Coleman's *The Adolescent Society.*" Pp. 150-54 in *Sport Sociology: Contemporary Themes,* edited by A. Yiannakis et al. Dubuque, IA: Kendall-Hunt.

Eitzen, D. S. 1987-88. "The Educational Experiences of Intercollegiate Student-Athletes." *Journal of Sport and Social Issues* 11(1 & 2):15-30.

Eitzen, D. S., and D. Purdy. 1986. "The Academic Preparation and Achievement of Black and White Collegiate Athletes." *Journal of Sport and Social Issues* 10(1):15-29.

Eliot, C. W. 1908. "Athletics Still Exaggerated." *Harvard Graduates' Magazine* 16:624-27.

Engstrom, C. M., and W. E. Sedlacek. 1991. "A Study of Prejudice Toward University Student-Athletes." *Journal of Counseling and Development.* 70(1):189-93.

Ewing, L. E. 1975. *Career Development of College Athletes: Implications for Counseling Activities.* Ed.D. Dissertation, Virginia Polytechnic Institute and State University.

Feltz, D. L. 1979. "Athletics in the Status System of Female Adolescents." *Review of Sport and Leisure* 4(1):110-18.

Figler, S. 1987. "The Academic Performance of Collegiate Athletes: Of Playpens and Backyards." *Arena Review* 11(2):35-40.

Figler, S. 1987-88. "Academic Advising for Athletes." *Journal of Sport and Social Issues* 11(1 & 2):74-81.

Figler, S., and H. Figler. 1991. *Going The Distance.* Placerville, CA: Petrel Press.

Figler, S., and T. Griffith. 1982. "Advising the College Athlete as a Special Population of Student." Presented at the annual meeting of the National Academic Advising Association, San Jose, CA.

Figone, A. J. 1988. "The 'Cooling Out' Function in Junior College: Implications for the Student-Athlete." Presented at the annual meeting of the North American Society for the Sociology of Sport, Cincinnati, OH.

Fletcher, H. J., and B. Mand. 1988. "Grade Improvement by Academically Endangered Student-Athletes Following Brief Study Skills Training." *Academic Athletic Journal* Spring:17–24.

Foster, W. T. 1915. "An Indictment of Intercollegiate Athletics." *Atlantic Monthly* 116:577–88.

Frey, J. H. 1987–88. "Institutional Control of Athletics: An Analysis of the Role Played by Presidents, Faculty, Trustees, Alumni, and the NCAA." *Journal of Sport and Social Issues* 11(1 & 2):49–60.

Gerber, E. W., J. Felshin, P. Berlin, and W. Wyrick. 1974. *The American Woman in Sport.* Reading, MA: Addison-Wesley.

Goldaper, S. 1974. "Pro Basketball: Diploma vs. Dollar." *New York Times* March 13:C46.

"Graduation Rates Jump by Six Percent." *NCAA News.* June 30:1, 22.

Green, H. 1986. *Fit for America: Health, Fitness, Sport and American Society.* Baltimore, MD: Johns Hopkins.

Gup, T. 1989. "Foul!" *Time,* April 3.

Gurney, G. S., D. C. Robinson, and L. M. Fygetakis. 1983. "Athletic Academic Counseling Within NCAA Division I Institutions: A National Profile of Staffing, Training, and Services." Presented at the annual meeting of the National Association for Academic Advisors for Athletics, San Diego, CA.

Hackensmith, C. W. 1966. *History of Physical Education.* New York: Harper and Row.

Hanks, M. P., and B. K. Ekland. 1976. "Athletics and Social Participation in the Educational Attainment Process." *The Sociology of Education.* 49:271–94.

Harrison, J. H. 1976. "Intercollegiate Football Participation and Academic Achievement." (Paper presented to the Southwestern Sociological Association, Dallas, TX).

Hart, A. B. 1890. "The Present Status of College Athletics." *Atlantic Monthly* 66:63–71.

Hartzell, M. J., and J. S. Picou. 1978. "Success in Interscholastic Sports and the College Plans of Women Athletes." *TAHPER Journal* Spring:12–13.

Henschen, K. P., and D. Fry. 1984. "An Archival Study of the Relationship of Intercollegiate Participation and Graduation." *Sociology of Sport Journal* 1(1):52–56.

Hickey, G. M. 1992. "The Role of Achievement Motivation in the Relationship Between Athletic and Academic Achievement." Ph.D. Dissertation, Pace University.

Hoch, P. 1972. *Rip Off the Big Game.* New York: Doubleday.

Jacobs, K. J. 1983. *A Comparison of the Graduation Rates of Student-Athletes with the Overall Student Body Who Enrolled at the University of North Carolina at Chapel Hill from 1966 to 1976.* M.A. Thesis, University of North Carolina at Chapel Hill.

Kiger, G., and D. Lorentzen. 1986. "The Relative Effects of Gender, Race and Sport on University Academic Performance." *Sociology of Sport Journal* 3(2):160–67.

Kingston, J. L. 1993. "Data Revealing: More Study Needed." *NCAA News.* June 30:4.

Kirshenbaum, J. 1989. "An American Disgrace." *Sports Illustrated* February 27:16–19.

Knapp, T. J., and J. F. Raney. 1987. "Looking at the Transcripts of Student-Athletes: Methods and Obstacles." *Arena Review* 11(2):41–47.

Lance, L. M. 1987. "Conceptualization of Role Relationships and Role Conflict Among Student-Athletes." *Arena Review* 11(2):12–18.

Landers, D., and D. Landers. 1978. "Socialization via Interscholastic Athletics: Its Effects on Delinquency." *Sociology of Education* 51:299–303.

Lapchick, R. 1987–88. "The High School Athlete as the Future College Student-Athlete." *Journal of Sport and Social Issues* 11(1 & 2):104–24.

Lederman, D. 1987. "Many Faculty Members Seek Greater Role in Athletic Decision Making on Campuses." *The Chronicle of Higher Education* February 4:29–30.

Lederman, D. 1989. "Nearly Half the Members in Top Division of NCAA Cited for Violations This Decade." *The Chronicle of Higher Education* February 22:A35.

Lee, C. C. 1983. "An Investigation of the Athletic Career Expectations of High School Student Athletes," *The Personnel and Guidance Journal.* May:544–47.

Lewis, G. 1966. "The Muscular Christianity Movement." *JOHPER* May:27–28.

Lewis, G. 1967. "America's First Intercollegiate Sport: The Regattas from 1852 to 1875." *Research Quarterly* 38(4):637–47.

Lucas, J. 1976. "Victorian Muscular Christianity—Prologue to the Olympic Games Philosophy." *Report of the Fifteenth Session of the International Olympic Academy:* 66–77.

Luther, O. B., and D. F. Alvin. 1977. "Athletics, Aspirations, and Achievements." *The Sociology of Education* 50:102–13.

Magner, D. K. 1989. "Bills Would Require Colleges to Report Athletes' Status." *The Chronicle of Higher Education* March 22:A35–A36.

Marks, S. R. 1977. "Multiple Roles and Role Strain: Some Notes on Human Energy, Time, and Commitment." *American Sociological Review* 42:921–36.

Mayo, A. M. 1982. *The Relationship Between Athletic Participation and the Academic Aptitude, Achievement and Progress of Male and Female Athletes in Revenue and Non-Revenue Producing Sports at the Ohio State University.* Ph.D. Dissertation, The Ohio State University.

McKinney, J. S. 1991. *Analysis of Career Maturity of Collegiate Student-Athletes and College Students Involved in Extracurricular Activities.* Ph.D. Dissertation, University of South Carolina.

Menke, F. G. 1977. *The Encyclopedia of Sports,* 3rd Edition. New York: A. S. Barnes.

Merton, R. K. 1938. "Social Structure and Anomie." *American Sociological Review* 3:672–82.

Messner, S., and D. Grossier. 1982. "Intercollegiate Athletic Participation and Academic Achievement." Pp. 257–70 in *Studies in the Sociology of Sport,* edited by A. O. Dunleavy, A. W. Miracle, and C. R. Rees. Ft. Worth, TX: TCU Press.

Meyer, B. B. 1990. "Idealism to Actualization: The Academic Performance of Female Collegiate Athletes." *Sociology of Sport Journal.* 7(1):44–57.

Monaghan, P. 1986. "Fired Teacher Wins Suit Against Officials at U. of Georgia, Is Awarded $2.5-Million." *The Chronicle of Higher Education,* February 19:29–30.

Naison, M., and C. Mangum. 1983. "Protecting the Educational Opportunities of Black College Athletes: A Case Study Based on Experiences at Fordham University." *Journal of Ethnic Studies* 11(3):119–26.

NASPE Coaches Council. 1993. "Position Statement: Exploitation of the Interscholastic Athlete." *AAHPERD Update: NASPE Supplement.* September:I.

NCAA. 1993. "Ergogenic Drug Use by Sport." *NCAA News* (Sports Sciences insert). September 1:1.

NCAA Enforcement Program, Part 2. 1978. Attachment "I." Committee on Interstate and Foreign Commerce, House of Representatives, 95th Congress, Serial# 95-160:1512.

NCAA News. 1989a. "In Texas, it's a felony to bribe prospective student-athletes." March 8:5.

NCAA News. 1989b. "State legislation relating to athletics." February 8:14.

NCAA News. 1989c. "Research Institute Releases Study of Black Student-Athletes." April 5:1, 19.

Padilla, A. 1989. "Controversy Over Proposal 42 May Lead to a New Role for College Presidents in Reforming Big-Time Sports." *The Chronicle of Higher Education* February 22:B1–B3.

Phillips, J. C., and W. E. Schafer. 1971. "Consequences of Participation in Interscholastic Sports: A Review and Prospectus." *Pacific Sociological Review* 14(3):328–38.

Picou, J. S. 1978. "Race, Athletic Achievement, and Educational Aspiration." *Sociological Quarterly* 19:429–38.

Purdy, D., D. S. Eitzen, and R. Hufnagel. 1985. "Are Athletes Also Students? The Educational Attainment of College Athletes." Pp. 221–34 in *Sport and Higher Education,* edited by D. Chu, J. O. Segrave, and B. J. Becker. Champaign, IL: Human Kinetics.

Rehberg, R. A., and W. E. Schafer. 1968. "Participation in Interscholastic Athletics and College Expectations." *American Journal of Sociology* 63:732–40.

Reilly, R. 1989. "What Price Glory?" *Sports Illustrated* February 27:32–34.

Rhoden, W. C. 1989. "Recruiting Extends Its Reach." *New York Times* March 6:C1, C4.

Roosa, D. B. 1894. "Are Football Games Education or Brutality?" *Forum* 16:534–42.

Rossi, R. J. 1989. "NCAA Forum," *NCAA News,* February 15:12–17.

Sack, A. L., and R. Thiel. 1985. "College Basketball and Role Conflict: A National Survey." *Sociology of Sport Journal* 2(3):195–209.

Savage, H. 1929. *American College Athletics.* New York: The Carnegie Foundation for the Advancement of Teaching.

Schafer, W. E. 1969. "Some Social Sources and Consequences of Interscholastic Athletics: The Case of Participation and Delinquency." *International Review of Sport Sociology* 4:63–79.

Schafer, W. E. 1973. "Sport and Youth Counterculture: Contrasting Socialization Themes." In *Social Problems in Athletics,* edited by D. Landers. Urbana, IL: University of Illinois.

Schafer, W. E., and M. J. Armer. 1968. "Athletes Are Not Inferior Students." *Transaction* November:21–26.

Schurr, K. T., A. F. Wittig, V. E. Ruble, and L. W. Henriksen. 1993. "College Graduation Rates of Student Athletes and Students Attending College Male Basketball Games: A Case Study." *Journal of Sport Behavior.* 16(1):33–41.

Segrave, J. O., and D. Chu. 1978. "Athletics and Juvenile Delinquency." *Review of Sport and Leisure* 3:1-24.

Segrave, J. O., and D. Hastad. 1982. "Delinquent Behavior and Interscholastic Athletic Participation." *Journal of Sport Behavior* 5(2):96-111.

Shapiro, B. J. 1984. "Intercollegiate Athletic Participation and Academic Achievement: A Case Study of Michigan State University Student-Athletes, 1950-1980." *Sociology of Sport Journal* 1(1):46-51.

Snyder, E. E. 1985. "A Theoretical Analysis of Academic and Athletic Roles." *Sociology of Sport Journal* 2(3):210-17.

Spears, B., and R. A. Swanson. 1978. *History of Sport and Physical Activity in The United States.* Dubuque, IA: Wm. C. Brown.

Spivey, D., and T. A. Jones. 1975. "Intercollegiate Athletic Servitude: A Case Study of the Black Illini Student-Athletes, 1931-1967." *Social Science Quarterly* 55(4):939-47.

Spreitzer, E., and M. Pugh. 1973. "Interscholastic Athletics and Educational Expectations." *The Sociology of Education* 46:171-82.

Stecklein, J., and L. Dameron. 1965. "Intercollegiate Athletics and Academic Progress: Comparison of Academic Characteristics of Athletes and Nonathletes at the University of Minnesota." *Reprint Series No. 3.* University of Minnesota: Bureau of Institutional Research.

Stephen, L. 1870. "Athletic Sports and University Studies." *Fraser's Magazine.* December:694.

Stevenson, C. L. 1975. "Socialization Effects of Participation in Sport: A Critical Review of the Literature." *Research Quarterly* 46(3):287-301.

Sutherland, L. W. 1983. *A Study of Scholarship Student-Athletes' Academic Progress from 1960 to 1982 at Texas A&M University.* M.S. Thesis, Texas A&M University.

Telander, R., and R. Sullivan. 1989. "You Reap What You Sow." *Sports Illustrated* February 27:20-26, 31.

Thirer, J., and S. D. Wright. 1985. "Sport and Social Status for Adolescent Males and Females." *Sociology of Sport Journal* 2(2):164-71.

Vance, N. S. 1983. "3 Institutions Find Athletes' Grades Low; Mixed Results in Big 10 University Study." *The Chronicle of Higher Education* May 11:17-18.

Veblen, T. 1965. *The Higher Learning in America: A Memorandum on the Conduct of Universities by Business Men.* New York: A. M. Kelley, Bookseller. [Original edition 1918; reprinted by arrangement with Viking Press.]

Waggoner, R. G., R. Ammon, and F. R. Veltri. 1993. "Perceptions of Student-Athlete Graduation Rates As an Evaluation Criterion for Head Football Coaches." *Sport Marketing Quarterly.* 2(1):27, 30-34.

Weber, L., T. M. Sherman, and C. Tegano. 1987. "Effects of a Transition Program on Student Athletes' Academic Success: An Exploratory Study." *Sociology of Sport Journal* 4(1):78-83.

Weistart, J. C. 1987. "College Sports Reform: Where Are the Faculty?" *Academe* 73:12-17.

Wulf, S. 1985. "The Diploma Bowl." *Sports Illustrated* January 7:7.

CHAPTER 7

Economics and Law:
The Other Side of Sport

Who is served by the structure and operation of what we shall generically call "economic sport?" The American economic system theoretically is based on supply and demand and the ebb and flow of a free marketplace, all for the ultimate benefit of the consuming, taxpaying, voting public. The result of this competition in the marketplace is the best product at the best price and availability, which should result in profit. Where inefficiency, a poor product, or a weak economy ensue, a business or even an industry might disappear. This, again theoretically, is modified with government intervention for the benefit of the public when the supposed balance of the marketplace swings one way or the other to the public detriment.

In this chapter we will discuss collegiate and professional sport separately. Although they are part of the same entertainment/sports industry (certainly the collegiate Division I level is), they differ in assumptions and ideals. A critical difference in ideals is that college athletics maintains an adherence, however tenuous, to educational and developmental goals for its athletes and even for some of its fans, while professional sport is purely and simply motivated by profit.

In the *pure description* phase of our analysis, we will introduce the concept of an economic cartel—the basic operational principle of both collegiate and professional sport. Our *evaluative commentary* will focus on how well and profitably the two industries operate, and on the evolution of the financial relationship between professional athletes and team owners. *Social critique* of the relationship between sport, the media, and the larger economy runs throughout the chapter. Specific suggestions for *social engineering* regarding both collegiate and professional sport will also be discussed.

Cartel Arrangements in American Sport

Before looking at specific figures, we must understand the economic environment of the collegiate and professional athletics industries. They are not, as some might expect, free and open markets. Rather, both collegiate and professional sport are run as *cartels,* an economic system that in America is generally illegal. As a form of market monopoly, cartels have been illegal since the late 19th century. This has not, however, prevented the United States government from allowing cartels and other monopolies to exist if they are deemed to be more beneficial than harmful in particular industries.

A cartel (Bye 1956:385) is an agreement or pooling arrangement among a number of firms in an industry in which competition is restrained regarding shares of the market, prices, and other matters important to the industry. The objective of a cartel is to assure each member an adequate share of the market by decreasing the forms of competition among the members. That is, while cartel members may compete against each other in the sale of their products, they agree, for example, not to compete over the raw material that forms the basis of their product. A clear example of this arrangement occurs in professional sports where teams agree to draft athletic "raw material" from high schools and colleges, avoiding competition among each other. In college athletics, a similar, if less competition-restricting, practice occurs when high school players sign "letters of intent" to attend a particular college.

Cartels are illegal in the United States because they interfere with the free market system. The competitive free enterprise system ideally provides the best product or service at the cheapest price. The economic mechanism of open competition is intended to ensure this. Those firms or industries that cannot compete flounder and die. Legislation such as the Sherman (1890) and the Clayton (1914) Antitrust Acts was passed to limit collusion, because agreements among competitors as to price, type, and quality of products or services and their availability might lead to poorer quality at higher prices.

Some industries by nature are more efficient as cartels under the legal sanction and control of the government. Among these industries are communications, transportation, and utilities. The government ensures the public's benefit through stringent controls of prices, product/service availability, and responsiveness to public needs. Although the government has granted cartel status (through certain specific exemptions from antitrust legislation) within the sports industry, it has seldom seen fit to institute controls ensuring the public's best interest (Johnson 1979).

The Question of Profitability

The amount of money spent annually on sports-connected advertising on U.S. television has grown explosively, from $2 million in 1950 to $1.59 billion in 1987. By the year 2000, sports advertising on U.S. television is expected to reach $11 billion a year (Rosner 1989).

TANK McNAMARA   by Jeff Millar & Bill Hinds

Copyright © 1980 Universal Press Syndicate.

While the magnitude of such spending is impressive, the profitability of sports teams is far from assured. Not only will costs rise, but the hope of great profitability will lead to greater competition, which will make the likelihood of achieving success even more problematic.

The Antitrust Question

A second issue is how the sports industry in general and particular sports organizations and leagues will fare in the searchlight of antitrust legislation. Within the antitrust issue, several questions need to be addressed. Antitrust laws exist to ensure fairness in the realm of business and trade. In the sports industry, the question of fairness breaks down into three areas:

1. Fairness to business competitors (other owners; other leagues or sports; groups, such as females and minorities, who might be disadvantaged by particular business practices)
2. Fairness to employees (athletes, game officials, etc.)
3. Fairness to consumers (i.e., fans)

The Question of Corruption

Corruption is a third issue. Here, also, the issue can be divided into subconcerns:

1. Corruption of the product—how athletic events are being altered in order to yield the most profit
2. Corruption of ethics—what unethical or illegal behaviors those in the sports business at any level are being driven to in order to achieve victory and profit

Given the magnitude of economics and influence of modern sport, any or all of these issues might arise when we look at a particular manifestation of sport. As we discuss the economics of sport, see which of these issues apply.

The Industry of Intercollegiate Athletics

Having established that cartel organization and media influence are key factors in the economics of both intercollegiate athletics and professional sport, we can now begin to evaluate in more detail each of those two related industries. While they have much in common, we shall see that each also has its own unique areas of concern.

NCAA: The Collegiate Athletics Cartel

The members of the NCAA cartel are its approximately 800 associated universities and colleges.[1] The cartel makes and monitors rules that restrict forms of competition among members. Limits are placed on the number of games (products) each school may offer the public. The cartel sets playing and eligibility rules, dictates how schools may obtain their raw materials, investigates and penalizes rules infractions, sanctions bowl games, runs postseason tournaments, and conducts other business intended for the common benefit of members (Koch 1971).

As noted in the previous chapter, until 1952 the NCAA was a weak cartel, having little effective power to control rulesbreaking from within or to regulate rewards. It was a watchdog with a bark, but no bite. During the early post-World War II sports boom, college athletic competitiveness spiraled out of control. NCAA members decided that to effectively govern, they needed punitive power. The member schools granted power to the NCAA cartel to restrict postseason play of transgressing members and to curtail the eligibility of players who had violated rules.

When the NCAA gained control of the televised marketing of collegiate athletics, it also gained economic power over its individual members, since large amounts of money could be earned from television appearances. Currently, the NCAA exercises legislative (rulemaking), executive (management), and judicial (punishment/reward) functions, all within the same body. Since the NCAA *is* its members, in most other American industries this would represent collusion and would be illegal.

There are no generally accepted reasons why the government allows this collusive cartel arrangement. Legislators have considered, but have been reluctant to vote for, governmental control or significant changes in collegiate sport for fear of "interfering" with sport and generating negative public reaction, while the NCAA jealously guards its self-governance.

Income and Expenses in College Athletics

It is a not-so-well-kept secret that college athletic programs have been in serious financial trouble for a long time (Farrell 1987a). The irony of big-time college athletics is that, although it is strongly motivated by economic goals, it

---

[1]The same cartel arrangement exists in the NAIA, which controls many small college athletic programs.

TABLE 7.1 *Revenue Sources of Government-Supported and Privately Financed Institutions* *

	Fiscal Year 1989												
							Division II				Division III		
Revenue Sources as a	I-A		I-AA		I-AAA		With FB		No FB		With FB		No FB
Percentage of Total Revenues	Gov.	Prvt.	Gov.	Prvt.	Gov.	Prvt.	Gov.	Prvt.	Gov.	Prvt.	Gov.	Prvt.	Gov.	Prvt.
Total ticket sales	35%	37%	17%	29%	9%	35%	12%	23%	9%	9%	6%	27%	2%	3%
Student activity fees	4	4	21	1	37	7	12	17	14	7	12	7	15	46
Student assessments	4	2	15	6	27	2	21	1	14	0	37	7	52	3
Guarantees and options	7	9	5	11	2	4	2	4	2	4	0	2	0	1
Contributions from alumni	16	13	10	16	7	15	9	46	7	30	9	19	3	11
Bowls, tournaments & TV	13	16	3	7	1	20	1	0	1	1	0	0	0	0
Government support	5	3	20	0	8	0	26	3	46	0	30	0	22	0
All other revenues	16	16	9	30	9	17	17	6	7	49	6	38	6	36
Total revenues	100%	100%	100%	100%	100%	100%	100%	100%	100%	100%	100%	100%	100%	100%

*Data from Raiborn 1990:17.

often fails miserably by economic criteria, but still remains a viable industry. Most other businesses or industries having the financial record of college athletics would have gone the way of the Pony Express and other glorious but inefficient enterprises.

Table 7.1 indicates how precarious is the funding of Division I-A college athletics. Seventy-one percent of the revenue at publicly supported schools and 75 percent at private universities in I-A athletics come from a combination of ticket sales, bowl\tournament\TV earnings, game guarantees, and alumni contributions. Each of these sources of income fluctuates with the success of football and basketball teams, "success" in the athletic big-time being defined more by championships and high ranking than by mere surplus of victories. Note also the disparity in funding from student fees and assessments between Division I (about 7 percent) and Division III (half to two-thirds). Similarly, government support to athletics ranges widely, from 0 to 8 percent at private colleges up to 46 percent at Division II schools without football. These stable forms of support—government and student fees—are the smallest sources of funding in the big-time of college athletics.

Perhaps that is as it should be at a level of athletics that operates as business and university public relations enterprises. However, this disregards a longstanding justification for the profit-orientation of football and basketball, i.e., that they "pay for" non-revenue producing and women's sports. If that were truly their justification, shouldn't we want big-time athletics on more firm economic footing than reliance on high ranking? If high ranking is not achieved—and by definition most schools cannot achieve it—it is women's and minor men's sports that suffer by being eradicated.

Relevance of Funding to Play and Exercise in Colleges.   If recreative or fitness-focused play and intramural sports were valued as highly as intercollegiate athletics, then they would also be a part of the picture of economic sport in colleges. However, greater cultural legitimacy is granted to organized athletics compared to the more personally focused recreative play and physical fitness. If public attention were drawn to such activities, a business could be made of them—as it was of regatta in the 1850s and football in the 1880s. High schools and especially colleges, however, devote millions of dollars to athletics while reducing or eliminating physical education requirements, because maximal striving fits our cultural bias. "Just playing" is what we do to rest from striving (athletics), and therefore it is not deemed worthy of economic investment, especially in times of crises in funding.

College Athletics and the Media

The prominent place of athletics on the college campus can be traced in large part to the influence of the communications media, historically newspapers, and, more recently, television. The newspaper industry grew up with collegiate sports, gaining widespread readership as it extolled the exploits of collegiate rowing and football (Lewis 1967). By the third decade of this century, newspapers and the new medium—radio—"whetted the sports appetites" of Americans (Edwards 1973:30–32).

College athletics, and particularly football, were wildly popular before the television age, but it is TV that may be credited with fostering the highly skilled, specialized, and expensive form of football we know today. When free-substitution, two-platoon football began in the 1950s, the size of squads more than doubled, as did the expenses of fielding the team. Since then, inflation plus the escalation in competitiveness have continued to drive up the costs as well as the revenues of all collegiate sport, although for "major" (meaning revenue-producing) sports more than others.

Our focus will be on the issue of television marketing of college athletics, which is essentially a consumer welfare question. From the inception of TV marketing of college football in the early 1950s to 1984, when the Supreme Court declared NCAA control over televised football to be in violation of the Sherman Antitrust Act, individual institutions were limited in the amount of money they could make through marketing their football teams.[2] Even if the entire nation wanted to see, for example, Notre Dame, UCLA, or Oklahoma play every Saturday, the NCAA limited their TV appearances—except for bowl games—to three in a particular year and five times over a span of two consecutive years. The rationale for limiting TV appearances was to "spread the wealth" among competitors so that less well-known teams could reap some of the monetary and recruiting rewards of TV exposure. This had the ring of a cartel. The NCAA's imposition of a limit on total number of games to be aired each week restricted the "supply" of televised games, which artificially increased the "demand" for those games. By interfering with the free marketplace of televised

[2]This case reached the Supreme Court as the result of a lawsuit brought by the Universities of Oklahoma and Georgia to gain control over the marketing of their respective football "products."

TABLE 7.2   *Two Conferences Compared Since NCAA Football TV Pact Voided* *

	Pacific-10 Conference				Southeastern Conference		
Year	Amount[b]	Appearances	$/Appearance	Year	Amount[b]	Appearances	$/Appearance
1983[a]	$7.27	20	$363,500	1983[a]	$10.3	30	$343,000
1984	7.35	37	198,648	1984	7.5	41	182,927
1985	6.85	21	326,190	1985	9.0	40	225,000
1986	6.50	26	250,000	1986	10.0	43	232,558
1987	6.50	25	260,000	1987	9.26	40	231,500

[a]Last year of NCAA monopoly
[b]Millions of dollars
*Data from *Sports, Inc.,* January 9, 1989, p. 17

college football games, the NCAA drove up the price of its product, which led to a four-year contract earning the NCAA $263.5 million for granting ABC and NBC the rights to televise college football (Vance 1984).

The result of the Supreme Court's order to have the NCAA football TV monopoly voided has been predictable: proliferation of the number of games being aired (benefiting the consumer), an increase in the number of games major teams have televised, along with a decline in the TV earning power of those games (supply and demand). Perhaps less anticipated was the effect on attendance, a decline from nearly 25.8 million among Division I-A schools in 1984 to less than 25.1 million in 1988. While this slide in attendance may not seem large, it represented a loss of $9 million to $10 million per year. Peter Dalis, athletic director at UCLA, claimed a $1 million loss in TV revenue alone as a result of the new free market for televised college football (*NCAA* 1989). John Weistart, a professor at Duke University specializing in sports law, sees "a natural contraction in the [college football] market," but warns that any attempt to control or reverse this by the NCAA represents "joint action to restrict output [which] is the 'original sin' of antitrust law" (*NCAA* 1988:4).

TV has clearly been quite profitable for college athletics, especially through the growth and profit of the NCAA postseason basketball championships, which have become a major media event each spring (touted as "March Madness"). In 1974 only 25 teams participated in the tournament with first-round losers taking home $11,000 and each of the four teams to reach the semifinals earning $64,000. By 1987 the tournament had expanded to 64 teams with first-round losers earning $200,675 for their trouble, while the "Final Four" each amassed $1,003,375 (Farrell 1987b). In 1991 128 teams were competing in the men's tournament. That year the NCAA decided to distribute the wealth more broadly across the spectrum of Division I, awarding money earned from the tournament according to a combination of basketball achievement, number of athletic scholarships given at the school, and the number of intercollegiate sports the school fields. An additional $30,000 for "academic enhancement" was given yearly to each Division I school to foster their athletes' progress toward their degrees.

Another source of media revenue for college basketball comes from radio and cable and local TV contracts signed by individual schools and conferences. The level of income varies widely by region and with each team. However, as televising of football and men's basketball increases, there is less room for women's sports, particularly if ratings remain low. In 1988 the men's NCAA semifinal (on a Saturday) drew a 12.8 viewer rating, while the women's *final* the following day drew only a 4.3 rating (Comte, Girard, and Starensier 1989).

(Un)profitability of College Athletics

Mitchell Raiborn, accountant and professor of accounting at Bradley University, conducts periodic research into the economics of NCAA intercollegiate athletics. Raiborn (1990) reports that the proportion of revenues from football—the "cash cow"—decreased between 1985 and 1989, while the percent of expenses increased everywhere except in Division I-A. In Division I-A, although average profits generated by football doubled over the eight years prior to 1990 ($1,342,000 to $2,771,000), the average deficit in programs operating at a loss grew by 250 percent ($251,000 to $638,000). In Division I basketball, profitable programs have increased their earnings threefold (average of $387,000 to $1,771,000), while average deficits have grown nearly as much ($88,000 to $238,000). These findings mean, simply, that the rich are getting richer, while the poor get poorer.

Raiborn (1990) compares revenues, expenses, and implied[3] profits or deficits between 1982 and 1989 at all NCAA levels. Table 7.3 shows that in Division I-A, athletic program deficits decreased through the 1980s, leading to an average yearly profit of $258,000 in 1987, only to drop to a mere $39,000 profit at the close of the decade. Perhaps more important for the total picture of intercollegiate athletics, in no other year at no other level of competition did an athletic program avoid a deficit. Of particular interest was the virtually relentless growth in the size of average deficits, peaking at $782,000 in 1989 at Division I-AA. This is clear, long-term evidence that intercollegiate athletics is "bad business," except perhaps at Division I-A, and even there it relies tenuously on high ranking of football and men's basketball teams.

Padilla concludes (1987:12–13):

> athletics do not pay for themselves at most colleges and universities in America. Indeed, a substantial subsidy of institutional resources must be injected annually to keep intercollegiate athletics programs operating at the current level of inflated and ambitious expenditures.

---

[3]Deficits or profits are called "implied" by Raiborn (1990:54) since they represent the differences between averaged figures.

TABLE 7.3 *Average Total Revenue and Expenses in NCAA Athletic Programs, 1982–1989** [Dollar amounts in thousands]

	1982	1985	1987	1989
Division 1-A				
Revenues	$4,916	$6,833	$8,351	$9,685
Expenses	5,054	6,894	8,093	9,646
Implied Profit or (Deficit)	(138)	(61)	258	39
Division 1-AA				
Revenues	1,170	1,616	1,949	2,409
Expenses	1,716	2,321	2,709	3,191
Implied Deficit	546	705	760	782
Division 1-AAA				
Revenues	402	609	941	1,197
Expenses	721	1,072	1,590	1,911
Implied Deficit	319	463	649	714
Division II – football				
Revenues	306	469	581	714
Expenses	580	875	929	1,161
Implied Deficit	274	406	348	447
Division II – No football				
Revenues	210	349	307	429
Expenses	353	547	594	797
Implied Deficit	143	198	287	368
Division III – football				
Revenues	35	70	86	118
Expenses	257	397	437	518
Implied Deficit	222	327	351	400
Division III – No football				
Revenues	42	97	56	133
Expenses	101	157	217	278
Implied Deficit	59	60	161	145
Average Implied Deficit	243 (÷ 7)	317 (÷ 7)	426 (÷ 6)	476 (÷ 6)

*Data from Raiborn 1990. All data include men's and women's athletic programs combined revenue and expenses. Deficits or Profits are called "Implied" by Raiborn since they represent the differences between averaged figures.

To better understand the meaning of these aggregate data, we should observe the economic conditions of athletics at the level of an individual university. At CSU–Sacramento (the academic performance of its athletes were compared to three other universities in Table 6.4), sought to elevate its athletic program from Division II to Division I, while nearly doubling its athletic budget between 1986 and 1993 ($1.4 million per year to $2.6 million). In 1993 the yearly cost of educating one student was approximately $7,000. An additional $7,500 was needed for a student-athlete. Meanwhile, varsity football, the "income engine" at CSU–Sacramento, as at most schools, incurred about a

TABLE 7.4   *How 'Crime' Doesn't Pay: Revenue Loss to Entire Big-8 Conference Resulting from 2-Year Probation of the University of Oklahoma**

	1989
Television	$1.5 to $2 million
Bowl	$1.6 to $3 million
	1990
Bowl	$1.6 to $3 million
TOTAL LOST REVENUE	$4.7 to $8 million

*Data from *Sports, Inc.,* January 9, 1989.

$200,000 yearly deficit (Philp 1993). The problem here, of course, is confusing a program that produces income with one that achieves a profit, or at least avoids a deficit. This pattern was repeated through the early 1990s during a funding crisis at CSU–Sacramento, which resulted in $20 million of budget cuts and the threatened loss of 30 academic programs (Lapin 1993). Both the campus funding crisis and the high cost of athletics at CSU, Sacramento has, in the 1990s, been reflected nationwide.

Revenue from television, which rises and falls directly with the competitive success of the major teams, is crucial to balancing athletic budgets. This could result in more pressure to be successful and, perhaps, less attention to ethical standards.

The cost of success is great, but the cost of getting caught pursuing success illegally is even greater. When Southern Methodist University was caught violating NCAA rules while already on probation for rules violations, the NCAA instituted the so-called "death penalty," which resulted in the school's not fielding a football team for two years. The University of Oklahoma football team was also placed on probation for 1989 and 1990 (avoiding the "death penalty" by cooperating in the investigation), which could cost the university $2 million in television revenue and as much as $8 million overall (see Table 7.4). The University of Washington was banned by the Pacific-10 Conference from bowl appearances for 1993 and 1994, forfeited approximately $1.4 million in TV revenues, and lost 20 scholarships for failing to control football boosters (Wieberg 1993). Auburn University received similar penalties for allowing ineligible athletes to compete, paying athletes performance bonuses, and exceeding grant limits (NCAA 1993).

College athletic programs seem to find themselves squeezed in a triple-jawed vise, with pressure exerted from (1) the economic need for unqualified success on the playing field; (2) judicial elimination of the monopolistic control of the college sports television marketplace; and (3) increasing attention to ethics from government, the NCAA and other athletic associations, and the public.

Avoiding Economic Disaster in College Athletics

The economic problems in college athletics are likely to continue and perhaps reach the point of disaster unless some creative solutions are found. The result could be bankrupt programs or the loss of major sports. This result would likely yield further reduction in the number of minor sports (i.e., those that cost but do not earn) offered to students and an increase in the number of income earning contests. Suggestions have been made to curtail the financial excesses of big-time college athletics, but none is without problems.

Drafting High School Players.   Colleges could begin to draft high school players. Since recruiting involves a major expenditure of money and time, drafting new players could significantly reduce expenses. By decreasing the pressure exerted on everyone involved in the recruiting game, much of the unethical behavior that is currently rampant might be eliminated. Unfortunately, this plan would also eliminate the free choice of high school student-athletes of where they will pursue their college educations, a consequence that is unacceptable to many people.

Subsidization by the Professional Leagues.   Professional leagues could underwrite the cost of collegiate athletic programs, since they serve as a minor league feeder system not only in football and basketball, but also in men's and women's tennis and golf. Major League Baseball and the National Hockey League have their own professional minor leagues, yet still draw talent from college athletics. College athletic programs might be subsidized directly by professional sports leagues, or they could charge professional teams or associations for each player drafted into the professional ranks.

Professional leagues, however, are unlikely to voluntarily pay in the future for what they now get for free. The only way of forcing them to purchase athletes' services may be to extend or eliminate the four-year limit on college eligibility, and many NCAA members are not willing to do that. Second, any influx of money from the professional leagues is likely to bring increased influence as well, and college administrators would be displeased with that development, since they have found it hard enough to keep boosters at bay.

Across-the-Board Reductions.   In 1993 the NCAA called for reductions in the number of scholarships and the size of coaching staffs. The first limitations in football scholarships occurred in 1973 when a cap of 105 players was instituted. Two decades later, the football scholarship limit was reduced to 85, yet costs and deficits continued to rise, despite the popularity of football. With the push over those same two decades to finally bring the funding and availability of women's athletics up to a par with men's athletics, it will be difficult to achieve overall reduction, unless men's programs are cut back even further. Questions are being raised whether four complete squads are required to field a football team, especially when the NFL competes well enough with squads of 47 players (Wolff 1993).

Restructuring of Intercollegiate Athletics. Complete restructuring of intercollegiate athletics has also been suggested in numerous forms to bring spending into line with fiscal responsibility. One example of some interest is the "Hofstra Plan" (Weiner 1973), which would recast athletics into four levels. The top level would have no spending limits and far fewer competitive limits such as now exist. The question remains as to whether it would then be subject, as are other businesses, to income and worker's compensation taxes. The middle two levels would be for large and small schools willing to limit their spending on scholarships and recruiting. The lowest level would be for schools offering no athletic grants and doing no recruiting: whoever shows up tries out for the team.

With this Hofstra Plan, only those schools opting for the highest level would encounter economic problems, to be balanced by their unlimited potential for earning profit. However, businesses go bankrupt, while failing athletic programs have had the luxury of reaching into their university's or their students' pockets to make ends meet. With the Hofstra Plan, presumably, a highest level athletic program not able to pay its bills would simply go bankrupt and cease to exist.

The Economic Dilemma of Intercollegiate Athletics: Unbalanced Budgets and Title IX

Two things are clear about the economics of intercollegiate athletics: (1) deficits must be reduced, which means that costs must be reduced; and (2) greater opportunity and equity must be provided in women's athletics. These two factors represent an apparent dilemma: how can we build up women's athletics while at the same time reducing the overall costs of athletics?

An answer, discomforting to many, is reduction in the costs of men's programs. An age-old argument for not reducing men's football, especially, is that it "pay for" minor sports. This may be true at a few Division I-A schools, but as we have seen, it is a fallacy everywhere else. Another argument is that men's athletics provide access to higher education for those who would otherwise not have the opportunity to get a college degree. To the extent that this is true for men, why should it also not be true for women? The trade-off seems to be eliminating the fourth-stringers in football who are not likely to get into even one game, and with the money saved from 10 or 15 football players, field a team of women athletes, all of whom will participate in contests and thus gain from the experience of intercollegiate athletics.

Over the 21 years that Title IX has been law, collegiate athletic programs have tended to fall short in providing this "boon" to representative numbers of female athletes. A question remains as to how much of a boon it would be for women's athletics to approach the men's model, particularly if, with additional money, it becomes "susceptible to the excesses and scandals that have plagued the big-time college game for men" (Blum 1993:A41).

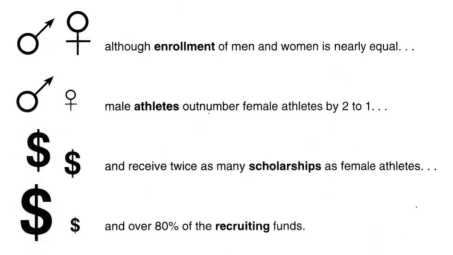

although **enrollment** of men and women is nearly equal. . .

male **athletes** outnumber female athletes by 2 to 1. . .

and receive twice as many **scholarships** as female athletes. . .

and over 80% of the **recruiting** funds.

FIGURE 7.1 *Distribution of Money in Men's & Women's College Athletics* (Chronicle of Higher Education, *March 18, 1992, Chronicle of Higher Education, Washington, DC: NCAA.)*

It becomes a particularly troublesome issue when a leader in women's collegiate athletics, such as Linda Bruno, Associate Commissioner of the Big East Conference, says: "Sex equity means that women have the same right as men to mess things up. . . . We had always hoped that corruption would be an equal-opportunity thing" (Blum 1993:A42). Perhaps this comment was made in jest. However, its humor pales when other leaders in women's college athletics admit, as does Judith Holland, Senior Associate Athletic Director at UCLA, that, "The only real model we have right now is what the men have done" (Blum 1993:A41). Women's athletics leaders knew in 1973, when Title IX became law, that they needed to develop a model less susceptible to exploitation than the men's. Yet in two decades they haven't found another way, perhaps because their energies were focused on actually achieving equity at the expense of how to use it.

The Industry of Professional Sport

"Whenever we call it a game, you call it a business! Whenever we call it a business, you call it a game!" (from the film *North Dallas Forty,* adapted from Gent 1973)

This statement from an NFL player to one of his coaches concisely summarizes the confusion surrounding the nature of professional sports from a legal-governmental control standpoint. Is professional sport a business or is it a pastime? If it is a business, should it be run by the same rules and tax obligations that most other businesses in America are subject to?

The Professional Sport League Cartels

Certainly professional sport is an industry, and a generally healthy one in which great sums of money change hands from consumers-fans to team owners and from owners to players, coaches, and support staff. Baseball has been expressly exempted from antitrust legislation since 1922. Football and basketball, although not protected in the same blanket way as baseball, have enjoyed specific exemptions, for example in the NFL's pooled television agreement and shared revenues, even though each team presumably competes in the marketplace against all others. Sports leagues, however, are not economic competitors, although their individual components (teams) do vie for a scarce prize (victory) on the field of play. Sports leagues are partnerships whose joint product is entertainment in the form of athletic conflict. Individual teams tend to succeed or fail economically as the league succeeds or fails.

As tacitly legal cartels, professional sport leagues control the raw material, the production, and the distribution of the product (games) through agreement among the individual team owners. Team rosters and the structure and availability to the public of the product are determined by collusion. Each team owner is assured exclusive operation within a geographical area, shares in lucrative television contracts, enjoys decision-making power in a popular national product, and enjoys the public esteem that comes from being one of the few people in control of a major league sports team. The federal government allows sports teams and leagues to function as monopolies and cartels, evading antitrust restrictions, because, presumably, the public benefits and the leagues could not function without such exemptions (Lobmeyer and Weidinger 1992; Jacobs 1991). A specific example is the NFL's ban on corporate ownership of teams to preserve the individual and family ownership pattern that has existed since the inception of the league (Krause 1992).

What is put before the public as professional league sport is wholly a product of the wishes of the sellers of that product, tempered only by tradition and the owners' beliefs concerning public tolerance. The public's sole choice is to buy or not to buy the product. Theoretically, if enough fans decide not to buy the product (reduced demand), an owner will feel pressured to enhance the product (improve supply). The owner, however, has other lucrative alternatives, such as moving the team to a newer and less demanding market or selling the team at a healthy profit.

The major sources of revenue for professional sport teams include the sale of television and radio broadcast rights, ticket sales (including season tickets and luxury boxes), parking and concessions at games, the sale of rights to club emblems (featured on merchandise sold to fans), and the sale of player contracts. Expenses are numerous, including payments to players (salaries, bonuses, benefits, pensions, etc.), coaching and administrative costs, game expenses, equipment and facilities costs, publicity, etc. Although teams are clearly in business to make a profit, accounting and tax avoidance practices (depreciation of players and other capital costs, amortization of financing costs, etc.) frequently allow them to show "paper losses" that can be used to offset profits in the owners' other businesses or personal income for tax purposes.

The Emancipation of the Professional Athlete

A functionalist view of professional sport would lead one to think that the owner-cartels of each league would have as their primary goal the maintenance, if not the increase in power over their own industry. Conflict theory would lead one to think that the "oppressed" workers would strive to destroy the system and recast it with themselves holding the reins and enjoying any profit. Changes have occurred in the realms of power and profit. However, neither outcome has transpired or is likely to occur, although players, with the help of the courts, have slowly eroded the economic and at least some of the job-security stranglehold that owners have traditionally enjoyed. Major League Baseball provides an instructive history in the development of owner-player relations.

The relationship between professional athletes (particularly baseball players) and team owners was virtually that of slave and master until the mid-1970s (Rottenberg 1956; Davenport 1969; and Scully 1978). The marketplace for the selling of athletic skills has been described in economic terms as *monopsony* (Daymont 1975), a situation in which a seller (the player peddling his skills) is limited to only one buyer, the owner to whom he is currently contracted or who has drafted him. The buyer controls contract negotiations since the seller-player cannot vend his special skills elsewhere in a free and open market.[4]

Aware of the exorbitant sums of money professional athletes get for their services, it may be difficult for us to feel sorry for them or to feel that they are somehow being "cheated" out of rights that the rest of us have. By 1993 average NBA salaries had reached $1 million, while the wire services reported that 100 Major League Baseball players had salaries of $3 million or more and 38 percent made at least $1 million. Many of us would gladly subject ourselves to such "slavery." Table 7.5 compares NFL team payrolls in 1993, with San Francisco 49er players averaging $880,000 in salary, while the Cincinnati Bengals were at the bottom of the earnings list, averaging "only" $406,000 (National Football League Players Association 1993).

Despite the high salaries enjoyed by current professional athletes, for over a century, the sports labor market was dominated by the owners. This bred a workers' revolution in which the underpaid and often oppressed players would not only seek a fair cut of the profits, but would grab as much of the owners' pie as they could.

---

[4]Those rare athletes, such as Bo Jackson and John Elway, who have the potential to play two sports professionally may bargain one opportunity against the other. The only other options for athletes are the professional leagues of considerably lower caliber, if not lower pay, in other countries.

TABLE 7.5 *Comparing Team Payrolls in the NFL—1993**

San Francisco 49ers	$41.4 million
Washington Redskins	$40.3 million
Buffalo Bills	$39.1 million
New York Giants	$38.5 million
New Orleans Saints	$36.3 million
Green Bay Packers	$35.3 million
Phoenix Cardinals	$35.2 million
Kansas City Chiefs	$35.1 million
New York Jets	$34.9 million
Cleveland Browns	$34.4 million
Miami Dolphins	$34.2 million
Atlanta Falcons	$33.9 million
Los Angeles Raiders	$33.3 million
Indianapolis Colts	$33.2 million
Chicago Bears	$31.9 million
Detroit Lions	$30.7 million
Denver Broncos	$30.4 million
Houston Oilers	$29.6 million
Los Angeles Rams	$28.4 million
Tampa Bay Buccaneers	$28.2 million
Minnesota Vikings	$26.7 million
San Diego Chargers	$26.2 million
Philadelphia Eagles	$26.2 million
Pittsburgh Steelers	$26.1 million
Seattle Seahawks	$25.7 million
Dallas Cowboys	$24.7 million
New England Patriots	$20.1 million
Cincinnati Bengals	$19.1 million

*Data from NFL Player's Association, 1993.

The Early Years.   The first professional baseball league was formed by players in 1870 to provide structure for what had been a loosely knit group of eastern and midwestern teams. Within five years, poor teams lost their best players to wealthier ones, destroying the league's competitive balance. The weaker teams folded, leaving a few stronger ones without sufficient opponents to play against, and thus no profit.

The National League was formed in 1876 with the new team owners determined to place severe restrictions on players switching teams to get the best deal. Owners shackled the players with restrictions rather than agreeing to control their own pirating of each other's players.[5] The reserve clause became the primary restriction on player-instigated movement between teams (as opposed to owner-instigated sale and trade of players). Through this reserve clause, which owners demanded be a part of every player's contract, the player could only go to another team if he was traded, sold, or released (which occurred only if he was deemed to have no value). A player had to work for the salary offered by management—having no other choice if he wanted to be a professional player. He was required to continue serving whatever new master his owner decided to sell or trade him to. Players were *chattel,* figuratively "cattle," bought, used, and sold, or put out to pasture.

The rationale for binding players to a team was the necessity to stabilize the league with more balanced competition, thus maintaining a better product (games) and encouraging fans to identify with particular players on "their team." This, in turn, would pave the way for greater profits. Not to be overlooked, however, was the tenor of the times—the 1870s and 1880s—an era of laissez-faire capitalism infused with Social Darwinism, which held that it was simply in the natural order of things to have those at the top of the socioeconomic ladder dominating and controlling those of a lower class. Consistent with this thinking was the belief that those engaged in manual labor—athletes—belonged on lower rungs of the socioeconomic ladder than those who worked with their minds—the owners or managers.

The Supreme Court, nearly half a century later in 1922, decided, based on Justice Oliver Wendell Holmes' opinion, that professional baseball was not subject to federal antitrust laws because (1) baseball was not a business in the nature of other businesses—Holmes didn't say what it was—and (2) no major league baseball stadium straddled a state line. No matter that teams crossed state lines to play each other, fans travelled to see the games, and radio stations had already begun to broadcast games heard beyond the state of origin. Since contests were not played outside the borders of a given state, baseball was not deemed to be engaged in interstate trade, and so was exempt from federal antitrust law, specifically the Sherman and Clayton Antitrust Acts. This rather creative reasoning has stood the test of time and several challenges, and to the present exempts baseball from these laws, although other professional sports are within the scope of antitrust laws.

In 1964, Major League Baseball began to distribute new players by draft, thus halting the owners' practice of bidding against each other for raw talent. Drafting players to their first professional contract has denied players the last vestige of choice about where they would be employed. According to Scully (1978:432), "No other occupation in America, except perhaps conscription into the military, is as restrictive [as professional sports]."

---

[5]This is similar to NCAA regulations, which historically penalized athletes for accepting the bribes of recruiters and coaches instead of penalizing those offering the bribes.

Changing the System of Owner Domination. The corporate model of ownership allowed team owners to dominate players in their legal and economic relations until the mid-1970s. Four times in the late 19th century, players formed their own cooperative, player-owned leagues. Each ended in failure. Without the capital to build their own enclosed stadiums and without the political clout enjoyed by capitalist owners (some of whom were also local politicians) to get trolley lines routed to their ball fields, they could not turn a profit (Vincent 1981).

The first and only successful challenge to the baseball monopoly held by the National League came in 1901 with the formation of the American League. The success of the American League can be attributed to its corporate rather than player-owned structure as capital and political clout created the conditions necessary for a successful business venture. Not surprisingly, the American League owners immediately adopted the reserve clause and arbitrary limits on player salaries.

Challenges to this organizational suppression of individual rights have occurred infrequently, considering the number of years these openly collusive and restrictive working conditions have existed. While labor in American industry was gaining rights, better salaries, improved working conditions, and the freedom to organize, the labor market of professional sports was docilely performing under a medieval system resulting from legal precedent (the Holmes decision), tradition, and inertia.

In 1949, a significant step was taken to change the players' subservient status, with formation of the Major League Baseball Players' Association. For over a decade, however, this union was less than dynamic in fighting for and achieving rights for players. Players chosen as shop stewards from each team often found themselves traded or released by owners in retaliation for their union efforts.

Occasionally, professional athletes used the courts to challenge owner domination. Among these were baseball player Danny Gardella (1949) and football players Bill Radovich (1957) and Jim Ninowski (1966), each directly challenging the written and unwritten rules that allowed players to be bought and sold like pieces of property. The Radovich case (*Radovich* versus *National Football League,* 352 U.S. 445) cracked the structure of NFL owner domination when the Supreme Court ruled that all sports, other than baseball, were subject to antitrust law.

In the mid-1960s, Sandy Koufax and Don Drysdale, the heart of the pitching staff on a weak-hitting Los Angeles Dodgers team, were each dissatisfied with the contracts they were offered. The two players decided to bargain in a unique way: to approach Dodgers' management as a single entity, knowing that the team could not afford to lose them both. Koufax and Drysdale received multiyear contracts (although the contracts were not linked), and forced the Dodgers to negotiate through their agent-lawyers. Both changes were unprecedented in owner-athlete contract negotiations, leading directly to other players also demanding legal representation and multiyear contracts.

Power in sports labor-management relations, however, had not yet shifted to the players. In 1970 Curt Flood, an all-star outfielder for the St. Louis Cardinals, and, not incidentally, a black man, sued to have baseball's reserve clause overturned, since it relegated players to the condition of slaves (albeit well-paid). The case went to the Supreme Court in 1972 (*Flood* versus *Kuhn*, 407 U.S. 258), where Flood lost. The courts, while beginning to question the *chattel* status of baseball players, felt that the reserve clause was still necessary to maintain stability and that owners were not making unreasonable demands in running their businesses (Rivkin 1974).

A 13-day players' strike at the start of the 1972 baseball season was a crucial event in giving power to the players. Their union and the owners' council agreed to collective bargaining for resolution of salary disputes, the owners' first concession to collective demands from their player-laborers in a century. Stalled contract negotiations would now be submitted to a neutral arbitrator who could decide for one side or the other based on such factors as comparable playing skills and existing salaries, cost of living index, and the ability of the team owner to pay the requested salary.

The key event in shifting power from owners to players—turning what had been a talent buyer's market into a talent seller's market—occurred in 1976 when arbitrator Peter Seitz decided that pitcher Andy Messersmith of the Dodgers could "play out his option" (i.e., play for one year without a contract) and then become a *free agent* to peddle his curveball wherever he might. Since 1976, owners have had to decide not only whether they could afford to meet a player's salary demands or be without his services, but also whether they could afford to have the player on a rival team.

Given this freedom to select their employer—a freedom enjoyed by virtually all other Americans except felons—salaries began to skyrocket. In 1950, amidst the era of owner domination, the highest team salary belonged to the New York Yankees, approximately $500,000 for the *entire* major league roster, with an average Yankee player earning $18,788 (Rottenberg 1956). By 1988, after more than a decade of free agency, the Yankees were still the highest paid team in the big leagues, their major league roster earning $19,441,152, the average salary *per player* of well over $600,000. Prior to salary escalation, major league baseball had its occasional Mickey Mantle or Ted Williams or Hank Aaron earning more than $100,000 per year toward the end of long and distinguished careers.

One need only hear the reactions of major league players to the 1993 income tax increase to see how far they have risen from the ranks of the oppressed and down-trodden. In 1983, the average major league salary was about $250,000. A decade later it had more than quadrupled to $1,120,247. In response to having his federal tax rate rise from 31 percent to 39.6 percent, Kent Hrbek of the Minnesota Twins, whose salary for 1993 was $3 million, said, "I'm working hard for the American dream, but it's being taken away" (Associated Press 1993).

"IT'S ALL IN HIS NEW CONTRACT."

Reprinted with special permission of King Features Syndicate.

NFL and NBA players are also riding the inflationary tide. Table 7.5 shows the salaries of NFL teams in 1993, while the contracts awarded NBA players at the beginning of the 1993–94 season do not bode well for the economic stability of that league. The year's top draft pick, Chris Webber, left college early (apparently wisely) to sign a $74-million, 15-year deal with the Golden State Warriors. A week later, second-year star Larry Johnson of the Charlotte Hornets renegotiated his contract to receive $84 million over 12 years.

Further proof in the shift of power in team sports can be seen in the content of players' contracts. Since the late 1970s players have demanded and won contracts giving them a voice in their working conditions, veto rights over trades, and performance bonuses as owners strive to hold onto their newly freed laborers.

The Owners' Perspective

Capital Gains. Lest one feel sorry for the owners, the value of their franchises has soared along with player salaries. The Seattle Seahawks of the NFL were sold in 1989 for $97 million, more than a 500 percent capital gain over the $16 million price paid for the franchise in 1974. The Portland Trail Blazers of the NBA brought its owner $70 million 18 years after the franchise was established for $3.5 million. The NHL's Hartford Whalers were sold for $31 million two years

TABLE 7.6   *What Sports Franchises Are Worth: Top and Bottom Dollar – 1993**

BASEBALL:	High	$225 million	New York Yankees
	Low	$80 million	Pittsburgh Pirates, Montreal Expos, Colorado Rockies, Detroit Tigers, Houston Astros, Florida Marlins
FOOTBALL:	High	$175 million	Dallas Cowboys
	Low	$100 million	Tampa Bay Buccaneers, Phoenix Cardinals, New England Patriots
BASKETBALL:	High	$140 million	Chicago Bulls
	Low	$50 million	Washington Bullets, Utah Jazz, Seattle Supersonics, New Jersey Nets, Indiana Pacers, Denver Nuggets
ICE HOCKEY:	High	$80 million	Detroit Red Wings
	Low	$35 million	Ottawa Senators, San Jose Sharks, Tampa Bay Lightning, Winnipeg Jets

*Source: Steinbreder 1993:69.

after *Fortune* magazine estimated its worth at less than $15 million (Moore 1986; Fichtenbaum et al. 1989). The Sacramento Kings were purchased (as the Kansas City Kings) in the early 1980s for $12 million, evaluated at $16 million three years later, and instantly became worth at least $32 million in 1988 when that price was set for four expansion teams to enter the NBA. In 1989 the Dallas Cowboys, which had won only three games the previous season, fetched $140 million. And the Baltimore Orioles were sold in 1993 for $173 million, the highest price to that point ever paid for a sports franchise (Steinbreder 1993). Table 7.6 shows the top and bottom prices for franchises in the four major sports. The total worth of all NFL teams was $3.64 billion, all Major League Baseball teams, $3.60 billion, NBA teams, $2.16 billion, and NHL teams, $1.42 billion. Entrepreneurs who pay high prices for sports franchises look to tax shelters, television receipts, depreciation of players, and sale of luxury boxes, along with their own eventual franchise sale to recoup the exorbitant cost of the team (Hayes 1989).

Collusion.   Besides selling their franchises, baseball owners have another strategy to combat escalating contracts and players testing their worth through free agency. Arbitrators found that, in 1985 and 1986 at least, the owners engaged in illegal *collusion*[6] to undermine the free agent marketplace. Arbitrator Robert Nicolau declared that, "As long as a free agent's former club demonstrated a continuing interest and retained negotiating rights . . . no other club

---

[6]Although owners have openly colluded on employment conditions and salaries throughout the history of professional baseball, it was not until the federal government began to show concern for the economic relationship between players and owners in the mid-1970s that legal sanctions have been applied.

bid for that player" (Bodley 1988:1C). Nicolau charged baseball owners with illegally attempting to rig the marketplace for baseball talent, which violated the existing labor agreement. When owners were not individually able to control the salaries they paid their players, they joined together in a secret—i.e., collusive—pact to do so (Gammons 1988).

A Solution to Runaway Salary Inflation: The Lackritz Model

The free agent system has clearly been an economic boon to players. Dire financial consequences for team owners was predicted over a decade ago (Wise and Cox 1978). Although this has not yet occurred, it may yet prove true if the salary trends, based on a free marketplace, continue. The NBA has tried to deal with this problem by instituting a salary cap for each team, although several unique accounting strategies devised by agents (e.g., deferred payments, performance bonuses) tend to undermine such attempts at controlling salary inflation, which will ultimately be paid for by fans. Decreased profit from national televising of baseball has also occurred, as CBS lost $500 million on a $1 billion contract ending in 1993. Conceivably, this could be the leading edge of a trend that might result in less free broadcasting of sports events, then to fewer teams, particularly with the government closing tax loopholes formerly enjoyed by owners. Ultimately, this would result in fewer positions for players.

Are multimillion dollar athlete salaries "fair"? Fairness can be defined in two distinctly different ways. In a free marketplace, price is based solely on whatever the buyer is willing to spend. If an owner is willing to spend $2 million or more for a player's services, that is the owner's choice. If fans are willing to spend $20, $30, or more for a ticket to a sports event, so be it. On the other hand, fairness can be defined more broadly than simply the immediate relationship between buyer and seller, particularly when such narrow interpretations may lead to widespread reconfigurations such as bankruptcies in the sports industry, movement of franchises, deaths of entire leagues, and outpricing the budget of the common fan. (Perhaps there was some wisdom, after all, in Justice Holmes' decision that baseball was more than a mere business and that sport should be governed with broader concern.)

According to James Lackritz, economist at San Diego State University,

> Most mediocre players make far more than the President of the United States.
> . . . If the clubs are to operate at a break-even level (many do not), then a realistic model must be established to monitor and control salary levels [based on an estimate of] a player's true value to his club (1987:1).

Salary would be determined by several performance variables compared with the average player in the league along with several franchise-related variables such as the percentage of games won by one's team, pennants won in recent years, and the number of other professional sports teams in the market. The resulting figure would be measured against the league average to determine how much above or below the league average that player should be paid.

Copyright © 1977 Washington Star. Reprinted with permission of Universal Press Syndicate.

Lackritz claims that this performance-derived model is more reasonable than the arbitrary free-market way in which salaries are currently determined, and that it would halt the inflationary salary spiral, for which fans ultimately pay.

A counterargument to this sort of salary-setting scheme is that the careers of athletes are short and they should be allowed to earn as much as they can while they can. Parallel is often drawn between professional athletes and popular music stars whose earnings are compressed over brief careers. Comparison is fatuous since music stars do not have minimum salaries, income guaranteed when they are ill or injured, or retirement plans that begin after only five years in the profession, all of which athletes in each of the major leagues enjoy.

Fans: The Ignored Constituency

While Peter Ueberroth, former commissioner of baseball, said of owners that, "They run their sports businesses less effectively than their primary business" (Sandomir 1989:3), owners are adept enough at either profiting from the operation of their team or making a killing by selling it. If players cannot be faulted for getting all they can while they can, should owners be criticized for maximizing their profits? Not according to one critic of sport: "Players, owners, sportswriters, and agents are paid more than teachers, nurses, and poets because the public—and that's you and me . . . —puts its wallet where its values are" (Barra 1989:44).

In the battle between players and owners, there are few monetary restraints, and, so far, the fan has been willing to pay whatever amount is asked. In other industries, prices and products are controlled to protect consumers, even though they might be willing, with some grumbling, to pay more. The government to this point, however, has been unwilling to protect the sports consumer.

It has been more than a decade since Ralph Nader briefly stepped into the breach with an organization called F.A.N.S.—Fight to Advance the Nation's Sports—which developed a Fans' Bill of Rights (Nader and Gruenstein 1978). This fan-consumer advocate stance, however, was met with stunning apathy. Born in 1978, it died the same year. More recently another organized effort has emerged, Sports Fans United, a not-for-profit organization with the goals of making sports more affordable, accessible, and accountable to fans and those affected by marketed sports. Their agenda is:

Sports Fans United
Principles & Legislative/Social Agenda[7]

FIRST PRINCIPLE: The fans' concerns should be foremost in all business decisions affecting them.

- All teams should establish Fan Advisory Boards that would be consulted on ticket prices and TV contracts.
- Fan Advisory Boards would collaborate on issues of fan safety, stadium amenities, and community programs.

SECOND PRINCIPLE: Sports fan-taxpayers need to be protected by federal law. Congress should enact legislation to:

- Repeal Major League Baseball's blanket exemption from antitrust laws.
- Give cities the right to buy a team or find a local buyer before the team's owner is allowed to relocate.
- Force all leagues to maintain a significant number of games on free TV (which would amend the 1961 Sports Broadcasting Act).
- Ban pay-per-view for all post-season championship events (such as the Super Bowl, World Series, Stanley Cup, and NBA Finals).
- Ensure competition between cable, telephone, microwave, and other telecommunication delivery systems.
- Include sports channels among those regulated by the FCC (i.e., amend the 1992 Cable Act).

THIRD PRINCIPLE: The antitrust division of the Department of Justice, the Federal Trade Commission, and the Federal Communications Commission should protect fan interests. Legal or regulatory actions should be taken to:

- Give any channel the opportunity to contract for the right to televise any game (thus invalidating the league's restrictive broadcast territories).

---

[7]Provided by Adam Kolton, Executive Director, SPORTS FANS UNITED, 352 Seventh Avenue, New York, NY 10001, 212/736-FANS.

- Challenge contracts between sports leagues and networks which limit the number of games on free TV and the overall number of games televised.

FOURTH PRINCIPLE: Fans and taxpayers should have a voice in stadium construction and lease negotiations between cities and sports teams. Leases should include provisions to:

- Keep tickets affordable and available to non-season ticket holders.
- Ensure that more than 50 percent of televised games are on free TV.
- Allow competition among concessionaires at all events.
- Give the home city a percentage of all stadium revenues.
- Limit the amount of in-stadium advertising.
- Make each team's financial information available to the public.

Few rights come to those who do not demand them and are unwilling to sacrifice for them. Whether sports fans feel that the economic warfare between owners and players is hurting them sufficiently to generate revolt, and whether fans are willing to forgo their spectating pleasures in order to gain some consumer control of the sports market, remains an open question.

Summary

We may wonder how many people retain the belief that marketed sport—collegiate, Olympic, professional—is anything other than big business. Justice Holmes in 1922 decided about baseball that it was "something" other than business, but the slow erosion of whatever it is that makes sport different is nearly complete. We have cartels throughout sport making decisions to maximize profits and control of their marketplace. Some legislation has modified this control, but as goes the tenet in big business that desires to remain big, other ways will be found to regain control and profit.

There are, however, two aspects of sport that are unlike most other businesses. First is the unique control that modern athletes have over the marketing of and compensation for their skills and personae. Second is the continuing health and even growth of elements in the sports industry—collegiate athletics, in particular—which often operate at a loss. The explanation in both cases may be attributed to inelastic demand for services and products. In the case of professional athlete-labor, the demand for talent among owners is such that no limit to salaries has yet appeared on the horizon. Perhaps this is so because the owners see little movement among fan-consumers to limit their consumption of the sports product. This situation, as in other aspects of economic life, leaves control, if it is to occur, in the hands of government.

References

Associated Press. 1993. "Players Bemoan Bigger Tax Bite." *San Francisco Chronicle.* August 22:C6.

Barra, A. 1989. "Killing Off the Fans." *New York Times Book Review* June 11:44.

Blum, D. 1993. "Backers of Women's Sports Wonder If Following in the Footsteps of Men's Programs Is a Good Idea." *Chronicle of Higher Education.* May 12:A41-42.

Bodley, H. 1988. "Owners Again Found Guilty of Collusion." *USA Today* September 1:1C.

Bye, R. T. 1956. *Principles of Economics.* 5th edition. New York: Appleton-Century-Crofts.

Comte, E., L. Girard, and A. Starensier. 1989. "Embracing Stars, Ignoring Players." *Sports, Inc.* January 2:41-43.

Davenport, D. S. 1969. "Collusive Competition in Major League Baseball." *The American Economist* 13:6-30.

Daymont, T. N. 1975. "The Effects of Monopsonistic Procedures on Equality of Competition in Professional Sports Leagues." *International Review of Sport Sociology* 10:83-99.

Edwards, H. 1973. *Sociology of Sport.* Homewood, IL: Dorsey.

Farrell, C. S. 1987a. "Big-Time Teams Will Fight Cuts in Football; Income Must Pay for Other Sports, They Say." *Chronicle of Higher Education* May 27:27-28.

Farrell, C. S. 1987b. "NCAA's First Basketball Millionaires." *Chronicle of Higher Education* March 25:37.

Fichtenbaum, P., R. Rosenblatt, and R. Sandomir. 1989. "How Golden the Goose?" *Sports, Inc.* January 2:29-31.

Gammons, P. 1988. "Inside Baseball: The Verdict Is In." *Sports Illustrated* September 12:60-61.

Gent, P. 1973. *North Dallas Forty.* New York: William Morrow.

"Get Sports Funds from Pros, Minnesota Panel Says." 1978. *Chronicle of Higher Education* May 15:2.

Hayes, T. C. 1989. "Cowboys' Sale Says Sports Is Business." *New York Times.* Reprinted in *The Sacramento Bee* March 6:C5.

Jacobs, M. S. 1991. "Professional Sports Leagues, Antitrust, and the Single-Entity Theory: A Defense of the Status Quo." *Indiana Law Journal.* 67(1):25-58.

Johnson, A. T. 1979. "Congress and Professional Sports: 1951-1978." Annals AAPSS, 445:102-15.

Koch, J. V. 1971. "The Economics of 'Big-Time' Intercollegiate Athletics." *Social Science Quarterly* 52(2):248-60.

Krause, D. D. 1992. "The National Football League's Ban on Corporate Ownership: Violating Antitrust to Preserve Traditional Ownership." *Seton Hall Journal of Sport Law.* 2(1):175-201.

Lackritz, J. R. 1987. *Salary Evaluation for Professional Baseball Players.* Unpublished paper.

Lapin, L. 1993. "Full Steam and Millions Ahead for Big-Time Athletics." *The Sacramento Bee.* October 24:A14.

Leonard, W. M. II. 1988. *A Sociological Perspective of Sport.* 3rd edition. New York: Macmillan.

Lewis, G. 1967. "America's First Intercollegiate Sport: Regatta." *Research Quarterly* 38(4):637-48.

Lobmeyer, H., and L. Weidinger. 1992. "Commercialism As a Dominant Factor in the American Sport Scene." *International Review for the Sociology of Sport.* 27(4):309-27.

Moore, T. 1986. "It's 4th & 10—The NFL Needs the Long Bomb." *Fortune.* August 4:160-67.

Nader, R., and P. Gruenstein. 1978. "Fans: The Sorry Majority." *Playboy* March: 98-100+.

National Football League Players Association. 1993. "Comparing Team Payrolls." *USA Today.* August 2:8C.

NCAA. 1988. "Opinions: Peter J. Dalis." *NCAA News* July 26:4.

NCAA. 1989. "Comment: It's Wrong to Try to Reregulate Football on TV." *NCAA News* July 20:4.

NCAA. 1993. "Auburn Football Receives 2-Year Probation." *NCAA News.* September 1:8.

Padilla, A. 1987. "On the Economics of Intercollegiate Athletic Programs." Paper prepared for the Amateur Athletic Foundation of Los Angeles and the Presidents' Commission of the NCAA.

Philp, T. 1993. "As College Budgets Shrink, Taxpayers Keep Sports Kicking." *The Sacramento Bee.* October 24:A1, A14.

Raiborn, M. 1990. "Revenues and Expenses of Intercollegiate Athletic Programs: Analysis of Financial Trends and Relationships, 1985-89." *National Collegiate Athletic Association.* Mission, KS: NCAA.

Rivkin, S. R. 1974. "Sports Leagues and the Federal Antitrust Laws." Pp. 387-410 in *Government and the Sports Business,* edited by R. Noll. Washington, DC: Brookings Institution.

Rosner, D. 1989. "The World Plays Catch-up." *Sports, Inc.* January 2:6-13.

Rottenberg, S. 1956. "The Baseball Players' Labor Market." *Journal of Political Economy* 64:242-58.

Sandomir, R. 1989. "Ueberroth's Parting Words: Decries Salary Escalation." *Sports, Inc.* March 13:3.

Scully, G. W. 1978, "Salary Arbitration in Major League Baseball." *American Behavioral Scientist* 21(3):431-50.

Steinbreder, J. 1993. "The Owners." *Sports Illustrated.* September 13:64-72+.

Vance, N. S. 1984. "TV Football Pact Is a Cooperative Venture, Not Monopolistic, NCAA Tells High Court." *Chronicle of Higher Education* March 28:27, 30.

Vincent, T. 1981. *Mudville's Revenge: The Rise and Fall of American Sport.* New York: Seaview.

Weiner, J. 1973. "The High Cost of Big-Time Football." *College and University Business* 55(3):35-42.

Wieberg, S. 1993. "Pacific 10's Harsh Sanctions Prompt Coach's Resignation." *USA Today.* August 23:8C.

Wise, G. L., and M. K. Cox. 1978. "Public Policy Questions Loom on the Horizon as the Consumer Confronts Selected Aspects of Major League Baseball." *American Behavioral Scientist* 21(3):451-64.

Wolff, A. 1993. "Trickle-Down Economics." *Sports Illustrated.* October 25:84.

CHAPTER 8

Sport and Aging

I would like to put in a good word for the thrill of learning something new after 45. I have watched many middle-aged men and women hoist themselves on skis and veer down the slopes behind an instructor, positively giddy with the delight of being learners again. They're never going to do dazzling jet turns, but so what! The same holds true for menopausal women who have told me about taking up golf or biking for the first time. One busy career woman who made time to start piano lessons enjoyed it so much that she has gone on to tap dancing. When undertaken in the right spirit, such activities have nothing to do with dilettantism. The point is to defeat the entropy that says, slow down, give it up, watch TV, and to open up another pathway that can enliven all the senses, including the sense that one is not just an old dog. (Sheehy 1976:501)

In her book *Passages,* Gail Sheehy describes what American adults can and should expect as they pass through the several stages of their lives. She shows that adult development is patterned, just as there are patterns in earlier stages of life. However, she argues that adults are more in charge and thus able to mold life to their own satisfaction with more freedom than children and adolescents have. This potential to better manage what happens to us is based on knowledge of life processes, what society does for and to us, and what factors are physically and emotionally unavoidable or changeable in the aging process.

The *pure description* phase of this chapter orients us to the meaning of aging and how the role and status of "elder" relates to other segments of life. Our *evaluative commentary* focuses on theories that apply to aging and what research says about the life and environment of the aged as it relates to physical activity and sport. Following the data we will engage in *social critique* on the position of elders in American society. Finally, we will describe several sports and exercise opportunities for elders, and we will offer suggestions for *social engineering* that might improve the lot of elders in American society.

What Is Old Age?

Since 1513, when Juan Ponce de Leon's troops swept ashore near what is now St. Augustine, Florida, seeking the Fountain of Youth, Americans have been clutching youth with one hand while pushing back old age with the other. Old age and the elderly have been alternately venerated and vilified throughout American history (Foner 1980), but the sanity of anyone in any era who looks forward to old age would be questioned.

We seem drawn to potions, massages and manipulations, water "cures," and exercises alleged to help us retain or regain youthful vitality. Approaching the 21st century, we still look to passive cures for fading youth through liposuction and facelifts and active means such as health clubs, spas, personal trainers, aerobics classes, and home exercise equipment. In the latter 20th century, a youthful, physically fit body is a status symbol, even to the elderly.

Can a person be healthy and happy without physical activity or exercise? Possibly. Can a person be healthy and happy without involvement in sports? Probably. Can sport foster health and happiness, especially in the elderly? We simply do not know yet. Little gerontological research has considered sports participation, and it was not until 1993 that a research periodical—the *Journal of Aging and Physical Activity*—focusing on physical activity in the elder years was begun.

An interesting new paradigm[1] is establishing a beachhead in the study of aging. Its prime spokesperson is physician Deepak Chopra, who argues in *Ageless Body, Timeless Mind* (1993), that people make themselves age and decline by their belief that aging and death are inevitable. According to Chopra, the problem lies in our mind-set that decline and death are our destiny to be faced in our sixth or seventh decades. This expectation sends a message to our cells, which dutifully begin to age. Without that message we would remain vigorous and youthful (if not young). Chopra's perspective suggests not so much mind over matter as mind influencing matter.

Clarifying Key Terms

Attempts to define terms clearly may yield more confusion than precision. Terms such as *young, middle-aged,* and *old* provide, at best, fuzzy distinctions. A person of 55 is old compared to one of 25, but may be young relative to a 70-year-old; conversely, the biologically older person may have more physical or mental capacity and "life" than the biologically younger one. Sixty years is near the upper range of age distribution, yet a person of 60 is too "youthful" to participate in the Kids & Kubs softball league of St. Petersburg, Florida, where 75 is the minimum age.

We will employ the generic term "elder" as a dynamic description of the later portion of life, rather than as a specific referent to biological age or a particular degree of infirmity. We must also distinguish among sport, exercise,

---

[1]Actually, this is an ancient Hindu paradigm, transported and translated into Western medicine and gerontology.

THE QUIGMANS

Could it be that negative feelings about aging make us age faster?
Copyright © 1988 Los Angeles Times. Reprinted by permission.

and physical activity. *Sport* refers to organized competitive contests having a physical component. *Exercise* is physical noncompetitive activity not bound by rules. *Physical pursuit*[2] will be used as a generic term encompassing both sport and exercise. The specific pursuit may be health, achievement, social involvement or ego gratification, but it must be purposefully focused on physical or mental health of elders to fit our conceptualization.

While elders' physical pursuit may be quite competitive, winning (*product-*focus), which characterizes much earlier-life competition, may be transposed

---

[2]"Physical activity" is, of course, relevant to the life of elders—as it is to anyone. This would include gardening, and possibly work or avocation endeavors, which are tangential to this chapter.

FIGURE 8.1 *George Bakewell, 101 years old, plays softball with the Kids & Kubs of St. Petersburg, Florida. Their minimum age for participation is 75, showing that there is indeed much joyful physical activity one can look forward to during the elder years. (Photo by Paul B. Good.)*

into participation for its inherent joy, health, and social contact (*process*-focus). This should not be considered as a regression to youth activity. Indeed, as we saw in Chapter 5, much childhood sport is quite adult-like. Rather, a "play-like" process-focus in elder sport can be the ultimate achievement of the potential for physical pursuit to reach one's personal potential, free of the expectations and restrictions of hierarchical goals. Elders are not likely to use competitiveness as a climbing tool, and so they can more truly "play" at their physical pursuit.

This is not to say that elders do not strive for success in sports. Clearly, many do, as indicated by the growth in elder competition, such as the Senior Olympics (detailed later). Our point is that even here there is not likely to be an ulterior or extrinsic motive, such as occurs in youth league, high school, collegiate, and professional sport. Youth and school sport is an avocation, something that may be pursued for inherent pleasure, but which may also provide extrinsic rewards ranging from social status to a scholarship, or even an eventual career. For the vast majority of young adults, sport and exercise are leisure activities that provide an interlude from work and career. For many elders, leisure is less interlude than a focal point of life, a fulcrum on which their lives balance (Rombold 1989). One retires from work, not from play (Harootyan 1982).

Differences Among Elders

Elders are not a single, homogeneously age-based group. They vary widely in employment and marital status, health and mobility, living arrangements (e.g., independent, elderly housed, nursing care), degree of contact with family and friends, vulnerability to and fear of crime, and the demographic variables of urban/rural, sex, race, socioeconomic status, religion, and education to which we more commonly pay attention. Each factor could affect degree and type of physical pursuit. Consider the following two examples: A recent retiree in Sun City, Arizona, fills her days with golf, while a 75-year-old in New York City ventures out of his apartment only in fear and trepidation, much less considers taking a "health" stroll in Central Park or attending a Yankee game in the violence-ridden South Bronx. It would be wrong to attribute the lower degree of physical activity in the latter example to advanced age, since other factors affect his decisions.

Very few elders are infirm or in need of supervised care. Merely 5 percent of elders are institutionalized (Harootyan 1982; Lammers 1983), which means that most elders function more or less on their own. Thus, the category of elderly should not be equated with loss or decline. Infirm or senile behavior in elders may be attributed to "learned helplessness" (McPherson 1984a:5). Remove that expectation and their "youthfulness" may return.

Age Cohorts

The elder years are a different experience for our grandparents and our parents than they will be for us, and these years will be different for our children. Such groupings are called *age cohorts*. Opportunities, attitudes and values, normative behaviors, and even variations in laws, family arrangements, and schooling paint diverse pictures of life for people born in different eras. For example, the attitude toward work and career, in particular job security, varies for people raised in the Depression compared to those raised in the affluent 1950s, which is also likely to differ from those raised in the fast-track 1970s and 1980s. As another example, elderly women consistently report little involvement in sport in their youth, as young adults, or in their later years

(Harootyan 1982). However, the age cohort of women raised in the 1960s and earlier did not have extensive opportunity for involvement in sport; they were less likely to value sports or physical exercise.

The well-observed pattern of decreasing activity with increasing age may change with the baby boom generation (those born between 1946 and 1964). This cohort will be reaching retirement in the second decade of the next century, but as they anticipate old age, baby boomers are likely to alter the cultural perception of aging well before they reach retirement. Along with its higher level of education relative to earlier generations (Lammers 1983), the baby boom cohort is particularly oriented toward health, exercise, and sport, which could reduce the apparent stigma attached to physical activity in old age. Baby boomers will also continue to be a politically powerful cohort, capable of reducing age discrimination that discouraged earlier elder cohorts from physical activity.

Following continuity theory, increased involvement in exercise and sport at younger ages is likely to translate into similar behavior in old age. The 20th-century trend toward earlier retirement may provide more time for leisure-oriented physical activity, especially during the middle-age years when exercise and sport habits can be solidified before physical decline begins. However, those immersed in work at the expense of physical activity until age 65 (to use a common marker for retirement) are unlikely to take up active exercise or sport at 66, despite their newly abundant available time.

The elderly should have their own standards of activity and performance. As Sheehy says, "Taking up an active pursuit in midlife doesn't mean falling into the trap of physical competition with one's younger athletic self" (1976:502). Perhaps in the process, the elderly will shed their current low status and ineffectual image. While these changes may occur spontaneously, they need to be anticipated and facilitated, especially as there is an aging pre-baby boom cohort that could benefit from a more positive attitude toward physical activity of the elderly.

Questions and Issues in Sport and Aging

Elders will have an increasing impact on society. In North America nearly 10 percent of the population has passed the age of 65, a figure predicted to rise to more than 15 percent by the second decade of the 21st century when the baby boom cohort reaches 65 (McPherson 1984a). By the century's third decade, those over 60 will be a larger segment of the population than the young in many countries (Levy 1984).

Mavis Lindgren is 81 years old. Since she began jogging at the age of 70, she has run more than 30 marathons (Whaley 1988). In her level of physical pursuit, Mavis Lindgren is far from typical of her age group, but we do not know how far. Elders who are past job and family-rearing responsibilities have more time for physical pursuits. Do they participate in these activities, or are they sedentary? To what extent is physical decline responsible for lack of activity? Can physical activity halt, or even reverse, physical or mental decline? How, in what forms, and to what extents do exercise and sport enhance their quality of life?

What opportunities for physical pursuit do elders have? Is society responsible for providing these opportunities, as it does for youth? How and in what forms could opportunities for exercise and sport be increased and made maximally beneficial for elders? Gerontologists are beginning to study such questions as the elderly more heavily influence society. We cannot provide answers to all these questions in this chapter; we can, however, answer some, put them into perspective, and suggest directions for the future.

Theories and Knowledge About Activity in the Life of the Elderly

Several theories attempt to explain patterns of involvement or lack of involvement of elders in exercise, sport, and other activity. We will focus on three theories explaining the activity patterns of the elderly: disengagement theory, activity theory, and continuity theory.

Disengagement Theory

Cumming and Henry (1961) say that elders withdraw from active involvement in a society as they lose their role responsibilities in work, family, and organizations. This withdrawal is bilateral: as society needs them less, elders voluntarily remove themselves from the mainstream of activity. Disengagement may occur because of (1) a shift in one's frame of reference (especially loss of friends and associations) resulting from retirement, institutionalization, or change of location; (2) redefinition of self from loss of roles; (3) questioning the value or cost of one's continued commitment in given activities; (4) finding a once-satisfying activity now disappointing, perhaps because of loss of ability or intensity; or (5) finding existing relationships to be inadequate (Prus 1984).

In functionalist terms (Curtis and White 1984), this mutual disengagement fits within the grand scheme of the social system; as their usefulness in the system wanes, elders withdraw to make room for new blood in a "symbolic preparation for death" (Seawell 1989:15). Elders in other societies function as repositories of knowledge, wisdom, and history, and as caretakers for the very young. In modern society, particularly in America, however, elders are seldom given responsibility for child care, while knowledge and history (if not necessarily wisdom) are gained from printed and electronic sources rather than from elders.

Disengagement, as conceptualized by Cumming and Henry, is something that society needs and imposes, which well-socialized individuals accept. It may be, however, that when and where disengagement occurs, it is "health factors and not aging per se [that] produce disengagement" (Fry 1992:256). Social disengagement may simply reflect a desire to ease the stress-inducing pace of the career and child-rearing years, although it also may reflect age discrimination in the form of fewer opportunities for participation than are available to other age groups (Atchley 1992).

Where disengagement is imposed on unwilling elders, it may be recast in conflict-coercion terms as abandonment, a "downward trajectory in life-style, with ever-increasing levels of abandonment and social isolation," because "industrial society has no use for older people. . . . Modern society provides no positive evaluation tailored for old age" (Fry 1992:258). Old is defined as obsolete.

While abandonment may never have been official national policy, it has been recommended. Witness the following missive from a 1966 Rand Corporation study (#RM-5115-TAB, cited in Butler 1975:13):

> A community under stress would be better off without its old and feeble members. . . . The easiest way to implement a morally repugnant but socially beneficial policy is by inaction . . . failing to make any special provisions for the special needs of the elderly.

Perhaps we are more enlightened as we approach the 21st century. Certainly, the baby boom cohort is likely to resist such Social Darwinism.

The American social system and its institutions make physical pursuit available for other segments of society—physical education and organized sports for youth, municipal or job-sponsored leagues for working-age adults—while elders tend to be left to fend for themselves, despite the societal benefits of healthier elders.

Harootyan's (1982) research shows that even among the elderly, many believe that "others like them" are less active than they report of themselves. Neither disengagement nor abandonment theories are supported by empirical studies, which show few elders feeling lonely or isolated (Atchley 1992; George 1990). Nevertheless, there is anecdotal evidence of both disengagement (accepted) and abandonment (resented) among elders. The question remains as to how prevalent is either form of elder withdrawal from active life.

Activity Theory

> The key to successful aging lies in the individual's motivation to stay physically and mentally active. Successful aging means the maintenance, as far and as long as possible, of the activities and attitudes of middle age (Fry 1992:263).

This conceptualizes activity theory, whose basic tenet is that both middle-aged and elders have identical social and psychological needs and may even have similar physical needs. The main difference between disengagement/abandonment perspectives and activity theory is that a strong and focused internal locus of control can help elders to maintain or build an active framework for their lives (Fry 1992). They will then have the opportunity to interact dynamically with each situation as it arises, choosing to (1) remain active, (2) withdraw or disengage in specific instances, or (3) substitute new activities and roles. However, if these roles and this active involvement in life are not maintained, the self-image of elders and their satisfaction with life will suffer (Barrow 1989; Burgess 1960).

Rosenberg (1981) sees the forced retirement of professional athletes as evidence of abandonment, particularly if the athlete is expected to depart "without making waves" (1981:121). From the activity perspective, the retired athlete needs to find some replacement for lost role and function, perhaps with the help of the sports establishment.

Disengagement and abandonment theories focus on the needs of society, while activity theory focuses on the needs of individuals. The former serve the social forces of equilibrium, compelling elders into a narrowed, culturally defined role of living out their years with little or no purpose—and without rocking society's boat. The latter pits the elderly against younger adults, subgroups competing for limited roles and resources.

Continuity Theory

A third perspective on aging, continuity theory, does not compete directly with disengagement or activity theories. It speaks less of macrosociological policies and prescription, instead focusing on early socialization patterns and psychological adjustment to aging. "Continuity theory presumes that people act in order to adapt, whereas disengagement theory presumes that people withdraw in order to adapt" (Atchley 1992:339).

Continuity theory says simply that whatever pattern of activity individuals exhibit in youth and middle age will be continued into their later years (Long 1987). A new form of activity is not likely to be "discovered" in later life. Those who are socially and physically inactive earlier in life, irrespective of the reasons (e.g., work commitments), are not likely to change this pattern even when the conditions change (e.g., retirement). Those who were active and involved before their elder years are likely to maintain some form of satisfying activity, which will help their adjustment, although they may have to find new roles and involvements (Barrow 1989). A study of the Canadian labor force showed that while the number of activities decreased with age, the frequency of involvement in retained activities increased (Curtis and White 1984). For those who did not pursue a physically active form of leisure or exercise earlier in life, retirement will likely be a time of substituted sedentary and perhaps worklike activity, e.g., writing, creative hobbies, etc. (deGrazia 1973). If one has not been socialized into sport, play, or exercise earlier in life, one is not likely to adopt those forms later in life.

A problem with each of these theories is their tendency to assume physical decline and the subsequent need for coping with that phenomenon. Chopra (1993) notes that normative decline in physical capacities amounts to about 1 percent per year after the age of 30, and he, along with Bortz (1991), question whether even that rate of decline can't be slowed. With maintenance, or at least markedly slowed decline over the years, perhaps through physical pursuit, resistance or adaptation as discussed in these theories might not be needed.

Patterns and Benefits of Sport Involvement Among the Elderly

The mass of evidence indicates that as age increases, people in America tend to reduce their involvement in physical activity, particularly sport (Kenyon 1966; Hobart 1975; Harootyan 1982; Curtis and White 1984; McPherson 1984b; Mobily et al. 1984; Ostrow and Dzewaltowski 1986). McPherson (1984b) relates that this decline in physical activity is most prevalent in women, those from lower-status occupations, and those living in smaller communities. Although the prevailing image is of increased leisure-driven physical activity in retirement, this does not seem to be the case, perhaps partly because reduced discretionary funds leaves less for formal physical pursuit, such as golf, tennis, bowling, etc.

While reduction in activity seems to support disengagement theory, it does not explain why some elderly are active and others inactive, or whether this phenomenon is reversible with programmatic changes. Continuity might better explain this phenomenon of low levels of engagement in sports among elders. However, this situation may change because of two factors: the aging of the health conscious baby boom cohort and the increased earlier life sports experience of females that began in the 1970s as a result of Title IX (see Chapter 12).

Type and Degree of Physical Pursuit among Elders. Few studies of the elderly consider such variables as degree and types of physical pursuit, and fewer still measure sports participation directly. Harootyan (1982) found among 60-and-over Southern Californians that walking, conditioning exercises, gardening, and dancing represent most of the physical activity reported, while none of the respondents in this study claimed current participation in fishing, canoeing, track, handball, tennis, skating, or team sports. Among the sports in which lesser participation was mentioned were swimming (12.3 percent), bicycling (5.5 percent), golf (2.7 percent), and bowling (outdoor, 2.7 percent; indoor, 1.4 percent).

Data from the National Sporting Goods Association (Table 8.1) covering 1984 to 1992 indicate overall participation in golf increasing, with participation of those 55 and older decreasing, then stabilizing. Participation in tennis also decreased, but at a much greater rate for elders and continues to decline. Note, also, that the tennis figures represent a small percentage of a smaller total. These decreases in numbers of elders in tennis and golf are occurring while their segment of the population is growing. In general, only about 10 percent of elders over 65 engage in active sports (Cutler and Hendricks 1990).

The pattern of elder participation in physical activity and sports (Table 8.2) is as we might expect, with individual, noncontact, cardiovascular activities showing the greatest popularity. It is interesting to note, and

TABLE 8.1 *Trends in Golf and Tennis Participation—
All Participants Compared to 55+**

	1984	1987	1992
All Golfers	18,990,000	20,258,000	24,000,000
55+	3,902,000	3,614,000	4,272,000
	29.5%	17.8%	17.8%
All Tennis Players	19,456,000	16,911,000	16,700,000
55+	919,000	714,000	651,300
	4.7%	4.2%	3.9%

*Source: Dan Kasen, National Sporting Goods Association, January 1994.

relevant perhaps for school physical education and sports programs, that the staple school sports of football, basketball, and baseball are the least engaged in by elders.

Physiological Benefits of Physical Pursuit

Several studies list benefits of physical activity for elders, while others suggest that physical decline can be retarded but cast some doubt as to how much improvement can be achieved once loss of structure or function occurs. Evans and Rosenburg (1991) list 10 "biomarkers of aging" that are controllable:

1. Bone density
2. Strength
3. Basal metabolic rate
4. Lean body mass
5. Aerobic capacity
6. Blood pressure
7. Body fat percentage
8. Total cholesterol and high-density lipoprotein (HDL) ratio
9. Insulin sensitivity
10. Body temperature regulation

Several of these factors interact. Since this is not a physiology text and because most research tends to consider several of these factors at once, we will present general findings rather than attempt to discuss each of these factors.

Osteoporosis—loss of bone matter and thinning of the mineral matrix—is a significant problem for elders, causing bone breakage, especially in the lower extremities, and subsequent falls. Around the age of 35 bone mass peaks then declines. While both sexes experience bone loss, especially after age 50, the yearly rate of loss is twice as rapid for women as for men (.5 percent for men and 1 percent for women). After menopause bone loss in women accelerates (Smith, Raab, Zook, and Gilligan 1989).

TABLE 8.2 *Most and Least Popular Physical Activity/Sports for 55+ (1992)* *

	Total Participation	55+ Participation
Exercise Walking	67.8 million	26.5 percent
Snowshoeing	.4	18.9
Golf	24.0	17.8
Sailing	4.1	15.9
Fishing	53.7	13.5
Baseball	16.5	0.9
Basketball	28.2	0.6
Football	13.3	0.4

*From Dan Kasen, National Sporting Goods Association, January 1994.

Lost bone density may be recoverable in elders with weight bearing activities (Hamdy, Beamer, Whalen, Moore, Hudgins, and Anderson 1993), although some recent research casts doubt on this. In one study, brisk walking did not reduce the loss of bone in elders (Drinkwater, Ready, and Brereton 1993), while a meta-analysis of 22 studies between 1968 and 1992 showed that moderate physical activity programs including walking, jogging, and conditioning did not slow age-related osteoporosis in the backbone or upper leg, although it did in the forearm (Berard, Bravo, and Gauthier 1993). Rikli and McManis's (1990) research indicated that moderate exercise can prevent further bone loss, but that intense exercise may be needed to recover lost bone density and girth. It may be unrealistic, however, to expect elders to participate in intense exercise over a period necessary to rebuild bone. It may be that a combination of aerobic exercise and weightlifting is the key to rebuilding or maintaining bone mass in elders.

George (1980) links good health directly to successful adjustment to aging. Tennis, particularly in singles, can maintain cardiovascular fitness (Friedman, Ramos, and Gray 1984). Marathoners over 60 years of age tend to be particularly health conscious (Hogan and Cape 1984).

Muscle strength can be improved in elders with significant changes occurring as early as after three weeks of weight training (Sharon, Boyette, Anderson, and Brandon 1993). While damaged or aged lung tissue cannot be restored, further functional loss can be slowed through fitness training to strengthen respiratory assist muscles (Shepard 1993). Arm strength and oxygen transport in elders can be improved, proportion of body fat reduced, work capacity increased, and blood pressure reduced in as little as six weeks of moderate training (DeVries 1970). Walford (1984) in his book *Maximum Life Span,* notes that the oxygen uptake and utilization of 50-year-olds who exercise exceeds by 20–30 percent that of younger sedentary men. He reports on a large-scale longitudinal study of

FIGURE 8.2   *Many participants in ultramarathons, such as the Western States 100-Mile Endurance Run, are over the age of 40. Some runners are even in their 50s. (Photo by Donna Lee Moore.)*

Finnish international athletes that found life-expectancy to be 75.6 years for those involved in endurance sports, 73.9 years for those in team sports with mixed training (e.g., soccer and basketball), 71.5 years for power sports (e.g., boxing and wrestling), and 69.9 for the referents drawn from Finland's armed services. While extending life may not be directly attributable to exercise, Walford suggests that human life expectancy can be extended, nearing 120 years, compared to the current mid-70s.

A problem inherent in getting elders to exercise is the fear of injury, as injury can be more devastating than for younger people since recovery is more problematic. Both elder men and women benefit physiologically from exercise, with men apparently gaining more than women (Davidson and Murphy 1989). The goals of elder exercise are to (1) improve daily function, (2) minimize and shorten disability, and (3) prolong independent living (Larson and Bruce 1989). We can be confident from the research that activity forestalls and in some cases reverses loss in physical function among elders. "At the very least, we know that inactivity makes worse any age-related losses in function" (Lenfant and Wittenburg 1989:9). Physical conditioning can begin at any age, even for those who were sedentary earlier in life (Shepard 1989).

Psychological and Social Benefits of Physical Pursuits

Psychological and social benefits can also come to elders from physical pursuit. There seems to be general support in the medical community for the antidepressant benefits of exercise, although the occasional study fails to show this (O'Connor, Aenchbacher, and Dishman 1993). Other recent studies, however, have corroborated the psychosocial benefits of elder exercise, including reduced tension and anxiety along with improved sense of well-being, life satisfaction, and internal locus of control (Perri and Templer 1985; Parnes and Less 1985; Riddick 1985; Pate and Pierce 1993; Nieman, Warren, Dotson, Butterworth, and Henson 1993). Whether benefits are shown may depend on payoffs that are meaningful to elders. Improved health may not be sufficient in the absence of social and psychological rewards (Pepe 1993).

Other psychological variables, such as happiness and coping ability, have also been linked to physical activity in elders (Ostrow 1980; Morgan 1984; Kelly, Steinkamp, and Kelly 1986). Rosenberg (1984) found that elderly involved in structured groups were happier than those not involved, although this did not particularly hold true for sports associations, perhaps because the inevitable loss in ability concomitant with aging reduced the happiness quotient. (The question remains as to whether socially involved elderly were happier because of their involvement or whether they were socially involved because they tended to be happy.) The differences between these findings on the psychological benefits of physical activity, exercise, and sport and Larson's (1978) earlier failure to show such benefits may reflect a shift in the more recent cohort of elderly.

While health is cited by the elderly as a primary reason for any involvement in physical pursuit, they do not seem to adopt and commit to such activities. Fewer than one-third of Harootyan's (1982) subjects considered themselves to be limited by health considerations from participation in physical activity, yet only 3 percent reported active involvement in sport. Perhaps as Snyder and Spreitzer (1983:283) have noted, people reduce their involvement in sport with advancing age in part because "society has defined sport as a youthful activity." It remains to be seen whether an aging baby boom cohort will change this.

Many of the physical symptoms and difficulties attributed to aging result from lack of cardiovascular and muscular fitness instead of accumulation of years. The 1982 Fitness Ontario report showed greater increases in physical activity among elders than among younger groups, stating that "Exercise is the closest thing to an anti-aging and anti-disease pill" (Levy 1984:20). Disengagement or withdrawal may be a self-fulfilling prophecy; alter the expectation and the outcome may change.

Social Critique

Aging is a physical reality, certainly for the vast majority of Americans who have a western scientific mindset. Perhaps we may some day adopt Chopra's position that "aging is nothing more than a set of mis-guided transformations" (1993:24) and that "our deep belief that we are meant to grow old may get transformed into aging itself" (1993:26). Chopra says further that, "if aging is something you learned, you are in a position to unlearn the behavior that makes you age" (1993:56). However, unless and until Americans learn to unlearn these expectations of aging, we must assume that the "old paradigm" (1993:4) holds, and that aging is inevitable.

Withdrawal from physical activity—particularly exercise and sport, because they are considered inappropriate beyond a particular age—has its source in the invented reality of culture and such concepts as disengagement theory. The physical reality of aging can be retarded or even reversed to some extent by a change in culture or by individual refusal to accept cultural restrictions (Ostrow 1980). This parallels Chopra's call for changing our awareness about aging.

While physiological decline may be inevitable with advanced age, it need not arrive as soon as we believe or fear, particularly with sufficient guided physical activity (Wessel and Van Huss 1969; DeVries 1970; Wantz and Gay 1981). Withdrawal resulting from the losses inherent in aging, e.g., death of family and friends, retirement, or loss of independence, may be moderated through participation in exercise and in sports that engage both body and mind. Exercise and sport provide goals that can, at least temporarily, provide respite from cares and fears and foster social interaction. Exercise and sport offer stability and regularity to lives that may no longer have the rhythm and structure of family and job responsibilities, and they provide a haven of familiar and pleasurable territory.

"With increasing age the need for physical activity as a component of one's lifestyle does not decrease" (McPherson 1984a:15). The need actually increases, yet the activity tends to decrease, even though elders benefit from regular physical activity that can mitigate or reverse physical problems associated with aging (Wantz and Gay 1981).

Evidence cited earlier indicates that physically active older adults are happier as well as healthier than their less-active cohorts. Harootyan (1982:143) is a staunch advocate of continuity theory: "If one's goal is to improve the general health and well-being of people in old age, it is clear that higher levels of consistent physical activity should be fostered during young and middle years."

"Ageism"

To the extent that the elderly are stereotyped and repressed, this is evidence of "ageism."[3] This phenomenon plays a part in the low proportion of elders who participate in exercise and sport. "Institutional ageism" has resulted in the low status of elders, giving them the least access to scarce recreational and sport resources (Harootyan 1982:126). According to Wallach (1986), the meager provision for the recreational needs of the elderly is at least partly attributable to an image of the elderly as a tax burden. Both Wallach and Govaerts (1985) foresee elders, particularly females, demanding more attention and resources in the future.

Even when institutional services for elders are provided, these services, according to some critics (Michener 1976; Levy 1984; Danigelis 1984), tend not to attend enough to the particular needs of the elderly. Ignored have been such factors as the heterogeneity resulting from various disabilities and the wide age range of the elderly—an activity appropriate for 55-year-olds will not likely be suitable for those in their 70s or older. Danigelis (1984:75) sees planners doing "for" the elderly rather than "with" them. Exclusion of elders from planning their own programs and facilities is demeaning, yet another manifestation of ageism.

Fostering Change in Physical Pursuit for the Elderly: Social Engineering

Man-in-the street interview with an elderly person:
"And what are your plans for the future?"
"Plans for the future? I don't even buy green bananas!"

Disengagement theory, and particularly its manifestation in abandonment theory, is itself a reflection of social engineering. An early form can be seen in the creation of mandatory retirement as a public policy, first developed in late 19th century Germany by Otto Von Bismarck (Butler 1975), who felt that room needed to be made in the workforce for younger workers raising families.

Approaching the 21st century, however, and with the recent demise of mandatory retirement, the future is looking longer and better for elders. As scientific advances extend the life span and the elderly segment of the

---

[3]The term *ageism* was coined by Dr. Robert N. Butler, author of the Pulitzer Prize-winning book, *Why Survive?: Being Old in America,* and the first director of the National Institute on Aging.

population grows in number, the status, and even the definitions of aging and elderly, are changing. From a focus on frailty and nonproductivity, old age is increasingly being seen as something that "is more positive, developmental, and less prejudicial" (Levy 1984:19). The commonly held belief in the inevitable decline of cognitive function with age has been challenged by research. Instead, activity and stable social interaction, especially during times of crisis and transition, enhance the stability of elders (Foner 1980).

The "Meaning" of Aging

Lammers (1983) notes several factors that will characterize elders over the next several decades. These factors include a higher level of education and more income than earlier generations of elderly, although this does not imply that they will be economically comfortable, nor does it deny the eroding effects of inflation. While the physical environment of aging is improving, the "meaning" to elders of that time of life remains crucial to their well-being. Besides a safe and appealing environment, life for elders should be challenging (McPherson 1984a). McGuire (1985) predicts that elders, given their growing power base, will demand an age-irrelevant society and increased options to continue a full life rather than an environment that encourages withdrawing to a marginal life. If social and physical activity are good, they are also good for the aged, and appropriate provisions should be made for them, at least to the extent that other age groups have structures that encourage physical pursuit. As a societal benefit, elders will be less likely to drain medical resources if they are more active and thus healthier.

Indeed, the order of life may be changing as people demand more "life" in their existence. Levy (1984:18) foresees a "harmonious blending of education, work, retirement, leisure, play, religion, and other profound ingredients for an optimal quality of life." People will be combining extended free time with a prolonged work life, departing from the "lock step" pattern of education, work, then retirement. With a pattern of interspersed work and leisure, there will be more time, energy, and inclination to include exercise and sport in the middle years, and thus a greater likelihood of continuing these activities into one's later years. Exercise and sport may not extend life, but they should make those later years more healthful and enjoyable.

Frequency of participation in exercise and sport is one issue, while the meaning of that involvement to the participant is quite another. Russell (1984) suggests that how elders perceive these activities has more to do with the value of the activities than does frequency of participation. How do elders define successful participation? What are they seeking from participation? One problem that may contribute to the currently low level of participation among the elderly in physical activity comes from comparing their performances to an earlier version of themselves. If comparison is to be made, it should be with one's elderly peers rather than with one's own performance in youth and middle years (Seawell 1989).

Why Elders Engage in Sport Activity

Snyder (1981) suggests four categories of reasons why elders commit to sports participation, beginning with the *joy or fun* inherent in physical contests. Two other motives for committing to sports participation are *social companionship* and *maintenance of identity*. The fourth reason Snyder identifies is *anticipation of extrinsic reward*. Attainment of rewards, however, depends on achievement of some externally defined measure of success. In some sports such rewards are limited to the few, as in tennis or golf tournaments, although there are often several created categories of success beyond simply the top scorer. In other sports and exercise forms, rewards can be achieved in unlimited numbers, based on completing the event or finishing within a particular time, by those who "survive," such as in endurance events.

In a study of older adults aged 50 to 82, Heitmann (1984) found both men and women listing *health* as their primary motive for participation in physical activity programs (not necessarily sports). Rating six motives, "achievement" was second and "social" fourth among men over 60, while women 60 and over ranked "social" second and "achievement" sixth. Those planning or providing physical activity for elders must be aware of the consistently high rating of the health motive, although as we noted above, health does not seem sufficient to lead elders to maintain exercise programs.

The nearly reversed rating of social and achievement motives by elderly men and women should also guide planners and providers; however, differences in cohorts could be a factor and should be kept in mind. Following continuity theory, we might expect those women in the baby boom and later generations to be more comfortable with achievement motives. To support this, Heitmann's study indicated that women in their 40s and 50s listed "achievement" as their third-ranked motive.

Continued participation in exercise and sport can afford elders enhanced self-worth, but this should be tied to their successes *as elderly athletes*. Being an athlete can provide a sense of self-worth, regardless of age. Not only does activity help delay infirmity and dependency, but exercise and especially sport are social endeavors often experienced with others who value the same activities. This is a return to the values inherent in participation—the process of sport—that may have been lost in the product-oriented young adult and middle years. (Among adult softball players, Purdy [1980] found extrinsic motivation—success and failure taken seriously—rather than a focus on fun.)

Snyder and Spreitzer (1983) submit that adult sport participants begin extrinsically motivated, i.e., for reward, but reverse that orientation as they come to appreciate the intrinsic enjoyment, health, and social benefits of their involvement. This may be explained by a shift in the meaning—the definition as adopted or molded by participants—of extrinsic rewards. Identity as an athlete may, in itself, be viewed as an extrinsic reward (Furst et al. 1988).

Provisions and Opportunities for Elderly Participation

We can now weigh what we know of participation in exercise and sport against the theories that attempt to describe the participation patterns of elders. While disengagement theory appears generally to describe the pattern of declining involvement with increasing age, it fails to predict where and under what conditions this happens and why it does not happen in some cases. Nor does disengagement theory predict whether this pattern is "natural," imposed by society (i.e., abandonment), or simply a self-fulfilling prophecy in which the phenomenon of withdrawal might disappear in light of an altered prediction.

Activity theory, on the other hand, suggests that increased participation will occur among the elderly and will benefit them, if it is allowed to happen. Continuity theory sets a precondition for this higher level of activity among elders based on a pattern of involvement earlier in life—elders are not likely to demand more physical pursuit resources and opportunities if they have not been integral to earlier stages in life.

How would we go about reversing the phenomenon of lower participation with age? By attacking or altering the factors that bring it about. Physiological decline can be retarded and to some extent reversed by continued physical activity *throughout* the life span. However, knowing this is apparently not enough to change the trend, in part because people in mid-life do not see themselves as having the time and energy to maintain the activity of their youth or because they become disenchanted with exercise (Pereira 1989). This may change, however, as leisure time increases. With increasing health consciousness, elders may see exercise and sport as more acceptable pursuits. This perceptual change is likely to occur slowly until a "critical mass" of elderly participants in physical activity is achieved (Snyder and Spreitzer 1983:284).

Current and Future Opportunities for Elderly Participation

Fine (1988) notes that the presence of a formal organization facilitates participation, since organizational imperatives tend to direct culture. This can be observed in the World Corporate Games. First held in San Francisco in 1988 and designed for annual competition, the World Corporate Games focused on corporate sponsorship of athletes but did not limit entrants to those sponsored by corporations. With corporate involvement sport participation among adults is likely to be seen both by employees and employers as adding to, rather than subtracting from, one's work life.

The World Corporate Games were designed to provide the adult segment of the population with athletic opportunity, which is seldom encouraged in a systematic way. In the inaugural 1988 games, Hewlett-Packard, for example, sponsored more than 400 athletes. Competition was held in 20 sports in 1988 and 1989, ranging from tennis, cycling, diving, and kayaking, to softball, basketball, volleyball, and soccer, to track and field.

FIGURE 8.3   *The World Corporate Games provides the opportunity for continued involvement in sports for people well beyond what is traditionally considered the "active years."*

The inaugural World Corporate Games drew 2,700 athletes. Four hundred eleven corporations and organizations were represented, as well as four countries, including the Soviet Union. Age-group participation in the first World Corporate Games was as follows:

Open Division (not age-graded) . . . . 38 percent

30 to 39 years of age . . . . 36 percent

40 to 49 years of age . . . . 16 percent

50 to 59 years of age . . . . 6 percent

60 years and older . . . . 3 percent

The relatively low percentage in the older categories was expected based on the presumption that relatively fewer people over 50 years old (i.e., those raised in the 1930s or earlier) grew up actively involved in competitive sport, compared to those raised in the post-World War II era. As opportunity and acceptability increase for later age cohorts, the cultural "message" that athleticism is not only acceptable but beneficial to adults and the elderly should swell the ranks of sports participants in the older population. In subsequent years, the World Corporate Games moved to Hawaii, France, and then South Africa, leaving a void where a need had been filled for all but the more-affluent Americans.

In the Senior Olympics participants enter as unsponsored individuals. The Senior Olympics began in 1969, offering competition in swimming, diving, and track and field for people over 40. Now run by the United States National Senior Olympics Foundation in St. Louis, the games have six age categories, ranging from 55 through 81+, with the oldest athlete being 91. The events drew 2,521 athletes over 55 in 1987, 3,396 in 1989, and 5,158 in 1991 (Knieim and Gandee 1993). Phil Mulkey, who competed in the 1960 Olympic Games in Rome, participated in his first Senior Olympics in 1989. Mulkey said, "The beautiful thing about this competition is, you never graduate, you just move on to the next class" (Stathoplos 1989:40).

The United States Tennis Association sponsors local, regional, and national tournaments for active players well into their 80s. During the 1993 national tournament in Cincinnati, Margaret Wickham, playing with Donna Moore (ages 71 and 74, respectively, see Figure 8.4), fell and broke her arm in the second set, yet finished the three-set match, a testament to the strength and resiliency that can come from a life of physical pursuit. Donna Moore said, "My son played linebacker for the San Francisco 49ers, and he can't keep up with me on the tennis court. Of course, that says something about what football can do to a body."[4] It also says something about what tennis can do for a body.

Organizational sponsorship, such as the USTA and the Senior Olympics, provides legitimacy. Increasing awareness of health and social benefits of sport is likely to yield greater demand for opportunities among elders, which in turn should yield increased sponsorship and legitimacy. Ultimately, this may lead to growing participation on the part of elders.

---

[4]Personal communication, October 31, 1993.

FIGURE 8.4 *Tennis, among other sports, is an excellent way to retain or regain vigor, health, and a positive attitude in later life.*

Adapting Sports to the Clientele

Increased participation of elders in sports can be encouraged by adjusting the activities. As noted above, one adaptation would be to redefine success. Participation awards can help to accomplish this, but who the "real" winners are remains apparent, and American culture extols winners at the psychological expense of others. Since the elderly have encountered this socialization throughout life, presumably they, too, have tended to internalize the status differences of traditionally defined winners and losers, although winning may no longer be as important to them.

The definition of success for elders and the opportunity for participation can be broadened. The competitive pyramid that progressively eliminates challengers should be discarded in favor of round-robin forms of competition in which winners are determined by cumulative scores. A number of sports—swimming, bicycle and foot races, golf tournaments, etc.—already use the round-robin format. However, other events, such as tennis and softball tournaments, eliminate competitors as they lose, which undermines the purpose of elder sports.

Playing fields, equipment, and rules should be altered to accommodate elders and promote their participation and enjoyment. In tennis, construction of clay or synthetic soft courts should be encouraged (Morton 1989). The

United States Tennis Association, cosponsors of the nationwide Volvo competition for club players, is well aware of the decline in participation among older players and has a pilot program designed to adjust the game of tennis to elders.[5]

Slow-pitch softball was designed specifically for post-youth participation. Adaptations for adult players include elimination of bunting, base stealing, and base running collisions, and a ban on metal spikes. Further adjustments were made to the equipment, with "limited flight" balls, and to the rules, with a further limit on the number of home runs allowed each team per game.

Baseball, traditionally a game played by youth, adolescents, and an elite of adult professionals, has become available to older adult males, with leagues designated for "over-30," "over-35," and "over-40" sprouting around the country. The rules of the Over 40 Baseball League, Inc., headquartered in Metairie, Louisiana, not only include a ban on bunting and stealing, but also prohibit advancing on passed balls and wild pitches, limit the number of innings a particular player can pitch each game, allow free substitution, and incorporate a 10-run-per-inning limit. Adapting the rules of baseball to older players maximizes the process of enjoyable and healthful participation, if not minimizing product-oriented competitiveness.

Basketball might also be tailored to elders, perhaps renamed *Golden Ball.* For the 55-and-over league the rim would be 9½ feet high. The court would be divided at midcourt into offensive and defensive zones with six-person teams split so that three players cover the offensive area and three the defensive area. To maximize activity, a fouled player would take a single free throw worth two points. This court arrangement resembles that of women's rules earlier in this century. However, while the women's rules place a false and stereotypical limit on the physicality of young females, these same rules more appropriately adapt basketball to the physical limits of elders.

For Golden Ball players 65-and-older, the rim would be at nine feet. The court and teams would be divided as with the 55-and-over group, but they would use a smaller ball (perhaps a women's ball), and possession would be retained after free throws. The 75-and-over league would use rims 8½ feet high and would play with a smaller ball, as used in youth leagues. Many other sports could be adapted to the physical limits and the competitive interests of elders.

As more populous age cohorts reach their later years, it is likely that more organizations will be formed addressing the physical activity needs and interests of elders. Existing organizations will be more attuned to elders, and sport and exercise equipment manufacturers will direct their attention to the elderly market. The late-1980s recession in the exercise industry may be attributable to the boredom inherent in exercise regimens. Sports, however, involve pleasurable activity that include elements of excitement and challenge along

---

[5]Personal communication with Susan Hahn of the USTA, May 25, 1989.

TANK McNAMARA   by Jeff Millar & Bill Hinds

with social interaction, although this comes at some cost to efficiency in fitness attainment. With sufficient organizational support and a joy-oriented approach, the conditions appear right for an upward spiral in active sports involvement among elders. Reversal of the cycle of disengagement from physical activity with increasing age can be aided by the thoughtful development of policies and programs.

Summary

With increasing age, some elders disengage physiologically, emotionally, and socially from active participation, although others may be substituting new roles and pursuits for old ones. The extent of disengagement and whether it is coerced or encouraged by society, subtly or otherwise, remains open to question. Yet, elders are less apt to be active if they have not developed these habits earlier in life. Continuity between activity incorporated into the pre-elder years leading toward similar activities during the elder years seems to be one's best path toward maintaining health, since in later life, health is even more dependent on physical activity (bone structure, circulation, muscle tone, etc.). Beyond the physical benefits, activity in the later elder years is also important as a substitute for lost or displaced roles and status. Simply put, the health and well-being of elders is more likely to be maintained, which also benefits society, if they are physically and socially active.

The belief that aging is inevitable is being challenged by the perception that aging is a state of mind. Our understanding of aging is likely to grow as a result of such challenges. Greater resources and more encouragement to elders to become or remain vigorous could benefit society by helping elders to maintain the productivity of earlier stages of life.

References

Atchley, R. 1988. *The Social Forces of Later Life.* Belmont, CA: Wadsworth.

Atchley, R. 1992. "What Do Social Theories of Aging Offer Counselors?" *The Counseling Psychologist.* 20(2):336–40.

Barrow, G. M. 1989. *Aging, the Individual, and Society* (4th ed.). New York: West.

Berard, A., G. Bravo, and P. Gauthier. 1993. "Meta-Analysis of the Effectiveness of Physical Activity in the Prevention and Treatment of Osteoporosis." Presented at the Stairmaster Conference on Aging and Physical Activity, October 21–23, Virginia Beach, VA.

Bortz, W. M. 1991. *We Live Too Short and Die Too Long.* New York: Bantam.

Burgess, E. 1960. *Aging in Western Societies.* Chicago: University of Chicago Press.

Butler, R. N. 1975. *Why Survive?: Being Old in America.* New York: Harper/Torchbooks.

Chopra, D. 1993. *Ageless Body, Timeless Mind.* New York: Harmony.

Cumming, E., and W. E. Henry. 1961. *Growing Old: The Process of Disengagement.* New York: Basic Books.

Curtis, J. E., and P. G. White. 1984. "Age and Sport Participation: Decline in Participation or Increased Specialization with Age?" Pp. 273–93 in *Sport and the Sociological Imagination,* edited by N. Theberge and P. Donnelly. Ft. Worth, TX: TCU Press.

Cutler, S. J., and J. Hendricks. 1990. "Leisure and Time Use Across the Life Course." Pp. 168–85 in *Aging and the Social Sciences* (3rd edition), edited by R. H. Binstock and L. K. George. New York: Academic Press.

Danigelis, N. 1984. "Sport and the Disabled Elderly." *Arena Review* 8(1):68–79.

Davidson, D. M., and C. R. Murphy. 1989. "Exercise Training in Elderly: Do Women Benefit as Much as Men?" Pp. 273–78 in *Sport and Aging,* edited by B. D. McPherson. Champaign, IL: Human Kinetics.

deGrazia, S. 1973. *Of Time, Work, and Leisure.* New York: Doubleday.

DeVries, H. A. 1970. "Physiological Effects of an Exercise Training Regimen Upon Men Aged 52–88." *Journal of Gerontology* 25:325–26.

Drinkwater, D. T., A. E. Ready, and D. Brereton. 1993. "A Six-Month Program of Brisk Walking Does Not Blunt Bone Loss in Postmenopausal Women." Presented at the Stairmaster Conference on Aging and Physical Activity, October 21–23, Virginia Beach, VA.

Evans, W., and I. Rosenburg. 1991. *Biomarkers: The 10 Determinants of Aging You Can Control.* New York: Simon & Schuster.

Fine, G. A. 1988. "Subcultural Penumbras: Servicing Leisure Worlds." Paper presented to the North American Society for the Sociology of Sport, November 9–12, Cincinnati, OH.

Foner, A. 1980. "The Sociology of Age Stratification: A Review of Some Recent Publications." *Contemporary Sociology* 9(6):771–79.

Friedman, D. B., B. W. Ramos, and G. J. Gray. 1984. "Tennis and Cardio-Vascular Fitness in Middle-Aged Men." *The Physician and Sports Medicine* 12(7):87–91.

Fry, P. S. 1992. "Major Social Theories of Aging and Their Implications for Counseling Concepts and Practices." *The Counseling Psychologist* 20(2):246-329.

Furst, D. M., J. E. Bryant, and B. Shifflett. 1988. "Career Contingencies: Patterns of Involvement in Competitive Distance Running." Paper presented to the North American Society for the Sociology of Sport, November 9-12, Cincinnati, OH.

George, L. K. 1980. *Role Transitions in Later Life.* Monterey, CA: Brooks/Cole.

George, L. K. 1990. "Social Structure, Social Processes, and Socio-Psychological States." Pp. 186-204 in *Handbook of Aging and the Social Sciences* (3rd. ed.), edited by R. H. Binstock and L. K. George. New York: Academic Press.

Govaerts, F. 1985. "Social Indicators of Leisure and the Quality of Life." *World Leisure and Recreation* 27(2):49-51.

Hamdy, R. C., J. Beamer, K. Whalen, S. Moore, L. Hudgins, and J. Anderson. 1993. "Does the Aging Process Affect the Response of the Musculoskeletal System to Physical Exercise?" Paper presented at the Stairmaster Conference on Aging and Physical Activity, October 21-23, Virginia Beach, VA.

Harootyan, R. 1982. "The Participation of Older People in Sports." Pp. 122-47 in *Social Approaches to Sport,* edited by R. Pankin. East Brunswick, NJ: Associated University Presses.

Heitmann, H. M. 1984. "Motives of Older Adults for Participating in Physical Activity Programs." Pp. 199-204 in *Sport and Aging,* edited by B. D. McPherson. Champaign, IL: Human Kinetics.

Hobart, C. 1975. "Active Sports Participation Among the Young, Middle-aged and the Elderly." *International Review of Sport Sociology* 10(3-4):27-44.

Hogan, D. B., and R. D. Cape. 1984. "Marathoners Over 60 Years of Age: Results of a Survey." *Journal of the American Geriatric Society* 32(2):121-23.

Kelly, J. R., M. W. Steinkamp, and J. R. Kelly. 1986. "Later Life Leisure: How They Play in Peoria." *The Gerontologist* 26(5):531-37.

Kenyon, G. S. 1966. "The Significance of Physical Activity as a Function of Age, Sex, Education, and Socio-Economic Status of Northern United States Adults." *International Review of Sport Sociology* 9(1):70-96.

Knieim, H., and R. Gandee. 1993. "Participation and Performance Change in the National Senior Olympics." Paper presented at the Stairmaster Conference on Aging and Physical Activity, October 21-23, Virginia Beach, VA.

Lammers, W. W. 1983. *Public Policy and the Aging.* Washington, DC: Congressional Quarterly, Inc.

Larson, R. 1978. "Thirty Years of Research on the Subjective Well-Being of Older Americans." *Journal of Gerontology* 33(1):109-25.

Larson, E. B., and R. A. Bruce. 1989. "Exercise in an Aging Society." Pp. 1-6 in *Physical Activity, Aging and Sports* (vol. 1), edited by R. Harris and S. Harris. Albany, NY: Center for the Study of Aging.

Lenfant, C., and C. K. Wittenburg. 1989. "Exercise and Cardiovascular and Pulmonary Health." Pp. 7-16 in *Physical Activity, Aging and Sports* (vol. 1), edited by R. Harris and S. Harris. Albany, NY: Center for the Study of Aging.

Levy, J. 1984. "Leisure and Aging in the Third Wave Society: A Look at the Future— Now." *International Journal of Physical Education* 21(4):17–22.

Long, J. 1987. "Continuity as a Basis for Change: Leisure and Male Retirement." *Leisure Studies* 6(1):55–70.

McGuire, F. A. 1985. "Constraints in Later Life." Pp. 335–53 in *Constraints On Leisure,* edited by M. G. Wade. Springfield, IL: C. C. Thomas.

McPherson, B. D. 1984a. "Sport, Health, Well-Being, and Aging: Some Conceptual and Methodological Issues and Questions for Sport Scientists." Pp. 3–24 in *Sport and Aging,* edited by B. D. McPherson. Champaign, IL: Human Kinetics.

McPherson, B. D. 1984b. "Sport Participation Across the Life Cycle: A Review of the Literature and Suggestions for Future Research." *Sociology of Sport Journal* 1(3):213–30.

Michener, J. 1976. *Sports in America.* New York: Random House.

Mobily, K. E., R. B. Wallace, F. J. Kohout, D. K. Leslie, J. H. Lemke, and M. C. Morris. 1984. "Factors Associated With the Aging Leisure Repertoire: The Iowa 65+ Rural Health Study." *Journal of Leisure Research* 16(4):338–43.

Morgan, W. P. 1984. "Athletes and Nonathletes in the Middle Years of Life." Pp. 167–86 in *Sport and Aging,* edited by B. D. McPherson. Champaign, IL: Human Kinetics.

Morton, J. 1989. "Standing on Shaky Ground." *World Tennis* June:98.

Nieman, D. C., B. J. Warren, R. G. Dotson, D. E. Butterworth, and D. A. Henson. 1993. "Physical Activity, Psychological Well-Being, and Mood State in Elderly Women." *Journal of Aging and Physical Activity* 1(1):22–33.

O'Connor, P. J., L. E. Aenchbacher, and R. K. Dishman. 1993. "Physical Activity and Depression in the Elderly." *Journal of Aging and Physical Activity* 1(1):34–58.

Ostrow, A. C. 1980. "Physical Activity as It Relates to the Health of the Aged." Pp. 41–56 in *Transitions of Aging,* edited by N. Datan and N. Lohmann. New York: Academic Press.

Ostrow, W. J., and D. A. Dzewaltowski. 1986. "Older Adults' Perceptions of Physical Activity Participation Based on Age-Role and Sex-Role Appropriateness." *Research Quarterly for Exercise and Sport* 57(2):167–69.

Parnes, H. S., and L. Less. 1985. "Variations in Selected Forms of Leisure Activity Among Elderly Males." Pp. 223–42 in *Current Perspectives on Aging and the Life Cycle. A Research Annual. Work, Retirement, and Social Policy,* vol. 1, edited by Z. S. Blau. Greenwich, CT: JAI.

Pate, D. W., and E. F. Pierce. 1993. "Mood Alterations in Older Adults Following Exercise." Paper presented at the Stairmaster Conference on Aging and Physical Activity, October 21–23, Virginia Beach, VA.

Pepe, M. V. 1993. "Payoff Index That Can Predict Older Women's Involvement in Physical Activities with Suggestions for Programming." Paper presented at the Stairmaster Conference on Aging and Physical Activity, October 21–23, Virginia Beach, VA.

Pereira, J. 1989. "Fadeout Sets In on Nation's Exercise Boom." *Wall Street Journal.* Reprinted in *The Sacramento Bee,* February 20:E1.

Perri, S., and D. I. Templer. 1985. "The Effects of an Aerobic Exercise Program on Psychological Variables in Older Adults." *International Journal of Human Development* 20(3):167-72.

Prus, R. 1984. "Career Contingencies: Examining Patterns of Involvement." Pp. 297-317 in *Sport and the Sociological Imagination,* edited by N. Theberge and P. Donnelly. Ft. Worth, TX: TCU Press.

Purdy, D. 1980. "Effects of Socialization on Attitudes Toward Failure and Work in Sport: An Analysis of Adult Softball Participants." *Sociological Symposium* 30(Summer):1-19.

Riddick, C. C. 1985. "Life Satisfaction Determinants of Older Males and Females." *Leisure Sciences* 7(1):47-63.

Rikli, R. E., and B. G. McManis. 1990. "Effects of Exercise on Bone Mineral Content in Postmenopausal Women." *Research Quarterly for Exercise and Sport* 61(3):243-49.

Rombold, C. 1989. "Leisure As an Emotional Experience: Expanding the Frame for Understanding and Studying Leisure." Presentation to the 6th Annual Conference of the Resort and Commercial Recreation Association, St. Charles, IL.

Rosenberg, E. 1981. "Gerontological Theory and Athletic Retirement." Pp. 118-26 in *Sociology of Sport: Perspectives,* edited by S. Greendorfer and A. Yiannakis. West Point, NY: Leisure.

Rosenberg, E. 1984. "Sport Voluntary Association Involvement and Happiness Among Middle-Aged and Elderly Americans." Pp. 45-52 in *Sport and Aging,* edited by B. D. McPherson. Champaign, IL: Human Kinetics.

Russell, R. V. 1984. *Correlates of Life Satisfaction in Retirement.* Re.D. dissertation, Indiana University.

Sarna, S., T. Sahi, M. Koskenvuo, J. Kaprio. 1993. "Increased Life Expectancy of World Class Male Athletes." *Medicine and Science in Sports and Exercise* 25:237-44.

Seawell, M. A. 1989. "Dispelling Myths About Old Age: Elderly Are Not More Stressed, Depressed, or Socially Withdrawn, Psychologist Says." *Stanford Observer* February:15.

Sharon, B., L. W. Boyette, and K. A. Anderson. 1993. "Effects of Strength Training on Muscle Fitness Development in Older Women." Paper presented at the Stairmaster Conference on Aging and Physical Activity, October 21-23, Virginia Beach, VA.

Sheehy, G. 1976. *Passages: Predictable Crises of Adult Life.* New York: Bantam.

Shepard, R. J. 1989. "The Impact of Aging on Physical and Sports Performance." Pp. 189-200 in *Physical Activity, Aging and Sports* (vol. 1), edited by R. Harris and S. Harris. Albany, NY: Center for the Study of Aging.

Shepard, R. J. 1993. "Aging, Respiratory Function, and Exercise." *Journal of Aging and Physical Activity* 1(1):59-83.

Smith, E., D. Raab, S. Zook, and C. Gilligan. 1989. "Bone Changes with Age and Exercise." Pp. 287-94 in *Physical Activity, Aging and Sports* (vol. 1), edited by R. Harris and S. Harris. Albany, NY: Center for the Study of Aging.

Snyder, E. E. 1981. "A Reflection on Commitment and Patterns of Disengagement from Recreational Physical Activity." Pp. 108–17 in *Sociology of Sport: Perspectives,* edited by S. Greendorfer and A. Yiannakis. West Point, NY: Leisure.

Snyder, E. E., and E. A. Spreitzer. 1983. *Social Aspects of Sport,* 2nd Edition. Englewood Cliffs, NJ: Prentice-Hall.

Stathoplos, D. 1989. "Silver Threads Among the Gold (Medals)." *Sports Illustrated* July 3:38–41.

Walford, R. L. 1984. *Maximum Life Span.* New York: Avon.

Wallach, F. 1986. "A Word to the Wise: Old Isn't Old Anymore." *Parks and Recreation* 21(1):62–64.

Wantz, M. S., and J. E. Gay. 1981. *The Aging Process: A Health Perspective.* Cambridge, MA: Winthrop.

Wessel, J. A., and W. D. Van Huss. 1969. "The Influence of Physical Activity and Age on Exercise Adaptation of Women Aged 20–69 Years." *Journal of Sports Medicine* 9: 173–80.

Whaley, M. 1988. "81-Year-Old Woman Is Inspiration to Others." *The Sacramento Bee* November 16:D14.

SECTION III

Sport and Social Issues/Problems

Sociologists examine truisms and myths; they question common, perhaps even comfortable beliefs about the way society works and people's place in the social order. Sociology asks us to look at beliefs that may seem self-evident and to consider these beliefs more fully, both in the way they help us to order our world and in the implications they have for our social world. In this last section of the text we will be examining such myths, especially those regarding the world of sport, as well as the media-generated making of cultural myths and heroes.

"Sport releases aggression," for example, says to us that sport provides a useful and even increasingly necessary function in this high-pressure world. The presumed release of aggressive tension supposedly is beneficial to individuals and to the society. An implication of this "truth" is perhaps that the most aggression-releasing sports should be provided, by those who have control of such decisions and resources, in areas where hostility is closest to the surface. But does sport really release aggression . . . or does it reinforce aggressive behavior?

"Sport must be kept free of politics" is not so much a myth as it is an ideal. We see sport as a pure endeavor with a level playing surface, fair rules, and equal opportunity for all, while politics is "dirty" in many ways. How far removed from reality, though, is this ideal that sport should be nonpolitical? How, where, and why does politics "intrude" on sport . . . or sport affect politics?

The United States and Canada were founded, in part, on the belief that through hard work and focusing on a goal, anyone can become successful. To prove this belief we can always point to individuals who came from meager beginnings to scale the mountain of success. However, this belief implies that other factors are equal, and that self-sacrifice and dedication to the goal (and to some extent, talent) are the primary variables. This belief in the primary effectiveness of personal striving leads to a disregard of societal factors, such as racism and sexism. It says that individuals can become successful *no matter what the society does to them,* no matter how tilted the playing field is in favor of people from other groups. Is the door to success as wide for minorities and for women as for others? How many are trying to squeeze through that door for the rewards on the other side? Are there as many doors to success for all people? Do we all begin with the same opportunities to achieve, or does our society in some way make it more difficult for some?

In each of these areas—aggression (Chapter 9), politics (Chapter 10), racism (Chapter 11), and sexism (Chapter 12)—we stand at different points along the path to knowing answers, corroborating or destroying commonly held beliefs and myths. These paths are well worth taking whether or not we know at this point "for sure" the degree to which particular beliefs are true. Even asking the questions—examining—takes us further along each path. We must do so even if asking the questions—which implies doubt about their veracity—pulls us from our accustomed intellectual comfort zones on these issues.

Finally, in Chapter 13 we consider cultural myth itself, along with a discussion of the heroes that populate myths and the media that relate their stories. This chapter delves into the origins and purposes of myth and media, ultimately comparing them to our modern era in which sport serves as American society's primary incubator of heroes. This chapter extends beyond the usual realm of sociology, the text's home discipline, but we see it as another one of those bridges we must cross in order to look back for a better view of the home territory.

CHAPTER 9

Aggression and Violence in Sport

London (AP)—Police arrested six people and seized an arsenal of knives, crossbows, and other weapons Wednesday in raids aimed at soccer fan violence. (Associated Press 1986)

Basel, Switzerland (AP)—Europe's governing soccer association on Sunday banned English club teams indefinitely from European competition because of a riot in Belgium last week that killed 38 people. (Czuczka 1985)

The most important function of sport lies in furnishing a healthy safety valve for that most indispensable and, at the same time, most dangerous form of aggression . . . collective militant enthusiasm. (Lorenz 1966)

The people of this country should realize that World War III has started. (Pete Cutino, coach of the U.S. Water Polo Team at the 1975 Pan American Games Jenkins 1975)

. . . Then King became Kong. Billie Jean grabbed umpire Howell and shoved him. Then she slammed her racquet on the table and uttered things that haven't been heard in public places since booze was 35 cents a throw in Butte, Montana, watering holes. (Rudman 1978)

America sets before the child the most aggressive kinds of models and then we wonder why we have such high rates of violent crime. (Montague 1978)

Physical aggression reflects the success of the socialization process. Players who have "guts," who "never back down from a fight," who never "give up," and who are otherwise consistently aggressive are breathing examples of the success of the prevailing system and its values and definitions of the game. (Vaz 1976)

What do these comments have in common? Obviously, each one addresses to some extent violent aggression. The differences among them are far more subtle than the similarities, yet a comprehension of these differences is imperative if we are to understand the significance of aggressive behavior in sport as it relates to players, fans, and society.

In recent years there has been increased concern over violence in American sports. It may be that more violence is occurring in sport, or perhaps violence of any kind is less acceptable to Americans today. Regardless, sport-related violence is considered a problem.

In the *pure description* phase of our analysis of this issue, we will describe and differentiate the types of aggressive behavior that characterize American sport and identify some key examples. Our *evaluative commentary* will focus on theories regarding the source and causality of aggressive behavior in humans as well as the role that such behavior plays in sport and the larger social order. *Social critique* is most evident in the discussions of legal perspectives on sport violence, fan violence, and cultural aspects of violent sport and war. Ideas for *social engineering* should arise from the synthesis of theoretical and practical considerations.

Considerations in Defining Aggression

A definition places "something" in a box, isolating "it" so that we can observe it and say what it "is" or "is not." Aggression, however is difficult to put in a definitional box, because it can appear to be so many disparate things. Is hitting a business competitor aggression if that person is selling a rival product? Is hitting a sports competitor aggression if that person is on a rival team? In either case, is hitting right or wrong? Does it depend on the activity, or perhaps on the situation within the activity? Does an act even have to include striking someone to be considered aggression? Is cheating aggression? Would we place verbal aggression in the same box? The problems in defining aggression are many, so while it seems reasonable to define something before discussing it, we will let the discussion, particularly in the first half of this chapter, lead us toward a conceptualization of what is and is not aggression.

Two Folk Beliefs Linking Sport and Aggression

To understand the place of aggression and violence in sport, we must first look at two common folk beliefs linking sport with aggression. The first folk belief suggests that sport *reduces* aggressiveness in participants and spectators, thus helping to keep them from behaving aggressively in the "real world" outside of sport. This belief implies that aggressiveness is an antisocial and harmful behavior, something to be "gotten rid of" in a safe manner through the setting provided by sport.

The second folk belief is that participation in sport *promotes* aggressiveness, i.e., teaches a pattern of behavior that helps the player overcome problems and frustrations while pursuing a particular goal. This folk belief holds aggressiveness in a favorable light, as a prosocial type of behavior to be achieved, benefited from, and carried into other, nonsports areas of life, rather than as a behavioral tendency to be reduced or controlled. On the surface, these two folk beliefs appear to be contradictory, yet they are both used to justify participation in sport. They are also the basis of much of the financial support provided for sport, especially within educational systems. Is aggressiveness something to be achieved or eliminated? Is aggression prosocial or antisocial, beneficial or harmful? While athletes, coaches, and athletic administrators use the term *aggression* freely, it is clear that they and others fail to distinguish among the forms and purposes of aggressive behavior.

A further difficulty arising from these two folk beliefs is that they both assume the *generalizability* of aggressiveness. In other words, that which occurs within sport is assumed to affect behavior beyond the realm of sport. It is just as reasonable, however, to assume that behaviors within sport are specific to the confines of sport. Aggressive responses in the sport context may have little or no relationship to aggressive responses in other contexts. Regarding the first folk belief, for example, it might be that the presumed sports-related reduction in aggressive tension will not serve to lower aggressive feelings toward job, home, or socially related frustrations. Similarly, regarding the second folk belief, if we learn assertiveness in sport (or simply have it reinforced) does it necessarily follow that this behavior pattern will generalize to nonsports activities? In this chapter we will examine the evidence for each side of this related issue.

Reactive and Instrumental Aggression

The problem of defining, understanding, and using the distinct facets of aggression can be aided by using modifiers to distinguish between two of its primary forms (Coser 1956; Buss 1961; Berkowitz 1962; Layman 1970; Alderman 1974; Schneider and Eitzen 1986). The antisocial, attacking, and hostile form of aggression is termed *reactive aggression*. This focuses on its emotional character and intent to do harm. The prosocial, problem-solving, nonemotional form of aggressive behavior is called *instrumental aggression*. It is task-directed and outcome-oriented with respect to the demands of the activity at hand.

Reactive aggression refers to the baseball "rhubarb" and the behavior of Billie Jean King mentioned at the chapter's opening. It refers to the behavior of a cornerback in football slamming a receiver to the ground out of frustration and anger. It also refers to the hostile responses of fans who, although not physically attacking the receiver or a referee, presumably might do so if they could and who, in Great Britain especially, are notorious for attacking each other. Particularly if the football receiver is a scoring threat or gains crucial yardage, he is an object of frustration to the opposition and to their supporters.

To the extent that the character of the cornerback's contact with the receiver is caused by frustration or anger, and particularly if the physical response goes beyond what is necessary to stop the receiver, this aggressive behavior is deemed reactive.

According to the reactive folk belief, sport provides a safe and appropriate outlet for "natural" hostile tendencies. Just how natural or safe the expression of these behaviors is can be debated. Furthermore, whether or not such hostile responses are reduced and controlled by their expression in the relatively safe setting of sport, or whether they are reinforced and generalized outside of sport, is a question we will address in this chapter.

Instrumental aggression is described in the quote by Vaz at the beginning of the chapter. It can refer to any athlete who needs to be assertive, to solve problems, and to display initiative. Here emotionality, hostility, and physical attack intended solely to inflict pain or harm do not motivate the behavior. To the extent that a defender is tackling a receiver because it is the defender's job, the tackle is considered instrumental.

Checking in hockey and blocking in football are among those physical attack strategies in sport that are usually motivated instrumentally with the intention of keeping opponents from functioning efficiently. These tactics may be performed in an intimidating manner, with the appearance of reactive behavior. Throwing at the baseball batter, knocking down the quarterback, and hitting one's opponent with the ball in squash all have the appearance of hostile attack, but tend to be done for the effect of forcing the opponent to change strategy, be distracted by feeling or thinking of pain and injury, or both.

The same aggressive act—tackling, for example—may *seem* identical in separate situations whether instrumentally or reactively motivated. However, as the *intent* differs in each case—halting an opponent's advance versus harming or retaliating against the opponent—the character of the tackle differs, what is done in addition to a simple tackle differs, and perhaps worst, the responses of the tackled player and that player's teammates differ. The accepted, instrumental, agreed-on norm of halting a player's advance has been violated, which calls for retaliation in the form of further, probably escalated, reactive aggression.

Still different is the instrumental effect that may result from reactive behavior. Baseball provides an example. The pitcher who has just yielded a home run aims a pitch at the head of the next batter. The pitcher is dually motivated since his response comes from anger and frustration and, additionally, he wants to upset the confidence and concentration of the next batter through intimidation. The situation becomes less instrumental and more reactive if and when it degenerates into a "beanball war" with both teams retaliating in kind.

Although it is difficult to distinguish between instrumental and reactive aggression in sport, it is important to do so. If we are to judge which instances of aggression are acceptable to us and which are not, we must consider the *intent* of the aggressive act as well as its form and outcome. Still, we cannot simply condemn all reactive aggression, since it may be completely within the rules and the law. Similarly, we cannot give blanket approval for all instrumental aggression, since it may be vicious enough that it is morally or legally suspect. (Some readers responding to football player Jack Tatum's 1980 book, *They Call Me Assassin,* find his revelations of intentional harm done to opposing players revolting, while others view Tatum's actions simply as a necessary part of doing the job required of him.) The following taxonomy of sport-related aggression provides further insights into the nature and acceptability of aggressive behavior.

A Taxonomy of Aggression in Sport

As shown in Table 9.1, aggression is a broad term that encompasses not only both instrumental and reactive behaviors, but also nonphysical as well as physical behaviors. It may involve only one person, two people, or many. Within sport, it may describe the behavior both of participants and of spectators.

Nonphysical aggression is evident on the *personal level* as a player's attitude toward the contest. It takes either the form of the so-called "killer instinct," which drives a player's intense efforts, or the more reactive form of vengefulness, the desire to get even after an opponent has made a player look bad. On the *interpersonal level,* nonphysical aggression between players usually takes the form of "psyching out" the opponent. "Working the officials," or hounding them about calls that go against one's own team and praising them for favorable calls, has developed into a key technique of the aggressive coach. On the *collective level,* nonphysical aggression may range from the aggressive team spirit of players or the intense cheering of supportive spectators, to the reactive booing of fans who are disappointed in their team's performance.

Physical aggression also occurs at the personal, interpersonal, and collective levels. Aggressive behavior by *individual* athletes includes both instrumental acts like spiking a volleyball or slam dunking a basketball, and reactive behavior such as tearing up equipment in frustration or leaping around in the now-illegal "sack dance" of the defensive football player who has just sacked the opposing quarterback. Most authors who have discussed aggression in sport, however, have focused on its physical (especially, violent) forms at the *interpersonal* and *collective* levels. A good example of such a focus, included within our general taxonomy in Table 9.1, is Michael Smith's "typology of sports violence" (1986).

Smith (1986) differentiates four increasingly questionable levels of violence. *Body contact* is defined as "all significant body contact performed according to the official rules of a given sport: tackles, blocks, body checks, collisions, legal blows of all kinds" (1986:223). Such actions may have reactive as well as instrumental intent. *Borderline violence,* Smith explains, includes "assaults which, though prohibited by the formal rules of a sport, occur routinely and are more or less accepted by league officials, players, and fans" (1986:225). Examples include baseball's "take-out slide," intended to knock

TABLE 9.1 *Taxonomy of Aggression in Sport*

Level	Nonphysical	
	Instrumental Aggression	*Reactive Aggression*
PERSONAL	Killer instinct	Vengefulness
(Attitude)	Aggressiveness	
INTERPERSONAL	Glaring, teeth-baring	Verbal threats
("Psyching out")	Catcher harassing batter	
	Working the officials	
COLLECTIVE	Aggressive team spirit	Fan booing
(May be personal or	Cheering, chanting	Mob mentality
interpersonal)	Fans heckling a free-	
	throw shooter	

Level	Physical	
	Instrumental Aggression	*Reactive Aggression*
PERSONAL	Tennis smash	Abuse of racket
(With equipment or	Volleyball spike	Sack dance
facilities)	Slam dunk	Kicking a locker
INTERPERSONAL	BC: Tackle, boxing punch	BC: Tackling in
Smith's typology:	BV: Take-out slide	retaliation
Body contact (BC)	QV: Illegal boxing blow	BV: Beanball
Borderline violence (BV)	CV: Monica Seles	QV: Marichal-Roseboro
Quasi-criminal violence (QV)		CV: Joseph Matteuci
Criminal violence (CV)		
COLLECTIVE	Full court press	Brawling
(May be personal or	Blitz defense	Fan rioting
interpersonal)		

down the infielder, and the more reactive "beanball," designed to hit the batter (usually in reaction to a perceived offense committed by the batter's team). Hockey fistfights and general brawling also constitute borderline violence. We call this borderline rather than criminal or quasi-criminal violence because it is accepted, if not tacitly condoned by the ice hockey hierarchy.

The third level of sports violence in Smith's typology is *quasi-criminal violence,* "that which violates not only the formal rules of a given sport but to a significant degree, informal norms of player conduct" (1986:226). A low blow in boxing is a relatively mild example of such violence, which also includes such incidents as the 1965 baseball scuffle which resulted in Giant batter Juan Marichal hitting Dodger catcher John Roseboro in the head with a bat, seriously injuring him. It also includes the 1977 basketball incident in which

Kermit Washington of the Los Angeles Lakers punched Rudy Tomjanovich of the Houston Rockets, causing serious damage to Tomjanovich's face. Both Roseboro and Tomjanovich won lawsuits resulting from those attacks.

The fourth level in Smith's typology is *criminal violence,* that which is "so serious and obviously outside the boundaries of what could be considered 'part of the game' that it is handled from the outset by the law" (1986:226). In extreme instances, such as the 1993 on-court stabbing of number one tennis player Monica Seles by a Steffi Graf fan who wanted Graf to regain the top ranking, even this level of aggression may be considered instrumental. It is almost always reactive, however, as in the 1993 death of 17-year-old spectator Joseph Matteuci after he was hit with a bat by an 18-year-old player during a brawl after a Little League-sponsored "Big League" baseball game in Castro Valley, California (Wilson 1993).

Player Violence

Football.   Violent aggression among players has been a concern in American sport for more than a century. In 1885, the faculty of Harvard University banned football for a year, largely because of the violence in that sport. In 1905, President Theodore Roosevelt (the famous "Rough Rider" who was no stranger to violent aggression) threatened to outlaw football nationwide if the brutality continued. More recently, common tactics like clotheslining and spear tackling prompted Pittsburgh Steelers' coach Chuck Noll to decry the "criminal element in football."

After garnering a reputation for rough, intimidating play, Oakland Raiders' defensive back Jack Tatum in 1978 brought his aggressive style to its culmination with a tackle that rendered the New England Patriots' Darryl Stingley a quadriplegic. Tatum's contact with Stingley was judged to be "clean," i.e., within the letter of the rules, but its intent clearly went well beyond simply bringing down the ball carrier. Tatum later suggested (1980) that a good defender must try to "destroy" receivers and runners who venture into his territory and that this is the goal of many players in his position. In 1993, Phoenix Cardinals free safety Chuck Cecil attracted similar controversy after being fined $30,000 for spearing, although many NFL coaches and players defended his style of play. San Francisco 49er Brent Jones commented, "I just think the guy plays hard. He's not dirty. He loves to hit people. A little crazy. The perfect safety" (Swan 1993:D5).

Baseball.   In spite of its status as a "noncontact sport," and despite strict rules intended to control player violence, incidents such as brushback and beanball pitches, take-out slides, and all-out brawls have been tolerated in baseball throughout its history. Most of the violent events seem to be absorbed into the framework of the game itself, answered with appropriate retaliation (as dictated by baseball's "code") and then forgotten. Even the most serious infractions soon pale in the collective memory. The 1965 bat-swinging incident in which Juan Marichal struck John Roseboro evoked "howls of indignation across the country" ("Bat Day" 1965). Nevertheless, two decades later Marichal was inducted into baseball's prestigious Hall of Fame.

Basketball. Both instrumental and reactive physical aggression have become a normal part of the game of basketball in recent years. Certainly it can no longer be considered a noncontact sport for either men or women. As rough physical contact becomes more tolerated and even expected, concern about violence grows accordingly. An extreme example is the Kermit Washington-Rudy Tomjanovich incident described earlier. In order to discourage such episodes, the NBA commissioner instituted heavy fines for any player becoming involved in a fight. Even in intercollegiate competition, though, on-court scuffles between players are becoming more frequent, and they raise the question of just how much violence is unavoidable, how much may be desirable, and how much should be tolerated in the sport.

Hockey. Ice hockey in North America has always generated fights. Contributing factors possibly include such things as the relatively uncontrolled actions resulting from the slippery medium of play, and the enclosed rink that presents sideboards to slam opponents into. Quite likely, however, a major determinant is the tolerance and even the expectation of violence among North American fans (since the sport is much less violent as played in Europe). The often-quoted one-liner, "I went to a fight and a hockey game broke out," is a clear indication of the general acceptance of violent aggression within the sport of hockey.

Some key examples illustrate the levels of violence that have been reached in hockey. In 1969, the St. Louis Blues' Wayne Maki struck Boston Bruin Ted Green over the head with a hockey stick after Green had backhanded him. Green suffered serious head injuries as a result of Maki's assault. Maki was suspended for one month by the National Hockey League, but he was acquitted of criminal charges (on the basis of self-defense) in a subsequent court case (Horrow 1981).

In a 1975 game between the host Minnesota North Stars and the Boston Bruins, Bruin Dave Forbes struck North Star Henry Boucha (with whom he had fought earlier in the game) in the face with the butt of his stick, knocking Boucha to the ice, then jumped on him and punched him until another player separated them. Boucha's face required 25 stitches, plus surgery to repair his right eye socket (Horrow 1981). In a resultant criminal assault case the jury became deadlocked. The prosecutor, predicting that another deadlock would be likely, decided not to retry the case (Horrow 1981).

Three National Hockey League players were suspended in 1988 for allegedly trying to injure opponents—eye gouging was one of the offenses. One of the combatants, Rick Tocchet of the Philadelphia Flyers, defended his

"And in this corner, wearing a face clouded by fear . . ."

Drawing by Mort Gerberg; copyright © 1980 *The New Yorker* Magazine, Inc.

actions: "I've been involved in 90 fights in the NHL, and to me, this doesn't seem any different from any other one" (*Sacramento Bee* News Services 1988). The suspensions suggest that league officials may be *beginning* an attempt to control player violence.

Boxing.   Perhaps it is ironic that boxing, the most openly violent sport legalized for humans, is among the least troubled by illegal violence between competitors. There are no "brawls" in boxing, because boxing by definition is a brawl, albeit a controlled one. Since hitting is not only legal but required in boxing—a boxer loses points for *lack* of aggression—any aggressive act that affords an unfair advantage (e.g., hitting below the belt, eye gouging) is clearly proscribed and severely sanctioned. In fact, anger leading to reactive aggression at the expense of well-considered strategy (instrumental aggression) has an inherently negative effect in boxing; a boxer who "loses his cool" is more likely to lose the fight.

Legal Perspectives

From a legal standpoint, are there reasons for treating assault among athletes any differently from assault in any other context? Also, why is it that in some instances (like the Marichal-Roseboro and Washington-Tomjanovich incidents), injured parties have been successful in related court cases, while in other instances (such as the Maki-Green and Forbes-Boucha incidents) they have not? Does the law offer any insights to help us determine how to evaluate violence within the context of sport and from one sport to another?

The legal system has been less than definitive, if not downright inconsistent, in its handling of sport-related violence. Nevertheless, a few key considerations have emerged from numerous court cases that help to explain, if not justify, the relatively high tolerance for violence in sport. First, the notion commonly exists that sport is a "different world" from that of everyday life, so different rules may apply there. Specifically, sport is inherently dangerous, therefore relatively high degrees of violence and injury are to be expected—it's all "part of the game" (Smith 1986). In the sport world the ethic of toughness prevails, and athletes are expected to "dish it out" and "take it" without complaint (Brown and Davies 1978). Bending and breaking the rules is also an accepted part of this unique world, and rules against violence are no exception. Legal defenses such as "self-defense" (as in the Maki-Green case) and "implied consent" (a common claim) are largely based on this consideration of a voluntarily elected, mutually combative situation in which a certain degree of violence must be considered natural. The question, then, is what degree of violence exceeds that which is natural and expected in a given sport. In the Forbes-Boucha case, the jury was unable to answer that question (Horrow 1981), perhaps because the answer is as much sociological as legal. Since fighting has become tolerated, if not expected and even anticipated, in the "separate world" of ice hockey, it is less subject to legal sanctions. The rules and the questionable applications of those rules send a mixed message to hockey players, which opens the gate to violence.

A second legal consideration is that of jurisdiction. Within organized sport leagues there is a clear preference for handling cases of violence internally by imposing fines, suspensions, etc. (Horrow 1981). Players have generally accepted this principle, with the fear of being cut, blacklisted, or branded a crybaby having a chilling effect on thoughts of taking a case to court. Only in extreme instances, such as those described earlier, have exceptions been made. Prosecutors have also been reluctant to file criminal charges against athletes for violent events that occur within the context of sport, agreeing that the leagues should be able to resolve most cases from within (Horrow 1981). Consequently, many violent occurrences within sport have received relatively little legal attention in comparison to similar occurrences outside of sport.

A third consideration is whether legal action would do any good. The question of whether legally imposed punishment is really a deterrent is only part of this consideration. The other aspect is that of the "continuing relationship" that exists among players in organized sport leagues (Smith 1986). Legal action may only increase the hostility between antagonists who, in their continuing relationship as competitive opponents, will probably meet again. Thus, any attempt to settle a violent score legally may only inflame the situation and make future encounters that much worse.

The social context within each sport, as well as the rules of the sport, help to determine how deviant aggressive behavior is. At one extreme are ice hockey and football, in which fighting is labeled as deviant by the rules (albeit with light punishments of mere minutes in the penalty box or a few yards of territory). In ice hockey the player who refuses to fight will not only be shunned by teammates but may also find his job threatened by team management. Toward the other end of the aggression-deviance spectrum is tennis, in which physical aggression is prohibited by rule and is anathema to social context.

Even if aggression is labeled deviant (i.e., against the rules), the relative punishment determines how acceptable within the context of specific sports a deviant act is. Jack Tatum's "assassin" tactics in football gave him an outlaw aura despite the high degree of actual pain and injury his physical aggression caused. Tatum was a villain to some but a hero to others; his aggressive-deviant tactics were considered "a part of football," worth no more than 15 yards apiece in penalties. In contrast, John McEnroe's mere verbal aggression made him, within the context of tennis, a criminal. His tactics of complaining, cursing, and shouting at match officials, fans, and opponents cost McEnroe many months of suspension from official competition. McEnroe never threw an elbow across an opponent's throat, as Tatum did on a weekly basis, yet McEnroe's act was considered far more deviant within its social context, judging by the relative penalties to Tatum and McEnroe.

Despite these reservations, the legal perspective does reveal a precedent of sorts for setting limits on the level of violence to which one can be expected to give consent. So-called *paternalistic laws,* designed largely to protect us from ourselves, exist in a number of arenas (Simon 1985). Dueling, for example, has been illegal for a long time, even though the participants "consent" to it, because it presents too great a potential harm. Motorcycle helmet laws and automobile seatbelt requirements in many states are also examples of paternalistic laws. It may be that, even given the implied consent of athletes to physical risk, paternalistic laws that define acceptable levels of violence and establish fair and consistent consequences for exceeding those acceptable levels can be designed.

Fan Violence

Just as aggressiveness among players occasionally erupts into physical violence, so does fan enthusiasm or crowding occasionally precipitate rowdiness and even rioting. Fan violence generally falls into the category of *reactive physical aggression at the collective level.* Fans typically have a significant emotional investment in a game's outcome, but they are not as able to directly influence the outcome by their own efforts, short of raising the noise level. Consequently, their role features inherent sources of stress and frustration.

Focusing on the dimensions and dynamics of crowds, Mann (1979) suggests five *situational factors* that, together, are conducive to the actual display of crowd violence. These include

(1)   A large crowd—irresponsible behavior brews from the anonymity of individuals, the power inherent in the mass of people, and the crowd's invulnerability to relatively puny authority.

(2)   A dense crowd—packed humanity is inherently frustrating as one's personal space is violated and needs are compromised (see also Dewar 1979).

(3)   A noisy crowd—not only is noise arousing in its assault on the senses, but it leads to further arousal regarding the content of the event. In other words, excitement leads to noise, leading to further elevated excitement, which is a likely precondition for violence.

(4)   A standing crowd—people on their feet tend to be active, while it is considerably more difficult for seated people to behave aggressively (and thus less likely that they will).

(5)   Crowd composition—sports crowds tend to be diverse, but an individual prone to violence—a likely candidate might be an unemployed male in his early 20s who has been drinking—would be more apt to become aggressive among a group of similar others than among a crowd comprised of families.

We can link Mann's situational factors to "the immediate environmental circumstances that may serve to facilitate or inhibit aggression," suggested by Gaskell and Pearton (1979:269). According to Gaskell and Pearton, a circumstance that is conducive to the outbreak of violence contains both an *instigation* to aggression (a drive or motivation) and an *inhibition* (a tendency against aggressive action). Within a sports crowd the instigation might be the contest itself, particularly when the circumstance is tense or rife with rivalry (Bryan and Horton 1976), and when those on the field of play are modeling aggressive behavior (Smith 1976). Inhibition stems from socialization (unless one is more heavily socialized by a violent subgroup than by society) and from the social control inherent in authority figures (police, ushers, school faculty) who are present. In the presence of the situational factors noted above (large and dense crowd, etc.), if the instigation has greater pull than the inhibition, aggression is a likely result.

Fan violence is similar to collective player violence in that it may be directly related to the sport contest or it may be incidental to sport. Incidents of *directly related* fan violence include a 1964 soccer riot in Peru, which killed 350 people and seriously injured another 500 (*San Francisco Chronicle,* May 30, 1985), and a 1974 "Nickel Beer Night" in Cleveland, which resulted in a fan riot and the rare forfeiture (to the Texas Rangers) of a major league baseball game. Fan violence that is *incidental* to the sport is exemplified by the riots, property damage, and personal injury surrounding

British soccer during the 1960s and continuing through the 1980s. It is the opinion of some that crowding and depressed economic conditions provide the excuses for hooliganism, while trips to and from the matches by rail provide the opportunity (Smelser 1963; Goodhart and Chataway 1968; Associated Press 1986). Examples of fan violence *both* directly and incidentally related to sport have occurred in Central America and Europe. In 1985 in Brussels, Belgium, a riot broke out between British and Italian soccer fans in which 38 died. In 1969 rioting at World Cup soccer matches between El Salvador and Honduras, largely an expression of increasing hostility between those two countries, led to an actual war, dubbed "the soccer war" (Lever 1983:149).

Theories Explaining Aggressiveness in Sport

The function of human society is, in part, an attempt to reduce destructive, hostile interpersonal aggression. The Golden Rule and the "social contract," under which people relinquish some of their freedom to live under moral or governmental rule and protection, represent efforts to realize this. Aggression is certainly less a part of our daily concerns than it was for cave dwellers, although over thousands of years we may have succeeded simply in changing the form of aggression. What we see as the drive to achieve may be a modern and "civilized" form of more primitive violent aggression. Present-day instances of violent aggression may be examples of primitive, nonevolved behavior. Whatever we choose to call it, and wherever we believe it comes from, aggression remains a part of our lives.

Where does such a durable phenomenon come from? Its very presence over the ages, against the teaching of many religions, and in spite of many laws designed to control its more hostile forms, suggests that aggression serves some biological or social purpose. A few explanations, some of which compete with each other, attempt to answer these questions about the origin and functions of aggression.

Catharsis Theory of Aggression

Earlier we explained reactive aggression as ridding oneself of aggressive tension. This view of aggression as something to be reduced through expression is called the catharsis (or drive discharge) theory of aggression. The human organism is seen as a steam boiler. While the boiler is operating (or the human is alive) it has a degree of internal pressure. In the process of operating, the pressure fluctuates: too little and the boiler will not function, too much and it may explode. To maintain optimal pressure, the boiler has a safety valve that reduces excess pressure. Analogous to the safety valve, according to this catharsis theory, is running amok or hitting a ritual tree in some primitive cultures, or playing sports in the modern and civilized world.

TANK M^cNAMARA   by Jeff Millar & Bill Hinds

Copyright © 1975 Universal Press Syndicate.

The catharsis theory describes humans as innately aggressive and in need of periodic release of aggressive tension (Freud 1922; Lorenz 1966; Ardrey 1966; Storr 1968). This interpretation provides the theoretical basis for the folk belief that sport dissipates violent, reactive aggression. Whether aggressiveness is innate or a result of the pressures and frustrations of modern life, it is seen as something requiring release, preferably in a safe setting such as that provided by sports. Lorenz (1966) and Goodhart and Chataway (1968) go so far as to suggest that sport provides a ready outlet for hostile aggressive tension of nations and is the best hope for humanity, given the pressures of modern life, politics, war, and weaponry.

The evidence that aggression can be released and reduced, or that sport provides a reliable avenue to accomplish this end, is not particularly encouraging (Bird and Cripe 1986; Bennett 1991). Physical exercise may produce a sense of physical and psychological well-being. Sport competition, however, generally involves a greater emotional investment and social significance than exercise, and these additional meanings prevent sport from being consistently cathartic. In fact, exercise through sport may produce a heightened arousal and readiness to be aggressive (Zillman, Katcher, and Milavski 1970; Ryan 1970; Pfister 1981). Sherif (1979) noted from a series of experiments with boys in summer camp that aggression of both a verbal and physical nature increased, rather than declined, following sports tournaments. In a study of homicide rates following heavyweight prize fights, Phillips (1983) found evidence to suggest that viewing such fights increases the incidence of fatally aggressive behavior in Americans. It appears that activities such as sport, which have the potential for reducing aggression through catharsis, also have the potential for increasing it by creating and/or intensifying the anxiety, tension, and hostility that feed aggressive behavior.

Frustration and Aggression

Probably each of us has experienced frustration followed by some aggressive behavior: lashing out either physically or verbally, becoming angry and wanting to lash out but not daring to, blaming and berating ourselves for creating the frustration, kicking the dog, breaking a dish, or similar behaviors. This link between a frustrating condition and an aggressive act is the foundation of the frustration-aggression theory (Dollard, Miller, Doob, Mowrer, and Sears 1939). The theory states that for every frustration, an aggressive act will necessarily follow. Although it does not state where or when the aggressive reaction will occur, the theory suggests that the closer in time to the frustration and the more closely the object of aggressive reaction resembles the source of frustration, the more satisfying the aggressive act will be.

While Dollard and his associates directed this theory toward hostile, reactive aggression, the model may also apply to instrumental aggressiveness. Calvinism and the Protestant work ethic are founded on the belief that deprivation (i.e., frustration) fosters hard work, assertiveness, and achievement (Slater 1970). Using sport and business as examples, one works hard in order to overcome the frustration presented by the opponent or competitor, who is impeding one's economic well-being. If the person in the next office drives a Mercedes, and we desire one, this is frustrating. The way to relieve our frustration is to (1) work harder or (2) slash his or her tires. Capitalism and the Protestant work ethic (as well as the law) assume we will do the former. Sport also fits well within the scope of the frustration-aggression theory, since every sport by definition is competitive and competition by definition is frustrating relative to the scarcity of the prize being sought.

Frustration in sports comes in many forms. Aggression in athletes and fans may be related to match scores or team standings (Russell and Drewry 1976), being the visiting team (Lefebvre 1974), or it may fluctuate according to crowd size in addition to other factors (Berkowitz 1976). According to Berkowitz (1976), aggressiveness in ice hockey increases when one's team is behind, but decreases as scores become closer, possibly because penalties are more harmful when the outcome is in greater doubt. While the behavior when the game score is closer may not be any less aggressive, the nature of the aggressiveness may be more instrumental and less hostile and reactive.

Catharsis as a result of sports participation might be contingent on the outcome of the contest. This conception marries the frustration-aggression and catharsis theories by suggesting that catharsis is contingent on the sports contest having a satisfactory conclusion. If we win, or if we play well, the contest might have a cathartic effect on aggression. If we lose or play poorly, however, a given sport experience might instigate frustration and aggressiveness. This frustration, according to Moyer (1972), causes the competitor's neural system to activate itself to prepare for aggressive behavior (possibly a vestigial response left over from when "fight or flight" responses were necessary for survival). Moyer believes that violence is likely to result unless the individuals involved have learned to inhibit violent behavior. While athletes may have the ability to cope with provocation, through their athletic training they may have lost much of their socialized inhibition of aggressive behavior (Zillman, Johnson, and Day 1974).

Standing alone, the frustration-aggression theory is somewhat limited in its ability to explain sport-related aggression. The theory implies that most aggression is reactive. Since it interprets sport as creating at least as much frustration in players and fans as it discharges, it contradicts the folk belief that sport reduces reactive aggression. Sport, then, could be seen as a potential social evil since it generates frustration, which leads to antisocial reactive aggression.

Social Learning of Aggression

Social learning theory (Bandura and Walters 1963; Bandura 1973) describes the social learning of behaviors in three ways:

(1) By direct instruction coupled with reward for approved behavior and punishment for disapproved behavior.
(2) By repetitive building of associations between certain circumstances and the behavior expected in those circumstances.
(3) By role modeling.

An example of this social learning process is the adoption of aggressive behavior in sport (McPherson 1978). The conditions inherent in playing (and watching) sport that may lead to the learning of aggressiveness include (1) a heightened state of arousal (inherent in physical and competitive activity); (2) numerous instances of aggressiveness being rewarded; and (3) a context for emulation (modeling behavior) of aggression that is not only accepted, but condoned (Gaskell and Pearton 1979). Players are respected and admired for aggressive behavior, and aggressive violence can be used as an effective intimidating competitive strategy.

The link between violence in adult hockey and early expressions of the same behavior in youth hockey is well established. The junior leagues feature a highly competitive atmosphere and seem to condone and reinforce both legal and extralegal violent behaviors (Vaz 1976). The McMurtry Report, commissioned by the Ontario government to investigate violence in amateur hockey, blames the high incidence of violent behavior in youth hockey on the violence in professional leagues and its effect, through role modeling, on young players (Smith 1978).

Smith (1974) found that among Canadian junior ice hockey players the more experience players had, the more they approved of assaultive (fighting) behavior on the ice. The opinions of significant others such as parents, coaches, and peers had less influence than years of play. Thus, the context of ice hockey reinforces and rewards violent play. Focusing on the learning of violent behavior from observation of professional athletes, Smith (1978:95) concludes that,

> The conditions for observational learning and modeling (i.e., Bandura's social learning theory) via TV are almost laboratory perfect: models who get money and attention for aggressive acts, observers' expectation of rewards for the same behavior, close similarity between the social situations portrayed on the screen and subsequently encountered by observers.

These findings and conclusions support the investigations of Berkowitz and his associates (Berkowitz 1964; Berkowitz and Geen, 1966; Geen and Berkowitz 1967; Berkowitz and Alioto 1973; Geen and Stonner 1974). Their research has consistently shown that observers of violent behavior who believe that hostility is a motivation for the actions being observed will behave in a more hostile fashion than those who have not been cued to the hostile overtones of the observed activity.

Does social learning theory imply that athletes, by virtue of their relatively more aggressive learning environment, are more aggressive *in general* than nonathletes? Bandura (1973) suggests that behaviors seem to be learned for specific situations. Bredemeier and Shields (1986) agree, arguing that sport introduces a unique moral context, called a "game frame," within which behavioral expectations regarding such things as aggression are understood by the player to differ from those expectations outside of sport. Zillman, Johnson, and Day (1974) found that nonathletes may be *more* reactively aggressive than athletes when provoked (a finding that also supports catharsis theory). Figler, in both an original study (1978) and a replication of that study (1979), found that high school athletes (both male and female) were neither more nor less reactively aggressive than nonathletes when faced with frustrating situations. However, male athletes in the original study, and both male and female athletes in the replication, were significantly lower in instrumentally aggressive response to frustration than nonathletes.

On the other hand, Bandura also says that behaviors such as aggression might generalize beyond the specific settings in which they were learned, especially if some guidance for such generalization is incorporated into the learning experience (1973). Athletes' display of aggression beyond the sports setting might be amplified when the learning of such responses is found in combination with anabolic steroids, given their aggression-inducing effects. As noted earlier, both folk beliefs regarding sport aggression carry the underlying assumption that this is true. It is known that aggressive parents tend to have aggressive children (Bird and Cripe 1986), an observation that indicates a transfer effect from the initial learning experience to a more generalized behavioral pattern. Parental influences, however, have a more encompassing effect on children than specific and isolated experiences such as sport. Furthermore, it may be that people who are already aggressive are attracted to and successful at sport, rather than sport involvement teaching general aggressiveness. Overall, the generalizability of the aggression learned in sport remains questionable.

Synthesis of the Aggression Theories

No single theory completely explains the presence and expression of aggressiveness. *Catharsis theory* seems subjectively to have some explanatory power in many of our experiences, yet it is not well supported by research, perhaps for methodological reasons. Frustration is clearly conducive to aggressive behavior,

DOONESBURY   by Garry Trudeau

Copyright © 1978 by G. B. Trudeau. Reprinted with permission of Universal Press Syndicate.

although the *frustration-aggression theory* does not explain the complexities of human aggression. *Social learning theory* appears to provide the best framework for considering the vast array of interpersonal and situational variables that determine and modify sport-related aggressive behavior, yet the greatest explanatory power probably will be found in a synthesis of the various theories.

Gaskell and Pearton provide a general synthesis (1979:276): "The balance of evidence from theories of aggression is that sports involvement may heighten arousal, produce instances of aggressive behaviors and their reward, and provide a context in which the emulation of such behaviors is condoned." More specifically, a combination of four contributing factors appears to be a particularly powerful predictor of aggressive behavior:

(1)   A *predisposition* toward aggression (as in the catharsis theory notion of natural aggressiveness, but recognizing individual differences).

(2)   *Early learning and reinforcement* of violent aggression (as explained by social learning theory).

(3)   An *environment* where aggressive others are rewarded for aggressive behavior (per social learning theory).

(4)   An emotionally charged, *frustrating situation* featuring heightened arousal, high stakes, hostility, etc. (as described by frustration-aggression theory).

We have seen that sport and its participants commonly feature this combination of factors, and so it is not surprising that there is so much aggressive behavior in sport. The question that remains, however, is what, if anything, can or should be done to change this.

Some aggressive behaviors are considered prosocial expressions of goal-striving, even when some of those behaviors have the appearance of antisocial violence (the New York Knicks of the NBA, the Philadelphia Flyers of the NHL, and the Los Angeles Raiders of the NFL are among the more notorious examples from professional sport). In order to control clearly improper violent expressions of aggression, we must consider which of the contributing factors above is modifiable, and how it might be changed. While nothing can be done about a person's predisposition toward aggression, we can, as a society, attempt to limit the degree of early learning and reinforcement of violent aggression (in children's sport programs, for example). Similarly, we can work to minimize the rewards for those who exhibit unacceptable levels of violent aggression in sport contests. Finally, although sport is naturally frustrating, we can try to reduce the accompanying hostility that so frequently precipitates into violence. In short, those negative factors that are controllable can be reversed with awareness and diligent effort, and both sport and the larger society will benefit.

Summary

Concerns about violence in sport can be illuminated within the broader concept of aggression. It is commonly believed that sport promotes positive, usually instrumental forms of aggression and discourages negative, usually reactive and sometimes violent forms. Historical examples in the annals of major American sport illustrate both the range and the complexity of the issue. Legally, characteristics of the sporting world introduce subtle variations on traditional concepts such as self-defense and consent. The potential effectiveness of paternalistic laws against violence is presented. While violence among fans has several identifiable variables, player violence is usually framed within catharsis theory, frustration-aggression theory and/or social learning theory. A synthesis of these theories clarifies their relative explanatory power.

References

Alderman, R. B. 1974. *Psychological Behavior in Sport.* Philadelphia: W. B. Saunders.

Ardrey, R. 1966. *The Territorial Imperative.* New York: Atheneum.

Associated Press. 1980. "A Deadly Rhubarb on the Diamond." *Sacramento Union* (April 29):1.

Associated Press. 1986. "London Police Target Soccer 'Fans.' " *The Sacramento Bee* March 27:D2.

Bandura, A. 1973. *Aggression: A Social Learning Analysis.* Englewood Cliffs, NJ: Prentice-Hall.

Bandura, A., and R. H. Walters. 1963. *Social Learning and Personality Development.* New York: Holt, Rinehart and Winston.

"Bat Day." 1965. *Newsweek* (Sept. 6):44.

Bennett, J. C. 1991. "The Irrationality of the Catharsis Theory of Aggression as Justification for Educators' Support of Interscholastic Football." *Perceptual and Motor Skills* 72:415-18.

Berkowitz, L. 1962. *Aggression: A Social Psychological Analysis*. New York: McGraw-Hill.

Berkowitz, L. 1964. "Aggressive Cues in Aggressive Behavior and Hostility Catharsis." *Psychological Review* 71:104–22.

Berkowitz, L. 1976. "Crowd Size and Aggression in Hockey." *Journal of Human Relations* 29(8):723–35.

Berkowitz, L., and J. T. Alioto. 1973. "The Meaning of an Observed Event as a Determinant of Its Aggressive Consequences." *Journal of Personality and Social Psychology* 28:206–17.

Berkowitz, L., and R. G. Geen. 1966. "Film Violence and the Cue Properties of Available Targets." *Journal of Personality and Social Psychology* 3:525–30.

Bird, A. M., and B. K. Cripe. 1986. *Psychology and Sport Behavior*. St. Louis: C. V. Mosby.

Bredemeier, B. J., and D. L. Shields. 1986. "Athletic Aggression: An Issue of Contextual Morality." *Sociology of Sport Journal* 3:15–28.

Brown, J. M., and N. Davies. 1978. "Attitudes Toward Violence Among College Athletes." *Journal of Sport Behavior* 1(2):61–70.

Bryan, C., and R. Horton. 1976. "Athletic Events and Spectacular Spectators: A Longitudinal Study of Fan Aggression." Paper presented at the American Educational Research Association.

Buss, A. H. 1961. *The Psychology of Aggression*. New York: J. Wiley.

Coser, L. 1956. *The Functions of Social Conflict*. New York: Free Press.

Czuczka, T. 1985. "Europeans Ban English Soccer Clubs." *The Sacramento Bee* June 3:A3.

Dewar, C. 1979. "Spectator Fights at Professional Baseball Games." *Review of Sport and Leisure* 4:14–25.

Dollard, J., N. Miller, L. Doob, O. Mowrer, and R. Sears. 1939. *Frustration and Aggression*. New Haven, CT: Yale University Press.

Figler, S. K. 1978. "Aggressive Response to Frustration Among Athletes and Nonathletes." *International Journal of Physical Education* 15(3):29–33.

Figler, S. K. 1979. "Aggressive Response to Frustration Among Athletes and Nonathletes: A Replication." Unpublished paper, California State University, Sacramento.

Freud, S. 1922. *Beyond the Pleasure Principle*. London: Hogarth Press.

Gaskell, G., and R. Pearton. 1979. "Aggression and Sport." Pp. 263–96 in *Sports, Games, and Play*, edited by J. H. Goldstein. Hillsdale, NJ: L. Erlbaum Associates.

Geen, R. G., and L. Berkowitz. 1967. "Some Conditions Facilitating the Occurrence of Aggression After the Observation of Violence." *Journal of Personality* 35: 666–76.

Geen, R. G., and D. Stonner. 1974. "The Meaning of Observed Violence: Effects on Arousal and Aggressive Behavior." *Journal of Research in Personality* 8(1): 55–63.

Goodhart, P., and C. Chataway. 1968. *War Without Weapons*. London: W. H. Allen.

Horrow, R. 1981. "The Legal Perspective: Interaction Between Private Lawmaking and the Civil and Criminal Law." *Arena Review* 5(1):9–18.

Jenkins, B. 1975. "Pan Am Water Polo: All Wet." *San Francisco Chronicle* October 29:52.

Layman, E. M. 1970. "Aggression in Relation to Play and Sports." In *Contemporary Psychology of Sport,* edited by G. Kenyon. Chicago: Athletic Institute.

Lefebvre, L. M. 1974. "The Effects of Game Location and Importance on Aggression in Team Sports." *International Journal of Sport Psychology* 5(2):102-10.

Lever, J. 1983. *Soccer Madness.* Chicago: University of Chicago Press.

Lorenz, K. 1966. *On Aggression.* New York: Harcourt, Brace and World.

Mann, L. 1979. "Sports Crowds Viewed from the Perspective of Collective Behavior." Pp. 337-68 in *Sports, Games, and Play,* edited by J. H. Goldstein. Hillsdale, NJ: Erlbaum Associates.

McPherson, B. D. 1978. "The Child in Competitive Sport: Influence of the Social Milieu." Pp. 247-48 in *Children in Sport: A Contemporary Anthology,* edited by R. A. Magill, M. J. Ash, and F. L. Smoll, Champaign, IL: Human Kinetics.

Montague, M. F. A. 1978. "Non-Violence, Like Charity, May Begin at Home." *The Sacramento Bee* June 15. Los Angeles Times News Service.

Moyer, K. E. 1972. *A Physiological Model of Aggression.* Pittsburgh, PA: Carnegie-Mellon University Report #72-3.

Pfister, R. 1981. "Agressivité et Pratique Sportive: Mise à l'Épreuve de la Valeur Cathartique du Sport." *Bulletin de Psychologie* 35:88-100.

Phillips, D. P. 1983. "The Impact of Mass Media Violence in U.S. Homicides." *American Sociological Review* 48(4):560-68.

Rudman, S. 1978. "Antidote for Oratory." *Seattle Post-Intelligencer* (August 11):C4.

Russell, G. W., and B. R. Drewry. 1976. "Crowd Size and Competitive Aspects of Aggression in Ice Hockey." *Human Relations* 29:723-35.

Ryan, E. D. 1970. "The Cathartic Effect of Vigorous Motor Activity on Aggressive Behavior." *Research Quarterly* 41:543-51.

Sacramento Bee News Services. 1988. "NHL Cracks Down on Violence, Gives Three Players Suspensions," November 1:F6.

San Francisco Chronicle. 1985. "Soccer Disasters," May 30:18.

Schneider, J., and D. S. Eitzen. 1986. "The Structure of Sport and Participant Violence." Pp. 229-43 in *Fractured Focus: Sport as a Reflection of Society,* edited by R. E. Lapchick. Lexington, MA: D.C. Heath.

Sherif, C. W. 1979. "Competition—Cooperation in Sports and Academia." Unpublished paper presented to the faculty of Dickinson College, Carlisle, PA (May).

Simon, R. L. 1985. *Sports and Social Values.* Englewood Cliffs, NJ: Prentice-Hall.

Slater, P. 1970. *The Pursuit of Loneliness.* Boston: Beacon Press.

Smelser, N. J. 1963. *Theory of Collective Behavior.* New York: Free Press.

Smith, M. D. 1974. "Significant Others' Influence on the Assaultive Behavior of Young Hockey Players." *International Review of Sport Sociology* 9(3-4):45-56.

Smith, M. D. 1976. "Precipitants of Crowd Violence." *Sociological Inquiry* 48(2): 121-31.

Smith, M. D. 1978. "Social Learning of Violence in Minor Hockey." In *Psychological Perspectives in Youth Sports,* edited by F. Smoll and R. Smith.

Smith, M. D. 1986. "Sports Violence: A Definition." Pp. 221-27 in *Fractured Focus: Sport as a Reflection of Society,* edited by R. E. Lapchick. Lexington, MA: D. C. Heath.

Storr, A. 1968. *Human Aggression.* New York: Atheneum.

Swan, G. 1993. "Cecil Calls His NFL Critics Hypocrites." *San Francisco Chronicle* Oct. 21:D1,5.

Tatum, J. 1980. *They Call Me Assassin.* New York: Everest House.

Vaz, E. 1976. "The Culture of Young Hockey Players: Some Initial Observations." In *Sport Sociology: Contemporary Themes,* edited by A. Yiannakis et al. Dubuque, IA: Kendall/Hunt.

Wilson, Y. L. 1993. "Spectator Dies After Youth Baseball Brawl." *San Francisco Chronicle* May 19:A1,9.

Zillman, D., R. C. Johnson, and K. D. Day. 1974. "Provoked and Unprovoked Aggressiveness in Athletes." *Journal of Research in Personality* 8(2):139-52.

Zillman, D., A. Katcher, and B. Milavski. 1970. "Excitation Transfer from Physical Exercise to Subsequent Aggressive Behavior." *Journal of Abnormal and Social Psychology* 14:101-11.

CHAPTER **10**

Sport as a Tool of Politics

In this chapter we will depart somewhat from our usual analytical approach. We begin with a brief *evaluative commentary* on the interrelationship between sport and politics. The entire chapter actually represents an extended *social critique,* exploring the interplay between these two social institutions. *Pure description* of the interconnectedness of sport and politics runs throughout the chapter, leading to various avenues for *social engineering.*

Does Politics Intrude on Sport?

Immediately following World War II the United Nations was conceived on the precept that future global conflict and devastation could be avoided by maintaining physical personal contact among representatives of nations. So long as these representatives of potentially hostile nations were speaking and meeting with each other, it was believed that fighting could be avoided.

Similarly, a central philosophy supporting international sport in general, and the Olympics in particular, is that meeting "on the fields of friendly strife" reinforces the mutual humanity and worth of global neighbors, some of whom maintain conflicting political ideologies. A second philosophy attached to the modern Olympic movement is that the friendly battles taking place within the arenas of sport provide an outlet for hostile tension, that is, a symbolic substitute for war (Lorenz 1966; Goodhart and Chataway 1968; Hoberman 1984). Thus, the philosophies supporting both the United Nations and international sport appear to coincide.

In light of this political affinity, the position of a number of writers decrying the "intrusion" of politics into sport is curious. Disgust at political involvement in sport has been voiced both journalistically and from within the power structure of international sports. Michener (1976:377) castigates our political leaders for allowing and fostering an "improper" and "unhealthy alliance" between sport and politics. A representative of the United States Tennis Association finds it "intolerable to mix politics with tennis" (Creamer 1976). Others find the mix of Olympic sports and politics so abhorrent that they suggest the United States withdraw from Olympic competition (Baley 1978).

Through the ages, sport has exhibited political importance in varying ways. The ancient Olympics, in that time of "purity and balance" we so often extol, were highly political, pitting Greek city-states (each called a *polis,* the root word for "politics") against each other. The Greek ideal was to excel, to defeat opponents in every walk of life in order to ensure fame for oneself— and for one's *polis* (Pfitzner 1967). The olive wreath awarded for athletic victory was merely a symbolic award. Often, significantly more tangible rewards went with victory, while disgrace, banishment, and sometimes death followed important defeats (Loy, McPherson, and Kenyon 1978). In the oppressed early years of Christianity, athletic training was valued for survival in a life that was viewed as a "race to be won" and "a battle to be fought" (Pfitzner 1967:79).

Sports in the Middle Ages were exemplified, at least for the European nobility, by tournaments in which knights championed their realms in competition with each other. The commoner's game of soccer (called Dane's Head in England) was abolished for some time so that the populace could practice and compete in the more militarily expedient sport of archery (Spears and Swanson 1978).

It is generally people with a Western European and American heritage who complain that sport and politics are strange bedfellows. Possibly, the root of this perception lies in the origin of the modern Olympic movement. Pierre de Coubertin, a French baron who was the motivating force behind the rebirth of the Olympics in 1896 (ending a 15-century hiatus), held an enamored view of English sports as a leisure class pursuit (Lucas 1976). The supposed purity of sports engaged Coubertin, although the political implications of Wellington's quote linking the Battle of Waterloo with the playing fields of Eton (see Chapter 6) should not have escaped Coubertin.

Sport and politics will be associated with each other, inexorably and inextricably, as long as people care about sports. Even in the mythical Panglossian "best of all possible worlds," sports would hold political meaning, if only to cement and maintain good international relations, as many sports leaders and politicians have suggested.

Sport has a chameleonic political quality, being associated with whatever values are endemic in a social system. Those values that permeate sport regardless of political context include perseverance, respect for authority, achievement

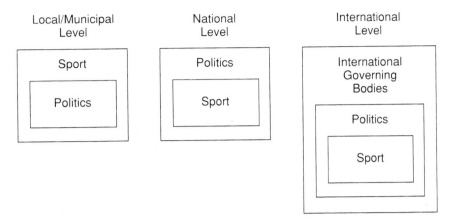

FIGURE 10.1 *Relationship Between Sport and Politics. (Adapted from Pooley and Webster 1976.)*

orientation, and support for the incumbent polity. (This is often confused with an attribute called "love of country"; when individuals oppose political positions taken by those in power, they are often accused of not loving their country.) Sport has been linked with values as disparate as democratic ideals in America, socialist ideals in the Soviet Union (Morton 1963), and fascist ideals in Nazi Germany (Mandell 1971). This flexible quality of sport—its ability to be attached simultaneously to political ideals that are anathema to each other—makes it, along with the popular attention paid to it, a perfect political tool.

Three Levels of Sport and Politics

Sport is neither devoid of politics, nor simply a tool of government. Politics is a "pervasive and characteristic aspect of international sport" (Shaw and Shaw 1977:58). In fact, all levels of sport are potentially influenced by political concerns. Pooley and Webster (1976) provide a useful scheme illustrating the lines of influence at work when the institutions of sport and politics interact at different levels (See Fig. 10.1).

At the local-municipal level, the interaction and influence of sport and politics are reciprocal and reflect a balance of power. The local politician or political structure regulates sport through zoning, permits, and other ordinances and financing. Local political leaders must identify and respond to the sports interests of their constituents if they want to remain in office, since at the local level even a small groundswell of public opinion can be sufficient to affect elections.

At the national level, sport and politics still influence each other, with agents in one institution making use of agents in the other. However, the balance of power has shifted in favor of the political sphere of influence, which, through regulations and financing, can for political reasons manipulate sports involvement and opportunities. Politicians at the national level are somewhat less accessible to individuals who do not favor their decisions, and it takes a larger body of public opinion to remove them from office.

At the international level, sport has no direct influence on politics, while politics influences sport and additionally is heavily influenced by international governing bodies (see Fig. 10.1). These imbalances of influence at the national and international levels might partially explain the stance of so many "sportsmen" decrying the influence of politics in sport. A relationship is likely to be distressing to those who see themselves as being manipulated. In particular, this may explain the critical posture assumed by many American athletes regarding the 1980 Olympic boycott while the American public tended to support the boycott.

At times the line between national and international sports is blurred. Unlike other nations, the United States exerts little governmental control over sports at the national level. The Amateur Athletic Union (AAU) and the National Collegiate Athletic Association (NCAA), as well as specific agencies that govern particular sports, have operated independently of national political concerns, including those concerns that have international implications. The primary "intrusion" of the federal government into national-level sports in the United States has been in a judicial role in the battle for control between the AAU and the NCAA. In 1978, President Carter signed a bill that gave the United States Olympic Committee (USOC) umbrella control over specific national governing bodies for each sport, thus undercutting the jurisdictional infighting that the AAU and NCAA had been engaged in for 50 years.

In the United States, national-level sports operate for the benefit of the individual athletes, or, in some sports, for the benefit of academic institutions that provide scholarship subsidies to athletes. When athletes reach international caliber in sports, however, the U.S. government and its agencies (whether or not under direct governmental control) take a greater interest. The USOC motto that "America doesn't send her athletes to the Olympics, Americans do" may have less validity now that federal decisions have established national Olympic training sites.

There are specific ways in which international politics influences sport. The remainder of this chapter considers these spheres of influence, which include the following:

1. Identity and self-image of nations
2. Dominance and propaganda among powers
3. Recognition of governments
4. Political sanction through the boycott
5. Sport as a stage for ideological expression
6. Sporting image of politicians

The first four political uses of sport are institutionalized and official or quasi-official in nature. We may consider these as institutional since they serve the values and needs of incumbent political groups or masses of people. Sport on an international scale could hardly exist, particularly in its currently well-endowed and spectacular form, without the support of governmental institutions and agencies. The final two political uses of sport are both collectively and individually noninstitutional. In the former, ideological stances of nongovernmental groups and individuals are linked with sporting events and accomplishments. In the latter, political individuals use sports in various ways to figuratively illustrate their political images.

Institutional Uses of Sport: The Diplomatic Bludgeon

National Identity and Self-Image

The seed of a sports consciousness was planted by Western European colonists. Sports served the colonists as a psychological link to the homeland and provided a release of tension for those in the diplomatic and military contingents in Africa and India. Assimilation of some of these sports was a natural response for the occupied and colonized populace, just as it was natural for newly emergent nations to assimilate some of the European political ideologies and forms. These patterns, along with industrial and economic modernization, were ways for emerging nations to become incorporated into the latter 20th-century international political mainstream.

We can assume that emerging nations need to establish national identity and to gain international acceptance, and many have chosen to direct efforts toward developing their athletic resources to address these problems. One reason that new nations use sports for recognition is that it is a resource that can be readily developed (Shaw and Shaw 1977); it also can be readily marketed. Compared to locating deposits of precious commodities (e.g., oil, gold, silver, etc.) and the problems of mining, refining, and marketing them, developing and marketing athletic prowess is a simple matter, given motivation and organized effort.

Developing prowess in athletics is a matter of first locating raw material within the population. This is easily done by the government's providing incentive and reward through institutional means (e.g., education, homes, and jobs). Second, after the raw material is located, it must be worked and shaped into a marketable (i.e., capable of performing well in international competition) form. This has been accomplished in some African, Latin American, and Caribbean countries through the importation of proven Western European, American, or Communist bloc coaches. Third, the product must be delivered to the market. This is perhaps the easiest problem to solve since the Olympics and other international forms of competition welcome new participants as long as they do not introduce political strife. The relative success of athletes from Kenya, Zambia, Nigeria, and other recently autonomous African states compared to the same countries' internal political and economic problems provides at least superficial evidence for the effectiveness of sport as a rapid means for achieving political identity and international recognition. With the merging of the two German states, the breakup of the USSR, and other events that have reconfigured national boundaries in Europe, the "new" nations resulting from those changes face the same challenge of building political identities. Their use of international sport to accomplish this will be a subject of continued study.

Cuba.   Cuba provides a specific example of an emerging country using sport as a means for achieving national prestige and international recognition. Sport and physical training in Cuba are organized by the state and are an integral part of virtually all children's and most adults' lives. Fidel Castro banned professional sports in part so that their best athletes may represent Cuba in international competition and particularly in direct competition with the United States, which prior to the Castro-led revolution had been regarded as an oppressive Big Brother (Komorowski 1977). Prestige has been gained in recent years by the successes of Cuban track and field athletes, boxers, and basketball teams. While baseball is the dominant team sport in Cuba and Castro has made numerous overtures to play teams from the United States, the American government has resisted head-to-head competition with Cuba outside of multinational events such as the Olympics and the Pan-American Games.

Little League Baseball.   Even on such a relatively modest scale as Little League baseball, national political recognition and esteem seem to flourish. The domination of the Little League World Series in the 1970s by teams from Taiwan brought great pride and prestige to that country. High-ranking officials of Little League baseball saw the Taiwanese domination as so threatening to the prestige of the United States that Taiwan was banned from participation in the World Series for a few years. After being reinstated, Taiwan resumed and continued its domination of the World Series.

An unmistakable example of the political importance of sport success was the scandal that surfaced after the Little League World Series of 1992. A team from the Philippines defeated a team from Long Beach, California and were declared world champions, returning to the Philippines as young heroes. Shortly thereafter, questions were raised regarding the eligibility of the players. Philippine officials admitted that the boys were not, as required by Little League rules, all from the same local league (Hoffer 1993). There was also evidence that the players were older than the 12-year-old maximum (Hoffer 1993). The team was stripped of its championship, and the Philippines was disgraced.

Multinational Alliances.   The use of sport for political identity and prestige transcends individual countries and functions also at the level of political and ethnic multinational alliances. The British Commonwealth Games, the Asian Games, the Pan-American Games, the Maccabiah Games, and the Third World Games are international sporting events that have among their purposes the reinforcement of political and ethnic solidarity and identity. Unfortunately, friction among participating nations frequently undermines that purpose.

As a case in point, the Pan-American Games (held every four years in the year before the Olympics) have been invested with political purpose, such as maintaining and increasing friendly contact among the nations of the Western Hemisphere. While this has been accomplished to a modest measure (although somewhat more so among the Latin American nations than with their North American neighbors), the Games are punctuated periodically by verbal and even violent conflict, usually between Cuba and the United States. The 1975 Pan-Am Games in Mexico City provide an example of the continuing hostility between the United States and Cuba. Brewing well before the competition began, fighting broke out during a water polo match and continued into the locker room following the match. "The Cubans were tremendously involved politically," Coach Pete Cutino said. "It was a life-and-death thing in every sport for them, a way to express their point of view" (Jenkins 1975). Players at the Mexico City Pan-American Games reported a general anti-U.S. sentiment also among Mexican athletes and spectators. Hostilities against the United States have erupted in basketball and other sports in other years. Recent Pan-American Games have been less openly conflictual, but the undercurrent of political hostility remains. The 1983, 1987, and 1991 Games all featured incidents that reflected continuing animosity toward the United States (Litsky 1983; Janofsky 1987; Wolff 1991).

The British Commonwealth Games (held every four years midway between Olympic years) have not been free of political strife. For a long time they were known as "the Friendly Games" (Macfarlane 1986), but tensions have increased in recent years. In 1977, a meeting of Commonwealth prime ministers was convened to avoid an African boycott of the 1978 Games similar to that which occurred at the 1976 Olympics. The meeting produced an agreement that each country would cease competing with racist nations, specifically South Africa and Rhodesia (Moore 1978). In 1986, 32 of 58 nations refused to send teams to the Games, protesting British Prime Minister Margaret Thatcher's "reluctance to impose economic sanctions on P. W. Botha's regime in South Africa" (Macfarlane 1986:255). England, which used to be viewed by many as a benevolent parent to its former colonies, seems to be facing increasing criticism as those newer nations pursue their own political agendas.

Propaganda and International Dominance Through Sport

Natan (1969:206) asserts that "There has never been any proof of sport contributing to peace anywhere in the world; it has merely incited previously latent chauvinistic impulses." Further support for this assertion is provided by the 1969 "soccer war" between Honduras and El Salvador, when a series of World Cup qualifying matches between the two neighboring countries ignited a smoldering fire of social, economic, and ethnic unrest.

Sport has never been shown to alleviate hostilities, while in rare instances it has created them. Sport in Cuba, for example, has three avowed political purposes: (1) rivalry with the United States; (2) representation of the Latin

American alliance; and (3) representation of the league of socialist nations. The Cuban success in the Munich and Montreal Olympiads were instrumental in what has been hailed as a "victory of socialism" (Komorowski 1977).

What is it that allows athletes to be considered "fleshly national assets" (Mandell 1971:288) and permits sport to become a tool for political ideological propaganda? Lowe (1977) suggests that it is the "zero-sum" outcome inherent in sports competition that makes it ripe for propaganda use. Zero-sum contests result in a winner and a loser, establishing a qualitative differential ("We are better!" or "We're number one!") with which political hay can be made, no matter how tangential accomplishment in sport is to the strength and utility of a political system.

Whether or not athletic superiority corresponds to political superiority is a moot point, and the extent to which any given populace believes the two are linked has yet to be determined. The important concern is that governments *behave* as if athletic superiority acts as propaganda to support their political system and way of life. The most apparent example of this use of sports for political propaganda has been the Olympic competition between the United States and the former Soviet Union. The Soviets entered Olympic competition in 1952 during the height of the Cold War. According to Strenk (1977:5), they used the Olympics as a "battle to prove that socialism was superior to decadent Western capitalism." The American psyche of the time, buffeted by both the Korean conflict and McCarthyism, found Communism particularly threatening.

National grouping in the modern Olympics was discouraged originally, although journalists began to keep medal counts by country around the 1928 and 1932 Olympiads (Lowe 1977). These tallies by country began as a curiosity, but they became an immediate propaganda tool for the Nazis at the 1936 Berlin Olympiad. Nazi leaders, following a strong showing by black American athletes, considered revising the scoring system to discount the performance of blacks. However, a late strong showing by Nazi athletes in gymnastics, yachting, and marksmanship provided the prestige they had promised the German people. According to Mandell (1971:ix), "German athletes . . . capped a festivity that at the time was a vessel without fissure, a seamless garment of happiness for the Nazis." The fact that Germany, Italy, and Japan garnered, respectively, more medals than the United States, France, and Great Britain led, according to Mandell (1971:281), to the "inescapable implication . . . that fascism and totalitarianism were more effective mobilizers of human energies."

What benefits of a tangible nature does symbolic sports supremacy provide to a nation? We might hope that momentous political decisions on the part of electorates or their governments would be decided on economic grounds, or human rights policies, or both. Lowe (1977) believes that the West has been naive in maintaining the separation of sport and politics. According to Lowe, Communist bloc coaches hired by nonaligned nations have been well schooled and active in politics and economics, while Western coaches know and care only about their sports.

The object of the propaganda may be a country's own populace, with sports supremacy simply a matter of creating or enhancing solidarity and commitment within a country's political system. Pride is indeed felt by a populace—capitalist, communist, or other—when its athletes perform well in international sports. However, this raises the question, "What price glory?" We know how efficient and technical athletic training was in the USSR. With the near collapse of that economy in the wake of the Soviet breakup, however, state support for training was seriously undercut (Swift and Lilley 1992) and a sporting powerhouse was humbled.

The End of Olympic Amateurism.　Since athletes are perceived as serving the propaganda needs of the nation, the athletes are often paid in one form or another, despite this being contrary to the notion of amateurism. Rule 26 of the Olympic Charter originally contained a strict interpretation of the regulation that Olympic athletes must not gain materially from their sport participation in any way (Strenk 1988). However, arrangements such as college athletic scholarships, subsidized training programs, travel allowances, sport-related or military jobs, and special living situations became accepted ways of compensating athletes for their efforts without jeopardizing their amateur status.

During the 1970s, the concept of amateurism was de-emphasized by the IOC in favor of the concept of eligibility, and responsibility for determining Olympic eligibility was shifted to the international sport federations (Strenk 1988; Taylor 1986). A baffling array of different eligibility rules then allowed athletes in various sports to accept huge amounts of prize and product endorsement money without sacrificing their Olympic eligibility (Strenk 1988). With the popularity of professional tennis players in the 1988 Olympics and NBA basketball players in the 1992 Games, the concept of Olympic amateurism has become a thing of the past.

So valuable are Olympic medals for propaganda purposes that countries now offer large amounts of money to their own athletes as incentives to earn them. Before the 1988 Olympics, the Philippines reportedly offered $100,000 to the athlete who could win the first Philippine Olympic medal; South Korea offered to pay all of its gold medalists $1,000 per month for life; and Taiwan promised its athletes $140,000 for each gold medal, $107,000 per silver, and $70,000 for each bronze medal (*Time* 1988). The USOC eventually followed suit, offering American Olympians a prize of $15,000 for gold, $10,000 for silver, $7500 for bronze, and $5000 for each fourth place finish in both the 1994 Winter Games in Norway and the 1996 Atlanta Summer Olympics.

Official Recognition of New or Changed Governments

When the Communist Chinese (later to form the People's Republic of China) forced the Nationalist Chinese to abandon the mainland in 1947, the United States' allegiance to the Chinese people shifted to the island of Formosa (now called Taiwan), leaving a huge void (i.e., mainland China) on the United States' diplomatic globe. While establishing economic and diplomatic ties with the Western world, Taiwan had both been a member of the United Nations and been active in Olympic competition. The People's Republic of China, however, whose population is more than 50 times that of Taiwan and whose land mass is 275 times as great, was hidden behind its Bamboo Curtain for three decades. The government of Mao Tse-tung welcomed its isolation while it remade the vast Chinese society in the communist image (Seban 1976). Then, during the 1970s, the People's Republic of China began attempting to merge into the political and economic mainstream of the world.

Ping Pong Diplomacy is a phrase coined during the Nixon Administration to describe the use of sports for establishing political ties between the People's Republic of China and the United States. The term can also be applied to establishing ties through sports between any two countries. For various reasons, not the least of which is political ego, competing governments seldom, in one stroke, initiate or reestablish full economic and political contact with a formerly hostile or unrecognized government. The term *Ping Pong Diplomacy* comes from the decision of both governments to have a table tennis team from the United States visit the People's Republic of China to symbolize reestablishment of contact between the two countries. This 1971 table tennis tour was followed by visits of basketball, track and field, volleyball, and swimming teams, and various cultural exchanges. Trade ties were opened and diplomatic contingents were exchanged to signify complete resumption of contact between the nations.

Why begin political contact with exchanges of sports teams? Possibly sport is used politically in this fashion because of the play aspect—the unseriousness—that is a vestige of all sport. Sending athletes seems to be the most innocuous way to institute official contact. Thus, sport provides a transitional step in the recognition of new governments.

Political Sanction: The Boycott

Probably the most heavy-handed political use of sports is the sanctioning[1] of governmental policies in other nations. The most widespread form of sanction is the boycott, in which a nation or group of nations severs relationships—including sports competition—with an "offending" nation and forces or cajoles other nations to follow suit. The purpose of the boycott is to force the offending nation to change a specific perceived illegal or immoral policy.

South Africa and Apartheid.   We mentioned earlier the 1986 boycott of the British Commonwealth Games by countries unhappy with what they

---

[1]The use of the word *sanction* may be confusing since it carries seemingly opposite meanings in different contexts. One definition is "authoritative permission" or "support." In contrast, the specific meaning of sanction in international law—the way we are using it here—is "action by one or more states toward another state calculated to force it to comply with legal obligations" (*Random House Unabridged Dictionary* 1973:1265). Notice, however, that the specification "legal obligations" has been expanded in the following discussion to include "moral obligations."

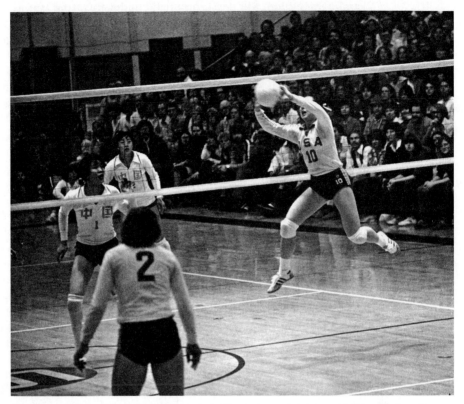

FIGURE 10.2   *"Ping Pong Diplomacy" allows countries that were formerly hostile or that did not officially recognize changes in government to ease into open economic and governmental contact. "Ping Pong Diplomacy" refers generally to any exchange of sports teams used partly to establish or cement relationships between nations. (Courtesy of Lynette Tanaka.)*

considered Great Britain's soft stance on South African racism. On a broader scale, the boycotts of South Africa and Rhodesia by the vast majority of nations that compete in international sport were prime examples of political sanction through sports.

In 1948, South Africa put into law an institutionalized system of racial segregation in which whites dominated, "brown" people (including Asians) were of middle status, and blacks (native Africans) formed a bottom caste. Called *apartheid*, this system restricted not only marriages and social contact but also places of residence, jobs allowed each group, and opportunities for competing in sports.

The move toward isolation of South Africa in international sports began in 1964 when it was banned from the Tokyo Olympics. In 1970, the IOC issued a "permanent" ban on competition with South Africa until its racial policies were changed, and particularly until apartheid was no longer a factor in the selection of teams and the opportunities afforded each athlete for training and competition. Rhodesia, originally under the same ban, is now Zimbabwe. Zimbabwe gained its independence as a non-apartheid nation in 1980, and the boycott against it ended. Throughout the 1970s and 1980s there were numerous indications that the grip of apartheid was loosening. A matter of debate, however, was whether the sports boycott was a major causal factor (Lapchick 1976; Krotee 1988). In 1991, with an end to apartheid in sight, the IOC lifted the ban on South Africa's Olympic participation—a move that was criticized by some as premature (Ramsamy 1992).

Apartheid and Olympic Politics.   The 1976 Montreal Olympiad provides a poignant example of how abhorrent South Africa's apartheid was to black Africans and how far they were willing to go to combat it. Shortly before the 1976 Olympics were to begin, 20 black African nations agreed to boycott the Games if New Zealand was allowed to participate. Why should New Zealand be boycotted when that country had an integrated sports policy and did not support apartheid? The reason was that New Zealand had broken the boycott imposed on all South African sports by allowing one of its rugby teams to journey to South Africa for a match. The commitment of black Africans to overcome apartheid can be measured by recalling our earlier discussion of the importance of Olympic acclaim to these emerging nations, many of which were expected to perform well. The black African nations as a group, if not as individuals, believed strongly enough in the importance of the boycott to relinquish years of athletic training, planning, and hopes through this political gesture.

Ironically, the pressure exerted to overcome apartheid in sports, causing numerous international sports governing bodies to sanction South Africa, at times worked against black South Africans. Sydney Maree, a black South African miler, was refused permission to compete in 1979 at the New Jersey Olympic Track Classic by the International Amateur Athletic Foundation (IAAF) because it had committed itself to a political stance against South Africa and its athletes (Moss 1979). According to the IAAF ruling, any athletes competing against a South African, black or white, could be suspended from all international competition. This "Catch-22" situation in which a rule instituted to help a group hurts a member of that group is one of the by-products of the interaction of sport and politics.

The Two Chinas.   The 1976 Olympics provides yet another example of political sanction, but one that does not concern South Africa in particular or racial policies in general. The conflict between Taiwan and the mainland People's Republic of China (discussed earlier) was a political sandwich with Canada in the middle. Canada's hosting of the 1976 Olympics happened to coincide with a trade bargain for mainland China to buy Canadian wheat, an agreement crucial to the Canadian economy. This provided mainland China with the necessary leverage to make its stance toward Taiwan felt in and through the world of sports. Mainland China threatened to withdraw from the wheat purchase if Canada recognized the entry visas of athletes from Taiwan should the Taiwanese claim to represent the Chinese people (i.e., compete under the flag and name of Republic of China).

Host countries of the Olympics must agree to welcome athletes from any country in good standing with the IOC, but Canada felt compelled because of this political/economic pressure to renege on that agreement. The IOC then had to decide whether to cancel or postpone the Olympics or accept the mainland Chinese and Canadian position. This issue came to a head during the week prior to the scheduled opening ceremonies.

The IOC first asked the Nationalist Chinese contingent to compete under the name of Taiwan. When this was rejected, the IOC suggested that the Nationalist Chinese compete under the banner of the IOC. The Nationalist Chinese stood by their name and flag, forcing the IOC to acquiesce to mainland China and Canada and ban the Taiwanese, since any delay of the Games, particularly because of the extensive television commitments, would have been unacceptable. With an eye toward the entry of mainland China into the Olympic fold, the IOC in 1979 ruled "permanently" that Nationalist China could no longer compete under its traditional name, flag, or with its anthem.

Thus, 20 black African nations, South Africa, Rhodesia, and Nationalist China all failed to compete in the 1976 Olympics because of political sanction. The government of the USSR promised the IOC not to deny entry in 1980 to any member in good standing of the Olympic community. At that time, however, one could not have anticipated that nations in the Olympic community would be boycotting the USSR.

U.S. Versus USSR.   The U.S.-led boycott of the 1980 Moscow Olympics,[2] prompted by the 1979 Soviet invasion of Afghanistan, drew severe criticism from some public and private sectors and most severely from many of the athletes affected. Numerous straw polls by American media, however, indicated that the public favored the boycott by about two to one. The old cry, that sport should be above and separate from politics, was heard widely. Concern was expressed that a U.S. boycott of the Moscow Games would threaten the 1984 Games scheduled for Los Angeles and endanger the very existence of the Olympics. From some of the athletes came the complaint that (a) they should not be used as political pawns and (b) there were other tactics, including economic and diplomatic sanctions, that could be used.

---

[2]A total of 62 IOC member nations sent no athletes to Moscow. However, it is estimated (Johnson 1981) that as many as half of those nations were not actually boycotting the Olympics since they would not have sent teams anyway. Among the most politically significant participants in the boycott with the U.S. were West Germany, Japan, Canada, and China.

Early in 1979, before the Afghanistan invasion, Cheffers (1979) wrote of the foolishness and futility of Olympic boycotts, pointing to the persistence of apartheid racial policies in South Africa despite 16 years of political, economic, and sports sanctions. Cheffers added that boycotts often have the greatest detrimental effect on the innocent athletes. He did suggest, however, that boycotts aimed at specific instances of intransigence (presumably, such as the Afghanistan invasion) may be more effective than those directed at general and longstanding policies. While the Carter Administration admitted that its 1980 boycott threat was not expected to result in Soviet withdrawal of troops, it felt that a stand had to be taken, one that would potentially do great harm to the Soviet economy and undermine the international prestige the Soviets were hoping to gain from hosting the Olympics.

Comparison was made between Soviet aggression in 1979 and Hitler's aggression in the early 1930s. Many nations threatened to withdraw from the 1936 Berlin Games to protest the Nazis' territorial invasions and racial policies toward Jews. Hitler wanted to legitimize his Nazi regime and policies by hosting the Olympics and showing the world that Germany was not in chaos, but rather was under complete and prosperous control. The United States and other world powers decided in 1936 that the best tactic would be to beat the Nazis in their own Games. The success of Jesse Owens is often pointed out as proof that the Nazi doctrine of Aryan superiority was a fiction. This victory was minor, however, since much of the world left Berlin in 1936 quite impressed with the apparent success of the Nazis in rebuilding Germany from the devastation of World War I and severe economic depression (Mandell 1971). A primary intention of the U.S. government and those nations supporting the boycott of the 1980 Olympics was not to make the mistake of 1936 again.

The political fallout from the 1980 Olympic boycott was perhaps most keenly felt in 1984, when the Soviet Union led a 15-nation boycott of the Los Angeles Olympic Games. Although the Soviets claimed that they were staying away from the Games because they feared that security would be inadequate to protect their athletes from terrorist attacks, it was clear that their action was primarily a retaliation against the United States for its boycott of the Moscow Olympics.

The 1988 Olympics, hosted by Seoul, South Korea, saw a return to almost-normal participation. South Africa was still banned, but only six invited nations (North Korea, Cuba, Ethiopia, Nicaragua, Albania, and the Seychelles) declined to participate. North Korea's boycott, motivated by displeasure over South Korea's unwillingness to allow them to cohost the Olympics, caused concern over the possibility of terrorist incidents. North Korea, however, kept its promise not to disrupt the Games. Cuba's athletes were missed to some extent, but the absence of the other countries was hardly noticed. All told, the 1988 Olympics were reassuringly peaceful, as were the 1992 Games in Barcelona.

Sport as an Ideological Stage

Not only governments but also politically oriented groups and individuals use sport and sport imagery to serve their own ends. At times, the link between sport and its use for ideological expression is quite tenuous, with sport simply providing a stage or a medium for politically motivated posturing. At other times, the ideological/political issues are central to the sports world. We will first discuss the use of sport by politically motivated groups and follow with a discussion of its use by individuals.

Collective Ideologies

Earlier we considered some instances in which groups supporting particular ideologies have had a significant impact on the sports world. The Berlin Olympics, as a political tool of the Nazi government, was used to further the belief in Aryan superiority and to indicate to the world that the Third Reich, represented by the Nazis, was civil and in control of Germany. The 1936 Olympics served to make legitimate the Nazi regime, if not the ideology, in the eyes of much of the world.

We have also mentioned the ideological stance of the black African nations taken in Montreal. The Olympic contingents, as adjuncts to each of the 20 national governments, withdrew from the 1976 Games to protest even the most tenuous support of South African racism. Numerous instances of ideological posturing occurred in the 40 years between the 1936 and the 1976 Olympiads, but we will focus on two: the political protests at Mexico City and the massacre of Israeli athletes at Munich.

Much has been made of the black-gloved salute of John Carlos and Tommie Smith on the victory stand at Mexico City. This symbolic gesture was the culmination—some might say the "residue"—of an abortive Black Athletes' Boycott instigated and orchestrated by sociologist Harry Edwards. The prospective boycott, building among American athletes many months before the Olympic Games, was intended to bring the plight of the American black community, and of black athletes in particular, to the attention of the world. Their contention was that white-dominated America used the athletic skill of its black citizens to earn international prestige through sports and, simultaneously, to create an illusion of racial equality in America, while in reality maintaining a system of oppression and lack of opportunity for nonwhites. In Edwards' words (Lipsyte 1975:128),

> It seems as though the only way we can reach a lot of the people is by showing them that all is not well in the locker room. No one attempts to change anything he's not in love with, and the Negro loves his country, fights for it in war, and runs for it. The tragedy here is that the country the Negro loves doesn't love him back.

As history shows, the black boycott of the 1968 Olympics never occurred. The reasons are numerous, ranging from Edwards' not appearing at the Games (he was strongly discouraged from entering Mexico) to the belief among the black athletes that political demonstration and failure to compete might undermine their scholarships, prospective careers in professional sports, or both.[3] In retrospect, following through on the boycott may not have been necessary to bring to public consciousness the treatment of black Americans. The threat of boycott, and the attendant publicity, may have been sufficient to effect a change in the racial-political atmosphere of America, while carrying out the boycott might have created more hostility and a climate of backlash.

Less has been written of the massacre of Mexican college students preceding the 1968 Olympics. In the weeks and months prior to the 1968 Games, thousands of Mexican college students publicly protested the Olympics, not because of any disaffection with sports per se, but because millions of dollars were being spent on this two-week extravaganza while millions of Mexican citizens lived in dire poverty. If the Mexican government could not care for the basic needs of its own citizens, they asked, how could it spend a significant portion of the gross national product entertaining foreign athletes, officials, and visitors? One official response might have been that Mexico needed to gain legitimacy and stature in the eyes of the world, with the possible tangible benefits of increased foreign investment in Mexico, a subsequent increase in employment, and a boost to the standard of living. Instead, the Mexican government answered its own students with bullets. The threat to disrupt the Games was intolerable to the government, as it would have created an image of instability and might have undermined subsequent investment and tourism.

The 1972 Munich Olympics are most famous for swimmer Mark Spitz's seven gold medals and infamous for the murder of 11 Israeli athletes by the Arab Black September Movement. The Israeli massacre differs from our previous consideration of politics in sport, not only because of the finality of the political act, but also because it was irrelevant to sports. Arab guerillas captured the Israelis as hostages for the exchange of imprisoned comrades, and the Israelis were killed during a bungled attempt to free them. The Olympics were used as a stage for this political action simply because the world was attuned to the Olympics, thus providing the widest publicity for the terrorists' cause. If the world had been attuned to a poetry reading, the terrorists would probably have used that as their stage. It is not that sport is inherently political, but it becomes political because of its utility as a widely observed medium for ideological expression.

---

[3]Evidence of subsequent job discrimination exists for Carlos and Smith as well as for Edwards and sports activist-social critic Jack Scott (Scott 1977). Former Olympic athlete and sports sociologist Phil Shinnick was jailed for his political activism and for his alleged involvement in the Patty Hearst case (Shinnick 1976).

The Politician as Sportsperson

A final irony linking sports and politics is that although successful athletes tend to be restricted in their use of sports for political purposes, politicians—at least *male* politicians—make free and frequent incursions into the sports world for their own political purposes. Politicians attempt to establish or exploit a personal association with sport or use sports imagery in their speeches for one general purpose: to foster an image that "I'm O.K." In particular, politicians attempt to use sport to create an image of health, virility, and stamina under stress (Petrie 1975). The boxing and basketball exploits of Uganda's ex-dictator Idi Amin and the pitching skills of Fidel Castro in baseball-crazy Cuba have been chronicled to the world. The intent was both to reinforce their own humanity (i.e., increase the citizens' identity with them) and to project an image of vigor and vitality.

American presidents have cultivated their sporting image since the time of Abe Lincoln and his alleged prowess in wrestling. Teddy Roosevelt's physical vigor was his hallmark. The post-World War II sporting boom seems to have made an association with sports, however tenuous, a near necessity for a successful presidential image. Truman's "constitutional" daily walks were marginally athletic at best, but in those years so was America. Eisenhower's primary association with sports as president was his fondness for golf. The Kennedy clan's love for touch football was widely extolled in creating an image of youth and vigor for John Kennedy. Lyndon Johnson may have been an exception to the post-war sporting image of presidents. Being a Texan, however, may have been enough to suggest his manliness and vigor.

President Nixon's years as a college football player, albeit a marginal one, were barely sufficient to provide him with athletic legitimacy. He more than embellished this image, however, by being football's "Super Fan" and "Armchair Coach," fulfilling an American fantasy of providing advice and secret plays to professional coaches in need of such insight.

Gerald Ford, the only president with true credentials as an accomplished athlete (most valuable player on the Michigan football team in 1934 and participant in two postseason All-Star games), also was an avid skier. During the 1976 presidential campaign, Ford's exploits as a skier may have been publicized to round out his well-known football image. Ford's loss of the 1976 election should not be attributed to his extensive prior association with football (in addition to playing football, he coached at Yale while in graduate school). However, Ford tells a story that may be indicative of the fine line between a sufficient sporting image for politicians and too great a one. While both were serving in Congress, Lyndon Johnson said of Ford, "There's nothing wrong with Jerry Ford except that he played football too long without his helmet" (Ford and Underwood 1974). Jimmy Carter seemed to be in tune with the times in his preferences for jogging, tennis, and swimming.

When former actor Ronald Reagan became president in 1981, the memory of his early role as "the Gipper" in a movie about football coach Knute Rockne was so vivid that many Americans thought Reagan actually had been a

"*Leading off, batting right-handed, playing second base, supporting the E.R.A., opposing wage-price controls, and favoring the windfall-profits tax—Willie Harper!*"

Drawing by Mort Gerberg. Copyright © 1980 *The New Yorker* Magazine, Inc.

star athlete. Of course, no concerted effort was made to correct that misconception. It was also no accident that we were periodically reminded of Reagan's love for horseback riding, and that the public was informed whenever he went for a ride at his California ranch. George Bush also followed the pattern of sport-associated presidential images. In addition to reminders of his experience as a baseball player during his undergraduate years at Yale, he presented himself to the American public as a swimmer and jogger who also loved to go fishing and played a mean game of horseshoes. Bill Clinton's routine of morning jogging and his enthusiasm for the University of Arkansas men's basketball team have offered the public an image to help offset his well-known affection for fattening foods.

Former NFL quarterback Jack Kemp and former All-America and NBA basketball player Bill Bradley both built careers in national politics following their competitive years. Numerous professional athletes have been elected to Congress, but the presidency may require a particular balance of athletic image minus the political stigma of extensive indulgence associated with professional athletics. This bias, to the extent that it exists, may have its origin in the English ideal of the gentleman athletes and their traditional leisure-class, elitist low opinion of the professional. To suggest that votes are cast and elections affected by athletic reputation or current involvement in sports is certainly speculative. However, involvement in sports and the cultural values attached to it would seem to be at least as important as other factors considered influential, including grooming, clothing, and camera angles, given the intense image-consciousness of politicians and their promoters.

Whether or not they are or have been athletes, many politicians like to attach themselves to winners. New York's former mayor John Lindsay became an instant and very public Mets fan during the Mets' drive to the 1969 World Championship. At the state level, governor Huey Long in Depression-riddled Louisiana publicly sought vicarious success through the LSU football team. Since the 1970s it has become standard procedure for the president to make congratulatory telephone calls to winning coaches and teams of the Super Bowl, the World Series, and other championships.

Finally, many politicians are prone to use sports terminology in their explanations of the machinations of government and politics, perhaps because they feel such terms (Balbus 1975) will make the intricacies of government more comprehensible to the populace and will reinforce their own sporting image and attach a positive value to their policies. The use of sports terminology to describe political or governmental activity projects an image of playing by the rules, attention to problem solving, and the beneficial effects of planning and strategy. In sports, the issues (i.e., the sides) are clearly defined and the outcomes are generally obvious, precise, and finite. In politics, the issues are seldom clear or concise. While the outcomes in political elections tend to be clear, the outcomes of government policy are seldom definite and often drag on—to their general detriment. Thus, sport—at least its imagery—may be used to portray politics as possessing a clarity and conciseness of issues and outcomes it does not actually possess. It can also be used to couch in more palatable and acceptable terms what amounts to transgressions of law, ethics, and trust, as when Richard Nixon described the illegal operations of his last months in office as "Operation Quarterback," a "team effort."

Summary

We have considered in this chapter the ways in which sport and politics interact, with politics generally having the greater influence on sports. It should be clear that sports and politics are not and cannot be separated, no matter how much we may wish they were. Nations use the sport arena to build their image and heighten their visibility in the international community, as a tool of political propaganda, as an ice breaker in establishing or reestablishing diplomatic relations, and to exert political pressure by threatened or actual boycotting of high-profile sporting events such as the Olympics. Smaller interest groups have used such events to stage incidents intended to send partisan messages to the larger political community. Finally, individual politicians have used their background as athletes and/or continued association with sport activities to portray themselves as robust and well-rounded leaders.

References

Balbus, I. 1975. "Politics as Sports: The Political Ascendancy of the Sports Metaphor in America." *Monthly Review* March:26–29.

Baley, A. 1978. "Suggestions for Removing Politics from the Olympic Games." *Journal of Physical Education and Recreation* 49 (March):73.

Cheffers, J. 1979. "The Foolishness of Boycott and Exclusion in the Olympic Movement." *Journal of Physical Education and Recreation* February:44–45.

Creamer, R. 1976. "A Matter of Politics." *Sports Illustrated* July 12:8.

Edwards, H. 1976. "Change and Crisis in Modern Sport." *The Black Scholar* 8:60–65.

Ford, G., and J. Underwood. 1974. "In Defense of the Competitive Urge." *Sports Illustrated* July 18:16–23.

Goodhart, P., and C. Chataway. 1968. *War Without Weapons.* London: W. H. Allen.

Hoberman, J. M. 1984. *Sport and Political Ideology.* Austin: University of Texas Press.

Hoffer, R. 1993. "Field of Schemes." *Sports Illustrated* Jan. 18:58–67.

Janofsky, M. 1987. "Stage Was Filled By Cuba and U.S." *New York Times* August 24:C4.

Jenkins, B. 1975. "Pan Am Water Polo: All Wet." *San Francisco Chronicle* October 29:52.

Johnson, W. O. 1981. "The Olympics/Troubled Games." Pp. 62–68 in *The American Annual 1981.* Danbury, CT: Grolier.

Komorowski, M. 1977. "Cuba's Way to a Country with Strong Influence in Sport Politics—The Development of Sport in Cuba Since 1959." *International Journal of Physical Education* 14(Winter):26–31.

Krotee, M. L. 1988. "Apartheid and Sport: South Africa Revisited." *Sociology of Sport Journal* 5:125–35.

Lapchick, R. E. 1976. "Apartheid Sport: South Africa's Use of Sport in Its Foreign Policy." *Journal of Sport and Social Issues* 1(1):52–79.

Lipsyte, R. 1975. *Sportsworld: An American Dreamland.* New York: Quadrangle.

Litsky, F. 1983. "Olympic Lessons in Pan Am Games." *New York Times* August 30:D19–20.

Lorenz, K. 1966. *On Aggression.* New York: Harcourt, Brace & World.

Lowe, B. 1977. "Sport Prestige: The Politicization of Winning in International Sport." *Arena Newsletter* 1(5):11–13.

Loy, J., B. D. McPherson, and G. Kenyon. 1978. *Sport and Social Systems.* Reading, MA: Addison-Wesley.

Lucas, J. 1976. "Victorian 'Muscular Christianity'—Prologue to the Olympic Games Philosophy." Pp. 66–77 in the Report of the International Olympic Academy. Athens, Greece: Hellenic Olympic Committee.

Macfarlane, N., with M. Herd. 1986. *Sport and Politics: A World Divided.* London: Collins.

Mandell, R. D. 1971. *The Nazi Olympics.* New York: Macmillan.

Michener, J. A. 1976. *Sports in America.* New York: Random House.

Moore, K. 1978. "Good Show in Edmonton." *Sports Illustrated* August 14:57–58.

Morton, H. 1963. *Soviet Sport.* New York: Cromwell-Collier.

Moss, A. 1979. "A Champion Miler Beaten by Catch-22." *San Francisco Chronicle* June 29:69.

Natan, A. 1969. "Sport and Politics." Pp. 203–10 in *Sport, Culture, and Society,* edited by J. Loy and G. Kenyon. New York: Macmillan.

Petrie, B. M. 1975. "Sport and Politics." Pp. 185–237 in *Sport and Social Order,* edited by D. Ball and J. Loy. Reading, MA: Addison-Wesley.

Pfitzner, V. C. 1967. *Paul and the Agon Motif: Traditional Athletic Imagery in the Paulian Literature.* Leiden: E. J. Brill.

Pooley, J. C., and A. V. Webster. 1976. "Sport and Politics: Power Play." Pp. 35–42 in *Sport Sociology: Contemporary Themes,* edited by A. Yiannakis et al. Dubuque, IA: Kendall/Hunt.

Ramsamy, S. 1992. "As South Africa Dismantles Apartheid, Sport Is First to Benefit." *CSSS Digest* Summer:11.

The Random House Dictionary of the English Language. 1973. New York: Random House.

Scott, J. 1977. "The Ramifications of Sports Activism: The Cases of Tommie Smith and Harry Edwards." *Arena Newsletter* 1(6):2–4.

Seban, M. M. 1976. "Political Ideology and Sport in the People's Republic of China and the Soviet Union." Pp. 306–15 in *Sport in the Socio-Cultural Process,* 2nd edition, edited by M. Hart. Dubuque, IA: Wm. C. Brown.

Shaw, T. M., and S. M. Shaw. 1977. "Sport as Transnational Politics: A Preliminary Analysis of Africa." *Journal of Sport and Social Issues* 1(2):54–79.

Shinnick, P. K. 1976. "Open Letter." *Arena Newsletter* 1(1):13–14.

Spears, B., and R. A. Swanson. 1978. *History of Sport and Physical Activity in the United States.* Dubuque, IA: Wm. C. Brown.

Strenk, A. 1977. "Sport as an International Political and Diplomatic Tool." *Arena Newsletter* 1(5):3–10.

Strenk, A. 1988. "Amateurism: The Myth and the Reality." Pp. 303–27 in *The Olympic Games in Transition,* edited by J. O. Segrave and D. Chu. Champaign, IL: Human Kinetics.

Swift, E. M., and J. Lilley. 1992. "Soviet Disunion: The U.S.S.R.'s Breakup Is Playing Havoc with a Sports Machine." *Sports Illustrated* July 13:46–48.

Taylor, T. 1986. "Politics and the Olympic Spirit." Pp. 216–41 in *The Politics of Sport,* edited by L. Allison. Manchester, England: Manchester University Press.

Time. 1988. "Just in Case the Glory . . ." 132(14):58.

Wolff, A. 1991. "Diplomatic Failure." *Sports Illustrated* Aug. 19:22–23.

CHAPTER 11

Racism in Sport

*I think racism is at its highest point since the civil rights movement in the
1960s and 1970s. I would call it our cancer. (Marcus Allen, NFL running back
[W. O. Johnson 1991])*

In April of 1987, Al Campanis, a 70-year-old executive with the Los
Angeles Dodgers, was interviewed by Ted Koppel on the "Nightline" television
program on the occasion of the 40th anniversary of Jackie Robinson's breaking
Major League Baseball's "color line." Asked about the scarcity of blacks in the
ranks of professional baseball management, Campanis said, "I truly believe they
may not have the necessities to be, let's say, a field manager or perhaps a general manager" (Chass 1987). In response to the resultant public outcry, Campanis was fired, and Baseball Commissioner Peter Ueberroth hired University of
California–Berkeley Professor Harry Edwards to investigate and recommend
changes in Major League Baseball to reduce racism and facilitate the ascension
of blacks into management positions. (In a move that shocked many people,
Edwards then engaged the services of Campanis as a consultant.)

Nine months later, in January of 1988, Jimmy "The Greek" Snyder,
who had for 12 years been the oddsmaker for CBS's "The NFL Today," was
interviewed at a restaurant by a Washington, DC, television reporter. Asked
"Why do blacks excel in sports?" Snyder replied, "The black is a better athlete to begin with because he's bred that way," and went on to explain how
this breeding dates back to the days of slavery ("Why Blacks Excel in
Sports" 1988). In the same interview Snyder also said that, if more blacks

were to become coaches, "There's not going to be anything left for the white people. I mean, all the players are black. The only thing that the whites control is the coaching jobs" (Uhlig 1988). Snyder's comments triggered an uproar, and he was fired by CBS Sports.

The combined effect of the Campanis and Snyder incidents—heightened in 1993 when Cincinnati Reds owner Marge Schott was suspended for racist references to players—was that America's attention was refocused on the issue of racism in American sport, a reflection of the renewed attention to racism in general. Raised anew were such questions as, why do blacks dominate certain sports, and why are they virtually absent from others? What part does sport play in the lives of black Americans, and what avenues does it open—or close—for them? Are blacks discriminated against in sport, and if so, what forms does this discrimination take?

In the *pure description* phase of our analysis, we will discuss the concepts of race and racism, and we will describe the overrepresentation and underrepresentation of black athletes in various sports relative to the general population. Our *evaluative commentary* will focus on the reasons (physical, psychological, and sociological) offered to explain the situation. In our *social critique* we will address the topics of financial discrimination and social mobility, which interrelate the factors of race, sport, and economics. Suggestions for *social engineering* will arise from our conclusions, and we will cite the advice of experts as well.

The Concept of Race

People tend to describe and categorize others initially by physical characteristics since they see peoples' appearance long before they know their substance. The genetic concept of race has been more one of degree than of absolute distinctions among groups of people, particularly in America, where genetic stock has been far from "pure" since the era of slavery (Holloman 1943; Montagu 1944; Brazziel 1969; Edwards 1973; Samson and Yerles 1988; Leonard 1988b). While certain physical characteristics such as facial features, hair texture and color, and skin color may place persons in one or another racial category having sociological meaning, there is more variation in physical appearance within each of those categories than there is between categories. Many blacks have lighter skin tone than some whites, or sharper facial features, or straighter hair. Even without the genetic mixing of interracial mating, we can see large differences in physical appearance within particular races. Possibly the most marked example of great physical differences within the same general racial category (i.e., Negro) is seen in the comparative sizes of Watusi and pygmy tribesmen in Africa: Watusi men frequently reach seven feet in height, while pygmies typically stand less than four feet tall.

Race as a Cultural Construct

The use of racial categories to describe physical characteristics is of less concern than the use of such categories to ascribe physical and mental abilities, because it is perceptions about abilities that lead to discrimination and racism. It is in such uses that culture intersects with biology in questionable ways.

The belief in America as a cultural "melting pot" is not always accurate. Although many immigrants have been assimilated into what is generally known as the American mainstream culture, many others have maintained their own ethnic identities, lived in self-imposed ghettos, and sometimes even continued to speak their native language to the exclusion of English. For blacks, life in ghettos has often been imposed by white-dominated society, while blacks' skin color has been a barrier to full assimilation not faced by European immigrants.

Ethnic or racial identity, however, too often becomes less a means for distinguishing physical and cultural characteristics and more a means for distinguishing social worth. From its origin as a genetic construct, race has become a social and political construct having meaning primarily in terms of social stratification (i.e., determining upper, middle, and lower classes) and in establishing access to wealth, status, and power. Social stratification and social mobility (movement between social classes) will be discussed with regard to the black athlete, his or her "place" in the American sports scene, and racism in America. Racism is described by Lapchick (1975:222) as "discrimination against a person or group of people based on that person's (group's) physical characteristics (such as skin color)." We would add only that discrimination is also potentially based on *perceptions* about a person's (or group's) mental and physical abilities, as well.

Race and Intelligence

Before the turn of this century and for a few decades after (during the time when Al Campanis, Jimmy "The Greek" Snyder, and Marge Schott were growing up), Social Darwinism was a popular belief in American scientific and educational circles. As described in Chapter 2, the underlying theory of Social Darwinism was that abilities, as well as physical appearance, were inherited. Probably the most important of these inherited abilities was believed to be intelligence. Since blacks were believed to be less highly evolved than whites, it was claimed that they were therefore less intelligent (Jensen 1969). Such claims have been shown to be based on falsified data (Hearnshaw 1979) and on tests that were biased toward their white middle-class authors. Nevertheless, the beliefs of Social Darwinism and its questionable conclusions regarding abilities of blacks compared to whites form a large part of the foundation of racism in America.

Attitudes toward Jack Johnson, the first African American to be world heavyweight boxing champion (1910–1915), epitomized the perceptions, fears, and bigotry of America toward blacks, and particularly black athletes.

Johnson was considered paradoxically both less than human and more than human. In many parts of the United States blacks were long considered subhuman, a lower, less intelligent form of life than whites. Seeing blacks as subhuman made it easier for whites to explain how and why Jack Johnson and other blacks could defeat whites in contests of physical skill—after all, the argument went, blacks were more "animal" than whites and thus should be expected to be more physical. This reasoning was partly responsible for the racial segregation rampant in sports from the post-Civil War Reconstruction period to the years just after World War II.

Blacks in American Sport

The fact that blacks do very well in a variety of sports is indisputable. Blacks constitute approximately 12 percent of the nation's population, yet according to recent figures, they make up about 16 percent of Major League Baseball players, 68 percent of the National Football League, and 77 percent of the National Basketball Association (Lapchick and Benedict 1993). Blacks also hold most major titles in boxing, and they represent 23 of the top 25 all-time men's 100-meter sprinters (NBC 1989). They also dominate the long jump (Samson and Yerles 1988). Black females dominate women's basketball and track as well. At the same time, blacks are proportionately *underrepresented* in a variety of other sports, notably tennis, golf, swimming, gymnastics, and the field events of high jump, shot put, discus, and javelin (Samson and Yerles 1988). Black males are markedly underrepresented in the pole vault and in ice hockey. Furthermore, blacks are sorely underrepresented in the coaching, management, and executive levels throughout collegiate and professional sport, as well as in sports broadcasting and sports journalism (Edwards 1987; Lapchick and Panepinto 1987; Ashe 1988; Eitzen and Sage 1989; Lapchick and Benedict 1993).

How can we account for these facts? Do they result from innate, racially linked genetic differences in anatomy, physiology, and/or psychology? Or are they culturally determined, and if so, what factors are the most influential?

Physical and Psychological Perspectives on the Black Athlete

Research aimed at measuring race-related physical and performance differences has been controversial. In a 1971 article in *Sports Illustrated,* author Martin Kane cited research findings indicating that black Americans tend to have longer and leaner arms and legs, broader and denser bones, and narrower hips than white Americans (Kane 1971). Kane argued that such differences, among other factors, account for much of the black dominance in sports such as basketball and sprint racing. Later studies have also suggested that blacks have greater bone density and different relative distributions of body fat than whites (Himes 1988), that blacks have higher percentages of fast-twitch muscle fibers (related to power) and lower percentages of slow-twitch muscle fibers (related to endurance) than whites (Boulay, Ama, and Bouchard 1988), and that blacks display advanced motor development as early as the first two years of life (Malina 1988).

Studies such as those just cited have been accompanied (and responded to) by numerous cautions about the complexity of related variables as well as methodological difficulties such as lack of control for racial purity, fitness level, and environmental factors (Himes 1988; Farrell et al. 1988; Samson and Yerles 1988; Boulay, Ama, and Bouchard 1988; Malina 1988). There continues to be considerable debate about whether the concept of race is scientifically useful at all (Bouchard 1988; Leonard 1988b). As Harry Edwards puts it, "When you say 'This is a black group,' you're already in trouble" (NBC 1989).

Psychological comparisons of blacks and whites have also met with problems, not the least of which is the predominance of racial stereotypes. The Harlem Globetrotters represent one stereotypical image of blacks as athletes. The "Trotters" are loose, rhythmic, happy-go-lucky (i.e., not serious), and very, very good. Along with the good will and good humor they spread, they also, unfortunately, perpetuate a "Sambo" or "Stepin Fetchit" view of blacks as docile, subservient, good-natured, childlike, and slightly exotic (Lombardo 1978). According to Kane (1971), this stereotype translates to a black attribute of being relaxed and thus less likely to become tense and to "choke" under pressure than the more serious whites. Edwards (1973), however, reports that on a validated psychological instrument (the IPAT), blacks appear to be more rather than less serious than whites.

Sport-related studies of race-linked psychological characteristics have focused on two hypotheses: (1) that black athletes exhibit different personality profiles from white athletes (especially, that blacks in sport emphasize individuality, style, and individual dominance more than whites); and (2) that blacks are psychologically better suited to reactive tasks than to self-paced tasks (Samson and Yerles 1988). Research does not support the first hypothesis at all (Samson and Yerles 1988). Regarding the second hypothesis, there is some evidence that blacks excel at reactive tasks such as baseball hitting and basketball field-goal shooting, and that whites do better at self-paced events like baseball pitching and basketball free-throw shooting (Worthy and Markle 1970). On the other hand, as Leonard (1988b) points out, the hypothesis falls short of explaining the predominance of whites in such primarily reactive sports as tennis, fencing, auto racing, and skiing.

If we try to characterize the sports in which blacks excel with regard to the physical or psychological demands of those sports, we quickly get into trouble. Do blacks excel at ball sports? Yes, except that tennis and soccer are ball sports, and blacks (especially in North America) are not overrepresented in those. Do they excel at leaping? Yes, except that they are underrepresented in high jumping. If blacks have longer arms as Kane suggested, does that give

FIGURE 11.1   *Arthur Ashe's success in the white-dominated sport of tennis helped to break stereotypes of black athletes. Later in his career, he urged black children and their families to concentrate on education rather than athletics as a road to success.*

them a mechanical advantage for throwing? That would be logical, and blacks are overrepresented as baseball outfielders, but they are underrepresented in javelin, discus, shot put, baseball pitching, and football quarterbacking. Do blacks excel at team sports? Yes, in football, basketball, and baseball, but ice hockey is a team sport and blacks are underrepresented there. Do they not do well at individual sports? Boxing is an individual sport, and it is dominated by blacks. Since blacks sprint so well, do they excel at all sports involving speed? No—cycling, skiing, and speed skating are speed sports, yet blacks are underrepresented in each of those.

Edwards argues that any view of blacks as physically superior is inherently racist, because the other side of that coin suggests that blacks are intellectually inferior. A belief seems to exist, according to Edwards (1973), that if blacks possess one attribute, they have been shortchanged on another. In other words, Edwards suggests that some whites will concede physical, animal superiority to blacks while maintaining a belief in their own intellectual superiority. In the modern, sophisticated world, mental ability is a more highly prized attribute than physical ability, bringing with it social and political dominance.

Certain research findings on average differences between blacks and whites may stand up over time, but overall such physical and psychological explanations for the differential participation patterns of blacks and whites in sport are woefully inadequate. The variation within races and the overlap between races are so extensive that they dwarf average differences anyway (Bouchard 1988; Samson and Yerles 1988; Himes 1988). As one research team (Samson and Yerles 1988:110) concluded, "it is virtually impossible to ascertain any type of relationship between alleged racial characteristics and specific athletic performances." We shall move on, then, to more plausible explanations for the pattern of black participation in sport.

Sociological Perspectives on the Black Athlete

Team Sports. Of the three major American team sports, baseball has the lowest percentage of blacks (about 16 percent) at the major league level. This is a third higher than the U.S.-population percentage of blacks (12 percent) but is significantly less than their proportions in pro football (68 percent) and basketball (77 percent). Furthermore, the percentage of blacks in baseball has declined over the past several years. According to Lapchick and Benedict (1993), the relative lack of urban youth baseball teams means that fewer black players are being developed. By contrast, the percentage of Hispanic players has steadily increased over the past decade to match the 16 percent proportion of black players in 1993, largely because of player development programs in Latin America (Lapchick and Benedict 1993).

Individual Sports. Boxing seems to be both an avenue to success and an outlet for frustration for whatever ethnic group is at the bottom of the socioeconomic ladder. At various times, Irish, German, Jewish, and Italian fighters have dominated boxing, with this dominance being exercised by whatever ethnic group was emigrating most heavily to America at the time (Weinberg and Arond 1952). Currently, blacks and Hispanics are dominant in American boxing.

Blacks are relatively scarce at the top competitive levels of tennis, golf, ice skating, gymnastics, and swimming. One possible reason is that opportunities for gaining wealth do not exist in swimming and gymnastics, are rare in ice skating, and only recently have become possible in golf and tennis. These sports may be too expensive for black youngsters and their families, while the

TABLE 11.1 *Rank Order of Prominent Boxers in Various Ethnic Groups During First Half of 20th Century**

| Year | Rank Order | | |
	1st	2nd	3rd
1909	Irish	German	English
1916	Irish	German	Italian
1928	Jewish	Italian	Irish
1936	Italian	Irish	Jewish
1948	Negro	Italian	Mexican

*Data from Weinberg and Arond 1952.

facilities are limited in areas where blacks tend to live. Another reason is that there are few black role models in these sports. Tennis has produced Althea Gibson, Arthur Ashe, and (more recently) Zina Garrison, Yannick Noah, and Lori McNeil. Golf has Jim Thorpe and Calvin Peete as male role models. Debi Thomas became a popular black role model in figure skating, and Charles Lakes was a highly touted black American gymnast at the 1988 Olympics in Seoul. These prominent athletes represent an encouraging increase in recent years, but compared to the large numbers of well-known black stars of football, basketball, and baseball, they may appear to be no more than "tokens" who do not represent a realistic model for young African Americans to emulate.

There is no shortage of black men and women in track and field, particularly in the sprints, hurdles, and long and triple jumps. Track has become a more profitable sport itself, with attractive prize and endorsement money, and its second-class status has faded. An interesting explanation for the overrepresentation of blacks in football, basketball, and baseball compared to the other sports mentioned (and also in comparison to their proportion of the American population) is that the best white athletes are spread across more sports (Phillips 1976; Edwards 1973), while top black athletes are concentrated in the more popular professionally oriented team sports. Phillips (1976) and Samson and Yerles (1988) suggest that if all sports were considered and the percentage of black participants in each were averaged, the overall proportion of top-level black athletes in sports would come close to the proportion of blacks in the U.S. population. In other words, they suggest that the appearance of black athletic superiority is an illusion created by the high black representation in the three major team sports, boxing, and track.

In summary, physiological and psychological differences are not sufficient to explain the pattern of black participation and excellence in sports, particularly at the professional level. A fuller explanation comes from inclusion of such sociological factors as geography (eliminating ice hockey for many blacks), access to individual coaching (particularly for tennis, golf, figure skating, swimming, and

FIGURE 11.2 *Jesse Owens undermined the Nazi theory of Aryan superiority in the 1936 Olympics in Berlin. Owens won gold medals in three dash events and the broad jump. Here he chats with Helen Stephens, winner of the women's 100 meter dash event. (From the Photo Archives of the United States Olympic Committee.)*

gymnastics), economics (e.g., the expenses of skiing and golf), lack of social mobility opportunities in some sports, as well as "good old, down-home bigotry." However, the most heavily emphasized reasons offered by sociologists seem to be the absence of black role models, along with the absence of moneymaking opportunities in these other sports. The rewards are exorbitant for success in professional baseball, football, and basketball. Five years as a major leaguer (roughly the average longevity rate) in any of these sports could provide more than a lifetime's earnings in the vast majority of other jobs most black youngsters, particularly those from a ghetto, see as attainable.

Racial Discrimination in Sports

Quotas

Bill Russell, former college All-America and NBA all-star player and coach, tells a story of the college basketball coach who played two blacks in front of the home crowd, three on the road, and five whenever victory was in jeopardy. Quotas have long been a part of American life in sport, schools, and other

FIGURE 11.3   *Physiological differences between blacks and whites are often used superficially to explain predominance in certain athletic activities such as basketball. (Photo by Faith Barbakoff.)*

institutions. For many years it was tacitly accepted that some private universities would admit blacks or Jews or women only on a quota basis, i.e., a limited percentage, which that particular school felt was an "appropriate" proportion. Federal law has since decreed these quotas to be illegal and established Affirmative Action guidelines to ensure not only that minority quotas are eliminated, but also that existing imbalances are reduced through a concerted effort to hire or enroll previously underrepresented groups.

While quotas have not always been illegal, they have been morally suspect, and the existence of quotas is often hidden or denied. For this reason, it is difficult to obtain hard evidence or specific examples of quotas. We are generally left either with impressions, such as Bill Russell's, or with the unmistakable evidence of total exclusion.

For example, prior to 1947, the quota for black players in Major League Baseball was zero. Although no written regulation existed, prohibition of hiring black players amounted to a "gentlemen's agreement." (The minor league International League in 1888 *officially* limited blacks to one per team [Scully 1974].) In 1947, Branch Rickey of the Brooklyn Dodgers brought Jackie Robinson of their Montreal farm team to Brooklyn to become the first black since the turn of the century (not the first black ever) to play Major League Baseball. Later the same year, the Cleveland Indians brought up Larry Doby from the minor leagues as the first black player in the American League.

One by-product of the racial integration of Major League Baseball was the rapid death of the Negro leagues, which had sustained black players for decades. Many outstanding black players such as Josh Gibson and Judy Johnson never played in the white major leagues. Other stars, such as Luke Easter and Satchel Paige, closed their careers in the white big leagues. Since they never played each other officially, comparisons between players in the black and white major leagues would be spurious. However, subjective views of many who saw them play suggest that the better black players could have excelled against white players of their day.

In football, the Washington Redskins franchise (ironically, since the majority of the population of Washington, DC, is black) was the slowest to accept blacks. Although the NFL had not completely excluded blacks as had major league baseball, a severe reduction of black players occurred during the Depression years and through World War II. Basketball, the "city game," began in earnest as a major league sport in 1949 and signed its first black player, Chuck Cooper of Duquesne University, in 1951.

Professional golf was much slower in opening its doors to black players. Charlie Sifford turned professional in 1948, but it was not until 1960 that the Professional Golfers' Association (PGA) allowed him to join the PGA Tour and eliminated the clause in its charter designating that the tour was for "professional golfers of the Caucasian race" (Ostler 1993:E7).

Quotas and simple resistance to black players without consideration of specific numbers seem, at least on the surface, to be a phenomenon of the past. However, this does not mean that discrimination toward blacks in sport has ended. Clearly, blacks still encounter resistance when they try to attain sports positions of importance, control, and higher status.

Stacking

The great influx of black athletes into professional sports since 1950 seems to indicate on the surface that they are becoming more acceptable to white society. However, even with these advances in opportunity for blacks, discrimination remains. Those playing positions to which blacks are given greater access tend to be those with the least power in decision making and those of least organizational influence. Thus discrimination in sport occurs when blacks are "stacked" at particular positions as well as when blacks are excluded from positions of power and leadership. Schneider and Eitzen (1979:137) define stacking (also called "positional segregation") as "situations in which minority group members are relegated to specific team positions and excluded from competing for others."

TABLE 11.2   *Stacking of Blacks in Major League Baseball (Percentage of Athletes Who Are Black)* *

Position	1967	1975	1984	1993
Outfield	49	49	70	50
Infield	17	24	38–40	12–14
Catcher	4	5	4	1
Pitcher	6	4	13	5

*Data from Loy and McElvogue 1970; Eitzen and Yetman 1977; Medoff 1986; and Lapchick and Benedict 1993.

Baseball. In baseball (see Table 11.2) blacks continue to be markedly over-represented in the outfield and underrepresented at pitcher and catcher, relative to their percentage of the total baseball population (Eitzen and Yetman 1977; Medoff 1986; Leonard 1988b; Lapchick and Benedict 1993). In 1993, for example, approximately 16 percent of Major League Baseball players were black, yet 50 percent of outfielders were black while only 5 percent of pitchers and 1 percent of catchers were black (Lapchick and Benedict 1993).

Medoff (1986) argues that this observation is best explained by the "economic hypothesis," i.e., that the economically disadvantaged black subpopulation is overrepresented in those positions in which skills cost the least to develop (i.e., the outfield) and underrepresented in those in which training is more costly (i.e., pitcher and catcher). As we shall see, a more common (though not incompatible with the economic hypothesis) explanation focuses on the implications of the central location of the pitching and catching positions and the peripheral location of the outfield positions.

Football. In football, positional segregation also continues to be prevalent. As shown in Table 11.3, blacks are stacked out of the central positions of quarterback, center, offensive guard, offensive tackle, and kicker, and into the peripheral positions of wide receiver, running back, and cornerback (Lapchick and Benedict 1993). In 1993, for example, the NFL was approximately 68 percent black. However, 94 percent of quarterbacks, 76 percent of centers, 62 percent of offensive guards, 50 percent of offensive tackles, and 83 percent of kickers were white (Lapchick and Benedict 1993). At the same time, 88 percent of wide receivers, 92 percent of running backs, and 98 percent of cornerbacks were black (Lapchick and Benedict 1993).

There is evidence that positional segregation occurs in college football as well as in the NFL. Jones et al. (1987) found that, in the Big Ten, Atlantic Coast, and Pacific Ten Conferences in 1982, 37.7 percent of the players were black. However, only 7.5 percent of quarterbacks, 6.3 percent of centers, 9.6 percent of left and 25 percent of right guards, 14 percent of left and 22.6 percent of right tackles, and 2.4 percent of kickers were black. At the same time

TABLE 11.3 *Stacking in NFL Football, 1993**

Position	Percent White	Percent Black
All Positions		68
Quarterback	94	
Center	76	
Offensive Guard	62	
Offensive Tackle	50	
Kicker	83	
Wide Receiver		88
Running Back		92
Cornerback		98

*Data from Lapchick and Benedict 1993.

they found 61.6 percent of wide receivers, 75.2 percent of running backs, and 67.5 percent of cornerbacks were black. A similar study of the 1983 Southeastern Conference (Vance 1984) revealed the same pattern of stacking.

Basketball.   Since 77 percent of NBA players are black, positional segregation is not the issue there that it is in other sports. Nevertheless, in 1992–93 only 55 percent of NBA centers were black, as compared with 80 percent of forwards and 83 percent of guards (Lapchick and Benedict 1993). The center position is generally considered to have the greatest control over the game's outcome, so the relatively low percentage of black centers is a possible indicator of some stacking.

Studies of more recent years indicate that stacking in college basketball is disappearing, at least among the men. Leonard (1987) found that in the early 1980s, NCAA basketball (both men's and women's) showed only a slight, statistically nonsignificant pattern of black overrepresentation at forward and underrepresentation at guard, and no stacking at the center position. Eitzen and Sage (1989) report, however, that in 1985, NCAA Division I women's basketball showed evidence that blacks were stacked into the forward and out of the center and guard positions, a finding consistent with that of Eitzen and Tessendorf (1978) about men's basketball 15 years earlier.

Volleyball.   Eitzen and Furst (1989) analyzed 1987–88 NCAA Division I women's volleyball, and found that blacks (6 percent of the overall sample) were significantly underrepresented (2.3 percent) at the setter position and overrepresented (7.4 percent) at the hitter position. They found no positional segregation among blockers or defensive specialists. Eitzen and Furst characterized the white-dominated setter position as the central position requiring the greatest leadership and intelligence and having the greatest outcome control. They described the black-dominated hitter position as requiring the greatest sheer physical skill. Eitzen and Furst indicated that racial stereotypes of different strengths among white and black athletes may be responsible for their findings of stacking in women's collegiate volleyball.

Centrality Theory

The theory of centrality provides some reasoning behind stacking. The theory of centrality is based on the work of Grusky (1963) and Blalock (1962). According to Grusky (1963:346),

> All else being equal, the more central one's spatial location: (1) the greater the likelihood dependent or coordinative tasks will be performed and (2) the greater the rate of interaction with the occupants of other positions. Also, the performance of dependent tasks is positively related to frequency of interaction.

Centrality in job situations is seen in (1) spatial location, (2) the nature of tasks to be performed, and (3) the frequency of interaction with other workers. Keeping these factors in mind, we can see that positions such as quarterback and center in football and catcher and pitcher in baseball are all high in centrality. Our previous discussion of stacking indicates that these central positions are highly represented by white players and underrepresented by black players. In the opinion of Loy and McElvogue (1970:22), blacks,

> because they are not liked by the white establishment, are placed in peripheral positions; and, as a result of this placement, do not have the opportunity of interaction with teammates, and do not receive the potential positive sentiment which [accrues] from such interaction.

Curtis and Loy (1978) and Leonard (1988b) offer alternative explanations for the existence of stacking of blacks in positions that tend to (1) be peripherally located on the playing field, (2) be peripheral to the decision and strategy process, and (3) have the least contact with teammates. These hypothesized explanations for the stacking phenomenon range from the psychological (where personality traits of blacks and whites are seen as conducive to different playing positions), to the biological (physical and mental abilities differing between the races), to the sociological (racial discrimination seen as resulting either from stereotyping, because whites prefer to interact with blacks as little as possible, because whites prefer to control outcomes, or from self-selection on the part of blacks). Each of these hypotheses may help to explain stacking, though at present they remain competing explanations.

Whether discrimination occurs because whites do not "like" blacks, whether they feel blacks are less capable of performing adequately or well in central positions, or whether they simply feel that blacks are better than whites at peripheral positions, and vice versa, the tangible result is that positions of decision-making importance and high status that are closer to the center of the field and the center of action tend to be populated by whites.

The Benefits of Central Positions.   There are benefits in playing positions high in centrality that are not afforded to those players who are kept in peripheral positions. Whether or not it proceeds from racial discrimination, central positioning in football tends to result in a longer playing career, since peripheral positions tend to be more susceptible to injury and age problems. Central positioning also provides players with (1) greater visibility, (2) greater influence, and (3) higher rank (Hopkins 1964). For athletes, this means not only that they are more likely to control the game and that they are more likely to be the focus of attention, but that they are perceived as more involved with the strategies in the game. This last factor is particularly important since coaches tend to be recruited from playing positions high in centrality. In Major League Baseball, Leonard, Ostrosky, and Huchendorf (1990), replicating and reinforcing a study by Grusky (1963), found that managers tend to be recruited more heavily from the positions of catcher and infielder (considered highly interactive) than from the less interactive positions of pitcher, outfielder, and designated hitter. In college football, a 1975 study of Division I teams found that 65 percent of head coaches and 63 percent of assistant head coaches had played central positions (Massengale and Farrington 1977). In basketball (selecting from coaches who had played professionally before 1975), 63.5 percent of coaches had played what was then the relatively central position of guard (Klonsky 1975).

Considering the great quantity of professional and intercollegiate athletes who are black, a disproportionately small number are in positions of authority. According to a report issued by Northeastern University's Center for the Study of Sport in Society (Lapchick and Benedict 1993), in 1992 only 2 of the NFL's 28 head coaches were black; 1 was Hispanic and 25 were white. The NBA in 1992-93, the report found, had 20 white, 7 black, and no Hispanic head coaches. In 1993, major league baseball had 22 white, 4 black, and 2 Hispanic managers. A study of NCAA Division I institutions (Anderson 1993) found evidence that intercollegiate athletics also underemploys black coaches and administrators. In 1990, the study revealed, 3.5 percent of head coaches, 7.2 percent of offensive coordinators, 6.9 percent of defensive coordinators, 21.4 percent of assistant coaches in football—and only 3.7 percent of athletic directors—were black.

Ability and Reward

We have alluded to two forms of financial disadvantage that result from the stacking of black athletes. First, the black-dominated peripheral positions in football depend largely on a player's speed and quickness, attributes that are especially vulnerable to injury and deterioration with age (Leonard 1988b). Consequently, players in peripheral positions have shorter average career lengths and hence both lower average career earnings and smaller pensions (Leonard 1988b). Second, the tendency for coaches and managers to come from the playing ranks of white-dominated central positions (not to mention the distinct possibility of Al Campanis-like racist stereotypes) greatly reduces the post-playing career options for black athletes, thus jeopardizing lifetime earnings from their sport expertise (Phillips 1987).

A third form of financial disadvantage might lie in discrimination in professional playing contracts. Does such discrimination exist? The answer is not simple.

Baseball. Boyle (1963) reports that in the days when bonuses were offered to entice young baseball players to sign their initial contracts (before baseball instituted a draft to eliminate competitive bidding for talent), white players received considerably higher bonuses than blacks. Analyses of salary data during the 1970s, however, point variously to (1) only slight discrimination (Hill and Spellman 1984); (2) discrimination only at the pitching position (Mogull 1975, 1979); (3) higher home run bounties paid to white infielders than to black infielders (Christiano 1986); and (4) no salary discrimination (Pascal and Rapping 1972).

One reason for the inconsistency of these findings regarding salaries is the complicating factor of performance. It is not enough simply to compare the contracts of white and black players at the same position. We must also consider the possibility that the black players had to perform better in order to obtain comparable contracts. Pascal and Rapping (1972) and Scully (1974) argue that this was true in the 1960s. Rosenblatt (1977) and Eitzen and Yetman (1977) provide further evidence that black players must be superior to whites, giving blacks with ability equal to that of white players less opportunity to compete.

This form of discrimination in baseball appears to be disappearing. Phillips (1987) notes a decline in marginality (the tendency to choose whites over blacks of comparable marginal ability) in professional baseball from 1960 to 1980. Raimondo (1983) and Cymrot (1985) argue that free agency, through which players can market themselves to the highest bidder, has made salary discrimination in baseball (at least for free agents) a thing of the past. In a study of 1987 nonpitching positions, Christiano (1988) found no evidence of systematic discrimination. Leonard (1988a) also analyzed 1987 major league nonpitching salaries and found no evidence of systematic discrimination against either blacks or Hispanics.

Nevertheless, among the players themselves the perception of salary discrimination continues. In a 1991 survey of professional athletes, *Sports Illustrated* found that although 84 percent of white Major League Baseball players felt that salary contracts were the same for blacks and whites, 61 percent of black players believe that whites have better salary contracts (W. O. Johnson 1991). In response to the survey, outfielder Deion Sanders said, "If you're black and in baseball, there is no in-between . . . You aren't going to be on the bench just drawing a salary if you're just so-so and black" (W. O. Johnson 1991:46).

Football. Lapchick (1986) cites evidence collected by David Meggyesy from the 1982 NFL season, indicating a clear salary differential favoring white players over black players. According to that data, white players' salaries league-wide averaged $100,730 compared with $91,980 for black players. Furthermore, according to the data, "It made no difference whether you played offense or defense or started or were a backup" (Lapchick 1986:113).

More recent information indicates that the NFL salary differential may be disappearing. Kahn (1992), using figures from the 1989 season, found the differential to be 4 percent or less and did not find it to be statistically significant. Kahn also found, however, that both white and nonwhite players made significantly more money in metropolitan areas where their respective percentages in the local population were relatively high.

In a study designed to test the "unequal opportunity for equal ability hypothesis," Kooistra, Mahoney, and Bridges (1993) compared 1991 NFL "protected" players (presumably the most talented) with "Plan B" free agents (the more marginal performers). Supporting the hypothesis, they found that Plan B players were disproportionately white. Thus, although overall salary differentials seem to be disappearing, evidence remains that black NFL players must perform better than whites to secure equal salaries.

Basketball. Lapchick (1986) and Leonard (1988b) are among those who argue that blacks in the NBA must be better players than whites in order to make the team. Mogull (1977) found no evidence that blacks were paid less than whites, but N. R. Johnson and Marple (1973) concluded that marginally skilled black players tend to be released more quickly than their white counterparts. More recently, Koch and Vander Hill (1988) analyzed the 1984–85 NBA salary structure and found that, at equivalent performance levels, blacks are paid significantly less than whites.

In summary, it appears that salary discrimination against black athletes is a reality, at least in professional football and basketball. Many observers of the situation feel that the only way to eliminate the financial barriers to blacks in sport, especially those that continue to keep blacks out of management positions, is for blacks to become owners of professional teams (R. S. Johnson 1987). Based on the evidence, it would be difficult to argue with that perspective.

Racism, Sport, and Social Mobility

The crime of racial discrimination in a nation like the United States, which prides itself on meritocratic ideals, is that racial discrimination focuses on ascribed characteristics (such as skin color) rather than on achieved characteristics (such as physical or mental skills). White male-dominated society has evolved social barriers that, intentionally or not, screen people on the basis of skin color, speech patterns, and sex rather than on merit or ability. While a few blacks may earn money and receive an education through sports, they cannot do much to overcome the barriers to social mobility that are blind to factors other than skin color. When skin color is no longer a matter of concern to whites or to blacks, blacks can begin to put greater faith in education, accomplishment in athletics or elsewhere, and earning power as useful means for social mobility.

Social Mobility

Socioeconomic classes are usually defined by social scientists on the basis of earning power and type of occupation. In lay terms, social class may also be measured by the neighborhood in which a family lives (e.g., we might refer to "a middle-class neighborhood"). Following the ideas of Loy (1968), we presume the direction of social mobility through sports participation to be upward, although it is unlikely that more than one status level will be gained. The socially mobile person hopes or expects this status change to occur within his or her own lifetime, or at least for the next generation. The status change may be a combination of economics, education, occupation, and prestige and power, although economic change alone might satisfy one's social mobility goal. The mechanism used to attain the status change of concern to us is the occupation, or "profession," of athlete. In some cases, mobility is a result of the education that may come along with training for professional athletics careers.

Upward social mobility has limits regardless of race. The upper class or "high society" is closed not only to blacks, but also to whites who do not have the proper "breeding," regardless of race or wealth (Aldrich 1988). Whether or not anyone, such as a newly wealthy athlete, would care to enter this upper echelon is irrelevant to the fact that he or she *could not* enter it. Therefore, when we speak of upward social mobility, we are discussing only movement from lower class to middle class, or at most to upper middle class.

Mobility Through Sport: A Myth?

Despite continuing economic discrimination against blacks in professional football and basketball, there is much money to be made in professional sports and many blacks are taking a healthy share of it. As one of the top ten male tennis players in the world, Arthur Ashe earned a small fortune and made himself—economically, politically, and humanistically—a strong role model for black youth. However, Ashe discouraged black youth from viewing professional sports as an avenue out of the ghetto (Ashe 1977). Why should Ashe discourage black youngsters from following in his footsteps?

Currently, the key issue for blacks is less a matter of overt discrimination (as it was in the past) than it is a problem of perceiving professional sports as a viable and accessible path for upward social mobility for significant numbers of black youth. There is a widespread folk belief, particularly among blacks, that sport is an accessible avenue for increasing socioeconomic status

(Loy 1968; Guttmann 1988). This belief is voiced by Richard Thompson (1964:12), who adds that "the national prestige" afforded superior black athletes "enables them to influence the pattern of segregation directly," and that blacks excelling in sports can lead to changes in social relations between blacks and whites.

However, gains for blacks in sports have been greater than their gains in society in general. Sports give "fulfillment and wealth and education to thousands of players" (Orr 1969:147), but what of the hundreds of thousands and even millions of blacks who, over the course of a decade or more, have bought the dream of professional sport but have failed to cash in on it because there is so little room at the top? Professional sport is more of a bottlenecked traffic jam than an avenue for long-term economic success. Guttmann (1988:138) states, "Of high school baseball, basketball, and football players, fewer than 1 in 10,000 succeeds at the professional level."

The crux of the problem, however, is that the bottleneck effect is greater for blacks than for whites (Edwards 1988; Leonard and Reyman 1988). While the chances for athletic success among the much larger white population are even less than for blacks, whites at least tend to perceive society as offering them many other opportunities. White youngsters striving to be professional athletes seldom see athletics as their only means for becoming successful in the world, no matter how great their desire. Many black youth, on the other hand, appear to see only athletics and entertainment as legitimate means to escape the ghetto. As Harry Edwards (Hamilton 1988:19) puts it, "To tie the aspirations of 30 million people to fewer than 2,000 jobs in three professional sports is an inhuman mockery." Stating the odds for aspiring black athletes somewhat differently, Edwards (1988:140) observes,

> Of the black athletes who participate in collegiate football, basketball, or baseball, only 1.6 percent ever sign a professional contract—less than *2 out of 100.* And within three and a half years, over 60 percent of those who do sign such contracts are out of professional sports, more often than not financially destitute or in debt, and on the street without either the credentials or the skills to make their way productively in our extremely competitive high-tech society.

The problem for the black community and for black individuals is that an inordinate amount of time and energy among black youth is devoted to sports and the dream of professional sports success, to the exclusion of other areas of development (Edwards 1988). Black youth tend to identify exclusively with black role models, while whites do not seem to limit their role models to whites (Castine and Roberts 1974). In addition there is some indication that black youth focus on sports role models, even to the exclusion of successful black politicians, scientists, and civil rights activists (SWOPSI 1974). This has led Arthur Ashe, Harry Edwards, and educator Roscoe Brown (1978), among many other black leaders, to suggest that other avenues for success be opened to black youth. Edwards (1988) challenges black families to place more emphasis on meaningful educational achievement. He states (1988:140),

> This does not mean that blacks should abandon sports, but that we *must* learn to deal with the realities of sports more intelligently and constructively. Black parents must insist upon the establishment and pursuit of high academic standards and personal development goals by their children.

For many black student-athletes, education is sound and will be an effective tool for taking a rewarding place in society. For many others, college educations appear to be wasted, partly because of poor preparatory education and partly because of a disproportionate amount of effort spent on athletics, even while in college. Edwards (1988) maintains that 65–75 percent of black scholarship athletes at four-year institutions never graduate. This point is brought home when scandalous educational practices in intercollegiate athletics surface, practices that are attempts to keep athletes eligible to play on college teams and foster their professional sports aspirations. The results of these practices, however, are that they subvert the athletes' educations, especially in the case of many blacks who are attempting to eliminate educational deficiencies rather than perpetuate them. These are not-so-subtle forms of racism, since education may be the most significant legitimate and generally obtainable means for blacks to achieve upward socioeconomic mobility (Guttmann 1988).

Whose responsibility is it to correct this situation? Edwards advises black athletes that they must take it upon themselves to bring about change. He asserts (1988:140) that

> it is black athletes themselves who must shoulder a substantial portion of the responsibility for improving black circumstances and outcomes in American sports. Black athletes must insist upon intellectual discipline no less than athletic discipline among themselves, and upon educational integrity in athletic programs rather than, as is all too often the case, merely seeking the easiest route to maintaining athletic eligibility. If black athletes fail to take a conscious, active and informed role in changing the course and character of black sports involvement, nothing done by any other party to this tragic situation is likely to be effective or lasting—if for no other reason than the fact that *a slave cannot be freed against his will.*

Allowing a youngster to choose between a profession in sports and a profession in medicine, science, law, or teaching is often like offering him or her a choice between ice cream and spinach. With this in mind, Brown, Edwards, and others have taken the radical and unpopular position that black youth should be actively discouraged from playing sports and actively encouraged to apply their curiosity and energy to developing talents that are more likely to be rewarding to the community as well as to themselves. Whether we agree or not is less important than our understanding that such a position stems from the belief that racism lingers in sport and that sport fails to provide the avenue of social mobility many people claim it does.

If racism occurs in sport—and there is ample evidence that it does in various if subtle ways—sport itself is not to blame. As one of American society's cherished institutions, sport simply reflects values and cultural attitudes and pressures. If coaches are racist, for example, it is because the society tolerates racism despite laws that are intended to prevent it. The institution of sport, at times, has led American society in the struggle to overcome racism, as with the removal of color lines in professional sports. Often, however, sport has had to be pushed to make changes by the efforts and sacrifices of such individuals as Jackie Robinson, Althea Gibson, Arthur Ashe, Lee Elder, Muhammed Ali, Curt Flood, John Carlos, and Tommie Smith. In some cases, such as the admittance of blacks to positions of responsibility, sport seems to be lagging well behind the rest of American society.

Summary

The past decade has seen a renewed awareness of racial discrimination in sport. Explanations for the overrepresentation of black athletes in certain sports and underrepresentation in others have included physical, intellectual, and psychological causes that are not well supported by disciplined inquiry. Phenomena such as quotas, stacking, and salary discrimination are best explained in a sociological context that views racism in sport as a reflection of a society that continues to harbor racism in general. The bottleneck effect makes upward mobility through sport a myth for most, and that myth's cruelty is intensified for those blacks whose aspirations are tied to little else besides athletic success.

References

Aldrich, N. W., Jr. 1988. *Old Money: The Mythology of America's Upper Class.* New York: A. A. Knopf.

Anderson, D. 1993. "Cultural Diversity on Campus: A Look At Intercollegiate Football Coaches." *Journal of Sport and Social Issues* 17:61–66.

Ashe, A. 1977. "An Open Letter to Black Parents: Send Your Children to the Libraries." *New York Times* February 6:E2.

Ashe, A. R., Jr. 1988. *A Hard Road to Glory: A History of the African-American Athlete Since 1946.* New York: Warner.

Blalock, H. M. 1962. "Occupational Discrimination: Some Empirical Propositions." *Social Problems* 9:210–47.

Bouchard, C. 1988. "Genetic Basis of Racial Differences." *Canadian Journal of Sport Sciences* 13(2):104–8.

Boulay, M. R., P. F. M. Ama, and C. Bouchard. 1988. "Racial Variation in Work Capacities and Powers." *Canadian Journal of Sport Sciences* 13(2):127–35.

Boyle, R. H. 1963. *Sport: Mirror of American Life.* Boston: Little, Brown.

Brazziel, W. F. 1969. "A Letter from the South." *Harvard Educational Review* 39(2):348–56.

Brown, R. C. 1978. "The Jock-Trap—How the Black Athlete Gets Caught!" In *Sport Psychology: An Analysis of Athletes' Behavior,* edited by W. F. Straub. Ithaca, NY: Movement Publications.

Castine, S. C., and G. C. Roberts. 1974. "Modelling in the Socialization Process of the Black Athlete." *International Review of Sport Sociology* 9(3–4):59–74.

Chass, M. 1987. "Campanis Is Out; Racial Remarks Cited by Dodgers." *New York Times* April 9: B13–14.

Christiano, K. J. 1986. "Salary Discrimination in Major League Baseball: The Effect of Race." *Sociology of Sport Journal* 3:144–53.

Christiano, K. J. 1988. "Salaries and Race in Professional Baseball: Discrimination 10 Years Later." *Sociology of Sport Journal* 5:136–49.

Curtis, J. E., and J. W. Loy. 1978. "Positional Segregation and Professional Baseball: Replications, Trend Data, and Critical Observations." *International Review of Sport Sociology* 13(4):5–23.

Cymrot, D. J. 1985. "Does Competition Lessen Discrimination? Some Evidence." *Journal of Human Resources* 20:605–12.

Edwards, H. 1973. *Sociology of Sport.* Homewood, IL: Dorsey Press.

Edwards, H. 1987. "Race in Contemporary American Sports." Pp. 194–97 in *Sport Sociology: Contemporary Themes,* 3rd edition, edited by A. Yiannakis, T. D. McIntyre, M. J. Melnick, and D. P. Hart. Dubuque, IA: Kendall/Hunt.

Edwards, H. 1988. " 'The Single-Minded Pursuit of Sports Fame and Fortune Is Approaching an Institutionalized Triple Tragedy in Black Society . . .' " *Ebony* 43(August):138–40.

Eitzen, D. S., and D. M. Furst. 1989. "Racial Bias in Women's Collegiate Volleyball." *Journal of Sport and Social Issues* 13:46–51.

Eitzen, D. S., and G. H. Sage. 1989. *Sociology of North American Sport.* 4th edition. Dubuque, IA: Wm. C. Brown.

Eitzen, D. S., and I. Tessendorf. 1978. "Racial Segregation By Position in Sports: The Special Case of Basketball." *Review of Sport and Leisure* 3:109–28.

Eitzen, D. S., and N. R. Yetman. 1977. "Immune from Racism?" *Civil Rights Digest* 9(2):3–13.

Farrell, S. W., H. W. Kohl, T. Rogers, and G. F. Knadler. 1988. "Cardiovascular Fitness and Maximal Heart Rate Differences Among Three Ethnic Groups." *Research Quarterly for Exercise and Sport* 59(2):99–102.

Grusky, O. 1963. "The Effects of Formal Structure on Managerial Recruitment: A Study of Baseball Organization." *Sociometry* 26:343–53.

Guttmann, A. 1988. *A Whole New Ball Game: An Interpretation of American Sports.* Chapel Hill, NC: University of North Carolina Press.

Hamilton, J. 1988. "The Season of Harry Edwards." *Image (San Francisco Examiner)* April 3:16–19+.

Hearnshaw, L. S. 1979. *Cyril Burt: Psychologist.* Ithaca, NY: Cornell University.

Hill, J. R., and W. Spellman. 1984. "Pay Discrimination in Baseball: Data from the Seventies." *Industrial Relations* 23(Winter):103–12.

Himes, J. H. 1988. "Racial Variation in Physique and Body Composition." *Canadian Journal of Sport Sciences* 13(2):117–26.

Holloman, L. L. 1943. "On the Supremacy of the Negro Athlete in White Athletic Competition." *Psychoanalytic Review* 30.

Hopkins, T. K. 1964. *The Exercise of Influence in Small Groups.* Totowa, NJ: Bedminster Press.

Jensen, A. R. 1969. "How Much Can We Boost IQ and Scholastic Achievement." *Harvard Educational Review* 39(1):1–123.

Johnson, N. R., and D. P. Marple. 1973. "Racial Discrimination in Professional Basketball." *Sociological Focus* 6(Fall):6–18.

Johnson, R. S. 1987. "For Blacks, Locker Room Doesn't Lead to Board Room." *New York Times* April 14:25+.

Johnson, W. O. 1991. "A Matter of Black and White." *Sports Illustrated* Aug. 5:44–47.

Jones, G., W. M. Leonard II, R. L. Schmitt, D. R. Smith, and W. L. Tolone. 1987. "A Log-Linear Analysis of Stacking in College Football." *Social Science Quarterly* 68:70–83.

Kahn, L. M. 1992. "The Effects of Race on Professional Football Players' Compensation." *Industrial and Labor Relations Review* 45:295–310.

Kane, M. 1971. "An Assessment of Black Is Best." *Sports Illustrated* 34(January 18):72–83.

Klonsky, B. 1975. "The Effects of Formal Structure and Role Skills on Coaching Recruitment and Longevity: A Study of Professional Baseball Teams." Unpublished paper, Department of Psychology, Fordham University.

Koch, J. V., and C. W. Vander Hill. 1988. "Is There Discrimination in the Black Man's Game?" *Social Science Quarterly* 69(1):83–94.

Kooistra, P., J. S. Mahoney, and L. Bridges. 1993. "The Unequal Opportunity for Equal Ability Hypothesis: Racism in the National Football League?" *Sociology of Sport Journal* 10:241–55.

Lapchick, R. E. 1975. *The Politics of Race and International Sport: The Case of South Africa.* Westport, CT: Greenwood Press.

Lapchick, R. E. 1986. "The Promised Land." Pp. 111–35 in *Fractured Focus: Sport as a Reflection of Society,* edited by R. E. Lapchick. Lexington, MA: D. C. Heath.

Lapchick, R. E., and J. R. Benedict. 1993. "1993 Racial Report Card." *CSSS Digest* 5:1,4–8,12–13.

Lapchick, R. E., and J. Panepinto. 1987. "The White World of College Sports." *New York Times* November 15:S12.

Leonard, W. M., II. 1987. "Stacking in College Basketball: A Neglected Analysis." *Sociology of Sport Journal* 4:403–9.

Leonard, W. M., II. 1988a. "Salaries and Race in Professional Baseball: The Hispanic Component." *Sociology of Sport Journal* 5:278–84.

Leonard, W. M., II. 1988b. *A Sociological Perspective of Sport.* 3rd edition. New York: Macmillan.

Leonard, W. M., II and J. E. Reyman. 1988. "The Odds of Attaining Professional Athlete Status: Refining the Computations." *Sociology of Sport Journal* 5:162–69.

Leonard, W. M., II, T. Ostrosky, and S. Huchendorf. 1990. "Centrality of Position and Managerial Recruitment: The Case of Major League Baseball." *Sociology of Sport Journal* 7:294–301.

Lombardo, B. 1978. "The Harlem Globetrotters and the Perpetuation of the Black Stereotype." *The Physical Educator* 35(May):60–63.

Loy, J. W. 1968. "The Study of Sport and Social Mobility." In *Aspects of Contemporary Sport Sociology,* edited by G. Kenyon. Chicago: The Athletic Institute.

Loy, J. W., and J. F. McElvogue. 1970. "Racial Segregation in American Sport." *International Review of Sport Sociology* 5:5–24.

Malina, R. M. 1988. "Racial/Ethnic Variation in the Motor Development and Performance of American Children." *Canadian Journal of Sport Sciences* 13(2):136–43.

Massengale, J., and L. Farrington. 1977. "The Influence of Playing Position Centrality on the Careers of College Football Coaches." *Review of Sport and Leisure* 2(June):107–15.

Medoff, M. H. 1986. "Positional Segregation and the Economic Hypothesis." *Sociology of Sport Journal* 3:297–304.

Mogull, R. G. 1975. "Salary Discrimination in Major League Baseball." *The Review of Black Political Economy* V(Spring).

Mogull, R. G. 1977. "A Note on Racial Discrimination in Professional Basketball: A Reevaluation of the Evidence." *The American Economist* 21(2):71–75.

Mogull, R. G. 1979. "Discrimination in Baseball Revisited." *Atlantic Economic Journal* 7(2):66–74.

Montagu, M. F. A. 1944. "The Physical Anthropology of the American Negro." *Psychiatry* February.

NBC. 1989. "Black Athletes: Fact and Fiction." NBC News Special, April 25.

Orr, J. 1969. *The Black Athlete: His Story in American History.* New York: Lion Press.

Ostler, S. 1993. "The Man Who Broke Golf's Color Barrier." *San Francisco Chronicle* Oct. 8:E1,7.

Pascal, A. H., and L. A. Rapping. 1972. "The Economics of Racial Discrimination in Organized Baseball." Pp. 119–56 in *Racial Discrimination in Economic Life,* edited by A. H. Pascal. Lexington, MA: Heath Lexington.

Phillips, J. 1976. "Toward an Explanation of Racial Variations in Top-Level Sports Participation." *International Review of Sport Sociology* 11(3):39–56.

Phillips, J. C. 1987. "Race and Career Opportunities in Major League Baseball: 1960–1980." Pp. 206–13 in *Sport Sociology: Contemporary Themes,* 3rd edition, edited by A. Yiannakis, T. D. McIntyre, M. J. Melnick, and D. P. Hart. Dubuque, IA: Kendall/Hunt.

Raimondo, H. J. 1983. "Free Agents' Impact on the Labor Market for Baseball Players." *Journal of Labor Research* 4:183–93.

Rosenblatt, A. 1977. "Negroes in Baseball: The Failure of Success." *Transaction* 4 (September):51–53.

Samson, J., and M. Yerles. 1988. "Racial Differences in Sports Performance." *Canadian Journal of Sport Sciences* 13(2):109–16.

Schneider, J., and D. S. Eitzen. 1979. "Racial Discrimination in American Sport: Continuity or Change?" *Journal of Sport Behavior* 2(3):136–42.

Scully, G. W. 1974. "Discrimination: The Case of Baseball." Pp. 221–73 in *Government and the Sports Business,* edited by R. G. Noll. Washington, DC: Brookings Institution.

SWOPSI (Stanford Workshop on Political and Social Issues). 1974. "Varsity Athletics, The Black Community, and Stanford University." Unpublished report.

Thompson, R. 1964. *Race and Sport.* London: Oxford University.

Uhlig, M. A. 1988. "Racial Remarks Cause Furor." *New York Times* January 16:47+.

Vance, N. S. 1984. "Football Study Links Race, Player Positions; Reasons Aren't Clear, 3 Researchers Caution." *The Chronicle of Higher Education* April 25:21+.

Weinberg, S. K., and H. Arond. 1952. "The Occupational Culture of the Boxer." *American Journal of Sociology* 57(March):460–69.

"Why Blacks Excel in Sports." 1988. *Ebony* 44(December):31–34.

Worthy, M., and A. Markle. 1970. "Black Americans in Reactive versus Self-Paced Sports Activities." *Journal of Personality and Social Psychology* 16:439–43.

CHAPTER 12

Women in Sport:
Sex Roles and Sexism

Why are we including a special chapter on women and sport? We have, after all, attempted to convey the fact that virtually all of the issues addressed in this text affect female athletes and women's sport as well as male athletes and men's sport. There are, however, circumstances and issues unique to females in sport that need to be discussed and evaluated in their own right.

Until fairly recently, a widespread belief held that strenuous sports activity was not only beyond the capacity of women but physically harmful to them. The belief, moreover, held that even if women could somehow find the physical endurance and emotional resolve necessary for high-level sports competition, it was still bad for them. It was, in a word, unladylike. Sport, of course, has been only one area in which women have been discriminated against, and although federal legislation now makes such discrimination illegal, legislation does little to change longstanding beliefs about the differences between men and women and their relative physical, mental, and behavioral attributes. Some of these perceived sex-related differences are real, others are mythical, and yet others are not really differences related to sex in the biological sense, but stem instead from different social perceptions and treatment of women and men.

The starting point of our analysis is this observation: that American girls and women are significantly less involved in sport than American boys and men, and have been throughout our history. There are fewer programs offered for females than for males, there are fewer numbers of female than male participants, and there is less societal emphasis placed on female sport in the form of funding, media attention, commercial and professional opportunities, etc. The question is, why? Is it a natural and right situation based on inherent differences between males and females in relation to the nature and demands of the sport experience, or is it an unjustified case of long-running but correctable discrimination?

In the *pure description* phase of our analysis, we will present a brief historical perspective on American women's sport, focusing on its current status. Our *evaluative commentary* will address three types of reasons—biological, psychological, and sociological—which are commonly offered to explain the continuing situation. *Social critique* will be discussed from two theoretical viewpoints, and suggestions for *social engineering* will emerge from politically based interpretations of what changes are needed.

Historical Perspectives on American Women's Sport

Prior to the Civil War, women as well as men participated in the physical activities that were popular in their country—and social class—of origin (Howell 1982). Typically, upper-class women danced and rode horses, but were not very active otherwise. Middle- and lower-class women led more physical lives by necessity. Their recreational activities often included dancing, riding, skating, foot racing, and early forms of such sports as bowling and baseball (Howell 1982; Gerber 1974). Overall, however, the activities considered acceptable for women were much more physically restricted than those engaged in by men (Howell 1982).

The Victorian Period
The post-Civil War period was characterized by the widespread adoption of Victorian beliefs, values, and ideals of womanhood. The hard physical labor commonly performed by lower-class and slave women belied Victorian notions of innate feminine weakness; nevertheless, those notions predominated and determined the patterns of physical activity among upper- and middle-class women (Smith 1988). Although Catharine Beecher and other proponents of physical fitness for females developed systems of calisthenics for schools and private clubs, most women of means rarely participated in any sporting activity more strenuous than croquet (Gerber 1974).

Growing Enthusiasm for Women's Sports
The late 19th and early 20th centuries brought some significant new trends in women's involvement in sport. Caught up in the growing popularity of such sports as archery, fencing, rowing, bowling, skating, bicycling, tennis, and golf, women increasingly joined private clubs where those sports were played (Gerber 1974). College men were developing baseball, rowing, track and field, and football into intercollegiate sports; meanwhile, private women's colleges, coeducational colleges, and teacher preparation schools (such as the Boston

Normal School of Gymnastics) offered women fitness and sport classes as well as intramural sport programs featuring the newly invented sport of basketball. Gradually, the connection between physical activity and women's health was established, and sport participation for females grew in acceptability (Gerber 1974).

Physical and Philosophical Issues

As the Roaring Twenties progressed, the trend toward women's participation in vigorous sports reached the point where concerns were raised as to how much physical competition should be allowed. Over the objections of Olympic founder Pierre de Coubertin, and despite resistance from the American Olympic Committee, American women had begun to participate in Olympic competition. Outstanding sportswomen such as Helen Wills (tennis), Sonja Henie (ice skating), Gertrude Ederle (swimming), and Amelia Earhart (aviation) became international celebrities and heroines. These developments were alarming to many people (including many women physical educators) who felt that (1) high-level competition was too stressful (both physically and emotionally) for women; (2) a focus on high-level competition was elitist, putting the interests of the highly skilled few ahead of those of the larger majority; and/or (3) high-level competition would breed corruption such as that which characterized men's intercollegiate athletic programs of the period. (These concerns are still being voiced today. Although we shall try and put the first one to rest, the second and third are not without continuing merit.)

In response to debates over these concerns, several women's sport organizations adopted position statements supporting a broad-based, egalitarian, educational approach to sport programs for girls and women (Gerber 1974). During the 1930s and 1940s, then, a common form of extramural competition for girls and women was the play day, which featured activities such as shuttle relays and low-level, modified sports played by teams formed on the spot with players from various schools (Gerber 1974). Somewhat more competitive was the sports day, which allowed representative teams but discouraged practicing ahead of time and downplayed contest results (Gerber 1974). A third alternative was the telegraphic meet, in which teams competed (typically in archery, bowling, or riflery) at their own campuses, then simply compared scores to determine the winner. Gerber (1974) points out that this competitive form was thought to avoid the danger of emotional stress that might result from face-to-face encounters with opponents.[1]

Although play days, sports days, and telegraphic meets sound quaint by today's competitive standards, they represented a significant historical period— one in which sport for girls and women was controlled and largely structured

---

[1]Telegraphic meets have also been used, by both men's and women's programs at various times, because they are a relatively inexpensive form of competition. It is impossible to know how often this justification has masked an underlying devaluing of women's sport and of men's "minor" sports.

specifically by and for women. Women held all of the leadership positions—administrator, coach, official—and protected their programs from the elitism, commercialism, and corruption that were so common in programs for males. This philosophical and programmatic control continued through the 1950s, during which time the major scholastic sport organization for girls and women was the Division for Girls' and Women's Sports (DGWS) of the American Association for Health, Physical Education and Recreation (AAHPER). DGWS established and modified rules, published rule books and other informational material, trained and rated officials, sponsored clinics, and promoted athletic programs at both the high school and college levels (Gerber 1974).

The Modern Era Begins

During the 1960s, American women such as Wilma Rudolph and Wyomia Tyus (track), Donna de Varona (swimming), and Peggy Fleming (figure skating) achieved Olympic fame. Golfers such as Patty Berg and Kathy Whitworth, and tennis players like Billie Jean King and Margaret Court, earned widespread recognition and a degree of wealth in the world of professional sport. In scholastic sport, DGWS gradually led the way toward more serious levels of competition, eventually (in 1969) sponsoring national tournaments in women's intercollegiate sports and (in 1972) establishing the Association for Intercollegiate Athletics for Women (AIAW) (Gerber 1974).

In the early 1970s, women first entered as active participants such previously all-male domains as horse racing and auto and motorcycle racing. The 1970s also brought experiments in women's professional team sports, especially softball and basketball. The Women's Professional Softball League, established in 1975, struggled along under difficult conditions (low pay, heavy playing schedules and promotional expectations, uncomfortable travel, and poor media coverage), and finally suspended play in 1979 (Boutilier and SanGiovanni 1983). The Women's Professional Basketball League, begun in 1978, also suffered numerous difficulties before folding in 1982.

Title IX

The major source of change in girls' high school and women's college sport in the 1970s was the passage of the Education Amendments Act of 1972 (amending the Civil Rights Act of 1964). One of the sections, or "titles," of that law is Title IX, which stipulates that

> No person in the United States shall on the basis of sex be excluded from participation in, be denied the benefits of, or be subjected to discrimination under any educational program or activity receiving Federal financial assistance.

As Title IX was interpreted for athletics, it focused on two areas: (1) proportional funding of athletic scholarships between the sexes, and (2) equivalent funding for all other aspects of school sports. Proportional funding of scholarships is to be determined by dividing the available money for athletic grants by the number of people of each sex in the athletic program. If a school that gives scholarships has 100 male athletes and 50 female athletes, then two-thirds of the scholarship money should go to men and one-third to women. In all other aspects of school sport, opportunities shall be essentially equal, according to Title IX. This includes opportunities for competition (i.e., teams), equipment, schedules of games and practice times, travel expenses, assignment and compensation of coaches and tutors, availability of facilities, medical and training services, housing and dining benefits, and publicity.

AIAW quickly realized the implications of Title IX for equity in girls' and women's sport. When the NCAA awakened to the necessity under Title IX to provide equal opportunity for females in sport, it lobbied to have revenue-producing sports exempted from the law. When that failed, the NCAA and AIAW began to battle each other over control of women's intercollegiate athletics. Beginning in 1980, the NCAA established national championships in women's events, thus openly competing with AIAW. Ultimately, AIAW was unable to compete with the NCAA's money and political power. It suspended operations in 1982, leaving the NCAA as the major governing body for women's intercollegiate athletics.

The 1980s

Developments in sport for girls and women in the 1980s were both hopeful and troubling. Sport programs for girls and women made gains in funding, visibility, acceptance, and popularity during the 1980s. There were more participants than ever before (Acosta and Carpenter 1989) and, at the college level, the average number of different sports offered per school increased from 5.61 in 1978 to 7.31 in 1988 (*Chronicle of Higher Education* 1988). According to a study funded by Wilson Sporting Goods (*The Wilson Report* 1988), the majority of American parents accepted the importance of sports for girls as well as for boys, and eight out of ten girls participated in sports. Prize money for women's professional sports continued to climb, and female Olympians like Mary Lou Retton and Florence Griffith Joyner were able to parlay athletic victories into major financial earnings.

On the other hand, at the 1984 Olympic Games in Los Angeles, only 23 percent of the athletes were female, and there were only 62 events in 15 sports for women compared with 220 events in 24 sports overall. (Probably related to this is the fact that, even in 1988, only 5 of the 92 members of the International Olympic Committee were women.) Advertisers continued to ignore the market for women's sport, and the attempt to establish the Women's Basketball League as a professional success failed (Comte, Girard, and Starensier 1989). Major League Volleyball, after a couple of promising years on the ESPN cable television network, also suspended operations, in 1989 (*San Francisco Chronicle* 1989).

Support for scholastic and intercollegiate sport programs for females still lagged far behind that provided for males. From 1982 to 1988, legal interpretations of the applicability of Title IX to athletic programs (especially a 1984

Olympiad

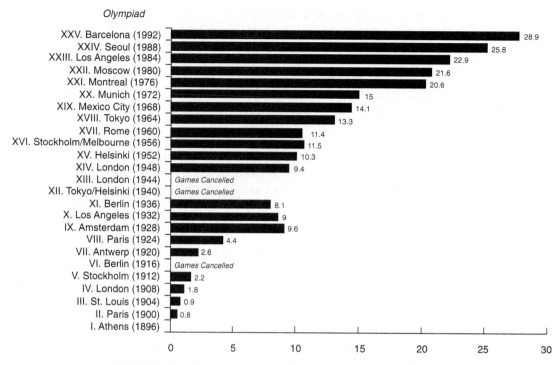

FIGURE 12.1 *Women's Summer Olympic Participation. (Information courtesy of* The Women's Sports Experience, *May/June 1993.)*

Supreme Court decision, *Grove City College versus Bell,* which asserted that only specific educational programs that receive federal aid are protected by the law) and presidential administrative reluctance to enforce Title IX resulted in a stagnation in the movement toward equity (NCAA 1988a). The Civil Rights Restoration Act of 1988 restored the relevance of the law to athletic programs, but good faith enforcement efforts on the part of the Bush Administration remained doubtful.

The 1990s

Sport for girls and women continues to show progress. By 1991, nationwide attendance at women's college basketball games had doubled from a decade earlier (Nakao 1993). At the 1992 Olympic Games in Barcelona, women represented 29 percent of the participants (Noel 1993).

The large-scale adoption of the business model by women's intercollegiate athletic programs appears to have destroyed any hope of reviving the broad-based educational philosophy of earlier decades of women's sport. In their eagerness to achieve equity with men's programs, women have added scholarships, letters of intent, competitive recruiting, slick publicity, and an emphasis on winning over all else, legacies of men's athletic history whose consequences include increasingly common NCAA sanctions for a wide range of infractions.

Meanwhile, gender equity in collegiate sport has remained elusive. In 1992, an NCAA survey of Division I programs revealed gross inequities in average numbers of participants (more than two-to-one male), scholarships (twice as many to males), operating budgets (three-fourths to males), and recruiting money (over 80 percent to recruit males) (Lederman 1992). The survey also found that Division I men's coaches made an average salary of $71,511, 82 percent higher than the $39,177 average for women's coaches (Sullivan 1992).

Out of concerns about such inequitable conditions have arisen a number of lawsuits, mostly based on Title IX. That law has been revitalized by a renewed commitment to enforcing it on the part of the U.S. Education Department's Office for Civil Rights (Blum 1993) and by rulings such as the Supreme Court's 1992 decision (in *Franklin* versus *Gwinnett County*) that monetary damages can be awarded in cases of deliberate violation of Title IX (NAGWS 1993). To date, lawsuits or the threat of lawsuits have resulted in gains (or successful defenses against losses) for women's athletics in the majority of cases settled (Blum 1992, Gottesman 1993, Reith 1993a, Reith 1993b).

Intercollegiate Coaches and Administrators

A serious concern dating back to the 1980s is the decline in women intercollegiate coaches and administrators (Bruce 1993). In 1972, over 90 percent of women's teams and programs were coached and administered by women. Twenty years later, women represented only 48 percent of coaches and 17 percent of administrators (Van Keuren 1992). As programs for women have taken on more of the character of men's programs, and as many men's and women's teams and programs have been combined under a single coach and/or a single administrator (almost always male), women have lost much of the control they previously held over women's programs (Potera and Kort 1986). According to a study conducted by Acosta and Carpenter (1989), men and women perceive the reasons for this differently. Men and women tend to agree that females "burn out" and leave the coaching and administrative professions sooner than men do. Men assume, however, that there are fewer qualified female coaches and administrators, that they fail to apply for job openings, and that they have greater constraints on their time from family responsibilities. Women, by contrast, cite the relatively greater strength of the "old boys club" network, the relative lack of support systems for females, and discrimination in the hiring process (Acosta and Carpenter 1989). Hasbrook (1988) supports this latter view and cites evidence (Acosta and Carpenter 1985) of gender role stereotyping among athletic administrators. Stangl and Kane (1991) report data supporting the theory of "homologous reproduction," i.e., the tendency for people in dominant positions to employ subordinates of like sex as well as other characteristics. They note, however, that the relatively

FIGURE 12.2   *Men coaching women's teams is not unusual, while women coaching men's teams is rare. (Courtesy of Lynette Tanaka.)*

greater percentage of women coaches hired by women athletic directors may also result from a "conscious commitment" by female administrators to hire women (1991:55). Nevertheless, the continuing dearth of women coaches and administrators is troubling as both a drop in professional opportunities for women and a scarcity of valuable role models for young female athletes.

Physical Considerations Regarding Sport for Women

It is often argued that sport is "naturally" a man's world because men are better "suited" physically to sport and superior to women in physical performance measures. This argument poses several questions for our evaluative commentary. First, how do males and females compare on physical and performance variables? Second, is there any evidence to suggest that females are in any way *unsuited* physically to sport competition? Third, what factors may bear on any significant differences in those variables? That is, are observable differences necessarily "natural" and immutable, or are they attributable to such potentially changeable factors as training and opportunity?

Physical and Performance Comparisons

From an anatomical and physiological standpoint, males and females are more alike than different. In fact, according to Wells, other than the obvious difference in reproductive organs, prior to adolescence there are only "minor" sex differences in body structure (Wells 1985). Even in adults, the type and functioning (although not the amount) of muscle fiber is the same in males and females (Carey 1983; Wells 1985). Also, "the cellular mechanisms that control the physiological and biochemical responses to exercise are identical for both sexes" (Wells 1985:35).

Nevertheless, when the sexes are compared, differences in certain average measures are statistically significant. On the average, men are stronger than women of the same size. This is attributable partly to greater muscle mass and partly to a relative lower percentage of adipose tissue (which is "nonperforming") in males (Wells 1985). Male and female muscles both benefit from training, although male muscles "bulk" more with increases in strength through training (Fox, Bowers, and Foss 1993). This is related to the larger testosterone levels in males (Fox, Bowers, and Foss 1993).

Wells (1985) observes that female athletes do not generally develop large muscles even on the heaviest weight training programs. She does acknowledge, however, that female body builders appear to achieve "rather remarkable muscular development" (1985:38). Wells attributes this phenomenon to genetic endowment (especially, unusually high numbers of fast-twitch muscle fibers); the likely use of anabolic steroids to enhance muscle development; the illusion of size that results when a muscle is fully developed, shaped, and defined; dieting to cut fat under the surface of the skin and emphasize the muscle; dehydration before competition, which tightens the skin around muscles; and "pumping up" techniques used by body builders before competitions to swell the muscles with blood, thus enlarging and distending them.

Females demonstrate better balance, which is usually attributed to their lower center of gravity (Wells 1985). The higher average percentage of adipose tissue in females gives them greater buoyancy and less drag in water (Fox, Bowers, and Foss 1993), and it insulates them better against cold temperatures (Wells 1985). The adipose tissue protects internal organs against extremes of heat as well as cold. Although females tend to sweat less than males, they dispel more heat through vasodilation in hot environments than do males, and, overall, adapt at least as well to heat as do males (Carey 1983; Fox, Bowers, and Foss 1993).

Males currently excel at endurance events, partly because it is difficult to separate out the related element of strength in such events. Nevertheless, males and females react similarly to endurance training, and the performances of females have been improving more rapidly than those of men in recent decades (Wells 1985). In fact, in the first year of the women's Olympic marathon (1984), winner Joan Benoit's time was better than the winner's of the men's marathon as recently as 1956 (NCAA 1988b). The question of whether women may eventually equal or surpass men in such events continues to be a matter of controversy and debate (Carey 1983; NCAA 1988b).

(a)

(b)

FIGURES 12.3a and 12.3b   *Strength and power are becoming more evident as women's sports become more socially acceptable and training techniques and tactics develop. (Fig. 12.3a: Photo by José M. Osario; Fig. 12.3b: Courtesy of Lynette Tanaka.)*

Women's Physical Suitedness to Sport

From a physical/physiological standpoint, there are no indications that highly competitive sport, including contact sport, is any more dangerous for females than for males. Injury rates for females are no greater than for males, especially in similar activities at the same level of training (Carbon 1992). Although arguments suggesting female physical vulnerability have been used to restrict their access to baseball, football, rugby, ice hockey, and other sports that incorporate physical contact or collision, it has also been noted that the male reproductive organs are far more vulnerable to damage in contact sports and by hard objects such as baseballs than are the female reproductive organs.

Although menstrual irregularities such as temporary amenorrhea (suspension of the menstrual cycle) have been associated with strenuous physical training, these irregularities are generally considered to be reversible, and athletes tend to have fewer problems with pregnancy and childbirth than nonathletes (Fox, Bowers, and Foss 1993). Even during pregnancy experts advise women to reduce active participation in training and competitive sports only gradually as the pregnancy progresses (Wells 1985). Overall, then, there is no validity to arguments that females are physically unsuited either to heavy physical training or to sport competition. In fact, as we have seen, women surpass men on some performance measures.

Nature Versus Nurture

There is a tendency, especially among natural scientists, to consider anatomical and physiological measurements and documented differences to be solely matters of nature, or genetic endowment. Recently, however, causal factors such as culture and lifestyle have been cited as significant contributors to such findings (Thomas and French 1985; Thomas and Thomas 1988; Toole and Kretzschmar 1993). For example, throwing a ball well is a much greater cultural expectation of males in our society than of females. Because of their greater average experience and practice with throwing, boys achieved significantly superior scores on the softball throw, which for many years was a typical component of physical fitness tests. It was eliminated from AAHPERD's fitness test battery as biased after research confirmed that sex differences disappeared when the nondominant arm was used (Wells 1985).

Wells (1985) observes that, after puberty, females tend to decrease their level of daily physical activity more than males do and that measured differences in average adipose tissue levels, strength, endurance, and related physical and performance measures between males and females can be attributed at least in part to that culture-related lifestyle change. In general, trained females and males show greater similarities than untrained females and males, and standards by which females are designated as "trained" are lower than those for males. According to Wells (1985:46),

> a proper equating of male and female groups relative to habitual activity, conditioning, coaching exposure, or competitive experience is rare, perhaps even nonexistent. Such unintentional biasing of samples in the scientific literature has no doubt *led* to the publication of differences in physiological variables that are *not* solely attributable to *biological* differences between the sexes.

In summary, females have been shown to be well suited physically to vigorous exercise and intense sport competition. Physical performance differences between women and men are relatively minor, especially compared to traditional views—and the gap is closing. Even measurable sex differences can be largely attributed to social expectations and resultant lifestyle differences which currently disadvantage women, but can be changed.

The question of whether women might eventually equal or exceed men's performances in sport is largely irrelevant. It is clear that women should be evaluated in their own right, rather than solely in comparison to men. We do not expect middleweight boxers to get into the same boxing ring with heavyweights, yet many middleweights are considered to be highly successful professional athletes. Just as we have weight classes in sports such as wrestling and boxing, we can adjust the structure of sport competition to allow women to compete with their physical peers.

The physical differences that exist between men and women are not sufficient to explain why women do not participate in sport to the extent that men have. We must look to other explanations for answers. Next, a look at psychological factors.

Psychological Considerations Regarding Women and Sport

Perhaps, it is sometimes argued, sport is dominated by males because females are somehow psychologically unsuited to the demands of sport competition. This type of argument tends to focus on three personality characteristics—aggressiveness, dominance/competitiveness, and success orientation—which seem to be demanded of the athlete in competitive sport situations. In our evaluative commentary, we will address these factors as we investigate the psychological "fit" between females and the competitive sport environment.

Aggressiveness

As we discussed in Chapter 9, aggression is a broad concept that takes many forms. It may be physical or nonphysical, personal or interpersonal, instrumental or reactive. Studies of differences in aggressiveness by sex have been inconsistent in specifying what is meant by the term, and they have measured it in different ways and under different circumstances. Consequently, it is difficult to know how to interpret the findings of those studies (Birrell 1983). For example, research indicates that males display more aggressive behavior than females (Maccoby and Jacklin 1974). It is not surprising, then, that both Silva (1983) and Rainey (1986) found that males are more approving of aggressive acts in sport situations than females. Generally, however, the aggressiveness measured in such studies is reactive, hostile aggressiveness, rather than the instrumental form of aggression associated with success in sport. It might be argued, then, that the greater reactive aggressiveness of males may actually disadvantage them within the controlled environment of sport.

It has also been widely assumed that aggressive behavior is linked to the high levels of testosterone characteristic of males (Birrell 1983). However, females with high levels of testosterone do not display unusually high aggressiveness (Money and Erhardt 1972). Apparently, aggressive behavior is determined by much more than hormonal factors.

It seems much more likely that the observed differences in aggressive behavior between males and females are the result of cultural expectations and conditioning, perpetuated by aggressive role models. For example, Birrell (1983) observes that the sports dominated by males in our culture (notably, contact sports) are structured to allow and even encourage highly aggressive behavior in participants. Research has shown, however, that where aggression is considered allowable behavior, sex differences usually disappear (Frodi, Macauley, and Thorne 1977). Such findings are clear indications that nurture is a powerful causal factor when it comes to aggressive behavior. Furthermore, regardless of the comparative aggressiveness of males and females,

BIZARRO By DAN PIRARO

The *Bizarro* cartoon by Dan Piraro is reprinted by permission of Chronicle Features, San Francisco.

it is obvious that females both learn and display aggressive behavior in a variety of situations, especially those in which aggression is considered appropriate.

Dominance and Competitiveness

The notion that females lack the competitive spirit and the drive to dominate, which are typically considered to be necessary for success at sport, was promoted by a variety of authors during the 1920s and '30s (Lenskyj 1986), and was still being supported in the 1970s (McClelland 1975). However, the body of psychological research surveyed by Maccoby and Jacklin (1974) showed men and women to be equally competitive.

In real-life situations, especially those that call for direct interpersonal confrontation, men appear to exhibit greater levels of overt competitiveness (Maccoby and Jacklin 1974) and greater interest in winning (Kidd and Woodman 1975). Three observations explain these findings. First, men have more socially approved opportunities to compete in life in a directly confrontational manner, and their greater size and strength have resulted in a history of greater success at such confrontations. Women, meanwhile, have learned to employ more subtle, emotionally manipulative forms of dominance. Second, for women who do compete overtly, the rewards have been fewer and less valuable. This has been particularly apparent in the different opportunities and payoffs for men and women athletes. Third, women's approaches to sport competition have not typically stressed winning so much as skill development, self-testing, fitness, and other less dominance-oriented motivations (Lichtenstein 1987). These observations indicate both that women *do* exhibit personality characteristics that lend themselves well to sport competition, and that dominance is *only* one of several motivations and approaches to the sport experience itself.

Success Orientation

Sport requires the purposeful application of skills toward a specific goal or objective, and it results in a definite measure of success or failure. Three concepts have been suggested in order to evaluate success orientation as a personality characteristic that may indicate a psychological suitedness to sport. *Achievement motivation* and *fear of failure* were explored widely during the 1960s as significant sources of a drive to succeed (Atkinson and Feather 1966; Maccoby and Jacklin 1974). A third concept, *fear of success,* was proposed by Horner (1968) and tested extensively during the 1970s as an explanation for what was considered to be a pattern among females of avoiding success-oriented pursuits. It was theorized that the anticipated outcomes of success for women included fears of such negative consequences as societal disapproval and loss of femininity, and that women therefore were not motivated to seek success.

Studies based on concepts related to success orientation were seriously flawed in that they tended to define success by criteria related to professional achievement, which at the time was a distinctly male standard. Overall, the results of such research are inconsistent, and they have failed to reveal any significant lack of success orientation in women as compared with men. They have, however, illuminated the connection between the value one places on the anticipated outcomes of a behavior pattern and the strength of one's motivation to pursue that behavior pattern (Birrell 1983). Perhaps more than anything else, this connection explains the effect of societal judgments about appropriate gender behavior in discouraging female athletes from seeking success at sport. No matter how attractive sport may be to girls and women, their enthusiasm for it can be seriously dampened by the expectation of disapproving responses to their involvement in it. The chilling effect of such anticipated disapproval is easily read as a lack of interest, and has been used to justify the shortage of support for girls' and women's sport programs.

Androgyny

Far from being psychologically unsuited to sport, many women demonstrate an especially good "fit" between their personalities and the emotional demands of sport. The concept of androgyny has been introduced to describe a personality that includes characteristics traditionally associated with masculinity *and* those traditionally associated with femininity (Bem 1977).

Androgyny appears to be an especially healthy personality profile, character-ized by a tendency toward "behavioral flexibility and psychological well-being in today's complex society" (Duquin 1977:49). Furthermore, research indicates that high-achieving women, such as scientists and athletes, tend to be androgynous (Helmreich and Spence 1977). Not only do such research findings negate the common conception of female athletes as overly mascu-line, they also imply that athletic participation tends to reveal a particularly positive personality pattern.

The concept of androgyny has met with some criticism since the 1970s. It is based in trait theory, a belief that personality is divisible into discrete fac-tors, or traits. Theoretical and methodological flaws have resulted from as-sumptions that every trait can be measured along a continuum (e.g., from dominant to submissive), that masculine and feminine traits are at opposite ex-tremes of the continuum, and that the "ideal" male and female are more differ-ent than alike in personality traits (Knoppers 1980; Birrell 1983). Androgyny studies have not successfully corrected or transcended such flaws. Neverthe-less, the concept has been useful in helping us break away from some of the most glaring misconceptions about personality profiles and psychological health in both males and females.

Sex-Role Socialization and Sport

In evaluating both physical and psychological factors related to female athletic participation, we have seen that societal expectations are a powerful influence on behavior patterns. Just how powerful an influence such expectations are be-comes obvious when we consider cross-cultural studies such as those conducted by Margaret Mead (1963). She points out (1963:286) that faulty reasoning has led us to some incorrect conclusions about sex roles and their cultural restrictions:

> We have assumed that because it is convenient for a mother to wish to care for her child, this is a trait with which women have been more generously endowed by a careful teleological process of evolution. We have assumed that because men have hunted, an activity requiring enterprise, bravery, and initiative, they have been endowed with these useful attitudes as part of their sex-temperament.

Instead of biological predestiny entirely determining sex roles, it is the im-print of traditional behavior patterns on people within cultures and the intricate weaving of relationships around and through these behavior patterns that foster sex-role socialization (Mead 1963). Temperamental traits that members of a sex tend to display and that have historically been useful have come to be consid-ered key aspects of sex-specific behavior, and any member of that sex not dis-playing these traits has come to be viewed as abnormal and deficient. Displaying behavioral traits of the opposite sex has also raised more than a few eyebrows.

Mead discusses three societies, each of which displays sex-role relation-ships very different from our Anglo-European tradition of male dominance and female subservice. Among the Mundugumor of New Guinea, both sexes val-ued aggressive and violent behavior and tended to act that way. In contrast,

Arapesh men and women both displayed mild, nonaggressive behavior and great sensitivity, traits Americans might consider feminine. The Tchambuli, however, provide us with the most interesting contrast because they displayed a complete reversal of our sex-role patterns. Tchambuli women were dominant, impersonal, and managing, while the men were less responsible and were "emotionally dependent" (Mead 1963:279).

Differential Sex-Role Socialization

It is through the process of socialization, specifically sex-role socialization, that we learn to do what is expected of us as men or women. From birth, parents direct their offspring toward masculine or feminine behavior patterns and interests. Probably the first question asked by or of new parents will be, "Is it a boy or a girl?" This indicates the importance of the child's sex and suggests how early sex-role socialization begins. From the color of the child's room and clothing, to the toys provided for play, to parental concerns over the child's degree of assertiveness and emotionality, parents shape children toward sex-specific behavior and become more or less disturbed by their child's deviation from cultural patterns of sex-specific behavior (Weitzman 1979; Toole and Kretzschmar 1993).

Other agents of sex-role socialization include media such as children's books, many of which portray stereotypical male and female characters. Television and movies tend to support a fluffy feminine image, and they tend to depict women as important only in support of men or as sideshow attractions. Men by contrast, are presented as dominant and decisive. Daytime television soap operas show women in a slightly more masterful light, but that image is undermined by commercials that depict women happily, if anxiously, chained to their children, dishes, dirty laundry, and still-to-be-perfected homes.

Schools often reinforce differential expectations of males and females. Teachers and guidance counselors may steer boys and girls toward different activities and future aspirations. Some textbooks still portray stereotypical situations such as math problems that feature boys calculating batting averages while girls figure out how to cut a cookie recipe in half. Boys' athletic teams are often celebrated in pep rallies where female cheerleaders leap around to generate enthusiasm for the male players.

The overall effect of differential sex-role socialization is that males are channeled into instrumental behavior and females into expressive behavior (Boutilier and SanGiovanni 1983). *Instrumental* behavior is associated with achievement, such as with tools or instruments. Males in our society are expected to play with instrumental toys (erector sets, trucks, tools, guns, etc.), do instrumental work (engineering, construction, auto mechanics, soldiering, etc.), and be instrumental people (i.e., independent, rational, competent, assertive, competitive, and achievement oriented). *Expressive* behavior is associated with appearance and with emotion. Females in our society are expected to play with expressive toys (cosmetics kits, dolls, tea sets, etc.), do expressive work (flower arranging, cosmetology, child rearing, care giving, etc.), and be expressive people (i.e., sensitive, intuitive, cooperative, sympathetic, and nurturing).

FIGURE 12.4   *The grace, beauty of form, and absence of direct confrontation in gymnastics account for its relative acceptability for females, while belying the strength, skill, assertiveness, and concentration required of performers. (Photo by Richard Fenker.)*

Sport, as we have structured and conducted it in our culture, is a highly instrumental activity. Consequently, there exists what Boutilier and SanGiovanni (1983:100) refer to as an "isomorphism between sport and masculinity." Sport is viewed as consistent with and reinforcing of what our culture has defined as masculine behavior, and as inconsistent with and contrary to our cultural definition of feminine behavior. Although in recent years it has become increasingly acceptable for American females to participate in sport (Snyder and Spreitzer 1983; *The Wilson Report* 1988), there is still a great deal of disapproval and even suspicion that frequently confronts the female athlete (Boutilier and SanGiovanni 1983; Bennett et al. 1987; Bennett et al. 1989). Aesthetically pleasing individual and dual sports such as gymnastics, swimming, and tennis are still more acceptable for women than team sports such as softball and basketball (Snyder and Spreitzer 1983; Kane and Snyder 1988). Probably the clearest evidence of continuing differential views of males and females with respect to sport involvement is the fact that, with few and relatively isolated exceptions, contact sports are still closed to female participation and are generally still considered to be inappropriate for girls and women.

Social Control over Female Athleticism

The socialization process operates through a number of mechanisms. We have discussed social learning theory (Chapter 3) and its three primary operations of direct instruction coupled with reward and punishment, repetitive building of associations between situations and appropriate corresponding behaviors, and role modeling. These operations are experienced somewhat differently by males and females. Males are frequently rewarded for instrumental behavior and punished for expressive behavior. They learn to associate masculinity with instrumental activities such as sport, and they tend to model their behavior after that of successful males such as athletic heroes. Females tend to be rewarded for expressive behavior and punished for instrumental behavior. However, since most instrumental behavior is also highly valued in society, high-achieving females in instrumental fields such as science, medicine, and engineering often receive ambivalent feedback—a sort of grudging admiration for their "inappropriate" but valued accomplishments (Weitzman 1979). Females learn to associate femininity with expressive activities such as child rearing, and they tend to model their behavior after that of women who are viewed as successful. As we noted earlier, the declining number of women coaches has alarmed many people concerned about providing successful role models for aspiring female athletes.

These processes of socialization are aided and reinforced by a number of related societal mechanisms that serve to maintain control over members of society by discouraging deviant behavior. Based on the conceptual framework developed by Parsons (1951), Whitaker (1982) has identified six such mechanisms that operate at both the interpersonal and collective levels to dishearten aspiring female athletes by conveying messages that female athleticism is of low value at best, and deviant at worst. The first is simply *silence*. Ignoring a behavior devalues that behavior. The female athlete often encounters parents, nonathletic friends, and male counterparts who may not argue with her involvement in sports, but don't discuss it or share her enthusiasm either. This form of silence, coupled with the obvious lack of media attention to women's sport (Dyer 1982) has a deadening effect on the female's sense of the importance of her sport involvement and her self-worth as an athlete. Second, *patronizing humor* is used to trivialize female athletes and their sport involvement by making fun of them (Whitaker 1982). From boys snickering at active girls to "ladies' day" golf jokes, poking fun at girls and women who are pursuing movement competence conveys the message that females and their sports "are entertaining but incompetent facsimiles of the real, male, thing" (Bennett et al. 1987:372). The third mechanism is *pseudo-logic,* the stringing together of observations so as to "prove" apparently that female athletics is a second-class proposition. As Bennett et al. (1987:372) describe it,

> In the case of female movement skill, we are reminded of presumed male superiority in speed, strength, skill, aggressiveness, interest to the public, or any number of other generalities which supposedly establish a stronger male claim to credibility as physically competent people. The real message is that winning against men is impossible, winning against other women is irrelevant, winning the public is unlikely, winning is everything, and therefore we do not even belong in the game.

The fourth mechanism is the *ritualizing of activities.* In our culture, as in many cultures, certain activities are associated with certain subgroups of the population. By this mechanism, they become reserved for some and restricted to others. For example, activities like dodge ball and tag are avoided by adults because they are thought of as "children's games." Similarly, competitive sports, especially contact sports, have been ritualized as male activities. As highly instrumental activities, sports are defended (and depicted in the media) as male rituals that confirm the masculinity of their participants. "The female who aspires to participation in such rituals encounters a barrier, a distinct message that she is encroaching on someone else's quasi-sacred rite" (Bennett et al. 1987). The female's place in sport—that of cheerleader—is also ritualized, thus channeling her away from direct sport participation by presenting a more acceptable (i.e., more expressive) alternative (Whitaker 1982).

As women have persisted in their sport involvement, the ritualizing of sport as an exclusively male domain has gradually been breaking down. Acceptance of women as legitimate participants in a variety of sports has improved significantly in recent decades, and some sports—tennis, foil fencing, swimming, equestrian sports, etc.—have been considered female as well as male sports for a long time. Nevertheless, sports magazines are still marketed almost exclusively to men (the notorious *Sports Illustrated* swimsuit issue being only one example of this), and media ads and commercials portraying sports-oriented scenes rarely feature women athletes. Overall, the tendency in our society to view athletes as male and cheerleaders as female continues.

The fifth, and probably the ugliest, social control mechanism is *slander.* Verbal abuse filled with allegations, epithets, and innuendo is a common response to any subgroup that offends or threatens the dominant group (Whitaker 1982). Whites have slandered blacks, gentiles have slandered Jews, Caucasians have slandered Asians, etc. Accusations against the target group range from laziness and stupidity to deviousness and sexual promiscuity. Slander against female athletes usually takes the form of describing them as mannish, butch, musclebound, unpretty, unnatural, and otherwise unfeminine. It contains two related messages: one, that to be a female athlete is to be a lesbian (or at least in danger of becoming one), and two, that to be a lesbian is

Doonesbury

BY GARRY TRUDEAU

Doonesbury. Copyright © 1989 G. B. Trudeau. Reprinted with permission of Universal Press Syndicate. All rights reserved.

wrong (Whitaker 1982). "Homophobic slurs contain the message that lesbians are unattractive, unfeminine, unpleasant, unhinged, and otherwise less than women" (Bennett et al. 1989:17). In the face of such messages, females who are not lesbians fear that sport participation will turn them into lesbians (or at least that people will assume that they are), and those who are lesbians are led to believe that it is unacceptable to be so (Whitaker 1982).

Finally, *coercion* (force or the threat of force) is used as a method of social control. Laws, ordinances, public policies, program rules and policies, and personal authority all have been used to deny people access to certain activities arbitrarily. We are not aware of any U.S. laws that expressly deny females access to sport, and rules and policies such as the pre-1974 Little League policy against female participants have largely fallen to pressures of the times. Private health and athletic clubs, once closed to women, are now mostly open in their membership policies. However, the example of San Francisco's Olympic Club is not unique. A private men's golf club, the Olympic Club, hosted the U.S. Open men's golf tournament in 1987. At that time (since the city of San Francisco was helping to finance the tournament), the Olympic Club came under fire from the San Francisco Board of Supervisors and others because of its men-only membership policy. Despite considerable pressure to change the policy, the club did not admit women to active membership until 1992 (Chapin 1993).

In general, high schools and colleges increased their support for female athletic programs during the 1970s and 1980s. Still, troubling incidents were reported from all over the country, involving arbitrary reductions in women's scholarships, the sudden and disproportionate (compared with men's teams) dropping of women's teams, and the firing of people who point out inequities between male and female programs (Hogan 1987). Such actions are clearly coercive.

Public policy at the community level determines the provision of recreational facilities and programs. "Even in small town recreational programs, we know that the pattern of access and use of community sports facilities is not random or haphazard but set by the town officials in alliance with the most 're-sourceful' group of organized citizens" (Boutilier and SanGiovanni 1983:240). Many local communities provide exemplary sport programs for girls and women, but many across the country do not. The scarcity of women in decision-making positions within policy-making bodies ranging from local town councils to the IOC leaves girls and women vulnerable to coercive restrictions on access to organized sport at all levels (Hall, Cullen, and Slack 1989).

The use of personal authority is a subtle but powerful form of coercion. There is evidence (*The Wilson Report* 1988) that the majority of parents would not forbid their daughters to play sports, but we dare say that there are still many parents who would and do—especially when the chosen sport is something like football, baseball, or wrestling. There is also evidence (*The Wilson Report* 1988) that female sport participation drops off dramatically during adolescence. Some of this attrition can probably be attributed to boyfriends who use a form of personal authority by threatening, directly or indirectly, to end relationships unless their girlfriends "quit the team." Although such coercive barriers to participation are gradually coming down, female athletes are still far from being free of such social controls.

Negative Effects on Girls and Women

The socialization process no longer sends uniformly negative messages to females about the role of athlete. Sport-related opportunities, role models, and positive reinforcement are increasingly available to girls as well as boys. Along with this, however, the continuing operation of the social control mechanisms described above cannot be ignored, for they have resulted in several unfortunate situations for girls and women with respect to sport. First, because so many females are steered away from sport participation, many of them have underdeveloped and ineffectual movement skills (Bennett et al. 1987; Gondola 1988). Not only are a lot of girls and women denied the joys of skilled movement experiences, they are left physically vulnerable, uneducated about even the most basic self-defense skills—skills practiced daily by young males (Whitaker 1982). Such vulnerability engenders anxiety, insecurity, self-doubt, and feelings of inferiority, thus robbing many women of the ability to move confidently and assertively in the world. Compounding this negative effect is the fact that women athletes, especially runners, have been targets of assault, rape, and even murder (Nelson 1991). In recent years women have become more acutely aware of this—and less and less tolerant of it. Books, videos, and classes on women's self-defense remain popular, providing evidence that women are attempting to make up for early deficiencies in skill development.

Second, Bennett et al. (1987) observe that, although girls and women have become more involved in sport in recent years, this does not mean that sport has become an activity feminists can endorse. To the extent that females have broken down barriers of structure and public opinion about women and sport, they have tended to adopt the approach to sport competition that has been ritualized for men (Blinde 1989). This version, which is based on dominance, authoritarianism, and elitism, is increasingly viewed as the only authentic model (Bennett et al. 1987). Despite evidence that this model is responsible for significant levels of conflict and feelings of exploitation among female athletes (Blinde and Greendorfer 1992), there appears to be no momentum for change.

Third, homophobia (fear and hatred of homosexuals) is rampant in women's sport (Bennett et al. 1989). As we have seen, unflattering characterizations of female athletes carry the insinuation that they tend to be lesbians. Homophobic jokes and slander frighten heterosexual females and intimidate lesbians. Women coaches are victimized as well (Bennett et al. 1989). High school players are steered away from college programs coached by women on the supposition that those coaches are lesbians (Griffin 1992). Athletic administrators may have other reasons (rational or otherwise) for not hiring female coaches, such as a belief that females are not skilled enough, not competitive enough, not serious or committed enough, or simply not members of the administrators' "old boy network." However, one of those reasons may also be a homophobic assumption that female coaches are likely to be lesbians (Griffin and Genasci 1990; Lenskyj 1991). In short, a hostile cloud of homophobic suspicion hovers over all of female sport. It disheartens female athletes, hinders female coaches, and is a likely factor in the reluctance of the media to promote professional sport for women (Bennett et al. 1989).

In summary, the process and mechanisms of sex role socialization explain much of our initial observation that American girls and women are significantly less involved in sport than American boys and men. Differential cultural expectations of males and females, and societal efforts to channel male and female behavior in different directions, have powerful effects. With respect to sport participation, these effects include restricted female access to programs, the dampening of female sporting aspirations and discouragement of females from seeking increased involvement, the inhibited development of female movement skills, a low social value on traditional women's approaches to sport, and a continuing societal image of women's sport as a hotbed of abnormal behavior.

The Functionalist Defense of Patriarchal Sport

Male dominance is called patriarchy, and Steven Goldberg (1973) argues that it is "inevitable." Goldberg's reasoning is as follows: Males have been dominant in all human societies past and present; this is not an historical accident, but arises from a biological (hence, inevitable) disposition of males to be more aggressive, and aggressiveness is the means by which humans dominate each other; therefore, males must inevitably dominate females.

Goldberg's argument breaks down when we begin to examine some of his postulates. First, not *all* societies display male dominance. In a few societies, women control both property and family. Second, Goldberg implies that men's physical dominance (stemming from biologically induced high testosterone levels relative to women) is transformed in modern societies into a drive for assertiveness and the necessary skills of leadership (e.g., manipulative ability and compromise). In complex societies, however, dominance is maintained through mutual consent, often by traditional role relationships and expectations, rather than by aggressive force (Maccoby and Jacklin 1974). If assertiveness and leadership are *not* primarily related to hormone levels, then women may achieve assertiveness and leadership abilities through nonbiological means (i.e., learning) and there is no need to believe in the inevitability of male dominance.

Another functionalist reason supporting patriarchy is that other male leaders or a male leader's followers would have less respect for or allegiance to a female leader (Goldberg 1973). In the political sphere, this argument is refuted by at least three examples in which women have successfully led nations: Britain, India, and Israel. Women perform well in Congress, as governors, and in municipal governments. In business and industry, women are thriving and becoming accepted at all levels. Even in the macho domain of manual labor, the image of "Rosie the Riveter" during World War II stands for the many crucial and tough jobs held by women while the men were fighting. Currently, women do well as truckers, in construction, in the military, and in other jobs traditionally the domain of men.

Sport is one of the last male-dominated strongholds in which women are surreptitiously kept from positions of power and control, even in the coaching of women's teams. One reason suggested for this is that in an era of transition in upgrading women's sports, men possess more knowledge about the intricacies of those sports. In their zeal to improve their product, even many women accept this argument. From at least one point of view, however, this rationale for male control of women's teams and female athletes is on shaky ground. Previous generations of female athletes have been coached by men, so why are those women who were then competing not now qualified to coach younger women? Where and when does this dependence on male coaches end?

Coercion and Conflict as Reasons for Patriarchy

Contrary to the belief that men dominate women because such a system works most efficiently, the conflict-coercion view suggests that men dominate and will continue to do so because they are unwilling to relinquish power and dominance gained in more primitive eras when brawn and physical aggressiveness were instrumental for survival. Dominance in social systems has since become more a matter of wit than of brawn, yet legal, governmental, and even religious authority tend to maintain patriarchy.

Bennett et al. (1987:376) locate the foundation of patriarchal society at "institutionalized heterosexuality." By this they mean more than simply male-female sexual relations, but rather the social construction of the definition of female as subordinate to the male, and "the control and use of women exclusively by and for men" (1987:377). This culturally based, institutionalized definition, they argue, has set up a male-female power differential that favors males and oppresses females. The result is patriarchal hegemony, a domination of society by male perspectives, priorities, values, interests, and agendas. In short, "it's a man's world" because women are understood only in service to men.

This description is an interpretation of conflict-coercion theory in which males represent the dominant class and females are the oppressed class. As predicted by coercion theory, males resist power gains by females because those power gains threaten the patriarchy. Especially troublesome are intrusions by women into areas of physical activity, such as sport, which were traditionally reserved for men.

> Sport's very physical nature gives it special significance because of the fundamental link between social power and physical force. Sport is a major arena in which physical force and toughness are woven into hegemonic masculinity and the resultant ideology transmitted. The celebration of "real men" as strong and tough underscores the fact that men are in positions (have the right?) to dominate (Bryson 1990:173).

Boutilier and SanGiovanni (1983) suggest three reasons for men's resistance to women's participation in sport. First, men wish to maintain the role of sport as a socializing agency for males that teaches male superiority and advantage. "In a society where the meanings and models of masculinity are more and more remote from the everyday lives of little boys, games and sports become crucial vehicles for teaching the virtues of masculinity and the principle of male dominance and privilege" (Boutilier and SanGiovanni 1983:101). To allow girls and women into this arena is objectionable, then, because it reduces the significance of sport as an agency of differential sex role socialization, specifically as a teacher of male supremacy. Second, the ritualizing of sport as an exclusively masculine domain has elevated its value, and to legitimate the presence of women in that domain would devalue it. "Men are what women are not; men do what women cannot" (Boutilier and SanGiovanni 1983:103). To admit that women *can* "do" sport is to nullify its specialness and the specialness of men for doing it exclusively. Third, men wish to preserve sport as a sanctuary for the expression of male emotionality and male-male intimacy. As Boutilier and SanGiovanni (1983:104) explain it,

> It is in sporting activity that men are allowed the rare opportunity to express those feelings forbidden in most of their other roles. They can embrace each other unself-consciously, holding and hugging, touching and kissing without threat of ridicule and suspicion. They can express fear, hesitancy, pain and doubt and be nurtured by other men. They can grieve together and be comforted . . . In sum, in the absence of women, they can allow themselves to express what sexist ideology insists must be suppressed if they are to lay valid claim to being "real men."

The presence of women in sport, Boutilier and SanGiovanni argue, is viewed as forcing men back into the behavioral expectations of the gender-mixed environment. It makes men self-conscious about expressions of emotion in one of the few places where such expressions have felt safe. Thus, they resent, resist, and revile women's increasing interest and involvement in sport.

Bennett et al. (1987) suggest a fourth reason for men's resistance to women in sport. Given the subservient definition of women institutionalized in our society, the very fact that women participate in the male preserve of sport with other women is threatening because it demonstrates the potential for women to form a female-female allegiance and free themselves from male control. "The allegiance itself is intolerable to a society which reserves the allegiance of women for men" (1987:377). In addition, the apparent autonomy of women in such a context represents a threat to the male hold on power.

Alternatives for Change

According to the conflict-coercion perspective, what needs to be done in order to make the sport experience what it should be for women? The answer is not easy. It is generally agreed by feminist conflict theorists that an ultimate solution must involve a major overhaul of society itself (Boutilier and SanGiovanni 1983; Bennett et al. 1987). As long as institutionalized heterosexuality and patriarchal hegemony continue, women will face male resistance to female involvement in such patriarchy-reinforcing activities as sport. It is unlikely that significant changes can be accomplished in mainstream (i.e., organized, commercialized, professionalized) sport while it still serves to affirm and perpetuate a large system of male dominance.

Nevertheless, some authors have made suggestions for possible transformations of sport, at least on the interpersonal, small group level. Theberge (1987) argues that by controlling sport at the local level women can build and strengthen community among themselves and focus on their own empowerment through the sport experience. Birrell and Richter (1987) cite examples of women's softball teams that have attempted to translate feminist consciousness into nonexploitative, mutually reinforcing competitive experiences. Through their investigation of such teams, Birrell and Richter (1987) identified the following six aspects of patriarchal sport that cause concern among feminists:

(1) The overemphasis on winning
(2) Hierarchies that subordinate players to coaches
(3) Skill-based elitism
(4) Exclusivity by which people are denied access to participation on the basis of sex, race, class, age, etc.
(5) The treatment of opponents as enemies
(6) The willingness to endanger players for the sake of a winning outcome

Whitaker (1989; 1991), observing that sport competition has been socially constructed to feature such aspects, argues that it can also be reconstructed so as to eliminate those oppressive features and focus instead on goals such as skill development, personal limit-testing, risk taking, personal expression,

---

POSITION STATEMENT
FOR GIRLS AND WOMEN IN SPORT

The California Association for Health, Physical Education, Recreation and Dance promotes and develops leaders and programs of sport and physical activity for all females.

Girls and Women in Sport advocate:

1. Equitable opportunities to develop and maintain desirable sport programs for girls and women.

2. Equitable use and time of facilities, equipment, athletic trainers, medical personnel, and other sport services for all females and female sports.

3. The participation in athletics for the development of the physical and emotional well-being of the athlete. Both communication and cooperation skills are learned and later used in the workplace and in society.

4. That there is a need to place women in leadership positions to ensure equitable role models as coaches, officials and administrators for the female athlete.

5. That all females participate in a daily quality physical education program in addition to the extra curricular school sponsored activities.

6. Sports programs and fitness activity designed to accommodate minority, disabled and mature women.

7. That professionals initiate, conduct and evaluate research in girls' and women's sports.

8. Promoting and conducting activities on February 4th of each year to honor National Girls and Women in Sport Day.

Revised: March 10, 1989

FIGURE 12.5 *Statement approved by the CAHPERD Representative Assembly, March 10, 1989, and reprinted with permission from the* CAHPERD Journal/Times, *Vol. 51, #8, (May 1989), p. 14.*

cognitive challenges, interpersonal cooperation, physical and emotional tenderness and sensitivity, and transcendental experiences. Whitaker (1989) suggests transformations of both text and context that show potential for equalizing access to sport, eliminating authoritarian lines of control, de-emphasizing the power implications of winning, and cultivating a spirit of equality and mutual empowerment among all participants.

Toward the Future

Not everyone embraces the goals and strategies of feminist conflict theorists regarding American sport. Even those who admire such a view as an *alternative* would not necessarily recommend it as a *replacement* for the current version of organized sport. Many women athletes, coaches, and athletic administrators have adopted and internalized the male model of sport to such an extent that they value no other approach. We have noted that women's intercollegiate programs are rapidly taking on the structure and priorities of the men's programs, and that this trend has been interpreted by many people as a move toward equality. The relatively few voices that denounce such developments as a co-optation of women's sport by the patriarchal order are, for the most part, neither heard nor heeded in the mainstream sporting world.

What lies ahead for women in sport? The restoration of Title IX's applicability to sport programs has given renewed momentum to the move toward equal opportunity for girls and women in sport. It is likely that the win-at-all-cost approach will increasingly characterize women's sport, and that a corresponding increase in corruption will occur. The acceptability of female athleticism will continue to improve, but resistance to women's equal claim on the sport world will not disappear. Homophobia will continue to victimize girls, women, and those who care about them. Opportunities for women coaches and administrators may eventually improve, but it will take concerted legislative and/or judicial pressures over a long period of time to accomplish this. In short, great strides have been made toward increasing the involvement of girls and women in the sport experience in American society, yet much remains to be accomplished.

Summary

The history of American women's sport reveals changing attitudes, alternative philosophies of participation, and ultimate adoption of the male competitive model. Despite legal protection under Title IX, however, girls and women continue to be significantly less involved in sport than boys and men, and gender equity remains an unrealized goal. Explanations based on physical and psychological comparisons have insufficient explanatory power. Sociological analysis, however, reveals the process and effects of differential sex role socialization, social control mechanisms, and patriarchal politics in perpetuating the second-class status of women in sport. Alternative transformations of the sport experience have been discussed, but the future does not, for now, point to major changes in approach.

References

Acosta, R. V., and L. J. Carpenter. 1985. "Status of Women in Athletics: Changes and Causes." *Journal of Physical Education, Recreation and Dance* 56(8):35-37.

Acosta, V., and L. J. Carpenter. 1989. "Perceived Causes of the Declining Representation of Women Leaders in Intercollegiate Sports—1988 Update." *NAPEHE Action Line* 12(1):8-10.

Atkinson, J. W., and N. T. Feather (eds.) 1966. *A Theory of Achievement Motivation.* New York: Wiley.

Bem, S. L. 1977. "On the Utility of Alternative Procedures for Assessing Psychological Androgyny." *Journal of Consulting and Clinical Psychology* 45(2):196-205.

Bennett, R. S., A. Duffy, D. Kalliam, M. Martin, N. J. W. Smith, E. L. West, and K. G. Whitaker. 1989. "Homophobia and Heterosexism in Sport and Physical Education: Why Must We Act Now?" *CAHPERD Journal Times* 51(8):16-18.

Bennett, R. S., K. G. Whitaker, N. J. W. Smith, and A. Sablove. 1987. "Changing the Rules of the Game: Reflections Toward a Feminist Analysis of Sport." *Women's Studies International Forum* 10(4):369-79.

Birrell, S. 1983. "The Psychological Dimensions of Female Athletic Participation." Pp. 49-91 in *The Sporting Woman,* by M. A. Boutilier and L. SanGiovanni. Champaign, IL: Human Kinetics.

Birrell, S., and D. M. Richter. 1987. "Is a Diamond Forever? Feminist Transformations of Sport." *Women's Studies International Forum* 10(4):395-409.

Blinde, E. M. 1989. "Participation in a Male Sport Model and the Value Alienation of Female Intercollegiate Athletes." *Sociology of Sport Journal* 6:36-49.

Blinde, E. M., and S. L. Greendorfer. 1992. "Conflict and the College Sport Experience of Women Athletes." *Women in Sport & Physical Activity Journal* 1:97-113.

Blum, D. E. 1992. "Education Department Says CUNY's Brooklyn College Discriminates Against Female Athletes and Coaches." *Chronicle of Higher Education* Feb. 26:A38.

Blum, D. E. 1993. "As far as Norma V. Cantu is concerned . . ." *Chronicle of Higher Education* Sept. 15:39-40.

Boutilier, M. A., and L. SanGiovanni. 1983. *The Sporting Woman.* Champaign, IL: Human Kinetics.

Bruce, T. 1993. "Title IX: 21 Years of Progress?" *Women in Sport & Physical Activity Journal* 2:73-79.

Bryson, L. 1990. "Challenges to Male Hegemony in Sport." Pp. 173-84 in *Sport, Men, and the Gender Order: Critical Feminist Perspectives,* edited by M. A. Messner and D. F. Sabo. Champaign, IL: Human Kinetics.

Carbon, R. J. 1992. "The Female Athlete." Pp. 467-87 in *Textbook of Science and Medicine in Sport,* edited by J. Bloomfield, P. A. Fricker, and K. D. Fitch. Champaign, IL: Human Kinetics.

Carey, R. A. 1983. "Physiological Aspects of Women and Exercise." Pp. 113-43 in *Exercise Medicine: Physiological Principles and Clinical Applications,* edited by A. A. Bove and D. T. Lowenthal. New York: Academic Press.

Chapin, D. 1993. "Women Scaling Olympic Heights." *San Francisco Examiner* Oct. 24:C1,17.

Chronicle of Higher Education. 1988. "Sidelines" 34(May 11):A32.

Comte, E., L. Girard, and A. Starensier. 1989. "Embracing Stars, Ignoring Players." *Sports, Inc.* January 2, 1989:41–43.

Duquin, M. E. 1977. "Perceptions of Sport: A Study in Sexual Attraction." Pp. 47–55 in *Psychology of Motor Behavior and Sport,* vol. 2, edited by D. M. Landers and R. W. Christina. Champaign, IL: Human Kinetics.

Dyer, K. F. 1982. *Challenging the Men: Women in Sport.* St. Lucia, Queensland, Australia: University of Queensland Press.

Fox, E. L., R. W. Bowers, and M. L. Foss. 1993. *The Physiological Basis for Exercise and Sport.* Madison, WI: Wm. C. Brown Communications.

Frodi, A., J. Macauley, and P. R. Thorne. 1977. "Are Women Always Less Aggressive Than Men? A Review of the Experimental Literature." *Psychological Bulletin* 84:634–60.

Gerber, E. W. 1974. "Chronicle of Participation." Pp. 1–176 in *The American Woman in Sport,* by E. W. Gerber et al. Reading, MA: Addison-Wesley.

Goldberg, S. 1973. *The Inevitability of Patriarchy.* New York: A. R. Morrow.

Gondola, J. C. 1988. "Homophobia: The Red Herring in Girls' and Women's Sports." Pp. 30–32 in *National Coaching Institute Applied Research Papers,* edited by M. J. Adrian. Champaign, IL: NAGWS.

Gottesman, J. 1993. "Gymnastics Rescued at UCLA." *San Francisco Chronicle* Aug. 21.

Griffin, P. 1992. "Changing the Game: Homophobia, Sexism, and Lesbians in Sport." *Quest* 44:251–65.

Griffin, P., and J. Genasci. 1990. "Addressing Homophobia in Physical Education: Responsibilities for Teachers and Researchers." Pp. 211–21 in *Sport, Men, and the Gender Order: Critical Feminist Perspectives,* edited by M. A. Messner and D. F. Sabo. Champaign, IL: Human Kinetics.

Hall, M. A., D. Cullen, and T. Slack. 1989. "Organizational Elites Recreating Themselves: The Gender Structure of National Sport Organizations." *Quest* 41:28–45.

Hasbrook, C. A. 1988. "Female Coaches—Why the Declining Numbers and Percentages?" *Journal of Physical Education, Recreation and Dance* 59(6):59–63.

Helmreich, R., and J. T. Spence. 1977. "Sex Roles and Achievement." Pp. 33–46 in *Psychology of Motor Behavior and Sport,* vol. 2, edited by D. M. Landers and R. W. Christina. Champaign, IL: Human Kinetics.

Hogan, C. L. 1987. "What's in the Future for Women's Sports?" *Women's Sports and Fitness* 9(6):42–47.

Horner, M. S. 1968. *Sex Differences in Achievement Motivation and Performance in Competitive and Non-competitive Situations.* Unpublished doctoral dissertation, University of Michigan.

Howell, R. 1982. "Generalizations on Women and Sport, Games and Play in the United States from Settlement to 1860." Pp. 87–95 in *Her Story in Sport: A Historical Anthology of Women in Sports,* edited by R. Howell. West Point, NY: Leisure Press.

Kane, M. J., and E. Snyder. 1988. "Current Attitudes Toward Female Sport Participation: The Case of Widespread Social Acceptance?" Paper presented at the North American Society for the Sociology of Sport, Cincinnati.

Kidd, T. R., and W. F. Woodman. 1975. "Sex and Orientation Toward Winning in Sport." *Research Quarterly* 46(4):476–83.

Knoppers, A. 1980. "Androgyny: Another Look." *Quest* 32(2):184–91.

Lederman, D. 1992. "Men Get 70% of Money Available for Athletic Scholarships at Colleges That Play Big-Time Sports, New Study Finds." *Chronicle of Higher Education* March 18:A1,45,46.

Lenskyj, H. 1986. *Out of Bounds: Women, Sport and Sexuality.* Toronto: The Women's Press.

Lenskyj, H. 1991. "Combating Homophobia in Sport and Physical Education." *Sociology of Sport Journal* 8:61-69.

Lichtenstein, G. 1987. "Competition in Women's Athletics." Pp. 48-56 in *Competition: A Feminist Taboo?* edited by V. Miner and H. E. Longino. New York: The Feminist Press.

Maccoby, E. E., and C. N. Jacklin. 1974. *The Psychology of Sex Differences.* Stanford, CA: Stanford University Press.

McClelland, D. C. 1975. *Power: The Inner Experience.* New York: Irvington.

Mead, M. 1963. *Sex and Temperament in Three Primitive Societies.* New York: W. Morrow.

Money, J. W., and A. Erhardt. 1972. *Man and Woman, Boy and Girl.* Baltimore: Johns Hopkins University Press.

NAGWS. 1993. "Title IX Implementation *Still* Demands Attention." *Update* Oct.:9.

Nakao, A. 1993. "Playing a Man's Game for Life." *San Francisco Examiner* Sept. 1:C1,7,10.

NCAA. 1988a. "Discrimination Complaints in Athletics Foreseen." *NCAA News* April 6, 1988:4.

NCAA. 1988b. "Women Eventually Could Equal Men in Sport, Researcher Says." *NCAA News* April 6, 1988.

Nelson, M. B. 1991. *Are We Winning Yet? How Women Are Changing Sports and Sports Are Changing Women.* New York: Random House.

Noel, A. V. 1993. "Women in the Olympics: Participation Patterns and Trends." *The Women's Sport Experience* May/June:11-13.

Parsons, T. 1951. *The Social System.* New York: The Free Press.

Potera, C., and M. Kort. 1986. "Are Women Coaches an Endangered Species?" *Women's Sports and Fitness* 8(9):34-35.

Rainey, D. W. 1986. "A Gender Difference in Acceptance of Sport Aggression: A Classroom Activity." *Teaching of Psychology* 13(3):138-40.

Reith, K. 1993a. "Title IX Tote Board." *The Women's Sports Experience* May/June:14.

Reith, K. 1993b. "Title IX Tote Board." *The Women's Sports Experience* July/August:8.

San Francisco Chronicle. 1989. "Pro Volleyball League Disbands" March 21:D6.

Silva, J. M. 1983. "The Perceived Legitimacy of Rule Violating Behavior in Sport." *Journal of Sport Psychology* 5(4):438-48.

Smith, N. J. W. 1988. "Discriminating Discourse: Toward a Pluralistic Model of the History of Women in Sport and Physical Education." Unpublished paper, San Francisco State University.

Snyder, E. E., and E. A. Spreitzer. 1983. "Change and Variation in the Social Acceptance of Female Participation in Sports." *Journal of Sport Behavior* 6(1):3-8.

Stangl, J. M., and M. J. Kane. 1991. "Structural Variables That Offer Explanatory Power for the Underrepresentation of Women Coaches Since Title IX: The Case of Homologous Reproduction." *Sociology of Sport Journal* 8:47-60.

Sullivan, R. 1992. "Toughening Title IX." *Sports Illustrated* Mar. 23:10.

Theberge, N. 1987. "Sport and Women's Empowerment." *Women's Studies International Forum* 10(4):387-93.

Thomas, J. R., and K. E. French. 1985. "Gender Differences Across Age in Motor Performance: A Meta-Analysis." *Psychological Bulletin* 98:260-82.

Thomas, J. R., and K. T. Thomas. 1988. "Development of Gender Differences in Physical Activity." *Quest* 40:219-29.

Toole, T., and J. C. Kretzschmar. 1993. "Gender Differences in Motor Performance in Early Childhood and Later Adulthood." *Women in Sport & Physical Activity Journal* 2:41-71.

Van Keuren, K. 1992. "Title IX 20 Years Later: Has Sport Actually Changed?" *CSSS Digest* Summer:9.

Weitzman, L. 1979. "Sex-Role Socialization." Pp. 153-216 in *Women: A Feminist Perspective,* 2nd ed., edited by J. Freeman. Palo Alto, CA: Mayfield.

Wells, C. L. 1985. *Women, Sport & Performance: A Physiological Perspective.* Champaign, IL: Human Kinetics.

Whitaker, G. 1982. "Social Control Mechanisms: Ties That Bind—and Chafe." *Perspectives* 83-84.

Whitaker, G. 1989. "Sport Without the 'Ism's': Defining a Different Future for Sport and Physical Education." Paper presented at the American Alliance for Health, Physical Education, Recreation and Dance, Boston.

Whitaker, G. 1991. "Feminism and the Sport Experience: Seeking Common Ground." Pp. 81-86 in *Rethinking College Athletics,* edited by J. Andre and D. N. James. Philadelphia: Temple University Press.

The Wilson Report: Moms, Dads, Daughters and Sports. 1988. Wilson Sporting Goods Co. and the Women's Sports Foundation.

CHAPTER 13

Heroes, Myths, and Media[1]

"Where have you gone, Joe DiMaggio? A nation turns its lonely eyes to you."
(Copyright © 1968 Paul Simon)

In the 1960s, a time of great turmoil and questioning in America, Paul Simon and Art Garfunkel sang of the loss of heroes, the dearth of exemplary individuals famous for their accomplishments, whose strength a distressed nation could borrow to endure a troubled world. Simon and Garfunkel ("Mrs. Robinson"), the Beatles ("Revolution"), the Beach Boys ("Heroes and Villains"), and other oral poets sang, as poets always have, of the anxieties of their society. Every age of humankind has had its heroes living out mythic stories and its "media" to tell of them.

This chapter proceeds with the premise that media transmit myth[2] to the populace, while media both make and break heroes. Media have served these functions throughout the ages. What has changed over the ages are the form and proliferation of media, the ebb and flow of myth's importance from one time and culture to the next, and the expectations that a populace has of its heroes.

How are these subjects relevant to the sociology of sport? For better or worse, athletes seem to be the prime occupants of the modern pantheon of

---

[1]In this chapter we will speak of heroes, human society, and gods. We are not speaking here of the monotheistic Judeo-Christian God, but rather the gods that populate the myths of many cultures.

[2]In this chapter we define *myth* not in the common sense of "falsehood" but rather as a depiction of events or explanation of human experience.

FIGURE 13.1 *"Joltin' Joe" DiMaggio was the classic American strong and silent athlete-hero. Perhaps his reputation has been untarnished because of the distance he maintained between himself and the public.*

heroes. This has occurred in a time widely bemoaned for its lack of myth and "true heroes." We will discuss specific conceptions of media, myths, and heroes shortly, but we begin with the observation that, through the ages, myths have been conservative, society-stabilizing messages (Bird and Dardenne 1988). As Silverstone colorfully puts it, "Culture is the seducer and myth its agent" (1988:21). Ironically, heroes of these myths often have been the agents of change, providing society with its life-enhancing flux (Nagy 1985).
As we proceed consider the following questions:

- What is the process of myth- and hero-making?
- What do we expect of our heroes?
- How and why do we choose athletes as heroes?
- What control, if any, do heroes have over their heroic status?

In the *pure description* phase of our analysis, we will describe the functions of media and myth, identify some classic heroes, and contrast those with more modern heroes, especially athlete-heroes. Our *evaluative commentary* focuses on alternative characteristics and depictions of heroes. *Social critique* is embodied in the comparison of functionalist and conflict-coercion views of modern athlete-heroes. The role of heroes, and especially anti-heroes, in *social engineering* is also noted.

The Functions of Media

The term *media* refers to the ways in which information such as news, sports, weather, and editorials is communicated to the populace. Modern media include television, newspapers, radio, movies, books, magazines, and music. Media not only convey news intended to inform us about events but also present events in progress, such as sports, concerts, political speeches, and even wars. Before, during, and after these events, media transmit impressions, opinions, and analyses that interpret the information as it is communicated. Media may even carry fictional or hypothetical renditions of such events intended not only to entertain but to sway opinion. "It is in [journalists'] power to place people and events into the existing categories of hero, villain, good and bad, and thus to invest their stories with the authority of mythological truth" (Bird and Dardenne 1988:80). Indeed, Bird and Dardenne observe, "One of the most productive ways to see news is to consider it as myth, a standpoint that dissolves the distinction between entertainment and information" (1988:70).

As long as there have existed human civilizations, there have always been media. While the names have varied, the functions have remained consistent. Media existed before television and even before the invention of movable type in the 15th century. The town crier was a form of media, as were the oral poets of Finland who told stories of the *Kalevala* (Friberg, 1988) and the medieval French *conteurs* (itinerant story-telling singers travelling France, England, and Scotland in the 12th and 13th centuries) singing of Roland and Charlemagne. The wizard Merlin foretold that the mythic tales of King Arthur would provide a "livelihood for story-tellers" (Loomis 1991:8), a function that media personalities such as Connie Chung and Bob Costas now serve on network television for seven-figure salaries. Sports media is the vehicle for relating to the modern public tales of their primary heroes—athletes. The result is a symbiotic relationship between the sports reporter/commentators and the sports organizations they cover (Wenner 1989b).

The Evolution of American Sports Media

The American sporting media has its own long history (McChesney 1989). The first American sports magazine appeared around 1820. By 1835 seven sports magazines existed, dominated by *Spirit of the Times,* which at first focused on horse racing, then helped to popularize baseball in the early 1850s as the American national game. The *New York Clipper* in 1853 was founded and employed Henry Chadwick as "the first full-fledged American sportswriter" (p. 51). In 1895, William Randolph Hearst's *New York Journal* had the first section in a major daily newspaper devoted to sports. That was also the time that youth sports fiction was blooming, creating a double-barreled impetus for disseminating the persona of athlete-as-hero.

The pattern of mutual and essentially free self-promotion between newspapers and sports—particularly baseball—was well established by the time the new medium of radio entered the scene in the 1920s, an era not coincidentally known as The Golden Age of Sports. At first, owners of major league baseball teams did not welcome radio broadcasts, seeing them as a threat to game attendance. However, they tolerated the broadcasts because of the free advertising they provided (Voigt 1983). Quickly, however, they came to realize that as a "hot" medium (McLuhan 1966:122), radio could bring an immediacy to the imagination of fans that newspapers could not. Of course, newspapers and sports continued their symbiosis, with estimates in the 1920s that as many as 80 percent of male readers looked at the sports pages, and a half a century later that 30 percent of newspapers were bought primarily for the sports stories (Wenner 1989a).

Media have considerable influence in the creation of heroes, especially in the minds of youth. Research by Harris (1986) found 60–80 percent of children choosing a public figure as a hero, especially athletes and entertainers, while adults preferred politicians. In research among high school students, about three-fourths of heroes identified were male, whether respondents were male or female, black or white (Balswick and Ingoldsby 1982).

Much of what passes for sports news relates pre-event commentary on athlete-heroes and teams or rehashes the tales of past contests rather than truly being "news." However, it all serves to keep sports heroes in the public consciousness, which further serves social stability through civic boosterism and cohesiveness (Tebell 1963).

The television era has brought an irony into the making of heroes by the media. As Rader (1990:330) points out, "television made myth-making, which is essential to hero-making, more difficult than in the past." The microscopic view that television gives the public of its heroes leads to their wealth and fame, yet it also displays their human frailties more easily hidden at a distance.

Modern media do far more than simply inform us of the day's events, just as ancient media did more than tell old tales. The commonality linking the ages and forms of media is that each of them also serve(d) to influence and entertain their respective populaces. The stories have remained consistent through the ages, only the details changing. They tell of achievement and failure, love and hate, physical struggle and mental anguish, joy and despair. Myths "deal with the greatest of all problems, the problems which do not change because men and women do not change. They deal with love; with war; with sin; with tyranny; with courage; with fate" (Highet 1957:540). Modern news and commentary, including those focusing on sport, are not so different. If they diverge, it might be in the nature of the heroes being regarded. Ancient heroes tended to be kings, warriors, knights, or even outlaws, while the modern heroes who populate so much of our media tend to be athletes and entertainers. With little effort, though—and modern media certainly helps us do this—we can see the warrior, knight, or outlaw persona in many of these athletes.

The Functions of Myth

> All primitive societies esteemed their storytellers as the purveyors and memorisers of tribal myths which explained human existence, natural phenomena, the character of the gods, their interference, benign or malign, in mortal affairs and so on. From the central myths radiated a huge and colourful assortment of lesser myths, what we call folklore; these lesser myths chart the development of society through change and growth and decay (Fife 1992:115-16).

The folklore of sport is "a vital source of myth in a nearly mythless country" (Oriard 1982:212). If America is, indeed, nearly mythless, it may be because our Anglo-European-derived culture transposed to the New World is relatively young and has not had the time to develop myths. But despite Americans' dearth of grand cultural myths—Paul Bunyan or even George Washington pale compared to King Arthur in the British mythic past—we still need myths and the heroes who populate them.

Rollo May (1991:30-31) sees four functions of myth[3]:

1. Explain natural phenomena
2. Provide bonding to one's community
3. Support a society's sense of morality
4. Provide a sense of personal identity

Let's look at each one.

Explain Natural Phenomena. Myth often blooms in the absence of scientific, supportable, and replicable proof. Humans are uncomfortable with chaos; we seek explanations. Prior to having access to scientific proof, we sought answers through myth. By its nature, myth is not empirical. Yet it serves to explain, however crudely or fancifully, the natural world. An example is the daily movement of the sun, explained in Greek mythology as Apollo's golden chariot pulling the fiery sun across the sky. Other prescientific myths sought to explain such phenomena as the seasons, the tides, and death.

Even today we manufacture explanations for things we cannot understand or seem to control. Our nonscientific explanations no longer have the elegance of myth, but have been reduced to the mundane of superstition. In the

---

[3]Myth has been conceived in many ways: anthropologically (e.g., Malinowski), linguistically (e.g., Levi-Strauss), and psychologically (e.g., Freud, Jung, Rank). While interesting, these interpretations are beyond the scope of our course. Therefore, we will limit our discussion to these four functions of myth.

modern era sports are among the human endeavors most wrapped in superstition, affording athletes, coaches, and fans a sense of power over outcomes that they sense unfolding beyond their control. Sport is rife with superstitions aimed at affecting events, such as the taboo of mentioning to a pitcher that he or she is in the midst of a no-hitter, for fear that this will "jinx" the effort.

Provide Bonding to One's Community. Mircea Eliade includes games and sports within his conception of a society's "sacred time and space" (1954:27–28). Participating in such activities includes ritual movements that have been performed through the ages of one's culture. Such seemingly mundane rituals as precontest warmups prepare the mind as well as the muscles for competition. The simple act of "playing catch" done by modern major leaguers as well as amateur baseball and softball enthusiasts of all ages can be seen also in grainy old films dating back to John McGraw's turn-of-the-century New York Giants. Playing catch was the linchpin linking the generations in the movie *Field of Dreams*—father with son and then, mystically, father with the ghost of Shoeless Joe Jackson of the 1919 White Sox.

Every sport has its own rituals passed down through generations, consciously or not, linking the past with the present. Following Eliade's lead, it does not matter whether the specific event is a casual game or a professional championship. Emulating timeless acts performed by heroes renders these acts mythic, even sacred, and thus provides a bond with our past and a link to the future.

Sports media make much of the linkages between past and current performers, particularly neophytes possessing great "potential." Specifically, their potential is to become as great for their own generation as past performers were for theirs. "The next Roberto Clemente," "the next Peggy Fleming" or ". . . Chris Evert" are all creations of the sports media serving to link generations, bonding them to a timeless, regenerating society of sport.

By linking generations, myth serves to support a continuous social order. The underlying message of such myth is to uphold the high standards set by those who have preceded and risen to the pantheon. "The hero's passage . . . serve[s] as a general pattern for men and women, wherever they may stand along the scale" (Campbell 1968:121). As is myth, sport is ideologically conservative (McChesney 1989). This may provide a clue as to why sports are so central to American myth. (Games and sports also frequently appear in ancient myth, such as Odysseus' athletic contests with the Phaiacians and the jousting tournaments of the medieval knights.)

"The mythic dimension of sport derives from two essential qualities: sport is both historical and religious" (Oriard 1982:220). History establishes standards within the collective memory, which is the particular domain of the sports media. These are the standards of judgment by which the past and present are bonded. Boris Becker as a youthful champion believed that he was Germany's first great tennis player, displaying ignorance of the path that Baron

FIGURE 13.2   *Chris Evert has not only served as a role model for female athletes, but has been raised to heroic proportions by the media, which christened her "The Ice Maiden." (Wide World Photos, Inc.)*

Gottfried Von Cramm trod before him (Fimrite 1993). When a modern athlete shows ignorance of the heroes who went before, the sports media note such disdain of respect for the heroic past.

Support a Society's Sense of Morality.   Ancient myths told of gods and heroes battling monsters or villainous enemies. These tales symbolized the contest between "good" (bravery, loyalty, honor) and "evil" (whatever threatened one's homeland or monarch). Good and evil are simpler, more concrete concepts than right and wrong. Good and evil are not relative. Morality, loyalty, and duty in ancient times were unquestioningly equated; witness the Crusaders, committing what today we would call atrocities in the name of a holy cause.

The function of myth in supporting a sense of shared morality is more problematic in the modern era than it was in medieval times. While ethnic, political, and religious slaughter continue, morality today is discussed more in terms of right or wrong than good or evil. Perhaps this is why we seem less certain of who our heroes should be, whom we should emulate, whom we should hold up as paragons to our youth, and what behaviors we should expect or demand of our heroes. Was Muhammad Ali right or wrong—moral or immoral—in refusing to be drafted into the armed forces during the Vietnam War because his religion forbids killing? Was Michael Jordan right or wrong to gamble hundreds of thousands of dollars? Although Jordan broke no laws, did he violate some public trust as a role model for youth? Was Mary Decker Slaney "ungenerous" in her response to colliding with Zola Budd in the Olympics?

Should Pete Rose, who collected more base hits than any professional player in history, be admitted to the Baseball Hall of Fame? His achievements certainly seem to qualify him, but Pete Rose also is a convicted tax evader, and by extensive gambling on sports while managing the Cincinnati Reds, he broke the rules of Major League Baseball.

Should Pete Rose's illegal off-field activities dispossess him of his place in the pantheon earned on the field of play? According to Snyder (1991:237), those who are enshrined in sports halls of fame are "defined . . . as socially acceptable. . . . Awe and reverence . . . are collectively associated with the behavior of sport heroes." This suggests a social control function of sport in which achievement, self-sacrifice, and perseverance are among the qualities of sanctified heroes. If good character is required in one era, perhaps that should be a requirement for enshrinement for players of that era, even if it was not for players in other eras. (Babe Ruth and Ty Cobb, it is argued, were far from saints.) Are members of the sports media (whose members elect players to the Baseball Hall of Fame) adhering to a moral standard that no longer applies within contemporary society by banning Rose from Cooperstown?

Provide a Sense of Personal Identity.

> Upon the hero . . . are projected the highest aims of the community. Without the hero the community lacks a crucial dimension, for the hero is typically the soul of the community. Heroes are necessary in order to enable the citizens to find their own ideals, courage, and wisdom in the society. . . . The hero carries our aspirations, our ideals, our beliefs. (May 1991:53–54).

In *The Hero With A Thousand Faces* (1968), Joseph Campbell claims that the heroes of cultures around the world are essentially the same hero appearing in different forms and contexts and serving the same purpose: to provide a model, if not a path to guide each of our lives. Whether we, as individuals, choose to follow that path determines whether we are worthy of heroic status. This fits well the American conception of meritocracy, the open society with a climbable socioeconomic ladder. If heroes suggest a path for the ordinary citizen, then how we conceive this path can be seen from several perspectives, which leads us to the topic of what heroes are like.

The Nature of Classic Heroes

We seem to feel ambivalent about our heroes. What do we want of them? Our media build up heroes, then sometimes seem to take pleasure in tearing them down, because we, the consumers of media, seem to have an appetite for "the dirt" that brings the hero back to earth, our own level. Then, reflected again in our media, we bemoan the absence of "real, old-time heroes." To understand modern heroes and their relationship to the society that venerates (or vilifies) them, we must first look at myths and heroes from the past as they appeared in their own societies.

In ancient myth, the hero took a risk by challenging an unfair, oppressive, or stagnant authority figure, which may appear in the form of a father, king, or evil shaman. In western myths these were sometimes represented allegorically as dragons,[4] which represent stagnation in a society. "The dragon to be slain by [the hero] is precisely the monster of the status quo" (Campbell 1968:337). The hero's journey and conquest allowed for the natural flow of change in a society. Laws, rules, wealth, and power—the tools of the status quo—were designed to halt change. The hero's boon to society was to foster change, bring life-giving motion to a society's stagnation. Character traits such as those we admire today were not required for heroic status, although one might argue that the ancient hero would have contributed more with better character. Let's look at several ancient heroes who provide an interesting contrast to our modern heroes.

Gilgamesh: The First Hero in Western Literature
The story of Gilgamesh, the great Sumerian (now Iraqi) hero, was written on clay tablets about 2,000 B.C. (Sandars 1972). Gilgamesh sought immortality, and in the process abandoned the people of the city he ruled, cost the life of his best friend, and angered the gods. Gilgamesh, although a great hero hailed by the poets of his time, was his own worst enemy. His human frailties—impetuousness, carelessness, emotion—helped to ensure his tragic failures.

---

[4]Eastern myths, in contrast, view the dragon as a benevolent power. Rather than a beast to be feared and defeated, the eastern dragon is to be praised and worshipped.

The Homeric Hero

Greek heroes are numerous; indeed all of their stories were of heroic proportion. An example of heroism in classic Greek literature is Atalanta, who bested
her male compatriots in a boar hunt by bringing down the prey with an arrow.
The problem of female heroism in male-dominated cultures, however, is evident in this story as several people die in conflict over her right to the prize
(Schwab 1974).

Homer cast his heroes as extraordinary humans, and it is primarily in the
works of Homer that Greeks were afforded heroic status while they lived (Nugent 1991). The *Iliad*, written in the 5th century B.C., is an account of the Trojan War, which occurred over a thousand years earlier (or even as early as
13,000 B.C., according to some accounts). For Greeks the Trojan War was their
own history, not fiction (Homer/Rieu 1951).

Within Homeric poetry, hero-status is earned by the living for their
deeds, who then get to enjoy their fame and honor. Thus, the Homeric hero-
model resembles the modern hero. Achilles and Odysseus were paragons, the
greatest heroes, but both their stories (the *Iliad* and the *Odyssey*, respectively)
are populated by heroic characters. These heroes, like modern heroes, had a
real place in the lives of their contemporary populace, and so were afforded
high status and rewards. This is explained in the *Iliad*, as one warrior-hero,
Sarpedon, speaks to his compatriot Glaucus about the rewards they receive.
As you follow Sarpedon's comments, try to see the parallels and divergence
with modern athlete-heroes.

> Glaucus, why do the Lycians at home distinguish you and me with marks of
> honour, the best seats at the banquet, the first cut off the joint, and never-
> empty cups? Why do they all look up to us as gods? And why were we made
> the lords of that great estate of ours on the banks of Xanthus, with its lovely or-
> chards and its splendid fields of wheat? Does not all this oblige us now to take
> our places in the Lycian van [the front line of war] and fling ourselves into the
> flames of battle? Only so can we make our Lycian men-at-arms say this about us
> when they discuss their Kings: They live on the fat of the land they rule, they
> drink the mellow vintage wine, but they pay for it in their glory. They are
> mighty men of war, and where Lycians fight you will see them in the van
> (Homer/Rieu 1951:229).

Greek heroes were rewarded in two ways, through enduring fame
(*kleos*) and material possessions (*timé*) that they looted from the conquered
or had given to them by grateful citizens in their own cities. They resembled
our own conception of heroes being well rewarded for their effort and risk.
Obviously, the material rewards given to heroes are relinquished in death.[5]
Kleos, or fame, however, can live beyond the hero's physical death. Babe Ruth
may live in the memories of more Americans than Herbert Hoover and a dozen
other presidents. The names of Knute Rockne (football), Helen Wills (tennis),
Mildred "Babe" Didrickson (track and golf), and Roberto Clemente (baseball)

---

[5]In ancient ritual the hero's wealth was buried with him, to be enjoyed in the next life.

have lived well beyond their mortal selves, as will the *kleos* of Arthur Ashe. While Larry Bird, Nolan Ryan, O. J. Simpson, and Billie Jean King are no longer active, or "alive" in a performance sense, their fame has outlasted their athletic preeminence and is likely to remain in the minds and on the tongues of the public beyond their mortal selves. The sports media will no doubt ensure that this occurs.

O. J. Simpson presents a special case of kleos in which the enduring fame from his athletic life led to the media circus surrounding the murder of his ex-wife and his subsequent capture and trial. In June of 1994, all of the major television networks simultaneously followed a slowly moving white Ford Bronco in which murder suspect O. J. Simpson was a passenger along a southern California freeway for 90 commercial-free minutes, then trained their cameras and commentators on that parked vehicle until after dark. A real sports event, the sixth game of the NBA finals between New York and Houston, was knocked off the air to cover this "event" simply because of Simpson's kleos, his fame as a former athlete. The electronic and print media continued daily to cover the court proceedings for weeks afterward.

The modern athlete-hero risks pain and injury, for which he or she is usually well rewarded, but seldom risks death. Those who do risk death, such as race-car drivers, do so not for the welfare of society, but rather explicitly for personal fame and wealth. Their boon for others amounts to little more than the vicarious, momentary joy of entertainment.

To appreciate our view of modern heroes, we must understand that Homeric heroes lived a social code freer than ordinary citizens, because of their bravery and loyalty. Not only were they allowed to brag, loot, rape, and murder, they were expected to. The story of the *Iliad* begins with a quarrel between Achilles and King Agamemnon over possession of a girl, Briseis, who was one of the spoils of war. According to Berlin (1991:66), "Achilles is cruel, violent, vindictive, concerned only with his own feelings, yet he is depicted as a blameless warrior, the ideal of the Homeric world" (1991:66). Today, we would call these heroic flaws, if not crimes. In the time depicted by Homer, however, men were "crude, boorish, savage, proud, stubborn" (Berlin 1991:66). Behaving this way was part of being a hero.

Medieval Heroes

Heroes of the Middle Ages were also warriors or knights. Roland served his uncle Charlemagne and France in their war with the Saracens (late 5th century A.D.). Roland insisted on leading the rear-guard protecting Charlemagne's troops as they slowly returned home from Spain through the Pyrenees. This was certainly a heroic act, which the modern mind can appreciate. However, when his troops were attacked and badly outnumbered by the Saracens, Roland refused to call for Charlemagne's help. Roland's pride doomed himself and his troops to death (Harrison 1970).

Joan of Arc, a teen-aged farm girl, led French troops to victory against the English at Patay and Orléans during the Hundred Years War. She claimed to be driven to this unusual female heroism by voices from heaven, which was considered heretical and evidence of witchcraft by the Catholic clergy. She was burned at the stake in 1431, evidence of western society's discomfort with female heroism. It was not until the 20th century that the Church officially recognized her valor, canonizing her as St. Joan.

King Arthur and the knights of his Round Table are the classic medieval heroes. Scholars continue to discuss who King Arthur was and when he lived (Barber 1986; Loomis 1991). By some accounts, Arthur was no more than a minor 6th century regional monarch who may have fought a battle against invading Saxons (Barber 1986). From this modest historical beginning, Arthur's legend grew through telling and retelling into the Arthur of Camelot, the Round Table, Guinevere, Excalibur, and the search for the Holy Grail.[6] Arthur's story is grander certainly than the myth of Abner Doubleday inventing baseball, but it is similar in that the telling and flowering of the tale served well those doing the telling (the media of their time) and those listening (a myth-hungry populace).

Monkey: A Hero of Chinese Myth

Monkey is a classic persona in ancient China. Although not human, he exhibits human behavior. Monkey begins his heroic quest by saving his herd, for which they come to venerate him. Tasting the rewards of heroism—high status, adulation, material rewards—whets Monkey's appetite for more. He becomes greedy, seeking to rise to the level of the gods, bragging, bullying, and using his wiles until he nearly gets what he wants. Monkey proclaims, "If might is honor, then none are mightier than I, or more honorable. This is why I dare to fight, for only heroes deserve to win and rule" (Kherdian 1992:79)

Buddha imprisons Monkey beneath a mountain to pay for his arrogance and his "corruptible, yet indomitable spirit" (Kherdian 1992:78). Despite Monkey's great physical ability and courage, he is a boorish, greedy braggart, lacking good sense and propriety. (Several modern athlete-heroes might come to mind.)

Imperfection of the Classic Hero

We have presented these classic heroes at length to make the point of the common trait they share: they are imperfect, flawed in some essential way. Unless the hero overcomes this flaw, doom awaits. Most do not, which is what makes tragedy. Odysseus is an example. Though a great warrior and leader, he is impetuous and egotistical, the traits of a boy, not a fully realized adult. He

---

[6]Among the five best knights of King Arthur's Round Table were Galahad, Percival, Gawain, Lancelot, and Bors, each of whom sought the Holy Grail. All were heroes, but four of them were flawed in some way and thus doomed to fail in their quest. Galahad, alone, was pure enough to find and carry the Grail to heaven. (Weston 1968).

FIGURE 13.3 *It took over five centuries for Joan of Arc's heroism to be officially recognized, which may say something about society's difficulty in accepting female heroes. (Bettmann Archive)*

finally grows into a manhood worthy of his wife, Penelope, and only then do the gods allow him to return to her. Unlike modern media and populace, the ancients accepted the hero's flaws, even expecting them.

Modern Media and Hero-Making

If there is a pervasive, enduring heroic legend in American society, it is the Horatio Alger myth.[7] According to this heroic model, the person most worthy of adulation and emulation is the one who lives the rags-to-riches story. Americans have always admired the individual who comes from poverty to achieve great economic success by dint of his or her own personal abilities and relentless drive. With some modification (notably, that a background of poverty is no longer a requirement), this sense of struggle for success survives in the American hero.

While a few scientists (e.g., Albert Einstein, Jonas Salk), politicians (e.g., Franklin Roosevelt, John Kennedy), industrialists (e.g., Lee Iacocca, Donald Trump), and military figures (notably World War II Generals Eisenhower, Patton, and MacArthur) have achieved heroic status in modern times, these are exceptions to the general shortage of contemporary heroes other than athletes. Bill Carpenter, the "Lonesome End" of Army's football team in 1958 and 1959, is a rarity as a hero in both athletics and war. Seven years after ending his collegiate football career as an All-American, he was serving as a company captain in Vietnam. On June 9, 1966, he called for a napalm strike on his own position to save 90 American soldiers. Carpenter did a second tour of duty in Vietnam, resisted the Pentagon's desire to use him for publicity—"The Athlete Hero"—and ultimately retired to northern Montana (Nack 1993).

Perhaps neither electronic media nor the popular press extol scientists because there is no microscope company willing to foot the bill. We have no king and our wars, which means our warriors, are increasingly impersonal, a condition not conducive to identifying heroes. Modern media require events to recount and individuals to extol. They are out of business without such fodder, resorting to scooping each other, sometimes creating news and controversy surrounding the heroes they have helped to create.

Heroic deeds and personas must be found somewhere. So Michael Jordan and Martina Navratilova (as well as entertainers like Madonna and Michael Jackson) become subjects of the modern media. When their stars fade or become tarnished, the media find others to extol as heroic, then to dissect.

Marshall McLuhan's now classic assertion that "the medium is the message" (McLuhan 1967) helps to explain why athletes and nonsports entertainers are our modern heroes and sources of myth. By devoting ink or air time to persons and events, media tell the public that these are worth our attention.

---

[7]Alger wrote children's stories during the latter part of the 19th Century. His heroes, invariably poor youth, found success as a result of strong character and hard work.

(a)

(b)

FIGURES 13.4a and 13.4b *Bill Carpenter, West Point's "Lonesome End" of the 1950s is rare as a 20th century athlete-soldier hero. (Fig. 13.4a: United States Military Academy at West Point; Fig. 13.4b: Wide World Photos, Inc.)*

How media choose to characterize them determines the public's perception of events and people. If media choose to ignore an event or person, that event or person will tend not be considered meaningful for the society. We can see an example of this in the lack of media attention paid women's sports relative to that afforded men's. The message is that men's athletic striving is central, or at least metaphoric of cultural values such as the Protestant work ethic, while women's athletic accomplishments are relatively insignificant.

Plight of the Modern Female Hero

Nina Boyd Krebs, author of *Changing Woman, Changing Work* (1993), describes the dissimilar approaches to heroism taken by men and women and their different and unequal regard in American society. The masculine is considered the norm, the standard to which everything else is compared. Women's ways are ignored or seen as deviant, whether in a sport or business context. Worse, they may be viewed as counterproductive to the bottom-line Lombardian Ethic. "You run like a girl," is not a compliment. "You run like a boy," is a compliment.

Occasionally, a Mother Teresa or Rosa Parks emerges as a heroic female figure. However, the feminine is not seen as newsworthy, other than in its Aphrodite incarnation, e.g., Marilyn Monroe or Madonna, or the evil seductress personified in recent movies such as *Fatal Attraction.*

Krebs relates that the inspiring myth of the masculine is the heroic journey, while the embracing myth of the feminine is the endless circle of giving birth, tending death, and giving birth. On TV it is the juicy stuff of afternoon soap operas, the laugh-tracked humor of evening sitcoms, and the ongoing dialogue of Oprah Winfrey—seldom reaching culturally lauded heroic proportions.

In sport there is no parallel for the feminine hero, or "shero." Sports events are pseudowars requiring victor and vanquished. To be considered heroic, especially by media, women must model the straight-line behavior of men. There is no culturally promoted heroism in unstructured play because there is no risk and no boon in play, at least none that our society recognizes. Perhaps this is where the potential for "sheroism" lies, in bringing back to sport civility, respect, and ethical behavior within the context of competition, values that seem to have been lost in recent decades. Leading sport back to its espoused ethics would certainly be a much-needed boon.

While women's athletic brilliance, regardless of level of performance or competition, is gaining recognition and reward, it remains insignificant, relative to men's or even to boys' sports. Exceptions include sports such as tennis, track, swimming, diving, and figure skating. Although Title IX has added support to women's athletics in schools, men's programs continue to dominate in money garnered and spent, media attention, and fan support.

The hero's journey—the masculine trek to bring back a "boon"—consumes the media's spotlight. In American culture, the cyclical nature of feminine heroism is ominous because it is not the norm and would require massive psychic upheaval to be elevated on a par with masculine hero-pursuit. The unrealized fear of such change often surfaces through hostile humor such as the wave of "Hillary" jokes and aspersions on President Clinton's masculinity that swept the country when he appointed her to pursue strategies for health care reform. Many new administration appointees attract criticism, but a less qualified man—even a relative—chosen for that job would not have been as controversial.

Since the feminine archetype tends to be demeaned rather than revered, women are unclear about how to honor themselves in deeply feminine ways, while the male-hero centered society has not even considered this question. Are heroes necessarily cast in the masculine mold? Must a girl or woman either relinquish her femininity—at least in the sports context—or overstress her traditional physical femininity through overt display, as did Flo-Jo Griffith in the 1988 Olympics? Even if she did, the media niche in which the "shero" would find herself likely would be secondary to the telling of the male hero's tale. Media, then, may be seen as the means of determining, as well as disseminating, a society's significant events and in turn its sense of self, purpose, and direction.

Media reiterate the cultural myth of sport as a male-appropriate domain (Messner, Duncan, and Jensen 1993; Sabo and Jansen 1992; Blinde, Greendorfer, and Shanker 1991). Men's sports predominate on television compared to women's sports as the media self-fulfill the myth by making it more profitable. In print media, too, the focus is on male athletes, and when females are personified as athletic heroes, they tend to be in the "sex-appropriate" sports of tennis, swimming, diving, and gymnastics (Kane 1988). In their analysis of 33 years of *Sports Illustrated*, Lumpkin and Williams (1991) found 90.8 percent of the 3,723 articles focused on male athletes. (Males wrote 91.8 percent of those articles.) Following our premise that media are responsible for creating particular heroes—or denying such status by ignoring individuals or groups of people—women athletes seem to be denied general access to the pantheon of cultural heroes. Being extolled in the media—"sung about"—is the society's evidence that such people are candidates for heroic status. Without it, the door to the pantheon is closed.

Two Paths to Modern Athlete-Hero Status

Modern American culture has modified the largely 19th-century Horatio Alger myth by adding two conflicting conceptions of who is worthy of heroic status: (*a*) those who achieve success irrespective of how they achieve it; or (*b*) those who behave honorably and bravely in crisis irrespective of their worldly success. The nature of sport creates artificial crises, offering for our vicarious pleasure daily opportunity for recognizing and exalting heroes.

Success at Any Cost.   Success in competitive American sports comes at the expense of others. This is also true in business, politics, and to some extent in the arts and sciences. Success in America is defined by a pyramid allowing successively less room as one ascends toward the peak. Our heroes stand at the pinnacle, but to get there they had to climb over the backs of others. As May says (1991:117), "Only a bold person would reach the top. When we had a pang of guilt at exploiting our fellow men, we could whisper to ourselves that we need not take the responsibility for others." From this perspective, heroic status in sport properly belongs to those who have *achieved the competitive pinnacle regardless of questionable or illegal behavior.*

Honorable Behavior above All.   The contrasting view is that heroism is measured against risk, challenge, and achievement, *but only in the presence of honor.* While there may be satisfaction and reward in pursuing and reaching a personal goal, it is not heroic without honor. Even if one undergoes personal risk, the status gained from achievement is diminished if it was gained dishonorably or if the hero displays noxious behavior.

DiMaggio and Williams: A Comparison of Two Classic Athlete-Heroes

The foregoing conceptions of what constitutes heroic stature suggest a comparison between two Hall of Fame baseball players who were contemporaries: Joe DiMaggio and Ted Williams. What did each do to deserve heroic stature?

Both came from the "hinterlands" of California to the urban east in the late 1930s. (At the time there was no Major League Baseball west of St. Louis.) Both immediately became stars in the American League and eventually were inducted into baseball's Hall of Fame. Williams' lifetime batting average is 19 points higher than DiMaggio's (.344 to .325) and Williams hit 160 more home runs, 521 to 361 (Turkin and Thompson 1979).

Those were personal accomplishments. What did Williams and DiMaggio risk for their society? Williams was a combat pilot in World War II and the Korean conflict, shot down one day and back in combat the next, while sacrificing five years from the heart of his career. DiMaggio served in World War II for three years, but not in combat. Significantly, DiMaggio played in New York, the hub of American media, while Williams labored in Boston his entire career, garnering far less national media coverage.

The personalities of the two men also diverged. DiMaggio was perceived as a gentleman by the press, an image that flowed from media to the public. Williams had a nearly continuous battle with the Boston press, which understandably was less likely to extol his heroic virtues. Lastly, DiMaggio played in ten World Series, while Williams appeared in only one, thus affording Williams far less national media coverage.

Should DiMaggio or Williams, then, be hailed the greater societal hero? Williams' individual achievements surpassed DiMaggio's. Williams risked his life for his country, while DiMaggio did not. Yet DiMaggio is an icon, a hero whose passing from the testing-ground is lamented in song (as were ancient heroes), while Williams is remembered simply as a great hitter instead of a societal hero.

We suggest that the answer lies in two areas. First, the media served to spread the public's awareness of DiMaggio more than it did Williams. Second, Williams was seen as flawed because of his acerbic personality, while DiMaggio was and remains the classic image of the perfected hero.

The Functionalist View of Modern Athlete-Heroes

Heroes, as the prime actors in myth, exist to transmit culture, most purposefully among a society's neophytes. This suggests an apparent paradox. Myths are conservative, reiterating their culture, providing society-supporting messages and lessons. Heroes, however, often are counted among a society's agents of change, the risks they encounter in seeking change being a key component of their heroism.

FIGURE 13.5 *Joe DiMaggio and Ted Williams, contemporaries as baseball stars, gained very different levels of heroic status. (National Baseball Library, Cooperstown, NY.)*

The stasis of myth and the flux of hero-action are not incompatible, however, because societies require flexibility. Without it they become brittle, in peril of shattering under their own weight and inertia. While some heroes at times seem to behave inconsistently with a society's mores to the point of deviance, they provide a necessary service. (Muhammad Ali's refusal of military service, daring the government to put him in prison, which influenced others to protest during the Vietnam War, is a case in point from sport.)

In a 1993 TV endorsement, intended to influence children to buy Nike basketball shoes, NBA star "Sir" Charles Barkley proclaims that he doesn't want to be a role model, in other words a hero (perhaps rendering his media-generated nickname apocryphal). Barkley asserts that a youngster's parents or teachers should be their role models. No doubt parents, teachers, scientists, fire and police personnel, nurses, and other such underpaid and overworked people *should* be the heroes of youngsters. However, media do not lionize these people as much or as frequently as they do athletes. "The hero is created by us; he or she is born collectively as our own myth. This is what makes heroism so important: it reflects our own sense of identity, and from this our own heroism is molded" (May 1991:54).

A similar point was voiced by Karl Malone, star basketball player of the Utah Jazz, in response to Barkley's comment. Malone said, "We don't choose to be role models, we are *chosen*. Our only choice is whether to be a good role model or a bad one" (Malone 1993:84). Heroes are created by their society, through its media. They cannot choose to be seen as heroes if the society is not ready or willing to see them in that light, nor can they shun heroism if media demand it of them.

The Media's Financial Interest in Athlete-Heroes

The modern hero's story-line is clearest in sport and other forms of entertainment. Their trials and successes happen in public (arena or stage) and over a defined period of time (season or career), which facilitates our evaluation of them. We not only witness their tests of heroism, we may see prizes conferred on them of money (golf and tennis) or symbolically through medals and trophies (the Olympics). All of this is presented through electronic media, which tend to spurn presentation of the Nobel Peace Prize for live public consumption. (College football's Heisman Trophy award has its own well-advertised show.)

This reiterates and contributes to the modern "gospel of wealth" (Oriard 1982:50), judging American heroes by their accumulation of assets. Perhaps we see a "boon" in this confluence between the American belief in the competitive system and our veneration of economic success. Perhaps we believe that, as individuals and as a society, we will benefit from the product—iron ore, personal computers, or an Olympic gold medal that make a few of us wealthy beyond our dreams. If we can assume that media give the public what it wants to revere, the proof of the above assertion lies in what is televised and what is not.

The mutually beneficial relationship between media and sports has been noted above and elsewhere (Eitzen and Sage 1993; Coakley 1990). In the first half of 1988, for example, $1.1 billion of sports advertising appeared on television in the United States, including the following amounts from the top 10 corporate and government contributors in millions of dollars (Real and Mechikoff 1992:327):

1. Chrysler—$72.0
2. General Motors—63.1
3. Philip Morris—54.7
4. Anheuser-Busch—54.3
5. Ford—29.0
6. AT&T—26.9
7. Sears—25.0
8. U.S. Armed Forces—23.9
9. McDonalds—23.0
10. American Express—20.0

This symbiosis among myth, heroes, and media is tied to the hope for, if not the realization of, profit.[8]

The Conflict-Coercion View of Modern Athlete-Heroes

In contrast to the functionalist perspective, conflict-coercion theory interprets the media as agents of dominant socioeconomic power holders who employ the media to parade athlete-heroes in front of the public for profit. Athletes are persuaded that the potential rewards are worth the risks to life and limb; although many are maimed in the pursuit of compensation, injury is rare and in any case insignificant compared to the profits generated. The public, for its part, is mesmerized by media presentations of athletic competition, oblivious to the oppressive circumstances under which it is duped into subsidizing the entire outrageous enterprise (Scott 1978). Not only is the public sold the idea that such spectacles are uplifting, it also buys the notion that the participant athlete-heroes are worthy of emulation. In fact, imperfections such as those we noted in classical heroes are no less present in modern athlete-heroes.

Character of the Modern Athlete-Hero

Christopher Lasch (1979) has described American society as a culture of narcissism, in which neither the benefits to others nor to society concerns us. We are immersed in a culture that venerates the self at the expense of our community. If that is true, should we expect any more from the athlete-heroes we venerate?

Research suggests that the behavior of the modern athlete is less than exemplary. The moral reasoning of athletes is suspect and seems to decay the longer they are involved in sport (Bredemeier and Shields 1986). Perhaps

---

[8]The $1.1 billion package for national televising of baseball signed in 1988 was renewed four years later at half that amount because of low ratings.

this results from athletes' conditional self-worth, which appears to depend on their continuously tenuous athletic identity. Selflessness and social awareness, while traits that we see as desirable in heroes, are contrary to those that tend to result in athletic success (Goodman 1993): "Despite their brilliance and (con)quests, even heroes cannot, in the end, shed their humanness" (Candelaria 1989:140).

By "humanness" Candelaria means the hero's essential flaws. The hero *must* be flawed in some fashion; flawlessness is the domain of the gods, not human heroes. (More precisely, a behavior, such as arrogance, which would be a flaw in a human, is the natural prerogative of a god. Humans who persist in displaying arrogance will be brought low by fate—"Pride goeth before a fall.") Although heroes cannot stand quite as tall as gods, acceptance of the hero's flaw by the populace is essential to the elevation of heroes above the public that needs them.

The Modern Anti-Hero

The American national hero-type is "egocentric rather than sociocentric" (Oriard 1982:43). This has been shown in modern adult sports fiction through the characterizations of Roy Hobbs (Malamud's *The Natural*), Henry Wiggin (Harris' *The Southpaw*), Jack Keefe (Lardner's *You Know Me, Al*), and Updike's Harry Angstrum of the "Rabbit" series.[9] Real-life athlete-heroes are also frequently egocentric, perhaps ultimately characterized by tennis player John McEnroe. While we laud athlete-heroes, such as Arthur Ashe and Roberto Clemente (who died while flying humanitarian supplies to the Nicaraguan people), who use their fame and sometimes their money to help others, such examples are rare.

There is no dearth of exemplary athlete-heroes. The long list of those who have lived (apparently) unblemished and exemplary lives includes:

Alan Page (football) Cheryl Miller (basketball)
Bill Bradley (basketball) Curt Flood (baseball)
Tom McMillen (basketball) Jack Kemp (football)
Lou Gehrig (baseball) Althea Gibson (tennis)
Jesse Owens (track) Nolan Ryan (baseball)
Billy Mills (track) Wilma Rudolph (track)
Joan Benoit (marathon) Babe Didrickson (track, golf)
Donna De Varona (swimming)

---

[9]Although three of the four novels cited depict baseball, this is not meant to imply that baseball players are more egocentric than other athletes. Baseball has yielded more fiction than other sports. Turn-of-the-century juvenile sports heroes were more sociocentric, although also more trivial (Higgs 1981).

However, the list of those we might call anti-heroes for challenging the status quo or simply daring to redefine their athlete role or persona could be as long, including:

Ty Cobb (baseball)	Ricky Henderson (baseball)
Jack Johnson (boxing)	Muhammad Ali (boxing)
Joe Namath (football)	Billie Jean King (tennis)
Jose Canseco (baseball)	Martina Navratilova (tennis)
Wilt Chamberlain (basketball)	Magic Johnson (basketball)
Eleanor Holm (swimming)	Babe Ruth (baseball)
Mary Bacon (horse racing)	Janet Guthrie (auto racing)
John McEnroe (tennis)	

Polking (1983:16) defines an anti-hero as someone who "might not live by society's values, [but] is true to the personal moral code that [s]he has established." A society's values change over time, and it is often a society's heroes who foster change. All of the female athletes noted above (and many more) might appear on the list of anti-heroes, since each in her time challenged the notion of female as nonathletic. They might even be considered more heroic than the males because their heroism came at additional risk to their feminine status, while promising a boon for other females who might also want to challenge the status quo. From the perspective of conflict-coercion theory, the anti-hero, by confronting the assumptions under which the power-holders control and oppress us, is the true hero of the people.

Summary

What, after all, was so classically heroic about Joe DiMaggio (or Joe Montana, or Flo-Jo, or even Jose Canseco)? Whether their personas are ideal role model or jerk, athlete-heroes tend to be little more than the sum of their competitive accomplishments. Oriard (1982) suggests that comparing the modern athlete-hero to the classic hero is justified because the heroic career, both ancient and modern, retells the process of maturation. If that is the case, then perhaps greed and egocentric behavior are not associated with immaturity in the realm of heroic stature.

The form of media changes over time; its function does not. The same can be said of myths and the heroes who populate them. "Where have you gone, Joe DiMaggio . . ." is an empty plea for "the good old days" and "the good old heroes." The heroes that our media extol are the heroes that our media, consciously or not, know we want.

Each society has its own expectations and requirements for exceptional status and reward and so defines its own heroes. If ancient Greek society accepted looting and slavery practiced by its warrior-heroes, who are we to say that they were unworthy of heroic status? If, in the early years of the 20th century, the media and the public ignored or accepted the carousing of their athlete-heroes, should we judge them by the standards of our own time? If toward the end of the 20th century, greed, selfishness, and arrogance are "normal" to our athletes and entertainers, and we don't exhibit much interest in heroes from other walks of life, should we rob ourselves of the age-old societal need for heroes? Consider heroes within the context provided here and be realistic about the role of athlete-heroes in the greater societal landscape.

References

Balswick, J., and B. Ingoldsby. 1982. "Heroes and Heroines Among American Adolescents." *Sex Roles.* 8(3):243–49.

Barber, R. 1986. *King Arthur: Hero and Legend.* New York: Dorsett.

Berlin, I. 1991. *The Crooked Timber of Humanity.* New York: Knopf.

Bird, E. S., and R. W. Dardenne. 1988. "Myth, Chronicle, and Story." Pp. 67–86, in *Media, Myths, and Narrative: Television and the Press,* edited by J. W. Carey. Newbury Park, CA: Sage.

Blinde, E. M., S. L. Greendorfer, and R. J. Shanker. 1991. "Differential Media Coverage of Men's and Women's Intercollegiate Basketball: Reflection of Gender Ideology." *Journal of Sport and Social Issues* 15(2):98–114.

Bredemeier, B. J., and D. L. Shields. 1986. "Moral Growth Among Athletes and Nonathletes: A Comparative Analysis." *Journal of Genetic Psychology* 147(1):7–18.

Campbell, J. 1968 (1949). *The Hero With a Thousand Faces.* Princeton, NJ: Princeton University/Bollingen.

Candelaria, C. 1989. *Seeking the Perfect Game: Baseball in American Literature.* New York: Greenwood.

Coakley, J. J. 1990. *Sport in Society,* 4th ed. St. Louis, MO: Times Mirror/Mosby.

Eitzen, D. S., and G. H. Sage. 1993. *Sociology of American Sport,* 5th ed. Madison, WI: Brown and Benchmark.

Eliade, M. 1954. *The Myth of the Eternal Return.* Princeton, NJ: Princeton University\Bollingen.

Fife, G. 1992. *Arthur The King: The Themes Behind the Legend.* New York: Sterling.

Fimrite, R. 1993. "Baron of the Court." *Sports Illustrated* July 5:56++.

Friberg, E. (transl.) 1988. *The Kalevala.* Helsinki, Finland: Otava.

Goodman, M. 1993. "Where Have You Gone, Joe DiMaggio?" *Utne Reader* May/June, 57:103–4.

Harris, J. C. 1986. "Athletic Exemplars in Context: General Selection Patterns in Relation to Sex, Race, and Age." *Quest* 38:95–115.

Harris, M. 1953. *The Southpaw.* Lincoln, NE: Bison.

Harrison, R. (transl.) 1970. *The Song of Roland.* New York: New American Library.

Higgs, R. J. 1981. *Laurel and Thorn: The Athlete in American Literature.* Lexington, KY: University of Kentucky.

Highet, G. 1957. *The Classical Tradition: Greek and Roman Influences on Western Literature.* New York: Oxford University/Galaxy.

Homer. 1951. *The Iliad.* New York: Penguin. Translation by E. V. Rieu.

Kane, M. J. 1988. "Media Coverage of the Female Athlete Before, During, and After Title-IX: *Sports Illustrated* Revisited." *Journal of Sports Management* 2:87–99.

Kherdian, D. (trans.) 1992. *Monkey: A Journey to the West.* Boston: Shambhala.

Krebs, N. B. 1993. *Changing Woman, Changing Work.* Aspen, CO: MacMurray and Beck.

Lardner, R. 1914 (1960). *You Know Me, Al.* New York: Scribner's.

Lasch, C. 1979. *The Culture of Narcissism.* New York: W. W. Norton.

Loomis, R. S. 1991. *The Grail: From Celtic Myth to Christian Symbol.* Princeton, NJ: Princeton University.

Lumpkin, A., and L. D. Williams. 1991. "An Analysis of *Sports Illustrated* Feature Articles, 1954–1987." *Journal of Sport and Social Issues* 8:16–32.

Malamud, B. 1952. *The Natural.* New York: Harcourt, Brace.

Malone, K. 1993. "One Role Model to Another." *Sports Illustrated* June 14:84.

May, R. 1991. *The Cry for Myth.* New York: W. W. Norton.

McChesney, R. W. 1989. "Media Made Sport: A History of Sports Coverage in the United States." Pp. 49–69 in *Media, Sports, & Society,* edited by L. A. Wenner. Newbury Park, CA: Sage.

McLuhan, M. 1966. *Understanding Media: The Extentions of Man.* New York: McGraw-Hill.

McLuhan, M. 1967. *The Medium Is the Message.* New York: Bantam.

Messner, M. A., M. C. Duncan, and K. Jensen. 1993. "Separating the Men from the Girls: The Gendered Language of Televised Sports." *Gender and Society* 7:121–37.

Nack, W. 1993. "The Lonesome End." *Sports Illustrated* October 4:64–72+.

Nagy, J. F. (trans.) 1985. *The Wisdom of the Outlaw: The Boyhood Deeds of Finn in Gaelic Narrative Tradition.* Berkeley, CA: University of California.

Nugent, G. 1991. *Heroes, Heroines, and the Wisdom of Myth.* Lectures at the Smithsonian Institution. Kearneysville, WV: The Teaching Company.

Oriard, M. V. 1982. *Dreaming of Heroes.* Chicago: Nelson-Hall.

Polking, K. 1983. *Writer's Encyclopedia.* Cincinnati, OH: Writers Digest.

Rader, B. G. 1990. *American Sports: From the Age of Folk Games to the Age of Televised Sports,* 2nd ed. Englewood Cliffs, NJ: Prentice-Hall.

Real, M. R., and R. A. Mechikoff. 1992. "Deep Fan: Mythic Identification, Technology, and Advertising in Spectator Sports." *Journal of Sport and Social Issues* 9:323–39.

Sabo, D., and S. C. Jansen. 1992. "Images of Men in Sports Media: The Social Re-Production of the Gender Order." Pp. 169–84, in *Men, Masculinity, and the Media,* edited by S. Craig. Newbury Park, CA: Sage.

Sandars, N. K. 1972. *The Epic of Gilgamesh.* New York: Penguin.

Schwab, G. 1974. *Gods and Heroes: Myths and Epics of Ancient Greece.* New York: Random House.

Scott, J. 1978. *Bill Walton.* New York: Thomas Y. Crowell.

Silverstone, R. 1988. "Television, Myth, and Culture." Pp. 20-47, in *Media, Myths, and Narrative: Television and the Press,* edited by J. W. Carey. Newbury Park, CA: Sage.

Snyder, E. E. 1991. "Sociology of Nostalgia: Sports Halls of Fame and Museums in America." *Sociology of Sport Journal* 8(3):228-38.

Tebell, J. 1963. *The Compact History of American Newspapers.* New York: Hawthorne.

Turkin, H., and S. C. Thompson. 1979. *The Official Encyclopedia of Baseball,* 10th ed. New York: Dolphin.

Updike, J. 1960. *Rabbit Run.* New York: Knopf.

Voigt, D. Q. 1978. "Myths After Baseball: Notes on Myths in Sports." *Quest: Literature\Myth* 30, Summer: 46-57.

Voigt, D. Q. 1983. *American Baseball, Volume II.* University Park, PA: Pennsylvania State University.

Wenner, L. A. 1989a. "Media, Sports, and Society: The Research Agenda." Pp. 13-48 in *Media, Sports, & Society,* edited by L. A. Wenner. Newbury Park, CA: Sage.

Wenner, L. A. (ed.) 1989b. *Media, Sports, & Society.* Newbury Park, CA: Sage.

Weston, J. L. 1983. *From Ritual to Romance.* Gloucester, MA: Peter Smith.

Index

Aaron, Hank, 183
Academics
  assessment of college athletes, 148-149, 157
  college athletics, 147-148
  and high-school sports, 142-143
  performance of college athletes by college/conference, 151-154
  standard setting for college athletes, 149-150
  support programs by college athletes, 156-157
Accreditation, college athletics, 157
Acosta, R. V., 297, 299, 320
Activity theory, of aging, 199-200
Adler, P., 147, 148, 159
Adler, P. A., 147, 148, 159
Aenchbacher, L. E., 205, 218
Age cohorts, 196
Agents, of socialization, 50
Aggression
  catharsis theory of, 237-238, 241
  frustration-aggression theory of, 238-240, 242
  generalizability of, 227
  instrumental aggression, 228-229
  reactive aggression, 227-228
  social learning theory of, 240-241, 242
  synthesis of theories, 241-243
  and women, 304-305
Aggression and sports
  folk beliefs related to, 226-227
  nonphysical aggression, 229
  physical aggression, 229
  taxonomy of behaviors, 229-230
  violence, levels of, 229-231
  See also Violence in sports
Aging
  activity theory of, 199-200
  and ageism, 207
  continuity theory of, 200-201
  disengagement theory of, 198-199
  future view for elderly, 208
  Hindu paradigm for, 193, 206
  and individual differences, 196
  social engineering of, 207-208

terms related to, 193
Aging and sports participation, 195-196
  adaptation of sports activities for elderly, 213-215
  generational differences, 196-197
  and life expectancy, 204
  motivations for, 209
  opportunities for, 210-212
  physical benefits from, 202-205, 206-207
  psychological benefits from, 205-206, 207, 209
  types of physical pursuits, 201-202
Albonico, T., 31, 45
Albrecht, R. R., 113, 126
Alderman, R. B., 227, 243
Aldrich, N. W., Jr., 33, 45, 285, 288
Alfano, P., 144, 159
Alger, Horatio, 337, 340
Ali, Muhammad, 97, 288, 331, 342, 346
Alioto, J. T., 241, 244
Allardt, E., 29, 45
Allen, Marcus, 268
Allison, M. T., 17, 23, 41, 45
Altherr, T. L., 66, 76
Alvin, D. F., 143, 162
Ama, P. F. M., 272, 288
Amateur Athletic Union (AAU), 250
American Alliance for Health, Physical Education, Recreation and Dance, 112, 113, 123, 124, 303
American Association for Health, Physical Education, and Recreation Commission on Desirable Athletic Competition for Children of Elementary School Age, 124
American Institutes for Research (AIR), 153, 154, 159
American League, formation of, 182
Amin, Idi, 263
Ammon, R., 158, 164
Anderson, D., 282, 288

Anderson, D. F., 113, 127
Anderson, J., 203, 217
Anderson, K. A., 203, 219
Androgyny, 306-307
Anomie
  and deviance, 89-90
  meaning of, 89
Antitrust issue, 166, 167, 181
Apartheid, South Africa, 256-258
Ardrey, R., 238, 243
Armer, M. J., 143, 163
Arnold, Thomas, 133
Arond, H., 274, 275, 292
Ashe, A. R., Jr., 271, 288, 345
Ashe, Arthur, 273, 275, 285, 286, 288, 334
Asian Games, 252
Asinof, E., 87, 99
Associated Press, 156, 158, 159, 183, 189, 225, 237, 243
Association for Intercollegiate Athletics for Women (AIAW), 28, 296
Association of Tennis Professionals, 42
Atchley, R., 199, 200, 216
Athlete-hero, 340-345
  anti-hero, 346
  character of, 344-345
  conflict-coercion view, 344-346
  examples of, 341, 345
  functionalist view, 341-343
  and media, 343-344
  theories of, 340
Athletic identity, 53
Athletics
  characteristics of, 15
  compared to sports, 15-16
Atkinson, J. W., 306, 320
Attitudes
  and early sport experiences, 113
  meaning of, 49
  transmission of, 50-51
Auburn University, 174
Austin, D. A., 66, 76
Authority, and sports, 14
Avedon, E., 60, 76